The Future of Lenin

The Future of Lenin

Power, Politics, and Revolution in the Twenty-First Century

Edited by

ALLA IVANCHIKOVA
AND ROBERT R. MACLEAN

SUNY
PRESS

Cover image (copyright Johann Salazar, taken in Bishkek, Kyrgyzstan)

Published by State University of New York Press, Albany

© 2022 State University of New York

All rights reserved

Printed in the United States of America

No part of this book may be used or reproduced in any manner whatsoever without written permission. No part of this book may be stored in a retrieval system or transmitted in any form or by any means including electronic, electrostatic, magnetic tape, mechanical, photocopying, recording, or otherwise without the prior permission in writing of the publisher.

For information, contact State University of New York Press, Albany, NY
www.sunypress.edu

Library of Congress Cataloging-in-Publication Data

Names: Ivanchikova, Alla, editor. | Maclean, Robert R., editor.
Title: The future of Lenin : power, politics, and revolution in the twenty-first century / edited by Alla Ivanchikova and Robert R. Maclean.
Description: Albany : State University of New York Press, [2022] | Includes bibliographical references and index.
Identifiers: ISBN 9781438488073 (hardcover : alk. paper) | ISBN 9781438488080 (ebook) | ISBN 9781438488066 (pbk. : alk. paper)
Further information is available at the Library of Congress.

10 9 8 7 6 5 4 3 2 1

Contents

Illustrations   ix

Introduction: Does Lenin Have a Future?   1
   Alla Ivanchikova

Part I. Lenin, Our Contemporary?

Chapter 1
Rejecting Lenin for the Left   27
   David J. Ost

Chapter 2
What Is Leninist Thinking?   55
   Jodi Dean

Chapter 3
We're All (Romantic) Socialists: Lenin and the Struggle with
Economic Romanticists Then and Now   75
   Christian Sorace and Kai Heron

Chapter 4
Whither the State? Steve Bannon, the Alt-Right, and Lenin's
State and Revolution   101
   Alexandar Mihailovic

Chapter 5
Saving the Vanguard: Lenin's Military Metaphors Today   125
   Daniel Egan

Part II. Centering the Black Leninist Tradition

Chapter 6
Elaborations of Leninism: Self-Determination and the Tradition
of Radical Blackness 151
    Charisse Burden-Stelly

Chapter 7
Black Leninist Internationalism: The Anticolonial Center 175
    Robert R. Maclean

Chapter 8
Lenin and East African Marxism: Abdul Rahman Mohamed Babu
and Dani Wadada Nabudere 205
    Zeyad el Nabolsy

Part III. The Actuality of Lenin's Theory

Chapter 9
"Withering Away": State, Revolution, and Social Objectivity 235
    Giovanni Zanotti

Chapter 10
Lenin and the Materialist Critique of Law 257
    Camila Vergara

Chapter 11
Facing the Test: The Leninist Party as Proctor 281
    Derek R. Ford

Chapter 12
The Production of "Leninism" and Its Political Journeys 299
    Zhivka Valiavicharska

Chapter 13
Looking for Lenin in Bishkek 323
    Text and Photos: Johann Salazar and
    Hjal(mar) Jorge Joffre-Eichhorn

About the Editors	339
Contributors	341
Index	345

Illustrations

Figure I.1	(copyright Alla Ivanchikova)	4
Figure I.2	(copyright Alla Ivanchikova)	5
Figure 9.1	(copyright Giovanni Zanotti)	239
Figure 9.2	(copyright Giovanni Zanotti)	243
Figure 9.3	(copyright Giovanni Zanotti)	249
Figure 13.1	(copyright Johann Salazar)	324
Figure 13.2	(copyright Johann Salazar)	324
Figure 13.3	(copyright Johann Salazar)	325
Figure 13.4	(copyright Johann Salazar)	326
Figure 13.5	(copyright Johann Salazar)	327
Figure 13.6	(copyright Johann Salazar)	328
Figure 13.7	(copyright Johann Salazar)	328
Figure 13.8	(copyright Johann Salazar)	329
Figure 13.9	(copyright Johann Salazar)	329
Figure 13.10	(copyright Johann Salazar)	330
Figure 13.11	(copyright Johann Salazar)	330
Figure 13.12	(copyright Johann Salazar)	332
Figure 13.13	(copyright Johann Salazar)	332
Figure 13.14	(copyright Johann Salazar)	333
Figure 13.15	(copyright Johann Salazar)	334

Figure 13.16 (copyright Johann Salazar) 334
Figure 13.17 (copyright Johann Salazar) 335
Figure 13.18 (copyright Johann Salazar) 336

Introduction

Does Lenin Have a Future?

ALLA IVANCHIKOVA

From Post–Cold War Leninology to the "Rebirth of History"

In October 2017, I attended a conference titled "the future of revolution," organized by the European University at St. Petersburg. This conference, which drew scholars from around the globe, took place not too far from the famous Winter Palace, which, in 1917, had been stormed by soldiers and workers—the same palace where the cabinet ministers of the Provisional Government bunkered, awaiting their fate. The lack of official commemoration of the October Revolution's centennial in Russia was palpable in St. Petersburg that week: while there were numerous events (conferences, museum exhibitions, readings) in celebration of the centennial, they all were happening indoors, while the outside—the public space—remained unmarked. I was aware of the official explanation of that fact: the October Revolution, it was said, was still too "controversial" an event in Russian public consciousness and memory. But the effect was still eerie. I could not help but remember cities awash with red flags on Revolution's Day every year in my childhood. The mood at the conference was energizing—rooms overflowing with attendees, presenters brimming with excitement. None of the presentations were nostalgic in their orientation or tone—it was future-oriented. And yet, there was also a yearning for the past: in the evenings, the crowd dispersed and most of us walked around the city looking for the memory of the revolution to come alive. And it did: on the evening of October 25, the Winter Palace suddenly glowed red. This change in lighting was subtle but powerful. I don't recall it being announced in the press, and perhaps it was, but it caught me off guard. The Revolution, I remember thinking that moment, will never leave this place. The Winter Palace will always remain a testament to the fact that things can change radically, the new replacing centuries-old, in a matter of months.

This edited collection of essays came out of this feeling, this sense of looking forward while also seeking inspiration in the past. It answers the following questions: Why do we still wander restlessly, looking for Lenin's ghost? What does "Lenin" and "Leninism" signify today and how has this changed in recent years? What does the future of Leninism look like? Why, after thirty years of iconoclasm (that involved the removal of statues of Lenin throughout the former socialist world), in spite of concerted efforts to demote, deconstruct, and discredit Leninist modes of thinking, does the figure of Lenin return to haunt our turbulent political present? The short answer is this: we are witnessing the end of what Alain Badiou, in *The Rebirth of History* calls "intervallic time."[1] Intervallic times are ones of reaction during which revolutionary energies become latent—rivers of lava flowing, invisibly, below ground. In 2021, when I am writing this, it is clear that the world-historical crises have arrived sooner than anticipated and are shaking up the post–Cold War global order, revealing its multiple cracks. Against the *longue durée* background of climate crisis and amid the immediate catastrophe of the coronavirus pandemic, the old world still struggles to reassert itself, but it is becoming clear that the postpolitical consensus and apathy of the post–Cold War era has come to an end, for better *and* for worse. Both those on the left and on the right are mobilizing, building capacity. This book, put together 150 years after the Bolshevik leader's birth, shows the actuality of Lenin, who has come back, for these new times. Whether arguing against, for, or with Lenin, the essays in this collection show that Lenin is our contemporary.

To many, this current return of Lenin comes as a surprise. Consider, for instance, Brian C. Anderson's essay, published in *National Review* in response to Slavoj Žižek's book *Lenin 2017*. Titled "Zombie Lenin," the essay invokes *The Simpsons* 1998 episode where both Lenin and the Soviet Union figure, quite literally, as zombies. A conservative thinker, Anderson finds Žižek's defense of, in Anderson's words, "Lenin's turgid and hate-ridden late writings" "preposterous and chilling." Anderson, for whom Lenin figures only as a symbol of political violence, repression, fanaticism, and gulags, insists, contra Žižek, that there was "no 'emancipatory potential' in Lenin's revolution."[2] In many ways, his surprise at Lenin's return is warranted. For the larger part of the last three decades, scholars and cultural commentators mostly agreed on what Ken Jowitt, in his eponymously titled 1989 essay, called "the Leninist extinction": the complete and final eradication of Leninism as a political form or a mode of thinking in the post–Cold War era.[3] Statues of Lenin were taken down everywhere throughout the former socialist world, his portraits destroyed or sold to private collectors as cultural oddities on the black market. As a teenager in the 1990s Russia, I personally witnessed ordinary citizens, institutions, and libraries taking their beautifully produced, meticulously annotated fifty-two volume collections of Lenin's writing to garbage dumps. In 1994, Boris Yeltsin ordered the removal of the famous "Lenin's Cabinet in the Kremlin" from the Kremlin, in an act of iconoclastic violence—a *coup d'état*, a symbol of the counterrevolution's victory over the Bolsheviks (the artifacts were salvaged and relocated to the Gorki museum in a suburb of Moscow). The iconic black marble statue of a brooding Lenin in the Kremlin was also removed in October 1994. The 1990s was the decade that Macedonian philosopher Jasna Koteska refers to as "Lenin's shame."[4] Koteska coined this phrase after having observed her five-year-old son, who had stumbled upon a statue of Lenin lying in the grass, proceeding to shake Lenin's hand and kiss Lenin's cheek—a gesture that she interprets as an attempt by the child to "restore" Lenin from his shameful state. This phrase captures the aspect of ritual humiliation that underlies acts of iconoclasm—the desire to not only remove symbols of communism from public spaces, but to also denigrate its very idea by shaming and punishing the body of the Bolshevik leader. As Russian philosopher Gleb Pavlovsky recalls, in the 1990s, Lenin was not to be argued with or refuted; he was to be laughed at.[5] Prominent thinkers on the Left distanced themselves from Lenin. Franco Bifo Berardi wrote, for instance: "I'm convinced that the twentieth century would have been a better century had Lenin not existed."[6] It is impressive that it is not Hitler, Mussolini, or, as a matter of fact, Reagan that Berardi singles out as the twentieth century's chief culprit. Instead of arguing with Lenin, Berardi psychologizes him: relying on a 1998 biographical source, he presents Lenin as melancholic and resentful, who, in Berardi's words, exemplifies "male narcissism . . . confronted with the infinite power of capital and emerg[ing] from it frustrated, humiliated, and depressed."[7]

Figure I.1.

What does the future of Lenin look like today? Built in 1989, on the eve of the Soviet Union's disintegration, the Lenin Museum in the Gorki complex outside of Moscow is a time machine. The monumental building is visible from afar, and as you walk from the parking lot, it dominates the horizon as if it were an alien spaceship, disconnected from the surrounding landscape. Upon entering, a visitor will walk up white marble steps, eventually glimpsing a circular opening where Lenin's statue appears, as if descending from a spacecraft hovering above (Fig. I.1). The museum's architecture and design capture the fantasy world of the late Soviet era—the fantasy of the revolutionary state as futuristic and of Lenin as an extraterrestrial, arriving on Earth from a faraway galaxy, or perhaps, from the future. The fantasy of Lenin we encounter in the 1989 museum contrasts starkly with the Lenin presented by the other, more terrestrial museum in the same complex—a museum commemorating Lenin's presence in the Gorki complex in 1921–24 (Fig. I.2). A small room, a single bed, a simple writing desk, and a modest library paint an image of Lenin as most comfortable in a humble environment—an ascetic, a workaholic, a writer, a revolutionary who despised luxury and excess.

Figure I.2.

A hundred years ago, in 1920, Lenin was visited by science fiction writer H. G. Wells, the author of *The Time Machine*. Lenin himself, however, is a time machine. He traveled through the twentieth century in various guises—as a revolutionary, a statesman, a cult figure, an extraterrestrial, a zombie, a figure of defeat and shame. And now he is back yet again—in what form? We assert, with and through the works in this collection, that Lenin belongs to the future. It is, of course, not the same future as seen from the depths of the Soviet era, in which the certainty of communism's arrival dominated the anticipatory horizon. This collection seeks to discern the contours of the future Lenin in various ways—by reclaiming the image of Lenin as future-oriented, flexible (despite the stereotype of the "rigid" Bolsheviks), and as a figure of survival and persistence in the struggle for a just world, rather than as a figure of melancholy and extinction. The Lenin of our collection is the opposite of the nostalgic Lenin of postsocialist studies: he is the figure of anticipatory hope that allows us to imagine something wholly other than the perpetual neoliberal present. Even those in this collection who argue against Lenin's ideas show a trend of renewed engagement that takes Lenin on a different set of terms, in the moment of capitalism's decline, as someone to be reckoned with. In the twilight of the intervallic era, Lenin resurfaces as a revolutionary figure once again—a human-sized figure, an analyst of the real conditions on the ground, a theorist of state and revolution, and one who provides manuals and blueprints for how to build a mass movement.

Lenin is also a political and intellectual giant to whom we must return, perhaps, every decade. By staging a conversation among a diverse group of scholars, we show that Lenin's thought today, as it was a century ago, sparks hope, raises controversy, and promotes intellectual debates. Aiming to produce an interdisciplinary collection of essays, we invited political theorists, activists, cultural and literary studies scholars, scholars of education, rhetoric scholars, and historians to assess the relevance of the Leninist legacy. Collectively, the authors in this collection debate whether Lenin's thought allows us to rethink political strategy for the Left, bring into view the rich yet silenced history of Black Leninism (both in the United States and on the African continent), and examine contemporary developments, such as right-wing Leninism (Steve Bannon) and the Bernie Sanders movement in the United States. Our scholars engage with specific concepts, such as "vanguard," "revolution," "withering away," "revolutionary state," "romantic anticapitalism," and "national self-determination"; they address specific texts, such as *State and Revolution*, "April's Theses," *The Development of Capitalism in Russia*, among many others; and they talk about the ways in which Lenin can be adopted, adapted, and re-envisioned for our times.

Lenin in Post-2008 Politics

This book also emerged as part of a continuation of the work started by *Lenin Reloaded*—a collection edited by Sebastian Budgen and Slavoj Žižek in 2007. The collection was groundbreaking at that time in that it sought to bring Lenin back from his shameful state and restore (reload) him as an interlocutor. From the perspective of the 2020s, however, it seems as if a vast epoch separates us from *Lenin Reloaded*, which was put together, as the editors note, during a time of profound disorientation when alternatives to capitalism seemed unimaginable to most, even on the Left. The collection's very title, the editors state, was somewhat scandalous in the context of post–Cold War capitalist-realist hegemony. Times have changed, however. The financial crisis of 2008 created the first ripples of mobilization on the otherwise smooth postpolitical surface. In *The Rebirth of History*, Badiou called the post-2008 moment "the time of riots"—a moment of "glorious but defeated mass mobilizations."[8] He writes: "As yet blind, naïve, scattered and lacking a powerful concept of durable organization," they nevertheless signal "a rebirth of History, as opposed to the pure and simple repetition of the worst."[9] Out of that crisis came the successes, failures, and contradictions of Syriza and Podemos; the mass Occupy protests of 2011; mass outrage at the banks, insurance companies, and the governments that bailed them out; Black Lives Matter; and the mass mobilizations around Bernie Sanders and Jeremy Corbyn that signaled the renewed visibility of the socialist alternative. Thomas Piketty's 2013 *Capital* became a *New York Times* best-seller in 2014. No longer in the age of postpolitical consensus, we are also no longer in the post–Cold War epoch. Some called the new era "the post-post-cold War,"[10] but surely a better term is needed.

The advent of Trump's presidency brought a new wave of popular mobilizations, with women's marches and antifascist protests. In upstate New York where I live and work, curators of the Women's Rights National Historic Park in the sleepy town of Seneca Falls, N.Y. (considered the birthplace of the U.S. women's suffrage movement) were awed, in January 2016, by the sight of almost twenty thousand people who poured into Seneca Falls' three-block downtown to protest Trump's inauguration. International Women's Day—a socialist holiday—is now marked by marches in U.S. cities and worldwide. In the 2017 centennial of the October Revolution, the time was ripe to rethink and revive the memory of October. The year saw a slew of publications—Slavoj Žižek (*Lenin*), Tariq Ali (*The Dilemmas of Lenin*), China Miéville (*October*), and Michael Hardt ("October! To Commemorate the Future"), among others—that assessed Lenin's thought and the legacy of the October Revolution of 1917.[11] Testifying to the potential for the return of Leninism today are also the critiques of the limits of horizontality and spontaneity that emerged in the aftermath of the Occupy movement (Nick Srnicek and Alex Williams) and the calls to return to the party form in political struggle (Jodi Dean). We have reasons to believe that the time of reaction, apathy, and Left retreat—where, in the absence of political organization, riots were the primary form that opposed, chaotically, the status quo—has ended. We are witnessing the return of both small- and large-scale Left organizing, and this is one of the reasons for Lenin's renewed actuality. Socialist organizations, such as The Democratic Socialists of America (DSA) and The Party for Socialism and Liberation (PSL) in the United States have reported exponential growth. Bernie Sanders's campaign drew into its vortex thousands of organizers while exposing at the same time the limits of elections as a vehicle of change. In 2020, as the coronavirus pandemic brought the global economy to a grinding halt, mass protests against racist police violence erupted all over the United States, shaking the system to the core. Reading Lenin in 2020, the 150th anniversary of his birthday, is instructive, as these overlapping crises expose the fragility of the current world system, similarly to the crisis unleashed, in Lenin's time, by World War I. For most of our authors, the actuality of Lenin seems beyond doubt, although it remains a point of debate as to which parts of his legacy we are to revisit, and to what ends. This collection starts precisely there: Which aspects of Lenin's thought are particularly relevant today, and for whom? Who has a legitimate claim to Lenin?

The first section of this collection maps the field of contemporary politics by charting four positions: a left-wing anti-Leninist, a left-wing Leninist, a right-wing Leninist, and a romantic anticapitalist. The left-wing anti-Leninist position is exemplified by David J. Ost, the left-wing Leninist position is articulated by Jodi Dean and Daniel Egan, the right-wing Leninist stance is described by Alexandar Mihailovic, and finally, the romantic anticapitalist position is examined by Christian Sorace and Kai Heron.

The first essay of this section begins by questioning whether a return to Lenin is warranted, and to what end. David J. Ost, a lifelong scholar of popular movements in Eastern Europe, and a self-described Left anti-Leninist, argues strongly that Lenin is more relevant to today's Right, who find inspiration in Lenin's program for taking over and dismantling the state, than to those on the Left, who, in fact, would have much to lose if the democratic institutions that exist today were dismantled. The contemporary Left, Ost believes, must continue on the Gramscian, reformist path that over the course of the post–World War II era proved successful. "Indeed, that the Left has succeeded with the Gramscian push is why the Right is today so enamored of Lenin: to smash those institutions and effect a (counter) revolution against the gains the Left has made," Ost asserts. He cautions against the temptation on the Left to return to Lenin, which he worries is already occurring: such return would be an act of self-betrayal. "[T]he resurrection of Lenin," he writes, "runs in the face of all the reasons why the Left abandoned Lenin in recent generations." Among these reasons are the rise of the *nomenklatura* in twentieth-century state socialist societies, in which the bureaucracy of the party assumed the rule over the proletariat and the people; the intolerance of dissent; and the generally antidemocratic outcomes of the October Revolution. The contemporary Left must learn from the failures of real existing socialism, argues Ost, and forcefully "object to parties with centralized leadership claiming a monopoly of knowledge that justifies efforts to limit opposition, and assigns to itself the sole right to decide not just the correct paths anti-capitalist practice should take but the nature of the political regime and what is or is not allowed once success is achieved."

We chose to begin this collection with Ost's provocative and rhetorically powerful essay, because it makes explicit the position that is shared implicitly by many on the Left: the belief that Leninism must be repudiated and purged from the Left's ranks in the aftermath of the collapse of large-scale state socialist projects. Leninism, for many, is associated with political violence, rejection of reformism, purges of opposition, and with such unsavory terms as dictatorship (of the proletariat). Moreover, Ost brings to the surface a sentiment, common to 1960s leftists but also to many of our contemporaries, namely, that Leninism seems rather straightlaced and old-fashioned when compared with the sexier, more nuanced pedagogies of anticapitalism developed from the 1960s on—by Deleuze and Guattari, Foucault, and many other post-Marxists—who were, some would argue, more radical in their analyses of power. Without providing definitive answers, we seek to start a debate about these shared assumptions and believe that Left anti-Leninism is a position we need to seriously engage.

It should be noted, however, that Ost's analysis, as he makes clear, focuses on the European and American intellectual currents that found their expression in the turmoil of the 1960s and resulted in the Velvet Revolutions of 1989. The Left that rejected Lenin, for Ost, is, consequently, the American and European Left. This qualification of the argument's scope is important: anticolonial movements in the global South that emerged victorious in the 1960-'70s, were more inspired by Lenin than Foucault or Deleuze. Zeyad el Nabolsy—an Egyptian Canadian scholar whose essay appears in Part 2, draws attention to the centrality of Lenin's thought for East African Marxists of that era. To add another example, the leader of Afghanistan's communist party, which was formed in 1965 and came to power in the Saur (April) Revolution of 1978, Nur Muhammad Taraki, was a proud Leninist who liked to boast that he had been born in 1917, in the days of the Russian Revolution.[12] In short, a global view of the 1960s–1970s era indexes that the Left rejection of Lenin in the Euro-American core was accompanied by political successes of revolutionary Leninism in the colonized world. And correspondingly, 1989 marks the advent of a dark era in the global South: while Velvet Revolutions were happening in Eastern Europe, many socialist countries in the formerly colonized world spiraled into civil wars as socialist governments were toppled by ultra-Right illiberal forces.[13] Fidel Castro, in his 1989 speech, said, in relation to these global changes: "Now imperialism wants the East European socialist countries to join in the colossal looting [of the Third World]. This apparently does not bother the theorists of capitalist reforms one bit. This is why in many of those countries nobody mentions the Third World's tragedy."[14]

Following Ost's provocative piece is an interview with Jodi Dean, titled "What is Leninist Thinking?" Dean, a self-identified Left Leninist and author of *The Communist Horizon* and more recently, *Comrade*, questions whether it is possible both to support Left politics *and* reject Lenin today. In contrast to Ost, Dean upholds the immediate importance of Lenin for the Left as an antidote to acceptable versions of Marx—"Marxism defanged, Marxism for liberalism, a Marxism without state and revolution." Lenin, for Dean, is also a vehicle of addressing large-scale, widely distributed crises, such as the climate crisis, that require scalable organizational forms. A theorist of the party organization as well as of communicative capitalism, Dean argues that Leninist thinking—with its focus on organizational capacity, whether it is building a mass movement or building a proletarian state—is both counterintuitive and especially valuable in the era of network-mediated communicative capitalism, where the hierarchies of followers that emerge through the seeming "democracy" of social media interactions mimic the larger social inequalities (and are produced by similar forces). Central to Leninist thinking, for Dean, is the idea of the future understood as the actuality of revolution—a paradoxical temporality that determines what needs to be done in the present. To think like Lenin is to take the revolution seriously, as a *future fact*; the Leninist party "anticipates the revolution, materializing the belief that makes revolution possible." The party, thus, is not, merely, an organization, but a force that makes the future present in revolutionary anticipation and concrete struggle. Attesting to the Left's re-energization in recent years, Dean believes that Lenin has much to offer to the contemporary "multinational, multigenerational, multigendered" working-class struggle.

No analysis of post-2008 Left politics would be complete without an engagement with the U.S. presidential election campaigns of Bernie Sanders (2016 and 2020), which popularized the idea of socialism in the U.S. context, galvanizing a progressive movement, especially among the millennial generation. In their chapter, "We're All (Romantic) Socialists," Kai Heron and Christian Sorace offer an analysis of Sanders's campaign by deploying Lenin's critique of the Russian Narodniks of the 1890s. Sanders's focus on mitigating the excesses of capitalism, they argue, is reminiscent of what Lenin calls "romantic anticapitalism"—an attitude that fails to think beyond a moral condemnation of capitalism. "[I]n both Lenin's time and in our own," write Heron and Sorace, "the pervasive dissatisfaction with capitalism tends to take the form of a sentimental anticapitalism through which capitalism is *simultaneously repudiated and preserved.*" While recognizing the significance of Sanders for U.S. politics, they are skeptical of his promises to mitigate capitalism's excess—via regulation, redistribution, and limited climate change interventions. Undergirding such hopes is the failure to recognize capitalism's inherent instability—brought into sharp relief by Marx, Engels, and Lenin—where excess and disruption (financial greed, environmental exploitation, necropolitical experiments) are constitutive of the very system and thus cannot be regulated away. By tracing Lenin's critique of Sismondi, the authors show that "Lenin demands that revolutionaries stay analytically within the *excesses of capitalism,* and refuse the temptation of seeking an imaginary resolution, whether *within* capitalism or *beyond* it." The desire to mitigate or escape capitalism, they remind us, with Lenin, can only be utopian and reactionary.

A curious issue that surfaced post-2016 is that of right-wing Leninism. Does Lenin belong to the Left only? Does the Right have a legitimate claim to Lenin, and what is the nature of that claim? In his fascinating chapter on the right-wing Leninism of Steve Bannon, Alexandar Mihailovic answers the question in the affirmative: the Right, he argues, does have a claim to Lenin. He then gives us a glimpse into the vast archives of right-wing Leniniana—a corpus of works, literary and theoretical, that, throughout much of the twentieth and twenty-first centuries, adapt Lenin for right-wing use. For many of us, the phenomenon of right-wing Leninism became visible after Steve Bannon claimed, in an interview with historian Ronald Radosh in 2013, that he was a Leninist. In this chapter, we learn of the history behind what seemed, to many, an odd claim. Lenin's revolutionary zeal and his belligerent, uncompromising stance appeal to the twenty-first-century "right-wing international" who see themselves not as traditionalists or defenders of the status quo, but rather as radical, countercultural, and against the status quo.[15] Paul Gottfried—the conservative thinker who coined the term *alternative right*—calls himself proudly "a Leninist of the Right," aiming to rouse the masses to bring on the "collapse" of the current regime.[16] Mihailovic explains the logic behind such statements. "Rebellion," Mihailovic writes, "now becomes the domain of the public-school scions of a 'decadent and dilettante political elite,' fully expressed by [Boris] Johnson's often puerile if not violent demeanor, and the deliberately fey yet strangely unembarrassed media maunderings of his pro-Brexit confederate Jacob Rees-Mogg. This is a push for revolution that is driven by the resolutely undemocratic impulse of *droit de seigneur*." Tory anarchists today share "many affinities with 'punk nihilism' from Thatcher-era England" and embody the rage of the disaffected white working class against the system that failed them. The list of things that those on the right adopt from the ultimate leftist revolutionary include his pathos, countercultural affect ("the drama of decision"), and his anti-statism, combined, paradoxically, with his willingness to take and hold on to state power. Among the aspects of Lenin's thought that right-wing ideologues have to dispense with to make him useful for their goals is his Marxist core: his commitment to universal equality, anti-imperialism, and working-class power. The Lenin of Bannon, who, according to Mihailovic, is drawn to "the negative core of Leninism," is thus a hollowed-out Lenin, hailed as a strategist and a warrior, above all, and a highly effective one. From this insightful chapter we draw the conclusion that anyone interested in twenty-first-century politics would be wise to take very seriously the Right's claim to, and fascination with, the Bolshevik leader.

The last chapter in this section returns us to the question of the party form. Lenin frequently talks about the party as a military force. In "A Letter to a Comrade on Our Organizational Tasks," he stresses the importance of "military discipline," noting that party members working in key areas such as factories should view themselves as soldiers "obliged to submit to all its orders and to observe all the 'laws and customs' of the 'army in the field' which [they have] joined and from which in time of war [they have] no right to absent [themselves] without official leave."[17] Later on, in the turbulent days of the February Revolution, as Lenin began to develop ideas about the proletarian state while still in exile, he imagined the entire victorious class of the working masses drawn into armed militias—an organization that "would enjoy the *boundless* respect and confidence of the people, for it itself would be an organization of the entire people."[18] The essay by Daniel Egan, "Saving the Vanguard," brings into view the technical and practical significance of Lenin's military metaphors. Specifically, Egan is interested in Lenin's concept of the vanguard, which he reads literally, as a military metaphor, explaining, with great nuance, its role in political struggle. "The vanguard," he writes, "keeps the memory of historical struggles alive during periods in which the masses, either out of exhaustion, disillusionment, or fear of repression, pull back from the revolutionary process—in other words, the vanguard ensures that a revolutionary movement's retreat is orderly and preserves its ability to fight another day." The vanguard thus is needed both in times of revolutionary offense and in times of defense, ensuring that the defeats suffered are tactical and temporary, and not a total capitulation resulting in a scattering of forces. In what amounts to a Left Leninist position, he argues against the turn to spontaneity that characterized much of post–Cold War left thought, where the party was viewed as necessarily authoritarian. While the way a vanguard functions in the twenty-first century might need to be rethought, revolutionary change will remain impossible without a vanguard, and various struggles will only have tactical significance, argues Egan.

Black Leninism and Anti-imperialism

Historian Carole Boyce Davies, in her 2007 book on Claudia Jones, finds an apt metaphor in the fact that Claudia Jones, a tricontinental Black revolutionary, is buried, in England, to the left of Karl Marx.[19] An immigrant from Trinidad and a prominent member of CPUSA, Jones was extraordinary, Davies argues, in her ability (widely recognized by her peers at the time) to theorize the superexploitation of the Black woman worker, linking "decolonization struggles internally and externally, and [challenging] U.S. racism, gender subordination, class exploitation, and imperialist aggression simultaneously."[20] She was clearly the model, Davies argues, for Angela Davis—another Black communist who, decades later, would theorize the "triple jeopardy" of the Black woman worker.[21] Like many other Black radicals, Jones paid a heavy price for her political organizing: arrested in 1948 for being a member of the Communist Party, she spent time in prison before being deported from the United States to England. The second section of our collection echoes and is in dialogue with the ongoing collective work of recovering the legacy of Black communism in the United States and beyond. As we turn to the past, we remain future-oriented, however: the three essays in this section construct a lineage, a legacy, and a past that is meant to inform and inspire the newly resurgent struggle for Black liberation in the United States and beyond. These chapters describe the moment where the history of tricontinental Black liberation struggle aligned with the organized Marxist Left in the aftermath of the October Revolution of 1917—an encounter of world-historical significance. The authors don't just assert that the story of Leninism and the twentieth century is *incomplete* without a chapter on Black Leninism. Their claim is much stronger: that the struggle for antiracism and anti-imperialism was *central* to twentieth-century revolutionary history.

How do we conceptualize this rich legacy of twentieth-century Black Leninism? The section opens with an essay by Black Studies scholar Charisse Burden-Stelly who proposes the term "the Tradition of Radical Blackness" to capture a lineage of "Black anticapitalist thought and activism rooted in and attendant to local, national, and global anti-Black political economies." This tradition, she argues, is conceptually distinct from the "Black radical tradition"—a term used by Cedric Robinson. This essay thus engages the theoretical debates stirring contemporary Black studies. Much of the latter is inspired by Robinson's concept of the "Black radical tradition" that he advances in his *Black Marxism*—a book that is, in part, a critique of Marxism and especially Marxism-Leninism.[22] While Robinson states that Marxism was at a certain point useful to Black radical thought and practice, overall, he detaches the Black radical tradition from Marxist thought, exposing, in turn, Marxism as a parochial European doctrine whose scope was circumscribed by its unique historical context and its Enlightenment prejudices, and thus unable to see the racial character of European capital accumulation. Marxism, and Leninism, in short, cannot provide the foundation for Black revolutionary struggle against what Robinson dubbed "racial capitalism."

Burden-Stelly's essay intervenes in this debate: it outlines the contours of what she proposes to call "the Tradition of Radical Blackness" through discussing the work of Black Communists, such as Harry Haywood, Doxey Wilkerson, Kwame Nkrumah, James Ford, Sojourners for Truth and Justice, and Claudia Jones. She traces how these twentieth-century intellectuals engaged with Marxism-Leninism, using it to frame their political views and to guide their analysis of racial capitalism. These thinkers deployed Marxist-Leninist vocabularies and epistemologies, while updating and deepening Leninist views on capitalist accumulation, imperialist war, and the national question, among other issues. The Tradition of Radical Blackness, as it emerges, Burden-Stelly argues, in their political and intellectual work, "theorizes Blackness as a special relationship to the capitalist mode of production; considers intraracial class conflict and antagonism; and strives for the eventual overthrow of racial capitalism." These thinkers placed particular emphasis on the specific character of Black oppression as *superexploitation* within the planetary capitalist formation, developing theories of worker organization attuned to this fact. Some of these Black communists used Lenin's pamphlet on the right of nations to self-determination[23] as they conceived of African American people in the U.S. South as a nationally oppressed group that must demand full emancipation and self-determination (the Black Belt thesis eventually formulated by Haywood). Others developed new theoretical paradigms in close connection to immediate political struggles, such as Kwame Nkrumah, who expanded Lenin's analysis of imperialism to U.S.-led neocolonialism after the political program of pan-Africanism and indigenous development he pursued as Ghana's first president was overthrown by a coup. These analyses thus connected the multiple local, national, and regional struggles to the global conditions that sustain racial and economic domination. Because the Tradition of Radical Blackness powerfully defies the regimes of superexploitation and dispossession, it has been, writes Burden-Stelly, "systematically targeted, often through discourses of anticommunism, by statist and imperial authorities as extremism, authoritarianism, and/or terrorism to rationalize the use of extraordinary force, violence, and exception."

In his chapter "Black Leninist Internationalism: The Anticolonial Center," Robert R. Maclean argues that there was an epoch of Black Leninism that to a certain extent spanned, and defined, the twentieth century. "As a thesis and a program," Maclean asserts, Black Leninism is "a necessary *re*statement of the subject of Black Communism that insists on the historiographic and conceptual overlap of mid-century Black struggle and Marxism-Leninism." Maclean insists that this juncture, in turn, is central to the historiography of twentieth-century communism. In centering Black Leninism as *the* subject of twentieth-century communism, Maclean's essay suggests that one cannot understand the twentieth-century worldwide communist movement without comprehending the centrality of the tricontinental Black anticolonial struggle, one that drew into its ranks Black intellectuals, revolutionaries, community organizers, militants, and artists, who analyzed the cataclysms of late colonial Europe as deeply rooted in (and rooted through) violent expropriations on the African continent and beyond. Maclean's is an effort to retheorize the revolutionary subject of Marxism as Black, anti-imperialist, pan-African—one that moved not only the struggle, but revolutionary thought forward by forcing a confrontation between Black revolutionary desire and the basic historical and philosophical principles of Marxism. Maclean asks what it would mean to view the short twentieth century—an epoch that includes countless anticolonial revolutions and antiracist mass movements—some successful, others defeated—as defined by the struggles (over, for, and against) Black Leninism around the world, sustained by an international formation of overlapping Black diasporas.

Zeyad el Nabolsy's "Lenin and East African Marxism" is fueled by a similar impulse—to center the conceptual and political legacy of Black Leninists. To the charge of Eurocentrism in relation to Leninist thought, el Nabolsy responds: We can only utter this accusation if we deliberately ignore the revolutionary and intellectual contribution of Black Leninist leaders, especially those from the formerly colonized world. By discussing the work of two such East African thinkers—the Zanzibari Marxist revolutionary Abdul Rahman Mohammed Babu (1924–1996) and the Ugandan Marxist theorist Dani Wadada Nabudere (1932–2011)—el Nabolsy shows that Marxism-Leninism was central to their struggle for African liberation; moreover, these African Marxists were not passive "adopters" of Marxism-Leninism but refined and expanded Lenin's ideas in relation to the African continent and beyond. First, Lenin's analysis of imperialism and the national question, el Nabolsy shows, provided a theoretical basis for their formulation of Pan-Africanism where the latter figured as "the expression of African nationalism vis-à-vis a racialized imperialism." Second, Lenin's critique of the Narodniks program allowed Babu and Nabudere to develop a comprehensive critique of "African socialism"—a doctrine that saw traditional *Ujamaa* ("familyhood," extended family) as the foundation for African socialism. While African socialism idealized the African village as communal and naturally socialist, stressed the lack of developed class relations in Africa, and charted a path for African liberation that, they believed, could avoid class struggle, Babu and Nabudere argued, via Lenin, that "the claim to uniqueness is not itself unique" but is a result of a certain stage of development in the relations of production. Nabudere wrote: "There is nothing uniquely African in an era where finance capital has united all the peoples of the world under its rule. An African proletariat is no less international than an Asian one or a European one. They are all exploited by the same monopolies, the same class, the same capital, only in different measure."[24] In contrast to the proponents of African socialism who argued that Marxism was a foreign ideological import into Africa, Babu and Nabudere used Marxist-Leninist methodologies to formulate their vision of African liberation.

The essays in this section thus center the Leninist tradition within the anticolonial, non-European tradition and canon—an important correction to the Eurocentric tilt of many accounts of Leninist thought, including those published in the recent decade. We decided to foreground Black Leninism specifically as it is particularly pertinent to today's struggles for Black liberation, of which the ongoing fight against racist police violence in the United States is an example. However, it needs to be noted that Leninist thought was important to countless other liberation movements around the world—in Asia, Central and Latin America, and in the Muslim world. Lenin was the first among his comrades to recognize the potential world-historical importance of non-Western countries in what he believed was going to be the inevitable march of workers' power in the twentieth century. And while the relation between communism and anticolonialism throughout the twentieth century was fraught with tensions and contradictions, anti-imperialism became a central tenet of global revolutionary struggle. Taken together, the three essays in this section present an argument that in the twentieth century the geographical reach of Marxism-Leninism was indeed planetary, anti-imperialist, and that Black struggles against superexploitation were central to twentieth-century communism.

The Actuality of Lenin's Thought

What are some of the other ways in which Lenin continues to be our contemporary? What other concepts, ideas, and analyses are particularly useful for today's political struggles and intellectual debates? The essays in this section focus on the following: Lenin's theory of the state, his theory of bourgeois law, and his theory of the party. We begin this section with Giovanni Zanotti's essay on "the two states" in Lenin's 1917 *State and Revolution*. *State and Revolution* and Lenin's conceptualization of the withering away of the state continue to spur debates among scholars.[25] For Badiou (*The Communist Hypothesis*) and Hardt, it is precisely the Leninist party's inability to bring about such withering away of the state that serves as evidence of the failure not only of twentieth-century socialism but of the party form more generally. As we saw in the chapter by Mihailovic, the ideologues of the Right find in Lenin's *State and Revolution* both an inspiration and guidance for their attacks on the state. "Criticized from the Right as utopian (since it allegedly postulates a full redemption of human nature)," writes Zanotti, "and from the Left as authoritarian (since it maintains the necessity of a state, however transitional, instead of invoking its *immediate* suppression), [the withering away thesis] touches the deepest layers of Marxist political theory and practice and has never ceased to challenge both of them." The question of the state, Zanotti argues, has acquired renewed significance in the current era of neoliberalism's crisis, where Left cosmopolitanism that previously celebrated the passing of nation-states into a globalized multitude is eclipsed, almost improbably, by the Left's defensive neo-statism, which now sees the state as not only "pivotal, but also as the proper space for democracy and even class struggle." Lenin's theory, for Zanotti, provides a key to some of these debates: Lenin's state always splits into two states, one that cannot wither away (the bourgeois state) and the other that *cannot but wither away* (the transitional revolutionary state). Via a careful reading of Lenin, supplemented by the conceptual apparatus borrowed from "New Marx Reading," Zanotti defends the "fundamental correctness and actuality" of Lenin's theory of the state.

Camila Vergara's essay on law argues, similarly, for the actuality of Lenin's theory of law. For Lenin, once again, there is not one law but always at least two juridical regimes: bourgeois law and proletarian law. By engaging with Lenin's three early essays, "Explanation of the Law on Fines Imposed on Factory Workers" (1895), "Draft and Explanation of a Programme for the Social-Democratic Party" (1895), and "The New Factory Law" (1897), Vergara asks, with Lenin, whether bourgeois labor laws offer protection to workers or whether they in fact serve to formalize exploitation. She argues, with and through Lenin, that within the context where workers are in a relation of dependence upon their employer, labor legislation becomes a form of legal domination: a legal "protection" formalizes a power relation, making it more intractable. A legal scholar, Vergara makes capacious connections across space and time, bringing into proximity today's platform capitalism and nineteenth-century factories discussed by Lenin. Within the gig economy, legal struggles surrounding megaplatforms such as Uber (a ride sharing service) and Handy (a housekeeping service), risk legalizing, via regulation, existing practices that are uniquely exploitative and disadvantageous to workers. For instance, Vergara shows, contracts in the new gig economy allows employers "to hire workers as 'independent contractors' but to discipline them as 'employees.'" In addition, Vergara points to and critiques the persistence of bourgeois laws in state socialist societies, highlighting how absenteeism laws, formulated in the late nineteenth century and critiqued by Lenin, persisted, in modified form, in the USSR, reflecting workers' subordination, not to the employer, but to the state.

In his essay "Facing the Test: The Leninist Party as Proctor," Derek R. Ford offers an insightful, dynamic account of Lenin's thinking about the Party—as "a kind of *teacher* who *teaches totally to the test: the test of revolution.*" Throughout the twentieth century, the Communist Party served as an educational institution for the masses. An education scholar, Ford argues that all revolutionary struggles are necessarily educational processes; yet in radical politics and research on Lenin these educational concepts are never brought into the foreground or deeply contextualized. Here, he fleshes out one pedagogical mode that figures prominently in Lenin's writings and that, he argues, undergirds his theory of the party: the protest as a test for the Party. Does the Party have the necessary capacity to organize a protest? Is the protest itself timely? Is there mass support for the action outside of the Party? What, essentially, is the role of protests in revolutionary struggle? These are the questions that Lenin had to answer, again and again, in 1917, as his thinking changed and adapted to the rapidly shifting conditions in the months preceding the October Revolution. These are the questions that are urgent today as well. In his 2017 *New Yorker* piece "Is There Any Point to Protesting?" Nathan Heller asks whether protests are a useful form of political action or a waste of everyone's energy and time. He recalls the president's inauguration day of 2016: "The boulevards in cities including New York, Washington, London—even L.A., where humans rarely walk—were riverine with marches. It was said to be the largest single-day demonstration in the history of the United States. Then Monday came, and the new Administration went about its work as planned."[26]

Lenin's theory of the Party as proctor preparing itself and the masses for the ultimate test—the revolution—allows us, according to Ford, to understand the significance of protests in the longer arc of revolutionary struggle. "Conceptualizing the revolution as a test and the revolutionary process as a series of pre-tests," writes Ford, "enables the Party to build its internal organization, learn the shifting coordinates within which it is operating, and intervene and push forward the revolution in response to these shifts." Most fundamentally, for Ford, Lenin's focus on protests evidences the dialectical nature of Lenin's conception of spontaneity and organization, centralization and decentralization, and theory and practice. Ultimately, Ford makes a case against depictions of Lenin as authoritarian, fleshing out the relation between the "iron discipline" of a political program and the "flexibility" or nimbleness Lenin demanded of a revolutionary organization: *embracing the test,* Ford insists, means effectively relinquishing control.

Zhivka Valiavicharska's essay, "The Production of 'Leninism' and Its Political Journeys," revisits Lenin to intervene in the debates surrounding the split between Western and Eastern Marxisms. By tracing the discursive production of Marxism-Leninism in Stalin's era, and by describing the ways in which Eastern Marxists from the 1950s on critiqued that doctrine and recovered an increasingly complex, dialectical Lenin and Marx, Valiavicharska demonstrates, with great effectiveness, that Eastern Marxism was a dynamic, evolving tradition. She draws attention to the Orientalizing view, prevalent among Western Marxists, of Eastern European and Soviet Marxism as dogmatic and unchanging—a view that is predicated on the continued erasure of thought that emerged from within the experience of actually existing socialism. In this, Valiavicharska is in the company of Alexei Penzin, Keti Chukhrov, and Maria Chehonadskih—contemporary Russian philosophers who have brought to the Western publics, for the first time, translations of some of these Eastern Marxist texts. Valiavicharska argues that "the disavowal of Lenin is foundational to the broadly accepted divisions between the 'good' Western Marxism and its bad, dogmatic, static, and historically catastrophic counterpart, Soviet Marxism." Ultimately, she states, her essay is an attempt at decolonizing Lenin and Eastern Marxism by tracing how Eastern Marxists, since the 1950s, recovered Lenin as a complex situational thinker and a dialectical philosopher (which, she points out, was recognized by Lukacs by 1967, when he became aware of Lenin's *Philosophical Notebooks*). This essay is an important, timely contribution to the dialogue between these two currents of Marxism that is just beginning.

The collection ends with a photographic essay about material memory as two artists set out on a quest to find Lenin's statues in Bishkek, the capital city of Kyrgyzstan. I'd like to supplement this lyrical essay with some additional context. Not everyone knows that Kyrgyzstan occupies a unique place among post-Soviet states: In contrast to other former Soviet republics—for instance, its neighbor Uzbekistan—Kyrgyzstan maintains a positive view on its Soviet history and has not tried to erase its communist past. The country's central monument in Bishkek—which mimics the one in front of the Finland Station in St. Petersburg—is adorned with flowers every year in April, to commemorate Lenin's birthday.[27] This attitude is generally shared by officials, experts, and ordinary people. Bakyt Bakhchiev, a history museum director in Bishkek, says: "Perhaps, we are the only country that did not demolish a single monument of Lenin."[28] Faculty of History of Osh State University chair Sydyk Smadiyarov says, in relation to Lenin's statue on Osh's central square: "Some young historians want to demolish Lenin, saying, it is in the way when the prayer takes place, but I told my students: it shouldn't be done because Lenin did a tremendous lot for the Kyrgyz people."[29] The October event is still referred to as a "revolution" rather than a "coup"; history museums maintain their collections of Lenin memorabilia; and the official position states that the formation of the Soviet era brought forth the revival of Kyrgyz statehood. Streets with Soviet-era names still populate the landscape: almost every town has a street named after Lenin. For those looking to see the remnants of the Soviet era untouched by post-1991 iconoclasm, Kyrgyzstan is a place to visit. By using a 35 mm

Soviet-era camera, the two artists in this final essay seek to recreate an image of the past that is at once intimate and inaccessible.

In sum, taken together, the essays in this volume paint a portrait not just of Lenin, but of our time. The question of the future of Lenin, ultimately, becomes the question, What kind of Lenin do *we* need? As we see from these interventions, the danger of the Left abandoning Lenin is that we can end up with the hollowed-out Lenin of right-wing Leninists—a formula for state takeover without the political commitment to workers' power, anti-imperialism, equality, and economic justice. However, the Lenin we need to recover is not the one of so-called Marxism-Leninism—not the dogmatic centralist, but the flexible, nimble Lenin who put his party, constantly, to the test. We need the Lenin who materialized the future—the revolution to come—through organized action in service of that goal. We need a decolonial and decolonized Lenin—one who recognized that most twentieth-century revolutions would take place in the East and the South, that the former periphery would lead the former core. We need the non-Eurocentric Lenin—a theorist of anti-imperialism who inspired Black Leninists and other oppressed people worldwide in their struggle. The Lenin who comes back is neither the larger-than-life Lenin of the late Soviet epoch, nor the Lenin in shame. He is a terrestrial, human-sized figure—an "actually existing revolutionary" for our times.

Notes

1. Alain Badiou, *The Rebirth of History: Times of Riot and Uprisings* (Brooklyn: Verso, 2012), 38.
2. Brian C. Anderson, "Zombie Lenin," *National Review*, Oct. 2 (2017): par. 9, https://www.nationalreview.com/magazine/2017/10/02/slavoj-zizek-lenin-2017/.
3. Ken Jowitt, "The Leninist Extinction," *The Crisis of Leninism and the Decline of the Left: The Revolutions of 1989*, ed. Daniel Chirot (Seattle: University of Washington Press, 1991).
4. Jasna Koteska, "Spaces without Time" (2009): par. 3, https://jasnakoteska.blogspot.com/2010/07/spaces-without-time-2009-video-lecture.html.
5. Gleb Pavlovsky, "Ot Sostavitelya," in Mikhail Gefter, *Neostanovlennaya Revolutsiya: Sto Let v Sta Fragmentah* (Moscow: Europa, 2017), 14.
6. Franco Bifo Berardi, *After the Future* (Oakland, CA: AK Press, 2011), 37.
7. Ibid., 37.
8. Badiou, 6.

9. Ibid., 5.

10. Stephen Collinson and Patrick Oppmann, "This Could Be the End of the Post–Cold War Era," *CNN*, Nov. 7, 2019.

11. In Russian, notable books that came out in 2017 include the already mentioned Mikhail Gefter's *Neostanovlennaya Revolutziya* (*The Revolution Unstopped*) and Lev Danilkin's biography *Lenin* (Molodaya Gvardiya, 2017). Also notable is a mini-series *Demon Revolyutzii* (*Revolution's Demon*) that as Alexander Mihailovic points out, in this volume, is part and parcel of the vast archive of right-wing Leniniana.

12. On the communist revolution in Afghanistan and Taraki's role in it, see Alla Ivanchikova, *Imagining Afghanistan: Global Fiction and Film of the 9/11 Wars* (Lafayette, IN: Purdue University Press, 2019).

13. See Fred Haliday, "Third World Socialism: 1989 and After," *The Global 1989: Continuity and Change in World Politics*, ed. George Lawson (Cambridge: Cambridge University Press, 2012), on the issue of the global 1989.

14. Osne Westad, *The Global Cold War: Third World Interventions and the Making of Our Times* (Cambridge: Cambridge University Press, 2007), 394.

15. See, for instance, David Horowitz's *The Black Book of the American Left* (New York: Encounter Books, 2016), 41.

16. Paul Gottfried, "America 2034," *American Renaissance*, June 10, 2014: par. 5–6. https://www.amren.com/news/2014/06/america-in-2034-2/.

17. V. I. Lenin, "A Letter to a Comrade on Our Organizational Tasks" (1902), par. 15.

18. Ibid., "Letters from Afar" (1917), Third Letter, par. 40, Marxists.org.

19. Carole Boyce Davies, *Left of Karl Marx: The Political Life of Black Communist Claudia Jones* (Durham: Duke University Press, 2007), 2.

20. Ibid., 2.

21. Ibid., 4.

22. Cedric Robinson, *Black Marxism: The Making of the Black Radical Tradition* (London: Zed, 1983).

23. V. I. Lenin, "The Right of Nations to Self-Determination," 1914, Marxists.org.

24. Dan Nabudere, *Essays on the Theory and Practice of Imperialism* (Western Cape, South Africa: Onyx Press, 1979), 93.

25. Consider, for example, A. J. Polan, *Lenin and the End of Politics* (Berkeley: University of California Press, 1984) and Lorenzo Chiesa, "Lenin and the State of the Revolution," *Crisis and Critique* 4, no, 2 (2017): 107–31.

26. Nathan Heller, "Is There Any Point to Protesting?" *The New Yorker*, Aug. 21, 2017, par. 4.

27. For more information on the peculiar history of this monument, see Sally N. Cummings, "Leaving Lenin: Elites, Official Ideology, and Monuments in the Kyrgyz Republic," *Nationalities Papers* 41 no. 4 (2013): 606–21.

28. Quoted in Alexei Tokarev, "Kyrgyziya: 25 Let Posle SSSR," *Vlast* 20, June 2016, my translation.
29. Ibid.

Bibliography

Ali, Tariq. *The Dilemmas of Lenin: Terrorism, War, Empire, Love, Revolution.* Brooklyn: Verso, 2017.
Anderson, Brian C. "Zombie Lenin," *National Review,* October 2, 2017. https://www.nationalreview.com/magazine/2017/10/02/slavoj-zizek-lenin-2017/.
Badiou, Alain. *The Communist Hypothesis.* Brooklyn: Verso, 2009.
———. *The Rebirth of History.* Brooklyn: Verso, 2011.
Berardi, Franco Bifo. *After the Future.* Chico, CA: AK Press, 2011.
Budgen, Sebastian, Stathis Kouvelakis, and Slavoj Zizek, eds. *Lenin Reloaded: Towards a Politics of* Truth. Durham: Duke University Press, 2007.
Chehonadskih, Maria, Keti Chukhrov, and Alexei Penzin. "Introduction: Antiquity and Modernity of Soviet Marxism." *Stasis* 5, no. 2 (2017).
Chiesa, Lorenzo. "Lenin and the State of the Revolution." *Crisis and Critique* 4, no. 2 (2017): 107–31.
Collinson, Stephen, and Patrick Oppmann. "This Could Be the End of the Post–Cold War Era." *CNN,* November 7, 2019. https://www.cnn.com/2019/11/07/world/meanwhile-in-america-november-8/index.html.
Cummings, Sally N. "Leaving Lenin: Elites, Official Ideology, and Monuments in the Kyrgyz Republic." *Nationalities Papers* 41, no. 4 (2013): 606–21.
Danilkin, Lev. *Lenin.* Moscow: Molodaya Gvardiya, 2017.
Davies, Carole Boyce. *Left of Karl Marx: The Political Life of Black Communist Claudia Jones.* Durham: Duke University Press, 2007.
Demon Revolyutzii, Directed by Vladimir Khotinenko. Rossiya 1, 2017. TV series.
Gefter, Mikhail. *Neostanovlennaya Revolutsiya: Sto Let v Sta Fragmentah.* Moscow: Europa: 2017.
Gottfried, Paul. "America 2034." *American Renaissance,* June 10, 2014. https://www.amren.com/news/2014/06/america-in-2034-2/.
Haliday, Fred. "Third World Socialism: 1989 and After." In *The Global 1989: Continuity and Change in World Politics,* edited by George Lawson. New York: Cambridge University Press, 2012.
Hardt, Michael, and Sandro Mezzadra. "October! To Commemorate the Future." *The South Atlantic Review* 116, no. 4 (2017): 649–68.
Heller, Nathan. "Is There Any Point to Protesting?" *The New Yorker,* August 21, 2017.
Horowitz, David. *The Black Book of the American Left.* New York: Encounter Books, 2016.

Ivanchikova, Alla. *Imagining Afghanistan: Global Fiction and Film of the 9/11 Wars.* West Lafayette, IN: Purdue University Press, 2019.

Jowitt, Ken. "The Leninist Extinction." In *The Crisis of Leninism and the Decline of the Left: The Revolutions of 1989,* edited by Daniel Chirot. Seattle: University of Washington Press, 1991.

Koteska, Jasna. "Spaces Without Time" (2009). https://jasnakoteska.blogspot.com/2010/07/spaces-without-time-2009-video-lecture.html.

Lenin, V. I. "A Letter to a Comrade on Our Organizational Tasks." 1902. https://www.marxists.org/archive/lenin/works/1902/sep/00.htm.

———. "Letters from Afar." 1917. https://www.marxists.org/archive/lenin/works/1917/lfafar/index.htm.

———. "The Right of Nations to Self-Determination." 1914. https://www.marxists.org/archive/lenin/works/1914/self-det/.

Mieville, China. *October: The Story of the Russian Revolution.* London: Verso, 2017.

Nabudere, Dan. *Essays on the Theory and Practice of Imperialism.* Western Cape, South Africa: Onyx Press, 1979.

Pavlovsky, Gleb. "Ot Sostavitelya." In Mikhail Gefter, *Neostanovlennaya Revolutsiya: Sto Let v Sta Fragmentah.* Moscow: Europa, 11–14.

Polan, A. J. *Lenin and the End of Politics.* Oakland: University of California Press, 1984.

Robinson, Cedric. *Black Marxism: The Making of the Black Radical Tradition.* London: Zed Books, 1983.

The Simpsons. Season 9, episode 19, "Simpson Tide." Fox Entertainment, 1998.

Srnicek, Nick, and Alex Williams. *Inventing the Future: Postcapitalism and a World without Work.* Brooklyn: Verso 2015.

Tokarev, Alexei. "Kyrgyziya: 25 Let Posle SSSR." *Vlast* 20, June 2016. https://www.kommersant.ru/doc/3008034.

Traverso, Enzo. "Historicizing Communism: A Twentieth-Century Chameleon." *The South Atlantic Review* 116, no. 4 (2017): 763–80.

Westad, Osne. *The Global Cold War: Third World Interventions and the Making of Our Times.* New York: Cambridge University Press, 2007.

Žižek, Slavoj. *Lenin 2017: Remembering, Repeating, and Working Through.* Brooklyn: Verso, 2017.

PART I

LENIN, OUR CONTEMPORARY?

Chapter 1

Rejecting Lenin for the Left

DAVID J. OST

It has been a while since the Left has revolved around Lenin. Fifty years ago, or fifty years after the Russian Revolution, young leftists were eagerly reading his works, wrestling over his ideas, assessing their contemporary relevance. That is certainly not the case today, and not only in the global capitalist core. Lenin does retain some hold on the Left in the global periphery, where his ideas on imperialism have long seemed more relevant. But global interconnections have made the possibility of Leninist revolution seem less likely everywhere, which explains why so much of the semi-peripheral Left has in recent years focused attention on viable social reform without regime transformation, such as with the so-called "Pink Tide" wave in Latin America.[1]

And so it was not so surprising that 2017, the centenary of the Russian Revolution, went by without much excitement or commemoration. Russia itself largely ignored the centenary, its leaders wary of any sympathy for revolutionary ideas that might infect the public. But even elsewhere the Left paid scant homage. Past triumphs and leaders were duly acknowledged, but few Left parties or papers treated the Revolution, or Lenin, as vital elements for contemporary political practice. China Miéville published a stirring popular book about the Revolution, *October*, appealing to Left sentiments, though as to why the Revolution deserves celebration today even he seemed rather stumped, meekly concluding: "The standard of October declares that things changed once, and so they might do so again."[2]

Yet if we look a little closer, we find a mini-revival of interest in Lenin, starting unexpectedly on the Right, but lately emerging in parts of the Left as well. As for the Right, this is the radical, illiberal, antidemocratic, essentially neofascist political Right that has lately been gaining in prominence.[3] This is a Right that promotes a powerful state and a belligerent, exclusionary nationalism, demands "national unity" around its own program, rejects liberal democracy's precepts of minority rights and rule of law, opposes feminism as a dire enemy, accepts a limited welfare state provided it is run only by the state (and not civil society actors such as trade unions), and rewards only those considered part of "the nation." This new Right seems to find Lenin almost irresistible. For them, Lenin appears as a contemporary figure with significance and relevance, not just historical mystique.

Here is former Trump strategist and would-be global "alt-right" organizer Stephen Bannon speaking in 2013: "I'm a Leninist. Lenin wanted to destroy the state, and that's my goal, too. I want to bring everything crashing down, and destroy all of today's establishment."[4] Before Bannon came Grover Norquist, the éminence grise behind the wedding of the American Right's corporate and religious tendencies into one happy family, who, in his home where such unity-building meetings took place, is reported by an ex-comrade to have had a "majestic portrait" of Lenin hanging in the living room.[5] Classic antistate liberals enamored with the market have long been fans of Lenin's passion and methods. "We can learn a great deal from Lenin and the Leninists," Murray Rothbard, the influential libertarian "anarcho-capitalist" advised his fellow free-market rebels already in a 1961 memo tellingly titled "What Is To Be Done?"[6] His 1977 *Toward a Strategy for Libertarian Social Change* is not only peppered with quotes from Lenin and other Bolshevik leaders, but for those who still did not understand, makes the point starkly: Those of us "who attack Communists for being willing to kill capitalists . . . are incorrect; the problem with the Communists is [only] . . . that their ends (the dictatorship of the proletariat) are incorrect."[7] Rothbard persuaded Charles Koch; in his memoir, Koch lists Marx and Lenin as two primary influences.[8] In the early 1980s, Cato and Heritage Foundation libertarians called for "a Leninist strategy" to dismantle the New Deal, the evolution of which Nancy MacLean documents in her recent book on the radical Right.[9] As Che used to do for the Left, Lenin does for parts of the intellectual Right: signal their membership in a special community with a clear mission, cause, and purpose.

Nor is the fascination limited to the American Right. Philippe Vardon, a leader of the French nativist "Bloc Identitaire" closely associated with the National Front, has boasted of being a "classic Leninist" political activist.[10] There is also Jarosław Kaczyński, architect and leader of Poland's Law and

Justice Party (PiS) which, since winning the 2015 elections, has been rapidly installing a Far Right regime. After an earlier attempt at holding power in the mid-2000s had gone awry, Kaczyński turned into a decided admirer of the organizational capacities of the Bolsheviks. "We became firmly convinced," he writes, "that in order to really accomplish something, we would need to have what Lenin called a 'party of a new type,' made up of people committed, attested for, and capable of disciplined action."[11]

What is it that today's "populist" Right so admires about the Bolshevik leader? Above all, his absolute conviction, his eyes always on the prize, his utter determination to attain state power regardless of the supposed impossibility of doing so. They salute his courage in trying not just to tamper with the system but to smash it. They revel in his plain and persistent insistence that rule by his party would be more democratic than any "so-called democracy" that results from elections. They do not especially care for democracy, but recognize that we live in a democratic age and that to some extent they must play by its rules. Such flexibility is what they also admire about Lenin, who, for all his implacable revolutionary ardor, was always able to temper his demands or make short-term coalitions in order to realize ultimate goals. What else, after all, was Lenin's concession of "land to the peasants," when socialist and Bolshevik policy had always treated private land ownership as a reactionary relic of the past?

For sociologist Cihan Tugal, the Right has turned to Lenin precisely because Leninism provides "the tools radicals need in an advanced democracy."[12] Conceptualizing the core of Leninism not as authoritarian zeal but as the need for elite/mass coalitions to build a new society, Tugal argues that the American Right has moved from a "primitive" antistate Leninism pushed by Rothbard to the "advanced" Leninism of the Koch brothers, focusing on the *capture* of state power. In this sense, Donald Trump's post-defeat determination to hold onto power regardless of the rules was an impressive performance of right-wing Leninism, on which Republicans then doubled down with a spate of new state electoral laws enabling them perhaps to even fix elections in the future. If the liberal-Left enemy must be defeated for the new order to take hold, then the Leninist readiness to throw away the rule book is a crucial part of the Right's new toolkit.

The Right can appeal to Lenin largely because the Left had so decisively given him up. The Left abandoned Lenin for four key reasons: his lessons failed, postwar social democratic capitalism seemed to render Leninism irrelevant, Gramscian cultural politics appeared to succeed as an alternative, and over time the Left grew more committed to the democracy that Lenin always distrusted.

Now, however, as the radical Right enjoys such success, some on the Left are beginning again to embrace Lenin. And precisely for the reason that the Right has done so: a focus on gaining power. I understand the temptation, yet I believe that would be a grave mistake. As a long-time and unapologetic Left critic of the "actually existing" state socialist societies that resulted from the Russian Revolution, I think the record shows that authoritarian state power, even in service of social justice, ends up catastrophically destructive for the Left, sapping it of its principles and almost invariably leading to a disastrous doubling-down on repression once new problems set in, as they must. The Russian Revolution brought gains to workers and set the stage for national development and modernization, while trampling democracy for workers and everyone else. It is hard to see how a renewed Leninism, whatever that might mean, can bring leftist rewards today.

This paper is set up as follows. First, I discuss reasons why the Left has largely given up on Lenin. Then I review three compelling left-wing and Marxist critiques of Leninism. I try to show both that there is not much in Lenin that today's Left might find useful, and that the Left knew what it was doing in abandoning Lenin. I then critically assess recent Left arguments for a Leninist revival.

The Leftist Turn against Lenin

The Left first turned away from Lenin when it became clear that his insurrectionary project of seizing state power, which succeeded in Russia, failed everywhere else. For the first two years after the Bolshevik Revolution it seemed plausible that the international revolution Lenin thought so crucial would in fact succeed. But a combination of fierce repression and revolutionary overreach led to the crushing of uprisings in Germany, Hungary, and in the Baltics. The *Biennio Rosso* of 1919–1920 in Italy culminated not in socialist power but in Mussolini's March on Rome, while in the U.S. rising militancy was met by the Palmer Raids and a comprehensive attack on civil liberties aimed at dismantling the Left. The Comintern, created in Moscow in 1919 to coordinate socialist revolution, having achieved no successes in Europe soon turned its attentions to China, supporting a Communist alliance with the Kuomintang that resulted in a rout and massacre of Communists in 1927. Communists built communist parties, but never again, in the capitalist core, did those parties try to seize power the way Lenin did. The last opportunity came right after World War II, when powerful Communist Parties in France and Italy, having played a leading role in the anti-fascist underground, appeared poised to take power, with many activists eager to do so. But they stood down on orders from Stalin, who sought a stable peace with the West and was concerned above all with consolidating Communist power in Eastern Europe.[13] Communist parties of course did seize power there, but only because the Soviet Union, whose Red Army occupied the land in the course of defeating the Nazis, insisted they try and made sure they succeeded.

In the core capitalist world the Left abandoned Leninism in the post–World War II era when Leninist parties no longer seemed central to securing the kinds of victories that *were* possible, given that the overthrow of capitalism was not.

World War II ended with a decided turn to the left. Outside of Eastern Europe, this meant a turn to social democracy, which did not end capitalism but managed, disciplined, and organized it. It was a stunning transformation from the interwar period. Marxist historian Eric Hobsbawm calls the thirty years after the end of World War II the "Golden Years"[14]—not just for capital, which experienced spectacular growth, but for workers, whose standards of living increased dramatically, and for trade unions, which attained unprecedented responsibilities and prestige under the emerging system of democratic corporatism.[15] Official communist parties were divided by these developments. On the one hand, they saw these changes as a sellout of the Revolution, propping capitalism up at a point when radical systemic change might be on the agenda. On the other hand, communist parties had long been making the kinds of social welfare demands that capitalism was now implementing. In Great Britain and Italy, postwar social democracy even went on a nationalization binge, with the state taking over the "commanding heights" of the capitalist economy in order better to be able to avert future crises through sophisticated Keynesian demand management. Communist parties had intended such calls for anticrisis action to be what Trotsky called "transitional demands": demands that capitalism could not implement but whose articulation would win the parties popular support, bringing their triumph closer. But with capitalism proving able to implement such policies (aiding chiefly, though not only, the male, dominant-ethnicity working class), Leninist parties and politics seemed increasingly irrelevant.

What did Leninism now mean? What did it want to achieve? Ostensibly still committed to the toppling of capitalism, in practice Leninist parties in the West became rivals of social democrats and even liberals in bringing more social reform. Just as had happened to classic Social Democratic parties in the early twentieth century, when they officially promoted Marxist revolution but slowly evolved into reformist ones due to the fact that they were able to flourish and make concrete gains for workers, so post–World War II Leninist parties became nonrevolutionary, too.[16]

It took the New Left to make communist parties aware of their de facto conservatism. Emerging in the 1960s, at the height of postwar class compromise, young leftists not without reason saw Western Communists as defenders of the status quo, fighting for jobs and wages while oblivious if not plainly hostile to the demands of youth—many of them children of those workers whom the Golden Years had elevated—for things such as autonomy, self-management, self-expression: precisely the sort of ultimate existential goals that communism supposedly would make possible. In 1968, while French students and young workers were pushing (incoherently, but still) for revolution, the communist-led General Confederation of Labor rushed in to try to settle the strike wave with a wage hike, which most workers were not even seeking. The Cohn-Bendit brothers aptly titled their book about France's 1968 "Obsolete Communism: The Left-Wing Alternative."[17]

By the 1970s, Western communist parties had become indistinguishable from social democratic ones. They might speak like Leninists, maintain internal party discipline like Leninists, but were or aspired to be players in a reforming capitalist system. It became increasingly hard to see these communist parties as antisystemic at all. When workers, both old blue-collar types and increasing numbers of higher-educated wage earners (the postwar boom had greatly complicated the old class structure), as well as women and ethnic and racial minorities, began pushing forth a host of new demands, Leninist parties, most still claiming loyalty to the Soviet Union, came to be seen as increasingly anachronistic, and began hemorrhaging members at high rates.[18] New social movements did not destroy Leninist parties, but laid bare Leninism's irrelevance for the Left in core capitalist countries.

The '68ers, of course, were no Leninists. They were not concerned with "taking" state power. State ownership of the means of production seemed irrelevant to whether work was alienating or emancipating. This New Left had contempt for any "dictatorship of the proletariat." All of this set the ground for the Left's Gramscian turn.

Those on the Right today look to Lenin in large part because the Left turned to Gramsci and succeeded. What this means is that the Left abandoned the pursuit of seizing state power and sought to capture key nodes in civil society instead. Jailed by Mussolini for his communist activities, Antonio Gramsci came to believe that the Party could not succeed in taking power—and that even if it did, it could not build a durable socialism—if the masses did not share socialist values. He thus urged the Left to work to transform people's ideas and change their notion of common sense, helping thereby build a socialist ideological "hegemony" that could sustain a durable Left project. "Changed people change the world"—this became the slogan of increasing sections of the Left. Shunning state power, the Left turned to the universities, the media, and the culture at large to try to build socialist, or "progressive," hearts and minds.

The point is not that existing communists and socialists flocked to this new vision, but rather that this is what leftism increasingly came to mean. Most of those *entering* the Left after the 1960s gravitated to grassroots activism and civic institutions, not to "the Party." While radicals in the 1930s got factory jobs, those in the 1970s and after sought a university or government job or a position in an NGO. Helping build communitarian sensibilities was now seen by most on the Left as a direct contribution to transcending capitalism. And there is no question it has had considerable success. Think of the way antiracism, which has historically so weakened and deformed the workers' movement, is now the default common sense, with racists, and not antiracists, now having to justify and finesse their positions. Of course, such "common sense" can serve liberal corporate ends too, not just socialist, but this confluence can itself be seen as a sign of success, though one that weakens the lure of communist parties that once played the leading role in the fight against racism and colonialism. Indeed, that the Left has succeeded with the Gramscian push is why the Right is today so enamored of Lenin: to smash those institutions and effect a (counter) revolution against the gains the Left has made.

Finally, the Left drifted away from Lenin over the question of democracy. Lenin always said he valued true democracy, real workers' democracy. It's just that he never encountered a democracy he liked for long. When the long-awaited Constituent Assembly was about to meet in Petrograd, Lenin disbanded it as obsolete bourgeois parliamentarism. In *State and Revolution* and other writings from 1917 before the October seizure of power, Lenin famously rejected parliamentary democracy in favor of the direct democracy of soviets. But when a year later some local soviets started voting against the Bolsheviks, Lenin turned against them too. Time and again, Lenin showed he approved of democracy only when the self-governing people came up with decisions he supported. In 1918, of course, a civil war had just broken out, so temporary abrogation of self-government might have been warranted. But when the war had ended, and the Bolsheviks had won, Lenin crushed the Kronstadt rebellion (with a level of bloodshed wholly unnecessary), smashed the Workers Opposition brewing within the Party (which was calling for worker self-management and less direction from above), and then pushed through, at the 1921 Tenth Party Congress, a ban on all "factions" that, while not yet eliminating internal disagreements, nevertheless stigmatized them, in yet another victory for centralization over democracy. The Left has had its doubts about parliamentarism, but never about democracy, understood as people governing themselves. Yet Lenin broke decisively with any kind of self-government within months of coming to power. Worker representatives in factories were replaced by party loyalists, a model broken only in 1921 when Lenin announced the New Economic Policy (NEP), which transferred control not to workers but to petty capitalists. While always paying homage to the principle of self-government, Lenin abridged the reality to the point that leftists truly concerned with democracy, starting with Rosa Luxemburg, increasingly rejected the Leninist reality.[19] For decades now, no leftist who champions democracy has been able to look to Lenin as a model.

The key argument for the superiority of the Leninist model has always been that it won power and toppled capitalism while other strategies failed. Yet even this is not quite true. The irony is that the Bolsheviks won power in 1917 by being a very different type of party than the one Lenin lauded. In his classic study of the day to day developments of 1917 that brought the Bolsheviks to power, Alexander Rabinowitch shows the enormous disparity between the Leninist notion of the centralized party confidently dispensing strategic advice to the rank-and-file faithful and the reality of the open, fluid, and generally quite democratic party that the Bolsheviks in reality were at the time. He describes how the Bolsheviks gained support by cooperating with Mensheviks and the Socialist Revolutionaries in the soviets, contrary to Lenin's recommendations. He notes how top Bolshevik leaders disregarded Lenin's insistence in August for a seizure of power against the will of the soviets. (Lenin had temporarily withdrawn the call for "all power to the soviets" when he thought the soviets were hopelessly opposed to the Bolsheviks.) He shows how it was the very openness of debate in the party, the *lack* of centralization, that in fact enabled the Bolsheviks to win. As Rabinowitch puts it, "The phenomenal Bolshevik success can be attributed . . . [to] the party's internally relatively democratic, tolerant, and decentralized structure and method of operation, as well as its essentially open and mass character—in striking contrast to the traditional Leninist model."[20]

In other words, the Bolsheviks won not by being a Leninist party but by being something very different. It was only after taking power that they created the myth of the centralized party guided brilliantly to success by Lenin, thus producing the model exported to Leninist parties elsewhere. Those Leninist parties then highlighted the principle of centralization, and all

Leninist parties have been marked by limited democracy within their ranks. The guiding principle of "democratic centralism" ostensibly means internal freedom of discussion until the top leadership makes a decision, but in practice that has always meant almost no freedom of discussion at all, since, once the Soviet Union was formed, every communist party had a "Party line" on everything. As late as 1990, rank-and-file members of the Communist Party USA were complaining that they were still not allowed to freely discuss their views on the rapid "perestroika" changes going on in the Soviet Union![21] Leninist parties maintained the proscription on internal democracy on the grounds that this was necessary for success, when, ironically, it was by not following such rules that the Bolsheviks had such success in 1917.

Left Critiques of Leninism

Lenin died in 1924. The only model he left for the political system he founded was that the Party had to maintain power at all cost. It might experiment with different forms: autonomous or subordinate soviets, war communism or NEP, private land ownership or forced grain acquisition, acceptance or repression of intellectual opposition (though never acceptance of political opposition). Indeed, what is striking is the diversity of arrangements Lenin sanctioned, from the complete statism without markets during 1919–1920 to the petty bourgeois NEP-men and kulak capitalism from 1921 till his death. The only constant was the maintenance of political power, because Party domination constituted for Lenin the only guarantee that socialism would triumph. Lenin differed from Stalin on numerous matters, but not on this: that the political form of the Soviet state had to guarantee Party power. Democracy mattered little. With their left-wing principles, Leninist states could and did make some astonishing historical advancements, on matters of education, employment, social policy, equality, opportunities for women. But there were no competitive elections, no right to free speech, and limited intellectual freedom. Professional and civil institutions lacked autonomy, while trade unions became little more than arms of the state.

I am aware that stressing Leninism's antidemocratic nature can sound to some Left ears old, trite, and mainstream. Lenin's dismissals of democracy are well known, but even so there is renewed interest in him from people on the Left looking for some way out of the global neoliberal trap that formal democracy seems to keep on perpetuating. Indeed, it is true that, to use the language from Marxist debates of the 1970s, the state may have relative autonomy from the capitalist class, thus allowing the space for democratic practices, but that in the end a democratic state in capitalist society does serve capitalism.[22] But if the aim of the Left is to build an authentic democratic society that is responsive to the needs of workers, and able to hear the voices of all its citizens, it needs to look closely at how Leninism was *unable* to do so. Socialism might well be necessary to save the planet, which is all the more reason to get it right.

Left-wing critics of Lenin are often met with the response that his deviations from democracy were all the result of contingency—the emergence of soviets justified the dispersal of the Constituent Assembly, civil war required the suppression of democracy in the soviets, economic collapse necessitated the abridgment of workers' control, imperialist encirclement required the ban on factions. There is always some "accidental" phenomenon, and Lenin is never to blame. The real Lenin, they say, can be found in his ultra-democratic *State and Revolution* written just before October, with its passages about cooks becoming ministers. If only Leninist principles could be introduced in different conditions, we hear, a democratic socialist outcome would be possible.

So let us take the discussion away from what happened when Lenin ran Russia and look more at Lenin's theories, with the help of three scholars, two of them Marxists. The central argument of all three is that classic Marxism's notoriously weak theorization of politics, as a superstructure phenomenon dependent on the economic base, along with Lenin's insistence that Communist Party power equaled working-class power, combined to make democratic government impossible.

I begin with an essay that ought to be an indispensable part of a Left political education but is in fact barely known at all. The author is István Mészáros, born in Budapest in 1930, a Marxist philosopher from the so-called Budapest School of critical theorists (largely students of Georg Lukács), who, upon leaving Hungary in 1956, differed from the path of most fellow émigrés by staying very much a Marxist. His 1978 *New Left Review* piece "Political Power and Dissent in Post-Revolutionary Societies" shows a pitiful total of nine citations on "Google Scholar" (eight in English, one of these mine), yet more than four decades later it still stands out as one of the best Marxist insights into the reasons for the systematic weakness of democracy in Leninist state socialist polities.

As Mészáros states at the outset, the crucial question of how political power is to be organized *after* a successful revolution "remains one of the most neglected areas of Marxist theory."[23] Marx devoted little time to the matter, either because he really thought it was no problem or just did not know how to address it. His few statements were clear but wholly unsatisfactory. After revolutionary success, writes Marx, there will no new class domination resulting in a new political power, since political power is the result of the class antagonisms created by capitalism and will no longer be necessary. "The working class . . . will substitute for the old civil society an association which will exclude classes and their antagonisms, and there will be no more political power properly so-called, since political power is precisely the official expression of antagonism in civil society."[24]

Since, however, contrary to Marx, neither political power nor the proletariat does disappear when a revolutionary party takes power, Mészáros, with no interest simply in bashing communist parties for any so-called betrayal, poses the question theoretically: "What happens to political power in post-revolutionary societies when the proletariat does *not* disappear?"[25] The Bolsheviks, of course, never contemplated that political power would disappear; thus "the severity of measures [they] devised to prevent" any eventual working-class eruptions.[26] That the proletariat does not disappear when communist parties take over, meanwhile, is obvious: social structures and economic relations do not and cannot change overnight. So, as a Marxist who in 1956 witnessed the Soviet Union not just crush a (socially and politically complicated) uprising in his home country but eliminate the workers' councils that arose in its wake, Mészáros asks why Leninist parties in power have always been so committed to stifling dissent. Does this follow from Leninist precepts? Mészáros shows how it does.

Lenin's theorization about postrevolutionary democracy was as confused as Marx's. In *State and Revolution* Lenin outlined a postrevolutionary polity of equality and flourishing participation, without the need for repression against anyone other than the bourgeoisie. This he called the "dictatorship of the proletariat," the social formation he asserted to be more democratic than any political order coming before it. Soon after completing the text, Lenin came to power, without the international revolution he hoped for. With the new regime facing enemies and obstacles, he authorized tough repressive measures against anything smacking of opposition, even among workers. Lenin tried to get around the apparent contradiction by insisting that the Party was the Proletariat, its most advanced and true embodiment, and thus its repressive activities were simply the Proletariat exercising its dictatorship against its enemies. Because proletarians in Lenin's theory are never the arbiter of "the Proletariat's" interests—only the Party, based on its "scientific" knowledge, is capable of that—Lenin simply "could not envisage the possibility of an objective contradiction between the dictatorship of the proletariat and the proletariat itself."[27] The Party's dictatorship was, for Lenin, by definition in the interests of the proletariat regardless of what individual workers think about things.

After October, Mészáros points out, almost all "positive references to the experience of the Paris Commune . . . disappeared from [Lenin's] speeches and writings; and the accent was laid on 'the need for a central authority, for dictatorship and a united will to ensure that the vanguard of the proletariat shall close its ranks.' "[28] Instead of the creative actors from *State and Revolution*, workers are now reduced by Lenin to "labor-power" which the state "distributes . . . among the various branches of the economy," and to consumers allocated goods "belonging to the state. The fact that the relationship of the working people to state power . . . was a relationship of structural subordination did not seem to trouble Lenin, who bypassed this issue by simply describing the new form of separate state power as 'the proletarian state power.' "[29]

The sophistry is plain, and unrelenting. Mészáros brings up Lukács's 1919 defense of postrevolutionary repression as a clear, if portentous, Leninist expression of the problem and solution. According to Lukács, workers in socialist society must either discipline themselves to do what the socialist state needs them to do (i.e., produce goods without resistance) or, "if they are incapable of [self-discipline], . . . they create a legal system through which the proletariat *compels* its own individual members, the proletarians, to act in a way which corresponds to their class-interests: *the proletariat turns its dictatorship against itself.*"[30] Both alternatives require the assumption that whatever the Party does is by definition in the "true" interests of workers. These are not theories of political power but rationalizations of postrevolutionary Party dictatorship.

Lukács's defense of dictatorship on the grounds of socialist economic rationality points to another problem: that conflicts between the Party and workers flow necessarily from the economic logic of state socialism. For while a capitalist state, Mészáros points out, "has no need to regulate *directly* the extraction of surplus-value"[31]—all it has to do is safeguard the economic system and the rule of capital—the socialist state must manage the economy directly in order to preserve political power. Why is this a problem for democracy? Because

> such a politically determined extraction of surplus-labor . . . inevitably sharpens the contradiction between individual producers and the state, with the gravest implications for the possibility of dissent. For under these circumstances dissent may directly endanger the extraction of surplus-labor . . . thus potentially depriving the dictatorship of the proletariat of its material base and challenging its very survival.[32]

So whereas the capitalist state "need not worry... about the manifestations of political dissent, so long as the impersonal mechanisms of commodity-production carry on their functions undisturbed,"[33] production in the socialist state is *threatened by dissent from the outset.* This is a problem, moreover, that increases over time. Individual workers, after all, especially those on the Left, are far more likely to accept Party dominance before revolutionary transformation than afterward, since in the earlier time they will feel the need to unite, while later, facing no class oppression, they are likely to assert their own interests, separate from the Party. *Lenin's theoretical model allows no ways for such contention to be expressed, much less democratically adjudicated.* State socialist economies, in other words, may *require* the absence of democracy.

All labor opposition in state socialist societies, from Kronstadt in 1921 to Gdańsk in 1980, has demonstrated the impossibility of the Leninist model to peacefully and systemically accommodate stark political disagreement. In 1981, Karol Modzelewski, the most prominent Left activist of Poland's embattled independent Solidarity trade union, saw the problem in all its tragic implications. The democratic rights that had been secured by Solidarity, he now realized, were the very thing *preventing* the Party from stabilizing the economic crisis, thus making a violent crackdown more likely: "For the state is capable of governing only in conditions where those rights are lacking."[34] The Polish United Workers Party imposed martial law a few weeks later.

Lenin's theory of the proletarian state, as articulated in *State and Revolution*, promises full democracy. With its vision of an egalitarian and participatory direct democracy, it has inspired leftist readers ever since. The usual charge is that Lenin betrayed this vision upon taking power. A. J. Polan, however, author of *Lenin and the End of Politics*, sees it the other way: that the glorious vision of democracy outlined just prior to coming to power is the problem. In that vision Lenin lauds unity too much. He categorically rejects parliaments and the very idea of representation on the grounds that they wrongly separate rulers and the ruled. He discards the concept of separation of powers for rendering impossible any true collective control over the state. Lenin instead proposes all state functions to be concentrated in a single institution in which everyone can and should participate, with rotation of office and payment of average salaries to all. But this very vision, Polan points out, leaves politics out. Instead of politics, understood as the free articulation of alternative and competing visions, Lenin's polity calls to mind Engels's idea of "the administration of things," supposed to happen when the state withers away. The problem, though, is that given the elimination of parliaments and bureaucracy, and the complete subordination of civil society to the state, which is now engaged in doing rather than deciding, how things will be administered must depend solely on the view of the Party. Why the Party? Because as Lenin insists in all his writings, and as follows if the Party is assumed to be the implementer of a "scientific" socialism, the Party has a monopoly on correct knowledge. It is the sole arbiter for determining the interests of the proletariat, as the universal class. As an arena for the articulation and defense of diverse ideas, politics outside of the Party thus disappears, even while economic equality might flourish. Although such a state need not result in Stalinism, "Lenin's theory of the state," Polan concludes, "rigorously outlawed all and any version of those political institutions and relationships that can make the triumph of the Gulag less likely."[35]

Even serious Left admirers of Lenin do not fundamentally disagree. In a sympathetic 2015 intellectual biography of the Soviet leader, *Reconstructing Lenin*, the contemporary Hungarian Marxist Tamás Krausz (b. 1943) points repeatedly to Lenin's inability, once in power, to countenance any genuine democratic practice.[36] Again and again, Party rule served for Lenin as both the necessary and sufficient condition of democracy. The process, for Lenin, was that "the Party . . . absorbs the vanguard of the proletariat, and this vanguard exercises the dictatorship of the proletariat."[37] Those who stay proletarians are not counted as the vanguard, and become the objects of policy, not agents. Krausz shows how democracy was always a minor concern for Lenin after October: the key tasks were promoting the European revolution, reorganizing the economy, winning the civil war, and reviving the socialist project afterward. There were crises nonstop facing Lenin after 1917, and every one of them was an excuse to put off any popular calls for participation. The contrast between writing *State and Revolution* just prior to the Revolution, when the democratic organization of society appeared to be of utmost concern, and after the Revolution, when democracy was among the least of his concerns, could not be more stark. Yet Lenin acted as if there were no contradiction at all. On the contrary, he claimed always to be building democracy, since he interpreted Bolshevik power as democracy's equivalent.

As for intellectual debate, Lenin did not try to stifle the expression of different opinions within the Party, though he expected his decisions on major issues to be final (and until his stroke in 1922, they were). Outside of the Party, things were different. While Lenin was generally sympathetic to technical experts—an economically struggling Russia needed them—he took a different view toward non-Party philosophers and social scientists. Initially, he neither bothered them nor cared much for what they had to say. Any who wished were free to emigrate. Lenin resisted calls to deport intellectual critics during the Civil War. Only after the war did he change his position, leading to the so-called philosophers' ships of 1922, or the involuntary deportation of hundreds of prominent nonsocialist intellectuals.[38] Why then? Probably because, with war over, he feared intellectual competition over the building of new durable institutions. The Bolsheviks may have been firmly in power, but having no idea what exactly the socialist future should look like, they were vulnerable to critique and alternatives issuing from outside the socialist camp. Also, young Bolsheviks were eager to take up the academic and editorial positions that the old intelligentsia had still controlled. The ensuing years, until the onset of Stalinism in 1929, became well known as a time of vibrant intellectual debate among Marxists, though the disappearance of nonsocialist intellectuals meant that when Stalinist orthodoxy silenced debates within the Party, no other intellectual public sphere even existed.

Complex as he always was, Lenin did have misgivings about his attacks on proletarian democracy. That is, he seems never to have recognized the contradiction at the heart of his understanding of democracy—namely, that workers would first have to voluntarily accept major Party decisions, organize no dissent, refuse to engage in any political competition. Still, if workers and indeed all citizens did that, he would have been happy to let them administer things "democratically." (This seems to have been Gorbachev's vision, too.)[39] And so, in his last active years, imagining that workers were fundamentally on his side and that an increasingly bureaucratic Party was stifling participation, Lenin made haphazard moves to undo the consequences of his past decisions. In 1920 he began pushing for a slightly more assertive trade union movement, striking a middle ground between Trotsky's call for the militarization of labor and the Left Opposition's demands for "economic democracy." He talked about the need for the proletariat—referring here finally to *real* proletarians, and not the Party as the Proletariat—to have organizations that "protect workers from their state," which he now saw as the condition ensuring that workers would "protect our state."[40]

Lenin's position was inconsistent. As Krausz laconically puts it, "It was a mistake to think that the workers could defend themselves from their own state without democracy."[41] At the end of his life, Lenin seemed to recognize, and rue, what he had wrought. "It is pathetic," writes Mészáros, "to see Lenin, a genius of realistic strategy, behaving like a desperate utopian from 1923 to the moment of his death: insistently putting forward hopeless schemes" to reduce the tendency to authoritarian rule by Party bureaucrats,[42] such as his call to increase working class cadre in the Central Committee, have a "workers' and peasants' inspectorate" fight bureaucracy, or his halfhearted effort to replace Stalin as General Secretary. The point is that he had put in place a polity that lent itself to unchecked Party power, and had no systemic way to reduce it. Lenin shouted endlessly about the dictatorship of the proletariat being more democratic than any bourgeois democracy, but neither his theory nor practice ever highlighted the existence, much less the superiority, of any institutions that could build such democracy. In the end, there is simply no Leninist legacy of support for democratic self-government.

A Left Re-Embrace of Lenin

Though most of the Left long ago moved away from Leninism, we are now witnessing a mini-revival, due to the sense of many that today's uncentralized Left cannot effect transformative change, and that the Right's increasingly prominent neo-fascist project can only be defeated by a radical break from capitalism. Of course, plenty of old Marxist-Leninist parties still exist, having never wavered from Leninist doctrine. I do not address them here, as they do not try to make a case for Leninism but merely insist on its relevance, without it being clear what "Leninism" actually means. For example, David North, chair of the Socialist Equity Party and chief editor of the World Socialist Web Site, regularly cites Lenin as the final authority, claims that history has "vindicated" Lenin's analyses, and denounces "pseudo-leftists" who challenge Leninism's relevance.[43] Among the "fake" leftists North denounces are two theorists who have been instrumental to the recent communist revival, Alain Badiou and Slavoj Žižek. The latter, labeled a "charlatan" by North, has had an outsized influence in the recent Leninist revival, if only because of the ubiquity of Žižek's voice in outlets that cater to a general left clientele.

Unlike those who have tried to present Lenin as a great defender of democracy, Slavoj Žižek does not claim to particularly care about democracy, and so his Leninism does not need to uphold it. For Žižek, there *is* no real democracy, and "Lenin" is needed simply to break the rigged game open. Žižek thus invokes the Lenin of *The Proletarian Revolution and the Renegade Kautsky*, Lenin's 1919 broadside which contends that any existing shred of democratic governance in the capitalist world is just a fig leaf masking the worst sort of class oppression (and boasting that the "proletarian democracy" then supposedly prevailing in Russia was "a million times more democratic than any bourgeois democracy"). For Žižek, existing democracy is a sham. The trap for the Left "is the belief that one can undermine capitalism without effectively problematizing the liberal-democratic legacy which—as some leftists claim—although engendered by capitalism, acquired autonomy and can serve to criticize capitalism."[44] In other words, Žižek is saying, let's be real: the political world has no autonomy, democracy cannot transform capitalism, and the sooner we admit it, the better. It's not clear what the alternative is, but it must be radical, because "the true utopia is the belief that the present liberal-democratic capitalist consensus could go on indefinitely, without radical changes."

Žižek wants a Lenin that can dispense with this bogus democracy. "The greatness of Lenin is that he *wasn't afraid to succeed*."[45] Succeed in what, we don't know. Lenin himself, after all, did not think he succeeded in much except obtaining and keeping state power for the Party. He exited the political scene without any socialist model to pass on to others. Neither war communism nor NEP were ever presented as such. The only models Lenin left the Left were the ideas of the centralized party guiding revolutionary collective action, and the seizure of power as opposed to the "waiting" for socialism that characterized most orthodox Marxists at the time. So when Žižek lauds Lenin's fearlessness to succeed, that is praise for what he destroyed, not what he created. Žižek's Lenin is thus quite similar to the Lenin the Right now admires. Does the Left really need such a Lenin? Today's Leninist Right does know what it wants to build: a plutocratic state providing minimal welfare protections and a sense of cultural superiority for accepted members of "the nation" or dominant race. It is unclear, from Žižek or others, exactly what kind of Left Lenin is supposed to enable us to build. This resurrection of Lenin runs in the face of all the reasons why the Left abandoned Lenin in recent generations.

Žižek is a famed provocateur, and sometimes the joke is on those who take him too seriously. But I think we must take seriously his resurrection of Lenin, precisely because at some level it makes so much sense. After all, it is not hard to agree with much of Žižek's diagnosis. Liberal capitalist democracy has not been able to challenge neoliberalism, much less provide an alternative to capitalism. Established Left parties play by the game and get nowhere. Even newer and more radical parties playing by the rules get trapped: Syriza in Greece won a popular referendum against Eurozone shock therapy only to sign a worse deal soon after. We do live in urgent times. These days there are many fascists, but few communists. With the Right gaining everywhere, it makes sense leftists would pine for a new Lenin. But if the real Lenin is one the real Left has turned away from, and if Lenin's legacy chiefly concerns the building of organizational power to effect the conquest of state power for the

Party, then Leninism is a fool's offer: unlikely to attract many activists, with no concrete vision to propose. The point is to make the next Left breakthrough successful in terms of what is created, not what is toppled.

Can a Leninist regime help workers? Of course it can. Particularly for lesser-skilled workers it can provide good benefits, educational opportunities, cheap housing, expanded healthcare, and elevate some to high positions in state institutions. But if leftists just want better things for the most exploited workers, they can sometimes support Far Right parties, too. The Right in the United States may be completely plutocratic (though Trump won in 2016 by promising to fight this), but the one in Poland, for example, has thought seriously of how to help Polish private-sector workers. Since coming to power in 2015, the Law and Justice Party (PiS) has criminalized most of the "junk contracts" private business used to overexploit labor, increased the minimum wage, introduced generous and universal cash payments for children, which has both reduced poverty and increased wages for single mothers (by strengthening their workplace bargaining power), and levied taxes on banks and corporations to make these expanded benefits possible.[46] The same government also denounces Muslim immigrants and refugees as an existential and biological threat, labels gays and "gender ideology" a scourge on society, rejects campaigns against domestic violence, imposes a total ban on abortion, promotes fascist and anti-Semitic figures from its past as models for schoolchildren, and treats both liberalism and the Left as the two greatest dangers to civilization. But if you are a "regular" blue-collar Polish worker, chances are your economic conditions have improved compared to those prevailing under the liberal and Left (former communist) governments of the post-1989 past. The government dislikes unions and other associations in civil society, but it likes providing directly to the people, and living conditions for the poorest have improved as a result. Should leftists therefore support this right-wing government? Some have. There were plenty of 2015 PiS voters whose second choice was the new left-wing party *Razem*, just as there were Trump voters in 2016 who considered Bernie Sanders an acceptable alternative. They wanted to help the most vulnerable workers, and opted for the Right.[47]

Many left-wingers were won over to fascism in the 1930s too, on the grounds that now *somebody* was finally doing *something* to help "our people" suffering from the ravages of the Depression.[48] National socialism is a socialism for "us," and if you belong to the in-group, it can definitely be a good thing, for you.

Most leftists, however, rightly reject right-wing governments that do good things for (some) workers. They do so because they are interested in power for the entire working class, not just a particular national, racial, ethnic, or gender component of that class. They do so because they are interested in democracy. And this same interest in democracy has led generations of leftists to reject Leninist models too.

The political theorist Jodi Dean has emerged as a leading theorist and proponent of communism in recent years, and one of her recent books is a paean to "the party." *Crowds and Party* is a critique of what Dean calls "left realism," a view based on hostility to "collectivity" on the grounds that it is both undesirable and impossible to achieve, and which supposedly recommends an ever-expanding fragmentation of Left politics into a myriad of independent initiatives, leading to the political toothlessness in which the Left is said to be mired today.[49] Against this self-defeating strategy, Dean recommends the model of "the party." Although nowhere precisely defined, Dean's idea is unmistakably Leninist: her party boasts a centralized authority to analyze the situation and coordinate activism, and a mass following ready to enact party commands.

Parties must lead, argues Dean, because recent experience shows that "crowds," such as Occupy, cannot get the job done. The party transcends crowds, for it is an "organizational form" that operates on both local and national scale, and embodies "knowledge that comes with political experience." The party "takes a position on that knowledge," and success comes when "the people" follow that position.[50]

Aside from the comment that the "party bureaucracy" is but the "institutional capacity necessary for political struggle and rule in a complex and uneven terrain,"[51] Dean provides no discussion of party leadership. Objections that focus precisely on leadership—on who will give the orders, the status and reliability of the party's knowledge base, the wisdom or legitimacy of the positions it takes—she treats largely as ill-willed distractions. The danger of "substitutionism"—that the party will substitute for the class, the bureaucracy for the party, and ultimately the leader for the bureaucracy, all of which actually happened in actually existing socialist societies—she dispenses by noting that "horizontalism" does not solve problems either, and that "political capacity always involves delegation."[52] What about the history of no democracy in the Party? This she rejects as an old critique (without saying why it is wrong), which she then minimizes by citing

Robert Michels's 1911 thesis on the "iron law of oligarchy," according to which all organizations, even the most ostensibly democratic ones, are run by hierarchies.[53]

It is hard to see how Dean's account of Michels's remarks—about how even the most democratic self-governing anarchist associations have hierarchies due to some individuals' better abilities at organizing or public speaking or some other valued capacity—is relevant to the question of potential party dictatorship over the proletariat and the people. Left-wing critics of Leninism, after all, do not object to leadership. They object to parties with centralized leadership claiming a monopoly on knowledge that justifies efforts to limit opposition, and assigns to itself the sole right to decide not just the correct paths anticapitalist practice should take but the nature of the political regime and what is or is not allowed once success is achieved. In other words, they object to parties that take Leninist precepts as their model.

To be sure, Dean addresses some genuine problems with the contemporary Left. A numerically strong but organizationally weak Left, offering "multitudes of opinions, suggestions, strategies, and critiques,"[54] is in a worse position to effect transformative institutional change than a smaller but organizationally tighter political movement with a base ideologically sympathetic to the principle of hierarchy. The utter diversity of left-wing activism may expand the terrain of contention, but Dean is right that the recurring problem with "localized political work is the way that it seems not to register."[55] Organizing local activism under the imprimatur of a national party clearly gives it more clout.

Still, Dean's re-embrace, with Žižek, of the hierarchical self-appointed Leninist party, her denunciation of "liberal democracy" ("in actuality the dictatorship of capital")[56] along with the pooh-poohing of Left uneasiness about an omniscient party introducing "real" democracy, the unwillingness to deal with the historical reality of Leninist regimes and the reasons (neoliberal individualism is not one of them) so many leftists have moved away from Leninism—all this turns Left political debate precisely the wrong way.

Like Žižek, Dean too sometimes relishes the role of provocateur. When an interviewer asks her, "How are [Party] comrades to deal with enemies?" she replies, "Gulag." And then, after a pause, "I'm joking." Any Left that jokes about the Gulag will fail, and should. I respect Dean a great deal (we have been colleagues at the same university department for more than twenty-five years), but her subsequent explanation does not help matters: "Really the way to deal with enemies is to change the structure that produces enemies."[57]

With this we get back to *State and Revolution*'s imaginary postrevolutionary outcome. Lenin too hypothesized a world whose participatory structures and absence of class divisions produced no enemies. Then his Party took power and he found that postrevolutionary structures still produced enemies. With the Party understood as the only institution to ensure socialism, he then began treating comrades who opposed Party power as enemies. Some years later, a new Party leader began sending them to the Gulag. Mészáros and other Marxists then began inquiring into Leninism, seeing the ways its very theoretical foundations denied the right to dissent.

If the aim is for the next Left to get things right, it has to learn from Leninism's antidemocratic past and reassess the theory that underpinned it. At some level, perhaps, neither Dean nor Žižek is concerned with getting things right. What they want is for the Left to succeed—at something!—and to stop the right-wing juggernaut ("The greatness of Lenin is that he *wasn't afraid to succeed!*"). The Right lionizes this Lenin and the Left's current Leninists want the Left to do the same. But the Left has different ambitions than the Right. We want to do more than just change some policies. Yet if we aim to transform institutions in a socialist direction, we need to understand power differently than Lenin, since his understanding of it allowed him and his successors to violate so many socialist, democratic norms. Rather than advising new anticapitalists to embrace some new Lenin ready to do anything to win and maintain power, the Left has a better chance of success by building mobilizational capacity behind a vision of deep transformative change aimed at creating institutions promoting collectivism.

In the end, one of the biggest problems with the Leninist revival is its total unclarity as to the aims. The interest in Lenin derives from a disappointment with the Left's long Gramscian turn, despite its considerable successes, and a desire to get back to the matter of power. The Left does need more power, but thinking about power means thinking about the state, and here the new Leninists have strangely little to say. The 1970s saw perhaps the last great Marxist debate—on the theory of the state, and specifically about what an emancipatory socialist project would actually entail, given the well-known deficiencies of Soviet-type state socialism and its failure in any case to mobilize new enthusiasts in postindustrial societies with complex class structures. Claus Offe alone authored numerous perceptive essays on these topics, in a brutally honest effort to imagine the socialist transformation of advanced capitalist societies in the face of obstacles caused both by capitalism's incredible durability and by statist socialism's failures.[58] The late Erik Olin Wright built on the contributions to this debate to come up with his plan of "real utopias," or new institutions that are both possible and fundamentally transformative.[59] The new Leninists talk about power and not fearing success, but without grappling with the diagnoses and proposals serious Marxists have offered in the relatively recent past.

One of the inconsistencies of Žižek's and Dean's Leninist revival is their sympathy with undeniably non-Leninist parties. Dean points to Greece's Syriza, which has distinguished itself as a reformist party par excellence, as an example of "the new relevance of the party form."[60] Žižek, meanwhile, defends his 2016 support for the election of Donald Trump (yes, support) on the grounds that "the Trump victory triggered a process of radicalization in the Democratic Party—and this process is our only hope."[61] Indeed, if all they were talking about were the importance of parties, few leftists would deny it. With the Far Right now winning through elections, leftists everywhere are trying to figure out the party vehicle that can defeat them. The Leninist party, however, is not just a vehicle for change but the embodiment of a model regime.

And that is what I treat seriously. I do not believe that just because the new Leninist calls are implausible we should treat them as mere useful provocations aimed at galvanizing resistance. I take them as proposals that can win the support of leftists, and thus as proposals that might someday really matter. And since we should want to make sure that the next Left survives, and is democratic, and really empowers and not just improves the lives of workers and others, it is incumbent on us to challenge, and reject, a renewed left Leninism.

The Marxist sociologist Nicos Poulantzas once wrote, "Socialism will be democratic or it will not be at all." Democratic socialism might be difficult to achieve; such is the power of capital and the capitalist state. But the risks of trying and failing are "in any case preferable to massacring other people only to end up ourselves beneath the blade of . . . some Dictator of the proletariat."[62] His language is a bit strong for me. He wrote these words in 1978, a time when so much of the Left was trying to understand why the old Left went wrong, and the words were intended as a cudgel against the still prominent defenders of state socialism. But as a signal that the next Left must not resort to "any means necessary" thinking, that in some conditions the Left has not just a right but a duty precisely to *be* "afraid to succeed," I think we must endorse the sentiment today. There is an urgent political struggle in the world today. The Left needs new ideas, new kinds of organizations, new leaders. But Leninism is a trap that will only defeat us, just as it defeated too many leftists in the past.

Notes

1. For an overview, see Rene Rojas, "The Latin American Left's Shifting Tides," *Catalyst* 2, no. 2 (Summer 2018).

2. China Miéville, *October: The Story of the Russian Revolution* (London: Verso, 2017), 317.

3. For an expanded discussion of right-wing interest in Lenin, see David Ost, "The Surprising Right-Wing Relevance of the Russian Revolution," *Constellations* 24 (December 2017).

4. Quoted by Ronald Radosh in "Steve Bannon, Trump's Top Guy, Told Me He Was 'a Leninist,'" *The Daily Beast*, August 22, 2016, last modified April 13, 2017. https://www.thedailybeast.com/steve-bannon-trumps-top-guy-told-me-he-was-a-leninist.

5. David Brock, *Blinded by the Right* (New York: Crown, 2002), 64–67.

6. Quoted in Nancy MacLean, *Democracy in Chains* (New York: Viking, 2017), 84.

7. Murray Rothbard, "Towards a Strategy for Libertarian Social Change" (unpublished manuscript, 1977). https://archive.org/details/Rothbard1977TowardAStrategyForLibertarianSocialChange. That communists generally did not "kill capitalists" is not the point; Rothbard admires and recommends Leninist determination and consequence.

8. Charles Koch, *Good Profit* (New York: Crown, 2015), 13.

9. Stuart Butler and Peter Germanis, "Achieving Social Security Reform: A 'Leninist' Strategy," *The Cato Journal* 3, no. 2 (Fall 1983). See MacLean, *Democracy in Chains*.

10. Nicholas Vinocur, "Marine Le Pen's Internet Army," *Politico*, February 3, 2017. https://www.politico.eu/article/marine-le-pens-internet-army-far-right-trolls-social-media/.

11. Jarosław Kaczyński, *Porozumienie przeciw monowładzy* (Poznan: Zysk i S-ka, 2016), 381–82.

12. Cihan Tugal, "The Counter-Revolution's Long March: The American Right's Shift from Primitive to Advanced Leninism," *Critical Sociology* 46, no. 3 (May 2020), DOI: 10.1111/1467-8675.12328.

13. Fernando Claudin, *The Communist Movement: From Comintern to Cominform, Part Two* (New York: Monthly Review Press, 1975).

14. Eric Hobsbawm, *The Age of Extremes: A History of the World, 1914–1991* (New York: Vintage, 1996).

15. Sheri Berman, *The Primacy of Politics: Social Democracy and the Making of Europe's Twentieth Century* (Princeton: Princeton University Press, 2006); Philippe Schmitter, "Still the Century of Corporatism?," *The Review of Politics* 36, no. 1 (1974).

16. This is Guenther Roth's classic argument about the unintended encroaching reformism of the German Social Democrats, in *The Social Democrats in Imperial Germany* (London: Forgotten Books, 2017; orig. 1963).

17. Daniel Cohn-Bendit and Gabriel Cohn-Bendit, *Obsolete Communism: The Left-Wing Alternative* (New York: McGraw-Hill, 1968).

18. Martin J. Bull, "The West European Communist Movement in the Late Twentieth Century," *West European Politics* 18, no. 1 (1995): 78–97. https://doi.org/10.1080/01402389508425058.

19. Even within the Party Lenin could not countenance objections. When his comrades opposed him in the months before the Revolution, rather than accepting their decision Lenin threatened to resign. Lenin had used his indispensability as internal blackmail many times in the past; see Victor Sebestyen, *Lenin* (New York: Pantheon, 2017).

20. Alexander Rabinowitch, *The Bolsheviks Come to Power* (London: Pluto Press, 2017; orig. 1976), 311.

21. Daniel Rosenberg, "From Crisis to Split: The Communist Party USA, 1989–1991," *American Communist History* 18, no. 1–2 (2019). https://doi.org/10.1080/14743892.2019.1599627.

22. For perhaps the best text on the matter, see Fred Block, "The Ruling Class Does Not Rule: Notes on the Marxist Theory of the State," *Socialist Review* 33 (1977); reprinted in Block's *Revising State Theory* (Philadelphia: Temple University Press, 1987).

23. István Mészáros, "Political Power and Dissent in Post-Revolutionary Societies," *New Left Review* 108 (March–April 1978), 3.

24. Quoting Marx's *Poverty of Philosophy*, in Mészáros, 4.

25. Ibid.; emphasis added.

26. Ibid.

27. Ibid., 10.

28. Ibid.

29. Ibid., 10–11.

30. This is Mészáros's translation of a Lukács essay unpublished in English, in ibid., 18; emphasis in original.

31. Ibid., 17.

32. Ibid.

33. Ibid.

34. Quoted in David Ost, *Solidarity and the Politics of Anti-Politics* (Philadelphia: Temple University Press, 1990), 130.

35. A. J. Polan, *Lenin and the End of Politics* (Berkeley: University of California Press, 1984), 130.

36. Tamás Krausz, *Reconstructing Lenin: An Intellectual Biography* (New York: Monthly Review Press, 2015).

37. Quoted in ibid., 329.

38. Ibid., 248–52. Trotsky defended the proposal on the grounds that, as implacable enemies of the Soviet state (which was decidedly not true of all of them), they would have to be shot in the event of a future war, so deportation was more

humane. For a popular account, see Lesley Chamberlain, *Lenin's Private War: The Voyage of the Philosophy Steamer and the Exile of the Intelligentsia* (New York: Picador, 2006).

39. Moshe Lewin describes the late Soviet period as a time when citizens knew "politics" was forbidden yet increasingly managed economic and cultural institutions on their own, leading to Gorbachev's efforts to decrease the role of the Party and let those citizens govern more democratically. This might be an argument on behalf of Lenin's vision, except that such reforms themselves prompted the return of politics, which led to the quick collapse of the system, thus providing additional evidence for the incompatibility of the Leninist model with democracy. Moshe Lewin, *The Gorbachev Phenomenon* (Berkeley: University of California Press, 1988).

40. Quoted in Krausz, *Reconstructing Lenin*, 330.

41. Ibid., 331.

42. Mészáros, "Political Power and Dissent," 13.

43. David North, "Lenin, Trotsky and the Marxism of the October Revolution," *World Socialist Web Site*, March 19, 2018; https://www.wsws.org/en/articles/2018/03/19/leip-m19.html.

44. This and other quotes here from Slavoj Žižek, "Repeating Lenin" (2002), available at https://www.marxists.org/reference/subject/philosophy/works/ot/Žižek1.htm.

45. Žižek; emphasis in original.

46. David Ost, "Thoughts on the Hungarian and Polish New Right in Power," *Public Seminar* (September 21, 2016). http://www.publicseminar.org/2016/09/thoughts-on-the-hungarian-and-polish-new-right-in-power/#.V_PHPvkrKM8; also Mitchell Orenstein, "What Europe's Populist Right Is Getting Right," *Project Syndicate* (March 15, 2019). https://www.project-syndicate.org/commentary/viktor-orban-family-policies-western-criticism-by-mitchell-a--orenstein-2019-03?utm.

47. For more on this, see David Ost, "Workers and the Radical Right in Poland," *International Labor and Working-Class History* 93 (Spring 2018). For the argument on behalf of a Left alliance with PiS, see Rafał Woś, "Lewico, czas na współpracę z PiS" (August 20, 2018), at https://wiadomosci.gazeta.pl/wiadomosci/7,161770,23791323,wos-lewico-czas-na-wspolprace-z-pis-trzeba-budowac-z-kaczynskim.html, and my response, "PiS to nie socjal, tylko antydemokratyczność" (August 26, 2018), https://krytykapolityczna.pl/kraj/lewica-pis-wos-ost/. Also, see David Ost, "The Attack on Democracy in Poland and the Response of the Left," *The Nation* (July 18, 2018), https://www.thenation.com/article/attack-democracy-poland-response-left/.

48. Berman, *The Primacy of Politics*.

49. Jodi Dean, *Crowds and Party* (London: Verso, 2016), 67–72.

50. Ibid., 26.

51. Ibid.

52. Ibid., 258.

53. Ibid., 170–82.

54. Ibid., 260.

55. Ibid., 263.
56. Ibid., 270.
57. "Jodi Dean Comrade," *State of Nature* blog, November 4, 2019. http://stateofnatureblog.com/jodi-dean-comrade/?fbclid=IwAR1O8VQWKzZW2pdzrnrTng_oWcFt-sxnmmoiduLl7xnCPl6r8xwuU3DJKSc.
58. Offe outlines the overall problem in "The Future of European Socialism and the Role of the State," in *The Future of Socialism in Europe?*, ed. André Liebich (Montreal: Interuniversity Centre for European Studies, 1979). See also his two collections of essays: Claus Offe, *Disorganized Capitalism* (Cambridge: MIT Press, 1985), and *Contradictions of the Welfare State* (Cambridge: MIT Press, 1984).
59. Wright introduced this project with the publication of *Envisioning Real Utopias* (London: Verso, 2010), and continued writing about it till his death in 2019. His final words on the topic are published posthumously in *How to Be an Anti-Capitalist in the Twenty-First Century* (London: Verso, 2019). All Wright's works are available for free at https://www.ssc.wisc.edu/~wright/.
60. Dean, *Crowds and Party*, 26.
61. Slavoj Žižek, "Was I Right to Back Donald Trump Over Hillary Clinton? Absolutely!" *Independent* (June 26, 2019). https://www.independent.co.uk/voices/trump-hillary-clinton-populist-right-left-democratic-party-civil-war-a8975121.html.
62. Nicos Poulantzas, *State, Power, Socialism* (London: Verso, 2014; orig. 1978), 265, quoted in Polan, *Lenin and the End of Politics*, 39.

Bibliography

Berman, Sheri. *The Primacy of Politics: Social Democracy and the Making of Europe's Twentieth Century*. Princeton: Princeton University Press, 2006.
Block, Fred. "The Ruling Class Does Not Rule: Notes on the Marxist Theory of the State." *Socialist Review* 33 (1977): 6–28; reprinted in Fred Block, *Revising State Theory*, 51–68. Philadelphia: Temple University Press, 1987.
Brock, David. *Blinded by the Right*. New York: Crown, 2002.
Bull, Martin J. "The West European Communist Movement in the Late Twentieth Century." *West European Politics* 18, no. 1 (1995): 78–97, https://doi.org/10.1080/01402389508425058.
Butler, Stuart, and Peter Germanis. "Achieving Social Security Reform: A 'Leninist' Strategy." *The Cato Journal* 3, no. 2 (Fall 1983).
Claudin, Fernand. *The Communist Movement: From Comintern to Cominform, Part Two*. New York: Monthly Review Press, 1975.
Cohn-Bendit, Daniel, and Gabriel Cohn-Bendit. *Obsolete Communism: The Left-Wing Alternative*. New York: McGraw-Hill, 1968.
Dean, Jodi. *Crowds and Party*. London: Verso, 2016.
Hobsbawm, Eric. *The Age of Extremes: A History of the World, 1914–1991*. New York: Vintage, 1996.

Kaczyński, Jarosław. *Porozumienie przeciw monowładzy*. Poznan: Zysk i S-ka, 2016.
Koch, Charles. *Good Profit*. New York: Crown, 2015.
Krausz, Tamás. *Reconstructing Lenin: An Intellectual Biography*. New York: Monthly Review Press, 2015.
Lewin, Moshe. *The Gorbachev Phenomenon*. Berkeley: University of California Press, 1988.
MacLean, Nancy. *Democracy in Chains*. New York: Viking, 2017.
Mészáros, István. "Political Power and Dissent in Post-Revolutionary Societies." *New Left Review* 108 (March–April 1978): 3–21.
Miéville, China. *October: The Story of the Russian Revolution*. London: Verso, 2017.
North, David. "Lenin, Trotsky, and the Marxism of the October Revolution." *World Socialist Web Site*, March 19, 2018. https://www.wsws.org/en/articles/2018/03/19/leip-m19.html.
Offe, Claus. "The Future of European Socialism and the Role of the State." In *The Future of Socialism in Europe?*, edited by André Liebich, 67–75. Montreal: Interuniversity Centre for European Studies, 1979.
Orenstein, Mitchell. "What Europe's Populist Right is Getting Right." *Project Syndicate*, March 15, 2019. https://www.project-syndicate.org/commentary/viktor-orban-family-policies-western-criticism-by-mitchell-a--orenstein-2019-03?utm.
Ost, David. "The Attack on Democracy in Poland and the Response of the Left." *The Nation*, July 18, 2018. https://www.thenation.com/article/attack-democracy-poland-response-left/.
———. "Workers and the Radical Right in Poland." *International Labor and Working-Class History* 93 (Spring 2018): 113–24, doi:10.1017/S0147547917000345.
———. "The Surprising Right-Wing Relevance of the Russian Revolution." *Constellations* 24, no. 4 (December 2017): 516–27. https://doi.org/10.1111/1467-8675.12328.
———. "Thoughts on the Hungarian and Polish New Right in Power." *Public Seminar*, September 21, 2016. http://www.publicseminar.org/2016/09/thoughts-on-the-hungarian-and-polish-new-right-in-power/#.V_PHPvkrKM8.
———. *Solidarity and the Politics of Anti-Politics*. Philadelphia: Temple University Press, 1990.
Polan, A. J. *Lenin and the End of Politics*. Berkeley: University of California Press, 1984.
Poulantzas, Nicos. *State, Power, Socialism*. London: Verso, 2014; orig. 1978.
Rabinowitch, Alexander. *The Bolsheviks Come to Power*. London: Pluto Press, 2017; orig. 1976.
Radosh, Ronald. "Steve Bannon, Trump's Top Guy, Told Me He Was 'a Leninist'." *The Daily Beast*, August 22, 2016, last modified April 13, 2017. https://www.thedailybeast.com/steve-bannon-trumps-top-guy-told-me-he-was-a-leninist.
Rojas, René. "The Latin American Left's Shifting Tides." *Catalyst* 2, no. 2 (Summer 2018).
Rosenberg, Daniel. "From Crisis to Split: The Communist Party USA, 1989–1991." *American Communist History*, 18, no. 1–2 (2019), 1–55. https://doi.org/10.1080/14743892.2019.1599627.

Roth, Guenther. *The Social Democrats in Imperial Germany*. London: Forgotten Books, 2017; orig. 1963.
Rothbard, Murray. "Towards a Strategy for Libertarian Social Change." Unpublished manuscript, 1977, https://archive.org/details/Rothbard1977TowardAStrategy ForLibertarianSocialChange.
Schmitter, Philippe. "Still the Century of Corporatism?" *The Review of Politics* 36, no. 1 (1974): 85–131.
Sebestyen, Victor. *Lenin*. New York: Pantheon, 2017.
Tugal, Cihan. "The Counter-Revolution's Long March: The American Right's Shift from Primitive to Advanced Leninism." *Critical Sociology* 46, no. 3 (May 2020): 343–58, DOI: 10.1111/1467-8675.12328.
Wright, Erik Olin. *Envisioning Real Utopias*. London: Verso, 2010. https://www.ssc.wisc.edu/~wright/.
Žižek, Slavoj. "Was I Right to Back Donald Trump Over Hillary Clinton? Absolutely!" *Independent*, June 26, 2019. https://www.independent.co.uk/voices/trump-hillary-clinton-populist-right-left-democratic-party-civil-war-a8975121.html.
———. "Repeating Lenin." Marxists Internet Archive (2002), https://www.marxists.org/reference/subject/philosophy/works/ot/Žižek1.htm.

Chapter 2

What Is Leninist Thinking?

AN INTERVIEW WITH JODI DEAN

Editors: *As we are having this discussion, we are nearly a year into the COVID-19 pandemic, more than 250,000 people in the United States have died, and there is widespread recognition, if not necessarily acknowledgment, that the government in the United States has failed at every level. While this is a global crisis that has hit several other neoliberal countries hard (Brazil, India, the UK, among others), the scope of the crisis in the United States is staggering. How do you characterize the crisis we are experiencing? What does a "Leninist" analysis of this historical moment reveal about what is happening?*

Jodi Dean: COVID-19 exposes the fact that the U.S. is a failed state. Its ruling class relies on force and fear. Force—the largest carceral apparatus in world history with the sort of aggressive policing seen primarily in apartheid regimes. Fear—of police, of job loss (which for those fortunate enough to have employer-based health insurance means that they lose that, too), of homelessness (because of inability to make rent or mortgage payments), of infection, and death.

Recall the two competing messages from the first months of the pandemic. Message one was that we are all in this together: people need to practice social distancing and stay at home for the good of all; essential workers are the most valuable members of society and must be respected, protected, and so on. Message two was a variation of the "borrowed kettle" that Slavoj Žižek frequently mentions when invoking Freud's account of dream logic: I didn't borrow your kettle; there was nothing wrong with it when I gave it back; the kettle was broken when I got it. The second version of the COVID message in the U.S. was precisely this: that the coronavirus is nothing serious, just another version of the flu, it would be gone soon; China was responsible for it; only "blue states" (states with Democratic governors and states that went Democrat in the 2016 election) were impacted; only old people got really sick so they should be willing to die for the sake of the next generation; getting the economy going was more important than a uniform response to the pandemic; a vaccine was imminent; the U.S. had developed such effective treatments that the virus was essentially curable—this last message came from U.S. President Donald Trump after he returned from the hospital following treatment for the coronavirus.

Message two demonstrates the illusory, ideological dimension of message one: it was never the case in the U.S. (unlike, say, in Vietnam or Cuba) that we were all in this together and that workers were recognized as essential. Had that been true, had "we all" been in this together, then U.S. billionaires would not have seen a pandemic wealth increase by $850 billion dollars.[1] The emergency aid packages passed by Congress would not have been a handout to corporations (driving a stock market boom) while small businesses collapsed and those most in need were left empty-handed. Over twenty million people would not have lost their jobs, with a quarter of them facing long-term unemployment and 850,000 women permanently leaving the work force. If "we all" had been in this together it would not have been the case that the dead would be those who had been warehoused in prisons and nursing homes, working in meat-packing plants, and more likely to be black, brown, and Native American. It would not have been the case that April would see hundreds of strikes as workers rejected their miserable working conditions. It would not have been the case that celebrities, professional athletes, and politicians would get tested daily while everyday people would have to jump through all sorts of hoops to get a test, which they would often have to pay for and which in many cases wouldn't provide results for at least a week, undermining the already inadequate efforts at contact tracing. If "we all" had been in this together, the approach to reopening public schools would have been a massive increase in the number and compensation of teachers and a dramatic expansion of education spaces instead of a fragmented and unequal response that left working-class parents in impossible binds, sometimes because schools were closed and learning was supposed to occur online and sometimes because schools were open but overcrowded and unsafe. Working-class children (especially black and brown children) will bear the brunt of the collapse of public education as they are pushed further behind their peers privileged enough to go to elite private schools, have a full-time stay at home parent who can guide remote learning, have their own laptops, functioning wifi, and quiet spaces for study and so on.

In a short piece from 1914, Lenin writes: "Every political crisis, whatever its outcome, is useful in that it brings to light things that have been hidden, reveals the forces operating in politics, exposes deception and self-deception, catch-phrases and fictions, and affords striking demonstration of '*things as they are*,' by forcibly driving them home."[2] Many have been asking why did the U.S. fail so badly, why has it been the worst country in the world at handling the virus? Typical answers focus on the multiple, serious, moronic errors of the Trump administration, errors resulting primarily from its intensely partisan approach, its unwavering focus on Trump's image and reelection above all else. But coronavirus didn't cause the crisis; it revealed the deep structural decay brought about by decades of neoliberalism, that is, of the failure to fund infrastructure maintenance and public goods while delivering massive tax cuts to corporations and the rich, privatizing basic services, eviscerating the remnants of the welfare state, and creating an economy where increasing numbers of people are stuck in low wage service sector jobs. Even more, it brought out the inequality baked into the fundamental premises of the U.S. political system—federalism and localism. The absence of a centralized and coordinated national-level response to the virus—a response that would have issued stay-at-home orders, mandated social distancing, ensured widely available free testing on demand, organized contact tracing, required masks, requisitioned and distributed equipment and PPE, guaranteed income so that furloughs didn't become job loss, supplied food and provisions for the infirm and isolated—led to the deaths of hundreds of thousands of people. Instead of the top-down effort the situation demanded, the response to the virus differed greatly from state to state. In some states, there were even county-level differences: some counties mandated masks while others stuck to business as usual.

Lenin supplies a method for thinking in a crisis: What appears more clearly than it did before? What does this new clarity tell us about the structures that produced it? How is the new truth driven home? About what were we self-deceived? A crisis is a crisis for the system or structure out of which it arises; it exposes its weakness, rupturing the ideological illusion that shapes the sense of what is possible and what is not. With respect to COVID, the most glaring self-deception was that federalization, decentralization, localism, and individual choice are attributes of freedom rather than the form of our political and economic deadlock.

Editors: *In some of your articles published this year, you revisit both Lenin and his revolutionary comrades, Krupskaya and Kollontai. Is it fair to say that Lenin, and the Bolsheviks' experience more generally, are becoming more important to your thought in this particular political moment? Can you talk briefly about why you choose to think with and through Lenin? For instance, in your recent article, "Revolution or Ruin," you coin the term "Climate Leninism." Can you clarify, Why is Lenin useful as we think of solutions to a climate crisis? After all, a hundred years ago, in 1920, Lenin announced a statewide electrification plan, which paved the way for an industrialization of the country that was not at all attentive to matters of ecology.*

Dean: The primary reason I turned to Lenin in my work is because his thinking is always oriented toward political action. It's not just "critique"—so popular among intellectuals. It is analysis with respect to an intervention, which means the action of a group in a specific context. Building, strengthening, energizing, and mobilizing this group—whether party, class, or people—is thus always an element of his thought. My academic field is political theory; this orientation toward collective mobilization has been missing from most political theory for at least forty years. Strangely, some of the most influential theorists have been more concerned with the agency of things than with the collective agency of people (a symptom of the constricted space of politics under neoliberalism, since the defeat of the USSR, etc.). The apparent "triumph" of capitalism and liberalism in 1989 (marked by Francis Fukuyama's influential article "The End of History") made it seem as if the primary questions of economic and political form had been settled; all that was necessary was smoothing out the rough edges and expanding the reach of the system, that is, including more people in a capitalism with a human face. It has taken decolonialist critics and anti-imperialist fighters to rupture this assumption, which, alas, is still dominant.

The most utopian thing in the world today is thinking that emancipatory egalitarian political change is possible through reformist, electoral means. It simply will not happen. The capitalist class has a firm grip on the governing institutions of the United States. Over the last forty years, productivity in the U.S. has increased over one hundred percent while workers' pay has essentially stagnated.[3] Even the slightest attempt to improve the lives of workers is met with vehement opposition. The police state has grown—more people incarcerated, more aggressive and militarized policing, harsher sentences and intimidation practices used to repress protesters. Let's not forget that this year (2020) unmarked vans were seizing protesters off the streets of Portland, detaining them in unknown locations. State terror—and permitted corporate terror—against environmental activists is widespread in the Americas, with some of the most visible cases being the assassination of Honduran organizer Berta Caceres and the militarized attacks on the Standing Rock Water Protectors. Every year we hear that the planet is getting warmer and yet internal documents released from Exxon show the company planning on increasing annual carbon emissions up to seventeen percent over the next five years.[4] Will that be stopped with a fine? Is there even a political entity in the U.S. with the will to slap them with a fine?

In "Revolution or Ruin,"[5] Kai Heron and I argue that we need a state to intervene against capital on behalf of workers and nature. And we need a revolutionary party with the capacity and will to seize this state. The turn to Lenin—and we advocate a Climate Leninism—is not a turn to the content of hundred-year-old policies but a turn to the form of power. The state is a ready-made apparatus for responding to the climate crisis. It can operate at the scales necessary to develop and implement plans for reorganizing agriculture, transportation, housing, and production. It has the capacity to transform the energy sector. It is backed by a standing army. What if all that power were channeled by the many against the few on behalf of a just response to the climate crisis?

Editors: *Some on the Left caution against the return to Lenin. What, in your opinion, does Leninist thought have to offer to the contemporary Left? What is Leninist thinking?*

Dean: To be honest, even as Western European Social Democrats have cautioned against Lenin since before 1917 (I'm thinking here of their betrayal of the working class when they reneged on their promise to remain unified in opposition to imperialist war), I am skeptical that anyone today who cautions against the return to Lenin is actually on the Left. I suspect that they are more likely liberals who think that electoral politics can facilitate radical change for the benefit of working people. This is delusional; it flies in the face of the last forty years of reaction and counterrevolution. Admittedly, sometimes anti-Leninists think of themselves as anarchists. They tend to view politics in terms of small groups and localized interactions, which means that they then have no way of dealing with the most pressing issues of our time—climate change, extreme economic inequality, imperialism, and pandemics. Today, more than ever, the only political line that makes sense is the one drawn by Lenin's name: for or against organization, revolution, and proletarian dictatorship, that is, the party, the seizure of the state, and working people's use of the state to abolish the conditions of oppression, exploitation, and extraction.

In the late eighties, Marxism became unfashionable among so-called Left intellectuals (some of who turned to Foucault or Habermas or Laclau and Mouffe as alternatives) in the so-called West. This change in fashion was no accident. It was the way that the defeat of the Soviet Union and of working-class struggles in the global North manifested itself in the academy. Fredric Jameson was right when he pointed out the link between postmodernism and late capitalism. More recently, however, the extreme inequality that has taken hold in the U.S., UK, Russia, parts of the EU (to stay with the global North here), has given new life to Marxism. Its analysis of the inequality that capitalism necessarily produces is now widely recognized—even in mainstreams newspapers and magazines—as common sense. Some "progressives" have also always been attracted to the early Marx's critique of alienation. But this newly acceptable Marx is Marxism defanged, Marxism as the completion of liberalism, a Marxism without state and revolution. For this we need Lenin.

Leninist thinking is thinking that is oriented toward the future that it brings into being. It has a principled and a tactical dimension. What's interesting about this principle is how for Lenin realizing it is always a matter of organization. This connects, then, to tactics—finding the best ways to reach or achieve the principle in a specific context. Lenin is always concerned with the details, "an objective analysis of the situation" or the concrete balance of forces.

Lenin's thinking can be periodized around forming the party, forwarding the revolution, and building the state. In each phase, Lenin's focus is on organization—how to organize the party, the organizational steps involved in revolutionary struggle, the organizational structures that will differentiate the workers' state from the state of the bourgeoisie.

This sort of structured organizational thinking has been missing on the Left. Or maybe it's more accurate to say that it has been channeled into directions that reinforce rather than challenge the hold of the bourgeois state. For example, issue campaigns generally want to raise awareness that will lead to legislative changes. Increasing fines, penalties, surveillance, etc.

appears as a viable solution to a host of different problems. But if we want to change the system, we have to organize for systemic change—and that is what we learn from Lenin.

Editors: *For many readers, Lenin is best known as the theorist of* Imperialism *(1916). He famously predicted it was the final or "highest" stage of capitalism, the era of capitalism as a world system. Now when commentators such as McKenzie Wark are suggesting capitalism may be transitioning to "something worse," and you have recently suggested we face the choice of "Communism or Neo-Feudalism," how should we view the central thesis of* Imperialism? *Are we still in capitalism's highest stage, inching toward the edge? Has capitalism entered a new stage, or will it?*

Dean: The language of "highest stage" makes it seem like Lenin has a rather linear conception of history, one where socialism necessarily follows from capitalism, as if this were a determined historical trajectory. But yet Lenin's own approach to revolution in Russia did not follow this trajectory. He famously disagreed with the Mensheviks that Russia needed to develop capitalism under a bourgeois parliamentary democracy and only after capitalism was fully developed would the time be ripe for proletarian revolution. In other words, he wasn't dogmatic about stages. I also think that we should not be dogmatic about stages. History isn't linear. Worse forms succeed "better" forms—as the neoliberal counterrevolution of the nineties makes clear.

So today we need to read *Imperialism* for its resolute internationalism, its attention to unequal and exploitative interconnections of the "global" economy. The dynamics that had been outward facing are now accompanied by an inward turn. Contemporary imperialism relies on producing indebtedness at home as well as abroad, for example. Similarly, the exploitation of raw materials is accompanied by the datafication of life and interaction, "big data."

Lenin theorized imperialism as an intensification of capital concentration, monopolies, and financial oligarchy. Today's complex networks—digital, communication, information—amplify these tendencies toward inequality as they result in powerlaw distributions (these follow the 80/20 rule or a winner-take-all/winner-take-most distribution pattern). For an example, just think of numbers of followers on Twitter: those at the very top have over a hundred million followers; most people have around two hundred. My argument is that current neofeudal tendencies are a continuation and reflexivization of imperialism under the conditions of communicative capitalism.

The structure of complex networks demonstrates why contemporary capitalism tends toward neofeudalism. As complex networks result in power-law distributions, they undermine equality and intensify hierarchy—and they do so by means of inclusion and democratic participation. Hierarchy is an *immanent feature* of networks characterized by free choice, growth, and preferential attachment (which explains why markets produce monopolies). It is not an external imposition. It is an emergent property. At the same time, in communicative capitalism practices associated with democracy—such as free speech and discussion—concentrate and detach themselves into affective networks where politics is reduced to the daily outrage. Liberated from democratic chains yet pretending to have democratic legitimacy, the state is then refined as an instrument of coercive force, surveillance, and control, a means for the maintenance of order amidst ongoing expropriation, dispossession, and fragmentation. In the U.S., this has meant funding prisons not schools, building up police not basic infrastructure like bridges and roads, and subsidizing corporations not social services. As the world's leading imperialist power, the U.S. pursues these same policies all over the world.

Editors: *Your professional roots are in the field of Soviet Studies. Everyone knows the Cold War roots of area studies in the United States and the anticommunist political character of Soviet history in English. What are the assumptions about Soviet society and state that continue to keep today's leftists from properly upholding the USSR as part of the history of socialism?*

Dean: There's a remarkable absence of knowledge about the USSR among today's leftists. Or, put a bit more generously, if the knowledge is there, it doesn't stick, it doesn't register. For starters, we can think of Soviet economic, technological, and scientific achievements—I've always had a warm place in my heart for the Soviet space program, Yuri Gagarin (the first man in space in 1961), Valentina Tereshkova (the first woman in space—in 1963!). When thinking about the Soviet Union, we need to keep in mind the dramatic improvement in women's lives and equality (shout out to Kristen R. Ghodsee's book *Why Women Had Better Sex Under Socialism*). Additionally, few seem familiar with the impact of the USSR on anticolonial and anti-imperialist struggles in the so-called Third World (as an example we might think of the training provided by the Communist University of the Toilers of the East). Instead, there is a stereotype of gray, flat, authoritarianism and deprivation.

This stereotype prevents people from knowing what they know; it stops anything that runs counter to the equation communism = Soviet Union = Stalin = gulag from registering (I discuss this in *The Communist Horizon*). So it's really a deeply flattening epistemological orientation that's at work here more than it is actual historical knowledge. An anticommunist, anti-Soviet, anti-Leninist orientation flattens the rich experience of the Bolsheviks, the decades of history of the USSR, even the tragic and conflicted legacy of Stalin into one uniform picture of totalitarian misery and political failure. So, for example, the "Leninist party" is misrepresented as some kind of antidemocratic machine. But what about the weeks of fierce debate in the Central Committee over signing a treaty with Germany to get Russia out of the war, which became the Brest-Litovsk treaty? The Central Committee deliberated for months. Arguing that the Russian Army was in no condition to continue, Lenin urged the conclusion of a peace, even with the severe annexationist terms demanded by the Germans. At various points numerous members of the Central Committee threatened to resign, including Lenin himself. Lenin won the final vote: seven in favor, four against, four abstentions. In response, the Moscow Regional Bureau passed a vote of no-confidence in the Central Committee. And all this happened in the "Leninist party," but those swayed by the image of gray totalitarianism don't see it at all. They either fail to acknowledge how Lenin was constantly arguing with his comrades—or, when they do see this, they trash Lenin for being too harsh and polemical. So they switch gears completely, doing everything they can to shore up their flattened-out view.

Another more obvious example: the flat presentation of the Stalin era ignores the leading role of the USSR in the war against fascism as well as the fact that the U.S. and the USSR were allies in WWII. This means that it ignores not just changes occurring within the U.S. during the Stalin period but also changes in the international arena. Leading cadre in anticolonial struggles from the thirties through the fifties received training and support from the Soviet Union.

Editors: *Lars Lih once said (back in 1991) that the most alien Bolshevik cultural value for Americans was the unparalleled importance of unity in the face of one's enemies. Americans lacked, the remark seemed to allege, the instinctual capacity to close ranks against a known foe. In your recent books, such as* Crowds and Party *and* Comrade, *you insist on the importance of solidarity and discipline characteristic of Bolshevik-style parties. But are there "cultural" impediments to* *the reconstruction of such parties in the U.S. (and in the so-called West world generally)? How could those on the Left address them if so, or rethink Marxist-Leninist categories and approaches? This is a "naive" question but we think it gets at many unspoken assumptions in everyday Left politics.*

Dean: The U.S. has long been dominated by various sorts of individualisms—the Protestant individual of religious faith as a matter of the individual's soul; the liberal legalism of basic rights as they attach to individuals; the individualism of the frontier (which should be recognized as premised on the genocide); the individualism of the capitalist who picked himself up by his own bootstraps and of the entrepreneur who did it all by himself; the individualism of the artist with his own unique creative voice; and these days the ever-present injunction toward self-branding—I should add that my choice of masculine pronouns here is deliberate; American individualism has been, let's just say it, stupidly and profoundly macho as it erases the fact that every woman knows people come tied together with other people. So the first problem is the cult of the individual. And you know, some who consider themselves leftists have not actually left this cult: they emphasize that everyone should speak for themselves; that no one should represent another person. These individuals, then, are primary cultural impediments to disciplined political collectivity of the kind constitutive of communist parties.

There are, of course, crucial exceptions—some immigrant communities, some communities of racialized minorities, some religious communities. And there has also been in the U.S. a wide array of civic and patriotic organizations. For the most part they have been presented as nonpolitical. Recognizing that they in fact affirm the power of collectivity can go some way toward dismantling the cult of individualism.

In the 1980s—in the face of the rise of neoliberalism and defeat of the working class—a number of European Left parties thought that giving more space to individual values, concerns, modes of expression, etc. would be a good idea. One of the theoretical resources for this shift was Ernesto Laclau's and Chantal Mouffe's *Hegemony and Socialist Strategy*. Their core idea was moving away from the centrality of class and emphasizing the need to construct hegemonic formations by linking together various identity struggles. They enacted in theory what neoliberalism was enacting in practice. In fact the slogan was the same: society doesn't exist.

What the Left should have done was double down on the need for solidarity at a time when the working class was under attack. Particularly in the U.S., it has been hard to rebuild the sense that political struggle requires solidarity. People have been reluctant to acknowledge how communicative capitalism pushes us toward individual opining and expressing but that individual voices and opinions are politically ineffective. Identity is presumed to be the basis of politics—not part of the field of contestation. And among some portions of the online Left and in some activist circles, there is a skepticism toward the discipline that an organized party offers, as if individual self-expression is more important for political efficacy than strong, united, organizations. Of course, there are and have been important exceptions. The Black Panthers are admired by everyone for their discipline even as other socialist groups are otherwise disparaged.

So as not to sound pessimistic, we should note that this dreary picture has been changing since the Occupy movement. Even with the defeats of Corbyn and Sanders, socialist politics in the UK and U.S. has been re-energized. And this re-energization has brought with it a new appreciation for the fact that the working class is multinational, multigenerational, multigendered and that struggles for an economic future, for economic justice, that is, against capitalism and for socialism are more necessary now in an era of pandemic and climate change than ever before. Another example: throughout 2020 there have been hundreds of strikes in the U.S., more work stoppages and strikes than the country has seen in decades. This is necessary and exciting. And of course during the summer of 2020, hundreds of thousands of people across the country demonstrated a remarkable capacity to coalesce in opposition to two main foes—the coronavirus and the police. In the wake of the murder of George Floyd, people risked their lives to come out in protest against racist policing in an extraordinarily powerful revolt against racism. This happened in large cities and small towns; it involved people of multiple races and ages. And it was consistent, frequent—not just one-off events. Particularly noteworthy is that no virus outbreaks or hotspots were associated with these gatherings. Even as they assembled in thousands, people wore their masks, practiced social distance, and took care of one another. The solidarity that comes from standing together in collective struggle won out over individualism and fear.

Editors: *You rightly point to U.S. individualism's macho character, which is an obvious facet of many of today's extremist organizations in the United States. As with the long-term U.S. experience of mass shootings, violent acting out is deeply tied to psychic "insecurity" and a fear of losing patriarchal privileges. You recently wrote on Lenin's wife Nadezhda Krupskaya and on Lenin's comrade Alexander Kollontai exploring their views on love, sexuality, gender, and* *comradeship in a proletarian state. Why did you decide to revisit these figures? How do they help us work through the social contradictions of misogyny and patriarchy in fear of losing itself?*

Dean: I should start by pointing out that there are good reasons for the "fear of loss," good reasons for people to feel insecure—"millennials" are the first generation of U.S. Americans to face a future where their lives are likely to be worse than those of their parents. Climate change is real; the absence of an economy where people without a college degree can earn enough for a decent quality of life is real and so on. There has not been a serious Left party with the capacity to give these fears political expression. The populist Right—like Trump and also in the form of various white supremacist groups like the Proud Boys all the way to conspiracy theories like QAnon—has filled the gap and offered people a way to understand why their futures look so dismal; it gives them people to blame, most typically Washington elites, people of color, and sexual minorities. So I'd say that there are significant material reasons for people's rage and political reasons for their attraction to the populist Right, namely, the Left position has been substantially blocked from political expression in the U.S. Bernie Sanders started breaking through this block, building a movement, and got trampled, shut down, by the Democratic Party.

Anyway, what I find refreshing in these Bolshevik women is their materialism and their emphasis on organization. To put it bluntly, they are political and today's dominant mode is moral (with aesthetic in second place). The emphasis on politics—division, organizing, struggle—is super refreshing given the tyranny of liberal feminism and identity politics (which actually reinforce each other). The former reduces feminism to women's (usually white women's) success in the capitalist economy and political system, seeking acceptance in that system rather than fighting to bring it down; the latter proceeds as if identities were unrelated to material economic conditions and that the forms of oppression linked to them can be addressed without changing the economy—in other words, it's idealist.

I'll say a bit more about this: I'm not persuaded of the political utility of "misogyny" as a category. What are women supposed to do about being hated? The options that the misogyny diagnosis presents repeat the traps of fairy tales: be the witch who draws power from her outcast position or the passive princess dreaming of love. Poison men or win them over. Mirroring the compressed possibilities of the world it claims to critique, the misogyny diagnosis compels us to accept a world of false choices. In so doing, it avoids the perplexing dilemma of how women are to wage a struggle against an aversion by sidestepping politics altogether.

In fact, the point seems to be that we can't do anything about being hated. Misogyny supplies an account of the world well-suited for the circulation of rage as a commodity. One gets a bit of a charge, a flash of indignation, while remaining free of any obligation to act. The misogyny claim suggests that the situation women face is moral, perhaps even ontological. Political struggle can't improve women's lives when the deepest problem we face is misogyny. No wonder liberal feminists find misogyny a compelling lens for understanding the contemporary world. It reflects it back to them while getting them off the hook for failing to fight to change it.

Kollontai is helpful for us here and now because she pointed out that women's subordination is anchored in economic conditions, that is, in the conditions of "the production and reproduction of immediate life," to use Frederick Engels's formulation. These conditions involve how both human existence is produced and reproduced and how the means of existence—food, clothing, shelter, tools, and so on—are secured and arranged. Women's position in the economy—which includes the sexual division of labor in the family—determines women's position in society. The repercussion is that women's liberation depends on the elimination of capitalism, of class society and exploitation, and the communist rearrangement of production and life. So her argument doesn't presume an unchanging patriarchy persisting throughout time; sexual relations, sexual liberation, are historical. When women are not economically dependent on men, when having children neither chains them to particular men nor dooms them to poverty (because it blocks them from income), then they can be free to love as they choose.

Incidentally, people assume that Kollontai had a "glass of water" theory of sex—sex should be as carefree as having a glass of water. It's not true (although a fictional character in one of her novellas had that view). Rather, her vision of love under communism is one of comradeship and solidarity. In "Make way for Winged Eros: A Letter to Working Class Youth" from 1923, Kollontai theorizes sex in terms of energy, wingless Eros and winged Eros. Wingless Eros is the natural and biological sex instinct. Kollontai associates it with a reproductive urge but also describes it as brief, simple couplings (we might say hooking up). Wingless Eros doesn't require emotional and psychological energy. And because it doesn't require emotional and psychological energy, this kind of casual sex is compatible with intense work elsewhere, with revolutionary work, for example. At the same time, the absence of intensity that gives wingless Eros this compatibility makes it unsatisfying.

People generally want something intensely satisfying and meaningful in their lives: "This extra energy seeks an outlet in the love-experience." So when our revolutionary work is done, or, when the movement ebbs, we long for something intensely satisfying and winged Eros come back in. Kollontai's goal is to find ways to transfer that energy to the collective, to make it the basis of our collective solidarity, what she calls love-comradeship.

In keeping with her historical materialist method, Kollontai places love-comradeship in historical context: it emerges as the proletarian ideal of love, the feeling of inner solidarity that derives from cooperative labor. It "involves the recognition of the rights and integrity of the other's personality, a steadfast mutual support and sensitive sympathy, and responsiveness to the other's needs." Love solidarity becomes for the dictatorship of the proletariat what competition was for the dictatorship of the bourgeoisie, the primary social tie, supposition, and expectation. Collectivism defeats individualism. Love and duty toward the collective takes the place of the isolated two of the couple.

Editors: *In recent months, the coercive side of the state apparatus became visible to the masses—photos of police in riot gear coming down hard on peaceful protesters speaking out against police violence are shocking. We are seeing a wave of politically motivated arrests of protestors, such as the ones in Denver. What is your analysis of the situation? Are we seeing the American equivalent of the Russian 1905, so to speak?*

Dean: Actually, what I've noticed is the dramatic instability of temporal reference. The present is analogized to the tumultuous time of the early seventies, to the age of the robber barons, to Reconstruction, to the U.S. Civil War, to the plantation—and these reference points just include the U.S.! What this assortment tells me is not that any one period is a more compelling reference point. It tells me that racism, struggle, and repression are continuous features of U.S. history. What's surprising is that something so frequent, so deeply ingrained into the U.S., continues to shock. Maybe we should ask who it shocks or what specifically is shocking? The politically motivated arrest of protesters stretches from the present, through the environmental movement, through Occupy, through the antiwar movement that sprung up after 9/11, through the Black Power struggle, through the arrests at Stonewall, through the arrest, prosecution, imprisonment of CPUSA members in the 1950s, beyond and in between.

Editors: *To continue on the topic of time here, Lenin's writing has a sense or tone of urgency that is unusual, perhaps unique. Can one speak of something like Lenin's "revolutionary temporality," perhaps akin to Walter Benjamin's concept of "Now-Time"? How does temporality work in Lenin's texts? If we assume the texts are urgent (not so much timely as anticipatory) interventions, what reading methods allow us to distil practical political applications to our present conjuncture?*

Dean: I think of Lenin as offering what I call the "temporality of the party." It combines a break in the present, response to the past, and projected future. The party anticipates the revolution, materializing the belief that makes revolution possible not as an overflow of present possibilities, but as an effect of the negation of some trajectories and the forcing of others. My idea here is informed by Jean-Pierre Dupuy's notion of "projected time" and Georg Lukacs's emphasis on the "actuality of revolution."

Dupuy introduces "projected time" as a name for "coordination by means of the future," that is, as a term for a temporal metaphysics wherein "the future counterfactually determines the past, which in turn causally determines it: The future is fixed, but its necessity exists only in retrospect." From the perspective of the future, what led to it was necessary. It could not have been otherwise because everything that happened led to it. Before an event occurs, there are possibilities, options. After something happens, it appears inevitable, destined. Projected time assumes a future inevitability, establishing this inevitability as the fixed point from which to decide upon present actions. Anticipation has practical effects.

When we turn to revolution, the immediate question arises: Whose anticipation? What carries the projected future? For the projected future to have coordinating effects, to generate the processes that will lead to it, it needs to be carried by a collectivity, some kind of institution or body. In politics, particularly revolutionary Left politics, this body has been the Party, a political organization mobilized by means of the future.

Consider the Bolsheviks. In the Party, historical materialism isn't an account of the past. It's a relation to a specific future, one where "revolution is already on its agenda." As Georg Lukács insists in a classic study, Lenin made the actuality of revolution into the point from which all questions were evaluated and all actions were considered. The fact of the approach of revolution cut through multiple tendencies, the manifold conflicts of groups and individuals within the masses, and the economic fatalism that contributes to capitalism's own response to crises. The certain future of revolution enabled Lenin's party to choose, to decide. The Bolsheviks weren't alone in anticipating the revolution. Various Left parties and tendencies throughout Europe and Russia thought revolution was imminent. Lenin's contribution lay in understanding revolution's coordinating effects, the way that its anticipation established the tasks that needed to be done. For the Bolsheviks, the fact of revolution operates as a force of negation within the present that pushes forth the practices necessary for revolution. Through the Party, the revolution produces its revolutionaries.

In the Party (and now I mean the party in its broader, more formal sense), anticipation of a certain future accompanies two other temporalities: the momentary and the retroactive. I designate "momentary" those disruptions to which the Party responds as if they are the actions of the people as their subject. In the history of Marxism, we see such responses to the Paris Commune, to mass strikes and demonstrations, to crowds of rioting women. Crowds do the unexpected, even the impossible, disrupting the given and installing a gap in the present. The Party responds to the crowds, reading the disorder they cause as the effect of the subject, the revolutionary people, the proletarianized, the oppressed (in *Theory of the Subject*, Alain Badiou describes this as subjectification). The crowd rupture is retroactively determined to be an effect of the people as its cause. The revolutionary divided people were the subject of the disruptive event. The event wasn't just something here and now; it was part of the subjective process of the people (to use Badiou's terms).

Editors: *One of Badiou's critiques of Lenin and the Leninist party form is that the latter failed to orchestrate the withering away of the proletarian state. People's democracy, of which Lenin had dreamed, never arrived, and the idea of centralization backfired when the party, effectively, became the apparatus of the state. In other words, Lenin is recognized largely as a theorist of state takeover. David J. Ost in this collection also argues that Left Leninists fail to address the "potential party dictatorship over the proletariat and the people" and that Lenin has nothing to offer in terms of how to build a socialist democracy after the revolution. Do you have any thoughts on these issues?*

Dean: These sorts of criticisms are so strange. It's like blaming people oriented toward victory for failing to prevent a future defeat. Lenin's task before he died was building the proletarian state, not orchestrating its demise. His initial goal was not socialist democracy but the dictatorship of the proletariat, which is the form for proletarian democracy. This democracy was always going to involve the forcible exclusion of the oppressors and exploiters of the people. At the heart of both of these criticisms of Lenin is the rejection of the dictatorship of the proletariat, a fundamental anti-statism. Fully rejecting the state (not just the party), Badiou goes in the direction of the communist Idea. Ost accepts a basically liberal (I think he qualifies his view as "corporatist" along the lines of the arrangements in Germany that give workers a voice in corporate decisions) parliamentary view of the state, but places his eggs in the basket of civil society—a move that was popular in the nineties among those who thought that the defeat of socialism in Eastern Europe and Russia was going to usher in democracy rather than ethnic conflict, austerity, and extreme capitalism.

From 1917 on, Lenin was massively invested in the details of building a working-class government. And this in a context of trying to extract the country from the imperialist war, fight the ongoing civil war with invasions from multiple other countries, and rebuild the economy after the wars utterly devastated it. His approach highlighted the need for control, accounting, and reporting—we might call this information sharing—and the importance of control, accounting, and reporting for production, distribution, and planning. This is an enormous operation whereby the people learn to produce and administer and thereby take over the functions of the state. To my mind, these remain the central issues of revolutionary self-governance: How exactly are we going to get things done, especially given people as they are and conditions not of our choosing? The CCP recognizes that this is a long task: the revolution reconfigures the terrain of struggle; building communism may take a hundred years.

Editors: *For many observers, even casual ones, these questions could articulate the quintessential "Leninist" question: Chto Delat? While it may not be a good idea to ground our idea of "Leninism" in "What Is to Be Done" alone, its title remains a perennial question, which we'd like to turn back to you: how are we going to get things done? What are the recipes for change in the United States, for instance? Let's say, if a Leninist party were to play a role in twenty-first-century U.S. politics, what would it have to do?*

Dean: The Leninist answer is always organize. At the end of the twentieth century, some on the Left thought that networked media was a work-around, a technological fix, a way to organize without having to do the serious work of connecting day-to-day to people's struggles. It was always like, "build a website," or "switch to a more secure channel," or "make an event page," or "create an efficient crowd-sourcing platform where users can rank preferences." I can't tell you how many discussions and events I was part of that fetishized technological solutions to the detriment of actual conversations with communities. But "organize" does not mean turn to technology. It means, always, be where the people are, because the goal is organizing the working class (broadly understood) to overthrow the ruling class.

The decades of attacks on unions make workplace organizing tremendously difficult. Nevertheless, in the last few years in the U.S., nurses and teachers have had very successful strikes. White supremacy has been on the rise, empowered of course by Trump. Yet the summer of 2020 saw the largest, most extensive revolt against racism and aggressive policing in U.S. history—and this during the coronavirus pandemic. The party we need is a party in and of the movements, one that is deeply involved in people's struggles, drawing out the ways that their success depends on overturning capitalism and building communism, making visible the red thread that unites them.

Editors: *An essay in this collection discusses the phenomenon of right-wing Leninism. Do you have thoughts on this concept? Why do you think is Lenin attractive to some on the ultra-Right end of the political spectrum? Do they have a rightful claim to Lenin?*

Dean: Historically, the Right has always taken ideas from the Left. We see this clearly with fascism as a "national" socialism. So there is nothing original or even interesting in saying that the Right is appropriating a figure, tactics, or strategies from the Left. What we should ask about is the perspective of the analysis; in other words, from what orientation does the attempt to discredit Lenin by linking him with political currents appearing nearly a hundred years after his death arise? It's a guilt by association argument rather than anything more substantial.

Editors: *If you were to recommend three to five of Lenin's texts to a young comrade today, which ones would you recommend she read and why?*

Dean: The 1920 interview with Clara Zetkin. It's crucial—in part because there are some weird and funny moments where Lenin says things like "and now I am the woman" or something like that and in part because it belies the myth that communists talk only about class and not about, say, "women's issues" (as if women's issues were not class issues). In it, Lenin provides the imperative reminder that household labor is drudgery and that socialism requires the socialism of reproductive as well as productive work. The early Soviets were absolutely correct in prioritizing childcare, nurseries, common kitchens and laundries, the right to abortion, and sexual freedom. These were not described in terms of individual rights. They were social conditions for liberation and equality. So there is a Leninist feminism articulated there that stresses the necessity of fighting to secure the conditions for liberation and equality—and organizing for that fight, analyzing the tactics that will be necessary to win it, and doing the work it requires.

So, to a young comrade, well, since she is a comrade I will assume that she has already read the classics: "What Is to Be Done?" (the Lars Lih version is great), "State and Revolution," and "Imperialism: The Highest Stage of Capitalism." These are indispensable for understanding the importance of organizing the party and the state and for grasping the international dimensions of the struggle for communism.

I also would recommend "A Letter to a Comrade on Our Organizational Tasks"—this is a shorter and more pointed version of the themes in "What Is to Be Done." Lenin's wife, Nadezhda Krupskaya, recommends it in her *Reminiscences of Lenin* because of the insight it provides into Lenin's attention to organizational detail and the importance of democratic centralism.

"Leftwing Communism: An Infantile Disorder" is crucial for recognizing the limits of anarchism or any kind of Left purism. "The Proletarian Revolution and the Renegade Kautsky" is important for understanding the argument for the dictatorship of the proletariat. I also really like Lenin's "Letters from Afar." They are models for "party time." Revolution is on the agenda—but not just the bourgeois revolution, the proletarian revolution. Lenin sees this when no one else does and his anticipation has practical effects as he organizes his party in preparation for it.

Editors: *Thank you for your thoughtful answers.*

Notes

1. https://inequality.org/great-divide/updates-billionaire-pandemic/.
2. https://www.marxists.org/archive/lenin/works/1914/may/03.htm.

3. https://www.epi.org/productivity-pay-gap/.
4. https://www.bloomberg.com/news/articles/2020-10-05/exxon-carbon-emissions-and-climate-leaked-plans-reveal-rising-co2-output.
5. "Revolution or Ruin." *e-flux* #110 (June 2020).

Chapter 3

We're All (Romantic) Socialists

*Lenin's Struggle against
Utopian Anticapitalism Then and Now*

CHRISTIAN SORACE AND KAI HERON

Introduction: The Once and Future Extinguished Hopes of Romantic Anti-Capitalism

"We are all socialists now," teased the British Liberal politician William Harcourt upon the passing of a modest piece of legislation authorizing the British state to buy private land for public use. The year was 1887, Lenin was just beginning his studies at Kazan University, and as Harcourt knew well it was hardly the case that Britain had turned socialist. Yet socialism was of such profound concern to Britain's propertied classes that its evocation in Parliament was enough to incite anxiety. No longer what one commentator at the time described as "a mere 'Utopia,' spun from the humanity-intoxicated brains of various French men," socialism had taken root among the working class and was becoming a political force of consequence across Europe. As Marx and Engels had written four decades earlier, a specter was haunting Europe, the specter of communism.[1]

Harcourt's words have acquired a life of their own since they were first spoken. For those on both the Left and Right they have offered support for arguments—not for or against communism, the abolition of property, or worker control of the means of production—but for or against modest state intervention in capitalist markets. We find the phrase peppered throughout parliamentary records; it was famously adapted by Milton Friedman to express his resentment at the spread of Keynesianism, and in the wake of the 2008 financial crash it sparked an international conversation after making its way onto the front page of *Newsweek Magazine*, which read: "We Are All Socialists Now."[2]

Recently, Harcourt's words have been recalled to discuss a new passion for "socialism" in the form of the democratic socialism of Bernie Sanders and the Green New Deal. In an *Intelligencer* article entitled "We're All 'Socialists' Now," media pundit Eric Levitz welcomed Sanders's policies. Levitz correctly observed that the state has always intervened in market dynamics and argued that to call this socialism is to do "violence to Marx's conception of socialism." For the Right (and many within the Democratic Party), however, Sanders and the Green New Deal represent an existential threat to capitalism and, for some, nothing short of a communist plot. Harcourt's words return to name the Right's fears and to associate them with a long struggle against communism. Take, for example, the right-wing think tank Acton Institute: "In 1888 [*sic*], the British Liberal leader Sir William Harcourt declared, 'We are all socialists now,' a similar claim could be made in America in 2018: We are all New Deal socialists now." Or consider the *National Review*'s call for its readers to "help . . . eradicate the socialist zombie resurgence." To galvanize its readership, the conservative magazine quotes the 2009 *Newsweek* headline before claiming that the situation is much worse a decade later, thanks to the threat of an ascendant socialist bloc led by none other than Bernie Sanders.[3]

Nevertheless, the 2020 democratic primaries, conducted haphazardly in the midst of the coronavirus pandemic, ended in Sanders's defeat, to the dismay of the numerous supporters he had inspired. As fanciful as the above accusations were—in that they misconstrued state intervention, a normal feature of capitalism, as "socialism"—it is true that Sanders identified as a "socialist." During the 2020 presidential primaries he distinguished himself from his competitor Elizabeth Warren by stating plainly that "Elizabeth Warren, I think, as you know, has said that she's a capitalist through her bones. I'm not." But what exactly is the *content* of Sanders's anticapitalism? In 2015 he dispelled concerns that his socialism was *actual* socialism with these words:

So the next time you hear me attacked as a socialist, remember this, I don't believe the government should own the means of production, but I do believe that the middle class and the working families who produce the wealth of America deserve a fair deal.

In the lead up to the 2020 Democratic primaries, Sanders renewed his commitment to "democratic socialism" by promising a "political revolution" that will make billionaires extinct, fight the "elite" and the "corrupt," introduce universal health care, and implement a Green New Deal to "avert climate catastrophe and create 20 million new climate jobs."[4]

Sanders's ability to locate and articulate the contradictions of global capital—a warming planet, escalating wealth inequalities, advanced medicine combined with deteriorating public health—has contributed to the growing popularity of "socialism" in the United States. In March 2019 *Intelligencer* ran an article entitled "When Did Everyone Become Socialist?" in which, as the title suggests, the author expresses bewilderment at the sudden popularity of "socialism" in the United States. Polls in 2019 suggested that more than one-third of U.S. millennials approved of communism, while 70 percent of millennials said they would vote for a socialist presidential candidate like Sanders. Having ignored Sanders's presidential run for months, by early 2020, the corporate U.S. press started to wake up to the fact that he was polling better than their preferred Democratic candidates. "Bernie Sanders Could Actually Win This Thing," confessed CNN, "Be prepared for President Sanders," warned the *Washington Post*. "The Media is Waking Up to a Possible Bernie Victory. Get Ready for the Backlash," replied the leading "democratic socialist" magazine, *Jacobin*.[5]

In the early months of 2020, Sanders figured as the U.S. Left's great socialist hope. His plans to rein in the excesses of capital, bring it under government control, and make it work for the many and not the few were, unquestionably, a thorn in the side of U.S. capital and a major departure from Wall Street–friendly Democrats. And yet, we suggest that it is precisely by promising to *manage* capitalism and remediate the worst of its effects that Sanders fails to follow his astute criticism of capitalism to its logical conclusion.

In this chapter, we ask: What would Lenin make of this resurgent interest in socialism? Though the stage and the actors might have changed, we think Lenin would have recognized the script. He might define today's manifold crises as a "fissure through which the discontent and indignation of the oppressed classes burst forth," but would also point out that this discontent has taken many forms, including what Lenin calls "romantic" attachments to a moral order and balance. In an early and seldom-discussed pamphlet entitled "A Characterization of Economic Romanticists: Sismondi and Our Native Sismondists," Lenin launched a stinging critique of Jean Charles Leonard de Sismondi's political economy exposing its influence over Lenin's contemporaries—the Narodniki—on precisely these grounds. According to Lenin, both Sismondi and the Narodniki—like Sanders—were keen observers of capital's contradictions yet shied away from pursuing their full political consequences. Rather than fighting for the proletarian abolition of capitalism they hoped to rein in capitalism's excesses. The system's contradictions, they argued, made it an irrational and therefore an *impossible* mode of production. They called for a balanced form of economic development sympathetic to precapitalist social formations. For Lenin, this was an essentially "romantic" or "sentimental" critique of capitalism. It was a politics that was at once utopian and reactionary. Utopian because of its fantasy of a future where capital's excesses had been brought under control. Reactionary because of its melancholic attachment to precapitalist practices that were being swept away as capital expanded across Russia.[6]

In this chapter, we argue that Lenin's critique of romantic anticapitalism at the turn of the nineteenth century is of renewed significance today. Despite a resurgence of interest in Lenin, his early writings, which are mainly devoted to the question of what to do with capitalism's excesses, have been largely neglected by scholarly and activist communities. Lenin's early work, it is widely believed, is too constrained by the "stagism" of the Second International to be relevant. His context, presumably, is just too different from our own. There is some truth to this. The early Lenin was investigating capitalism's expansion into Russia and how to respond to it. Today, we struggle to imagine an alternative to a globalized capitalism in the aftermath of the defeat of large-scale socialist projects.[7] But in both Lenin's time and our own, the pervasive dissatisfaction with capitalism tends to take the form of a sentimental anticapitalism through which capitalism is *simultaneously repudiated and preserved*. Here, we return to Lenin not to reenact the costume and scripts of 1917 in 2021 but to inquire whether our own supposedly anticapitalist impulses can stand up to Leninist scrutiny.

In the end, which effectively arrived on the eve of the Super Tuesday primaries in March 2020, Sanders was defeated by forces who fear even minor incursions into the vast landscapes of their privilege and wealth; however, this chapter's core insight remains valid. Our point is not to provide a critique of Sanders and the Green New Deal—one does not need Lenin for this—but to think with and from Lenin's early works to illustrate the continued relevance of his thought in our struggles with romantic anticapitalism. The resurgence of socialist politics in our era does not, after all, begin or end with Sanders, the Green New Deal, or even "democratic socialism." Even as socialist resurgence is not encompassed by the Sanders phenomenon, the "romantic" limitations it exhibited continue arguably to constrain the former. Our wager is that the "ruthless" critique of utopian/reactionary expressions of anticapitalism that we find in Lenin's early work will have continued relevance as late-stage capitalism's contradictions deepen.

The chapter is divided into four sections. First, we summarize Lenin's reading strategy—which we regard as a kind of revolutionary practice—and explain how and why this practice needs to be turned back onto Lenin today. Then, in the following three sections, we explore how Lenin's early critique of nineteenth-century romantic anticapitalism can help us to make sense of the romantic anticapitalists of today and of Bernie Sanders and the Green New Deal in particular. In the first of these sections we discuss Lenin's understanding of capitalism as a form of social organization that is constantly in motion, at once creative and destructive. In the second we discuss how, for Lenin, this means that we cannot hope to escape capitalism or return to precapitalist social formations but rather that we must move dialectically *through* capitalism. In the third we demonstrate the relevance of this approach through a discussion of surplus populations and Sanders's Green New Deal.

Reading as Revolutionary Practice

This chapter unapologetically aims to repeat Lenin. But as Slavoj Žižek has argued, to repeat Lenin does not mean to turn to him for "dogmatic certainty"; rather, "*the* Lenin to be retrieved is the Lenin whose fundamental experience was that of being thrown into a catastrophic new constellation in which the old co-ordinates proved useless." Contrary to those who maintain that Leninism is a stage in Marxism's scientific development, we do not believe that Lenin provides us with a road map to revolution. Nor do we think that by reading *What Is to Be Done?*, *The April Theses*, and *State and Revolution* we will unlock the secrets to an authentically "Leninist" or "Marxist" revolution. Rather, what we take from Lenin is a *form* of militant engagement with the "concrete conditions" of struggle that can guide—without prescribing—our political practice.[8]

To read Lenin in this way is to read him as he read Marx and Engels. While hiding in Finland from persecution during the exhilarating months of August and September 1917, Lenin wrote *State and Revolution*, which begins not with an incendiary call to arms as one might expect but with instructions on how to read Marx. As Lorenzo Chiesa writes, "This text primarily and intentionally amounts to a close reading of Marx and Engels. Lenin here is returning to the revolutionary core of their teachings" against "reactionary readings." Lenin even apologizes to his readers for the "cumbersome" exegesis, which he insists is absolutely necessary to counter accounts that "omit, obscure or distort the revolutionary side of this theory, its revolutionary soul." As the Revolution swept across Russia, Lenin felt compelled to salvage Marx from the dual threats of opportunism and revisionism (to give a sense of the conditions under which he was writing: Lenin did not even have time to finish the final chapter on the state, because he was in charge of it).[9]

Lenin embodied the rare example of *reading as revolutionary practice*. In the words of French communist philosopher Louis Althusser, by 1894: "Lenin had not read Hegel, but he had read Marx's *Capital* very closely, and understood it better than anyone else ever had—he was twenty-four—so much so that the best introduction to Marx's *Capital* is to be found in Lenin." In addition to citing Marx and Engels, Lenin's early texts extensively quote from his political rivals and polemical targets. As Yuri Tynanov put it in a 1924 volume by *The Journal of the Left Arts* (LEF) dedicated to "Lenin's Language," part of Lenin's polemical force is derived from his use of "quotation marks," or what we now call scare quotes. Tynanov writes: "[In Lenin's prose, t]he word is taken out of the opponent's phrase and is put into quotation marks . . . .Lenin likes to speak in the words of his opponents, but he makes their words look suspicious, deprives them of their power and liberates them from their 'husk.'" To most readers, especially those lacking context, Lenin's style can be in turns intimidating, exhilarating, and boring. Lenin has a habit of approaching the same idea repeatedly from different directions until the truth of his position and the falsity of his opponents' becomes beyond doubt, as much because the point has been made so frequently as because of the sharpness of Lenin's argument. To borrow from Nietzsche, Lenin *philosophizes with a hammer*. What emerges from the rubble is a space for revolutionary movement of both thought and practice.[10]

As discussed in the introduction to this volume, the targets of Lenin's polemics were, mainly, other socialists and Marxists. Lars T. Lih argues, for example, that one of Lenin's most famous texts *What Is to Be Done?*, cannot be accurately understood if it is divorced from "the large context of international Social Democracy and the small context of the polemical in-fighting among Russian Social Democrats in late 1901."[11] Lih reminds contemporary readers that Lenin was arguing with people who shared the same political objectives, assumptions, and sensibilities, but differed on how to achieve them. This means that when reading Lenin, it is necessary to ask: Whom was Lenin reading and for whom is he writing?

As Lih provocatively puts it: Why does everyone regard *What Is to Be Done?* as a doctrine of Leninist Thought, when Lenin does not mention it again after 1907? For Lenin, Lih surmises, it was a political intervention at a specific moment in history, which had scant intrinsic value beyond it. In addition to reducing Lenin to specific works and passages, the "selective tradition" leaves out Lenin's early work. In this early period Lenin seems less worried about reactionaries, whose logic is transparent, than about fellow travelers who are unable to draw the necessary consequences from their insights into the contradictions and horrors of capitalism. As he says in *State and Revolution*, the gravest danger to the revolution may not be a counter-revolution from *without* but a counterrevolution from *within*. The Marxist tradition is full of thinkers and practitioners who water down Marxism to create formulas that they imagine would not upset bourgeois sentiments. For Lenin, such so-called Marxists end up "robbing the revolutionary theory of its *substance* . . . blunting its revolutionary edge."[12]

Of particular importance is Lenin's discursive struggle against the Russian Narodniki of the 1890s—as distinct from their 1860s predecessors—who espoused a vision of utopian peasant socialism premised on the refusal of capitalist development. According to Michael Löwy and Robert Sayre, Lenin was unconvinced by the "Narodniki wager on the possibility of sparing Russia all the horrors of capitalist civilization."[13] For Lenin, the suggestion that capitalist development could be avoided in Russia overlooked the reality of it already being present in the farthest reaches of village society. Lenin wrote off the Narodniki as "*utopians*" who dreamed of a society already lost and impossible to achieve in reality. Richard Swedberg explains: "Lenin objected to the fact that the Narodniki constructed an ideal society first and then criticized the existing society."[14] As a dialectician, Lenin believed that communism would emerge from the contradictions of existing society. Idealists, meanwhile, obscured these contradictions by imagining a future unblemished by them. Lenin adhered to Marx's 1845 insight in *The German Ideology*: "[C]ommunism is for us not a *state of affairs* which is to be established, an ideal to which reality [will] have to adjust itself. We call communism the *real* movement which abolishes the present state of things. The conditions of this movement result from the premises now in existence." The Narodnik political vision was utopian because it failed to establish a relationship between present and future. Extending this line of criticism, in a pamphlet, Lenin pilloried Swiss economist Jean Charles-Leonard Simonde de Sismondi (1773–1842). Published in the spring of 1897, during Lenin's first exile in Siberia, *A Characterisation of Economic Romanticism (Sismondi and Our Native Sismondists)*, claimed to discover the same romantic anticapitalist disposition in Sismondi and in Lenin's contemporaries, the Narodniki. Like Marx before him, Lenin argued that Sismondi keenly observed capitalism's contradictions but that his essentially bourgeois disposition prevented him from seeing the true consequences of his own analysis. Lenin then claims to find the same mistake in Narodnik political economy. Like Sismondi, they are said to harbor a hopeless attachment to a "precapitalist Golden Age" and "dreams of a patriarchal society of small artisans and peasant landowners." In Sismosndi's view, via Lenin's recounting of it, capitalism's drive to accumulate for accumulation's sake, to produce for production's sake, lost sight of the human needs and ends that production ought to serve. Lenin praised Sismondi's insight into capitalism's impersonal structure: workers' lives do not have value apart from their capacity to labor and create value for others. As Marx put it in 1844, we have yet to "make man's *sense human*"; instead, we sense the world through the mutilated and amputated limbs of the infinite process of capital's self-valorization.[15] Lenin faulted Sismondi, however, for failing to think beyond a *moral condemnation of capitalism*. For Lenin, morally denouncing capitalism is equivalent to dreaming of a world without contradictions. It fails to think strategically from *within* and *against* the material conditions of capitalist society.

Is this not similar to our situation today, in which people condemn capitalism for its immorality and yet are resigned to its existence? This is precisely the message of Bernie Sanders and his Green New Deal: yes, capitalism is exploitative, it produces gross inequalities and destroys the environment. And for these reasons, Bernie argues, we need a socialism that can make life under capitalism bearable. For Lenin, this is a deeply romantic approach to capitalism because it is animated by the hope that we can keep the world as it is (e.g., not socializing the means of production) but do away with capitalism's excesses (e.g., offer, as Sanders says, "a fair deal" for "the working families"). Commodified labor, yes. But billionaires, no. Ecologically devastating resource extraction, yes. But fossil fuels, no. Lenin rejects this kind of critique from the Left as a form of "economic sentimentalism," which "replaces an economic analysis with sentimental values" and utopian wishes.[16] However, this does *not* mean that Lenin dismisses the realm of emotion in favor of a harsh rationalism. As Žižek argues, if anything, Lenin's infamous reaction to Beethoven's *Appasionata*—to well up with tears before explaining that he cannot listen to classical music because "it affects your nerves, makes you want to say stupid and nice things and stroke the heads of people who could create such beauty while living in this vile hell"—suggests a heightened sensitivity to the affective and sensuous dimensions of human existence.[17] Lenin's point is that our utopian impulses for a better world cannot replace the political work that needs to be done to build it. Rather than remain in a state of perpetual heartbreak about the world, Lenin's point is that such affective intensities must find revolutionary conduits in the struggle to build communism.

Agitated and Feverish Life

In the popular imagination, it is often forgotten that Marx and Engels praised capitalism and the bourgeoisie as "the first [class] to show what man's activity can bring about. It has accomplished wonders far surpassing Egyptian pyramids, Roman aqueducts, and Gothic cathedrals" by creating more "colossal productive forces than have all preceding generations together." The rise of capitalism generated "an impulse never known before," one that dialectically combines creation and destruction.[18] In his early works, Lenin adopted this perspective on the revolutionary force unleashed by the historical necessity of capitalism. Two years after his polemic against Sismondi, Lenin published *The Development of Capitalism in Russia* (1899), an account of capitalism's penetration into Russian society. Against detractors who professed that capitalism could be avoided, or was categorically evil, Lenin welcomed the revolutionary potential of capitalism tempered "with the full recognition of the negative and dark sides of capitalism, with the full recognition of the profound and all-around social contradictions which are inevitably inherent in capitalism, and which reveal the historically transient character of this economic regime." In this work, communism figures as the positive overcoming of the negativity unleashed by capitalism.

Lenin underscores that capitalism's positive and negative valences are parts of the same process. In one of the most poetic and prescient lines of *The Communist Manifesto*, Marx and Engels write that capitalism's power derives from its "constant revolutionizing of production, uninterrupted disturbance of all social conditions, everlasting uncertainty and agitation [that] distinguish the bourgeois epoch from all earlier epochs."[19] On the basis of their insight into the laws of capitalist political economy, Marx and Engels describe capitalist life as one of *disturbance, uncertainty, agitation, fluctuation, upheaval,* and *crisis*. The "revolutionary impulse in the heart of capitalism"—its dynamic of perpetual motion, self-revolutionization, and expansion—means that the slow-moving tectonic shifts of historical change have become earthquakes happening all of the time, at disparate intensities in different locations. Marxism distills political economy into its basic laws: competitive advantages are temporary. To earn profit, the capitalist must invest in new technologies, expand production, find new markets, and reduce costs. "That is the law which again throws the bourgeois production out of its old course and which compels capital to intensify the productive forces of labour. And because it has once intensified them, this law gives capital no rest and continually whispers in its ear: 'Go on! Go on!.'"[20]

The generation and accumulation of wealth is simultaneously a process of dispossession, extraction, and exploitation; extension of capitalist relations "over the whole surface of the globe" and its ability to "nestle everywhere, settle everywhere" is simultaneously the process of de-territorialization, uprooting, and displacement. Capitalism's biopolitics is twofold: on the one hand, it involves improvement of living conditions and develops technologies that prolong life; on the other hand, it transforms people into commodities "constantly exposed to all the vicissitudes of competition, to all the fluctuations of the market."[21] Life is thus structurally exposed to capitalism's negativity at all times. Although we need sleep, capitalism does not rest. Although our bodies suffer from overwork and stress, capitalism further intensifies the "feverish simultaneous agitation on the whole world market." Life under capitalism is *agitated, feverish,* and *unable to rest*. Also, under capitalism, as Jacques Lacan argued, we are compelled by a superego injunction to "Enjoy!" irrespective of who or what is produced, destroyed, or left behind.[22]

Lenin develops Marx's insight that capital's expansionary movement—now referred to by the benign term *globalization*—means that there is no place beyond its reach. It does not remain "limited to the village community, to the patriarchal estate, to the tribe, to a territorial area or state" and "draws the most remote localities into the sphere of exchange," whether they desire to be included or not.[23] Capitalism "*compels* every entrepreneur to strive to expand production unlimitedly, to go beyond the bounds of the given country, to set out in the quest of new markets in countries not yet drawn into the sphere of capitalist commodity circulation."[24] In *Imperialism, the Highest Stage of Capitalism* (1916), capitalist compulsion is tracked in imperial conquest, colonization, and war. As a de-territorializing flow, capital destroys both the imagined sanctity and real barriers of spatial enclosure. Commodities appear where one might least expect to find them, making the search for a space untouched by capitalism a *sentimental* one. Economic sentimentalism thus includes dreams, desires, practices, and modes of critique that promise respite from capitalism by withdrawing into a place *outside* of it that is nevertheless entirely *within* it. In Lenin's day, the Narodniki longed for a populist mode of production that developed prior to capitalism's devastation of the traditional countryside. Today, anarchists aspire to create communism at the abandoned edges of capitalism; Bernie Sanders's social welfare proposals aim to carve out sanctuaries from the vagaries of capital; while exhausted corporate workers seek to preserve their "inner peace" by engaging in New Age versions of Buddhism, yoga, and self-care (epitomized in Erik Olin Wright's description of the "wilderness hiker who flies into a remote region with expensive hiking gear in order 'to get away from it all' ").[25]

Capitalism has not only transformed our conceptualizations of space but also of time.[26] We cannot accelerate the arrival of the future, escape capitalism by carving out spaces free from its influence, retreat into the past, or remain complacent as if the present were eternal; instead, Lenin suggests that we must *move through*, in, and against capitalism's destabilizing contradictions. For Lenin, capitalism severs all linkages to a time before it or to a place outside of it, or indeed to a time after it. To view capitalism otherwise is to adopt a *utopian* perspective, a view from nowhere. From Lenin's perspective, it was not only that utopians failed to see that they were already irreversibly swept up in the tide of capital's expansion but that in their blindness they forfeited the political opportunity, the very rift in world history that capitalism had created. "Attacks of this kind betray the romanticist who fearfully condemns precisely that which scientific theory [i.e., Marxism] values most in capitalism: its inherent striving for development, its irresistible urge onwards, its inability to halt or to reproduce the economic processes in their former, rigid dimensions."[27]

Capitalism detonated the old world of localities, traditions, and self-sufficient economies. Both Marx and Lenin glimpsed the shimmering image of communism in these shards and fragments that capitalism churned into profits. After the first attempt at communism was defeated in the Soviet Union and Leninism was proclaimed dead, the specter of communism, as Derrida stated in 1994, was still there, haunting.[28] But specters are ephemeral: murmurs of discontent, whispers of hope. Post-2008, and especially post-2020, however, socialism is no longer just a phantom: the discontent and hope of the 99 percent is being articulated in promises, uttered by left-wing social movements, coalitions, parties, and politicians, to use the state to save the environment and alleviate the crushing debts and anxieties of the working class. While supporting all of these initiatives, we must ask: Can these goals be achieved within capital's restless, expansionary and ecologically devastating dynamics? And if not, why do parts of the Left keep acting as if they can?

Dreaming of Life Beyond Capitalism

As Lenin observed, one can be sentimentally anticapitalist in a way that reinforces its power over us. In part, this is why Lenin's early works are not treatises against capitalism as such but rather *criticisms of criticisms* of capitalism. For instance, capitalist ideology inheres in the belief that capitalism is a system through which goods are efficiently produced in response to demand for consumption. Lenin rejects this premise. Instead, he considers the idea of economic proportion and balance to be an anachronism. The dyadic and static image of production determined by consumption "directly applies the ethics of the frugal peasant to capitalist society." The frugal peasant does not produce more than is needed to survive or can be sold on the market; the artisan craftsman only makes what clients order. This model of finite quantities, face-to-face exchanges, and consumption-based production is a vestige of precapitalist modes of production. The ethical/aesthetic criterion of proportion masquerades as an economic concept; it is not an accurate reflection of the dynamics of capitalist production and exchange. "This true proportion between supply and demand which is beginning once more to be the object of so many wishes, ceased long ago to exist. It has passed into the stage of senility."[29]

The fact that Lenin refers to political economic categories as "wishes" indicates an awareness of the role affective attachments play in capitalist ideology. Lenin stipulates: "Production creates a market for itself and determines consumption." The origins of capitalism are not the production of use-values to satisfy needs but, to use Lacan's terms, the superego injunction to "Enjoy!," to produce *more*, to accumulate *more*. The drive to produce and the desire to consume develop each according to its own internal logic and do not necessarily map onto each other. They interact but not in any reciprocal or balanced fashion. The periods of crisis punctuating the history of capitalist development confirm, time and again, Marx's and Lenin's insight that "accumulation and production *outstrip* consumption."[30] Capitalism is structurally haunted by the permanent threat of overproduction in which goods are unable to realize their value in consumption. Gathering dust in warehouses and on store shelves, their value is wiped out as prices plummet. In his response to Sismondi, Lenin delves into tremendous detail about how excess production can be absorbed by the needs of "productive consumption" in which capitalists produce the means of production for other capitalists rather than for consumption by private individuals. In today's hyperfinancialized capitalism, overproduction is often incorporated into the everyday realities of production (consider, for example, the vast tracts of unoccupied apartments in China that serve as instruments of value creation and investment),[31] or it is warded off by turning to just-in-time production. Regardless of the methods by which the threat of "overproduction" is managed, Lenin's key point remains valid: capitalism's productive capacity is also the reason for its internal contradictions and instability. Capitalism and crisis cannot be analyzed separately because, as the Occupy Movement put it, capitalism *is* crisis.

Along with Marx, Lenin acknowledges that Sismondi was among the first to have insight into these dynamics. He rejects, however, what he regards as Sismondi's sentimental impulse to return to a natural balance that has been disturbed. Whereas Sismondi, in Lenin's words, argues that "disproportion is not a law of the present system of social economy, and of its development, but a 'mistake' of the legislator,"[32] Lenin insists that disproportion is a law of capitalism. "[Sismondi's] theory that production must conform to revenue naturally led to the view that crises are the result of the disturbance of this balance, the result of an excess of production over consumption." For Lenin, no such balance is possible. In Lenin's eyes, Sismondi recoils from his own insight into capitalist excess by embracing a utopian vision of balance and harmony. Addressing a broader tendency among his contemporaries, Lenin writes: "Their failure to understand that this 'instability' is a *necessary* feature of all capitalism and commodity economy in general brought them to *utopia*." Lenin's argument here is profound: under capitalism, *instability is primary* and stability is a secondary effect or "object of so many wishes."[33]

Economic romanticism uses figures of excess to shift the blame to an extraneous element, which perturbs the presumably proportional logic of capitalist development. These figures of excess contain a promise: if only [*name your excess*] is eradicated, capitalism would function smoothly. The culprits (and their solutions) range from excesses of human greed (more regulation); financial capital (more productive capital); state intervention (more free markets); inequality (more taxes); corrupt officials (more meritocracy), and so on. This is not to argue there is no room for improving people's lives under capitalism but to caution that such gains do not redress the structural problem of *capitalist excess*, and remain permanently vulnerable to being undone by it.

For Lenin, another version of economic romanticism is the idea that one can voluntarily escape from the contradictions of capitalism. Today this kind of romanticism comes in various forms: conservative republican, libertarian, and anarchist. In all three, the fantasy of autonomy (whether participating in the market as entrepreneur or withdrawing from it in pursuit of self-sufficiency) is offered as an antidote to capitalism's heteronomy. In one of the most influential cases for anarchist withdrawal, political scientist James C. Scott argues that it is possible to achieve a "precious zone of autonomy and freedom in state systems increasingly dominated by large public and private bureaucracies." For Scott, people prefer being "largely in control of their working day and work with little or no supervision" to being a "clerk" or "factory worker."[34] Instead of Scott's anarchist vision of tending a plot of land and consuming what is harvested, the "live and let live" libertarian variant is an imaginary laissez-faire capitalism; both anarchist and libertarian "imaginaries," however, romanticize the figure of the individual who exists in an *external* relationship vis-à-vis capital and power.[35] The Leninist response is that the autonomous individual required by both contrasting visions simply does not exist. Scott's claim that "no one wants to work for the man" may very well be true in certain contexts (it is also well known that people enjoy the power that comes from authority), but it does not reflect the *objective conditions* in which people find themselves. Lenin criticizes his contemporaries who "invent for themselves a sort of abstract small production existing outside of the social relations of production, and *overlook* the trifling circumstance that this small production actually exists in an environment of *commodity production*."[36]

Thus, in his early works, Lenin demands that revolutionaries conduct their analyses from within the *excesses of capitalism,* and refuse the temptation of seeking an imaginary resolution, whether *inside* capitalism or *beyond* it (or for that matter, *before* it). This is not only because at that time Russia needed to accelerate the development of its forces of production and resolve the problem of material scarcity but also because communism only becomes *thinkable* from within an analysis of capitalism's excess. To avoid thinking through the excesses of capitalism is thus to forfeit the possibility of communism.

Capitalist Excess/Excess People

As we have argued throughout, many of Lenin's criticisms of Sismondi remain relevant to contemporary struggles. Perhaps one of the most salient criticisms of Sanders's democratic socialism and the Green New Deal relates to what Lenin calls the problem of "capitalist overpopulation." Sismondi, Lenin shows, grasped that *capitalism does not need people to be profitable* but failed to draw the correct political conclusions from his insight. Whereas for Lenin this made capitalism a uniquely dynamic mode of production, for Sismondi it made it an *impossible* one. Today, we know that capitalism does not need to reproduce the living conditions of large parts of the world's population. In João Biehl's words, capitalism routinely produces "zones of social abandonment," which Tania Murray Li describes as a process of "letting die," and Achille Mbembe categorizes as the "necropolitics" of dividing humanity into "useful" and "useless" populations. Advances in the organic composition of capital, meanwhile, throws off living labor, driving people into unemployment or casualized and precarious labor conditions.[37]

Lenin gives Sismondi credit for being an early critic of these processes. As machine industry was developing toward the end of the eighteenth century, early political economists such as Sismondi were tasked with explaining how such industry "led to the formation of a surplus population, and political economy was confronted with the task of explaining this phenomenon." Evaluating competing early interpretations, Lenin dismisses Malthus's natural-historical account and praises Sismondi's political-economic explanation of surplus populations as the product of "displacement . . . by machines." Repeating Marx, Lenin argues that the surplus population makes up *"an indispensable component part* of the capitalist machine" and that capitalism generates superfluous people according to two laws: the first is the revolution of technology and modes of production that wipe out entire industries and jobs; the second is what Lenin refers to as a "fluctuation" in production which requires a "surplus population . . . ready at any given moment to provide hands for any industry, or factory."[38] This fluctuating level of unemployment is what Milton Friedman detestably called the "natural rate of unemployment."[39] Lenin, however, follows Marx, distinguishing between (1) the "industrial reserve army," whose function is to regulate the labor market, and (2) "surplus populations," who serve no function whatsoever to capital. As Marx and Engels wrote:

> The greater the social wealth, the functioning capital, the extent and energy of its growth, and therefore also the greater the absolute mass of the proletariat and the productivity of its labour, the greater is the industrial reserve army. The same causes which develop the expansive power of capital, also develop the labour-power at its disposal. The relative mass of the industrial reserve army thus increases with the potential energy of wealth. But the greater this reserve army, the greater is the mass of a consolidated surplus population, whose misery is in inverse ratio to the amount of torture it has to undergo in the form of labour. The more extensive, finally, the lazarus-layers of the working class, and the industrial reserve army, the greater is official pauperism. *This is the absolute general law of capitalist accumulation.* (638)

Homeless encampments dotting the urban landscape of the United States would not surprise Marx, Sismondi, or Lenin. All three were attuned to capitalism's indifference to human life when it is no longer profitable, and understood what Marx in the above passage calls the "*absolute general law of capitalist accumulation*" to produce a reserve army and surplus populations. After this point of agreement, however, Lenin begins to part ways with Sismondi. Lenin shows that for Sismondi capitalism's tendency to produce surplus populations makes it a self-undermining, contradictory, and thus *impossible* mode of production. Lenin refutes this: "Capitalism gives no employment to displaced workers, they say. This means that capitalism is impossible, a 'mistake,' etc. But it does not 'mean' that at all. Contradiction does not mean impossibility." In positivist logic, contradiction does mean impossibility: one cannot be A and not A at the same time. For the dialectical Lenin, however, positivist logic cannot capture the real world of forces of production and relations of production. It is pure idealism, he argues, to believe that naming objective inconsistencies will make them vanish: "Capitalist accumulation, i.e., real production for the sake of production, is also a contradiction. But this does not prevent it from existing and from being the law of a definite system of economy." Sismondi rejects the contradiction he discovers on moral grounds. But doing so leaves the world to remain as it is.

The problem of reserve armies of labor and surplus populations is of renewed importance today. The writing collective Endnotes, for example, has argued that contemporary capitalism is defined less by its tendency to proletarianize than by its tendency to produce a population that is "absolutely redundant to the needs of capital." According to Endnotes, postindustrial capitalism is failing to draw living labor into expanding circuits of capital accumulation and is instead forming what they call "abject" groups on the margins of capital, workers who are surplus to the requirements of capital. For Endnotes, this shift from proletarianization to abjection signifies the "tendential disappearance of the previous revolutionary horizon."[40] Whereas it was once possible to imagine a collective proletarian subject arising out of capital's tendency to proletarianize increasing numbers of the world's population, Endnotes argues that it is now much more likely that capital will produce populations whose only possibility of employment lies in precarious labor. This raises important questions about what kind of revolution—if any—is possible in our time.

Endnotes does not argue that the "abject" will come to constitute a new revolutionary subject or that capitalism will collapse under its own weight. Others, however, are not as circumspect. Like Sismondi, Robert Kurz and Anselm Jappe have argued that capitalism is self-undermining and thus, ultimately, *impossible*. In 1986, Robert Kurz had predicted a crisis in capitalist accumulation brought about by its inability to reabsorb living labor. The result would be a "new and final crisis of capitalism," that would be "no temporary crisis of overaccumulation or overproduction, but rather a crisis of the creation of value itself, from which there can no longer be a way out for capital."[41] More recently, Anselm Jappe has argued that "[c]apitalism has *visibly* become what it *essentially* was from its inception: a beast that devours itself, a society that, over the long term, cannot be endured by anyone, since it consumes all social bonds and all natural resources in order to preserve the mechanism of value accumulation, which becomes increasingly difficult. With each passing day capitalism is undermining its own foundations."[42] Neither Kurz nor Jappe falls for the sentimental illusion of trying to save capitalism from its contradictions. From a Leninist perspective, however, they are the inheritors of Sismondi's legacy insofar as they replace the political task of building revolutionary movements and subjectivities with the revolutionary self-undermining of capital as subject.

Like Sismondi, Kurz and Jappe underestimate capitalism's capacity to find new and unexpected ways to boost profitability and absorb surplus populations. Sanders's Green New Deal is one such method. Like Roosevelt's New Deal before it, the Green New Deal is an effort to stave off a social, political, and environmental crisis by absorbing surplus populations back into capital's circuits of accumulation. Sanders's Green New Deal includes a federal jobs program that promises to create twenty million "good paying, union jobs with strong benefits and safety standards in steel and auto manufacturing, construction, energy efficiency retrofitting, coding and server farms, and renewable power plants." The plan also promises to create "millions of jobs in sustainable agriculture, engineering, a reimagined and expanded Civilian Conservation Corp, and preserving our public lands." Suspending comment on the environmental or social desirability of these proposals for a moment, Lenin's work helps us to see them for what they are: a social compromise, an effort to contain capital's excesses. Lenin's critique of Sismondi also helps illustrate why the Green New Deal is a "romantic" criticism of capitalism. It is romantic precisely because it tries to ward off what Marx called the "absolute general law of capital accumulation." By creating millions of climate jobs and investing in massive industrial development, the Green New Deal promises to launch a new cycle of accumulation, ushering in a period of greener, friendlier capitalism. With Lenin we see that it is a major error to conclude, as Kurtz does, that capitalism is in its "final crisis." And contrary to Jappe, it is patently not the case that "capitalism does more harm to itself than all of its enemies put together."[43] From a Leninist perspective, even if capitalism throws more and more of its workforce into a condition of precarity and even if climate change brings about the deaths of millions and displacement of billions, we cannot count on either to abolish capitalism for us. A Leninist concludes that only a revolutionary struggle can halt capitalism's dialectical spiral.

Conclusion: Romantic Impulses and Restraints

In 2019–20, Sanders and his Green New Deal symbolized "hope"—for a way out or forward beyond late-stage capitalism—to many of his supporters, reviving the idea of socialism in the United States and responding to concerns about the climate crisis. We do not deny this. From the perspective that we have elaborated here, however, this does not take away from the fact that Sanders represents the epitome of capitalist ideology in the guise of critique. Like Sismondi and the Narodniki before him, and consonant with more recent diagnosticians of capitalism's "impossibility," Sanders and the Green New Deal promise to save capitalism from its own excesses. Lenin shows us that this is a romanticist trap. Recovering the early Lenin helps us think through how *romanticism* at the level of political practice enables us to imagine that we can have our cake and eat it too. What we must do instead is learn to exercise what Frederic Jameson, inspired by Lenin, calls "dialectical ambivalence" about capitalism. We must train ourselves to find traces of the communist horizon[44] in capitalism's forces and relations of production. This is precisely what Lenin famously did with the Russian banking system:

> This apparatus must not, and should not, be smashed. It must be wrested from the control of the capitalists; the capitalists and the wires they pull must be *cut off, lopped off, chopped away from* this apparatus; it must be *subordinated* to the proletarian Soviets; it must be expanded, made more comprehensive, and nation-wide. And this *can* be done by utilizing the achievements already made by large-scale capitalism (in the same way as the proletarian revolution can, in general, reach its goal only by utilising these achievements).[45]

Although in this passage Lenin focused on *cutting off* control over the means of production, in his early works he urges us to *sever* our sentimental ties that reproduce the status quo in the guise of opposing it. Even so, the violent image of *chopping off* may misleadingly evoke a one-time, eruptive event rather than an ongoing process of *loosening* and *dissolving* the affective and intellectual bonds that ensnare us in the dominant order. This is why Lenin devotes precious amounts of time and effort to the revolutionary practice of reading. Lenin's critique of economic romanticism is a salutary reminder that capitalism is incapable of rescuing itself from its destructive excesses, and that it will not collapse under the weight of its own contradictions and moral impossibility but requires a push from within that opens a line of sight to the future.

Notes

1. HC Deb, "Bill 329 Second Reading—Hansard," 1887; Sidney Webb, "Socialism in England," *Publications of the American Economic Association* 4, no. 2 (1889): 7–73; Karl Marx and Friedrich Engels, *The Communist Manifesto* (London and New York: Verso, 2012).

2. Milton Friedman, "The Economy: We Are All Keynesians Now," *Time*, December 31, 1965; Jon Meacham, "We Are All Socialists Now," *Newsweek*, February 6, 2009.

3. Eric Levitz, "Bernie Sanders Is Right—We're All 'Socialists' Now," *Intelligencer*, June 13, 2019, https://nymag.com/intelligencer/2019/06/bernie-sanders-socialism-speech-gwu.html; Joe Carter, "We Are All New Deal Socialists Now," Acton Institute PowerBlog, July 26, 2018, https://blog.acton.org/archives/102909-we-are-all-new-deal-socialists-now.html; Jim Geraghty, "Help National Review Eradicate the Socialist Zombie Resurgence," *National Review* (blog), May 8, 2019, https://www.nationalreview.com/2019/05/spring-webathon-help-fight-socialist-resurgence/.

4. Adam Kelsey, "Bernie Sanders Draws Contrast with Elizabeth Warren: She Says 'She Is a Capitalist through Her Bones.' I'm Not," *ABC News*, October 13, 2019, https://abcnews.go.com/Politics/bernie-sanders-draws-contrast-elizabeth-warren-capitalist-bones/story?id=66217140; Andrew Prokop, "Read Bernie Sanders's Speech on Democratic Socialism in the United States," *Vox*, November 19, 2015, https://www.vox.com/2015/11/19/9762028/bernie-sanders-democratic-socialism; David Choi, "Read Bernie Sanders' Full Speech From His First Iowa 2020 Campaign Rally," *Business Insider*, March 8, 2019, https://www.businessinsider.com/bernie-sanders-iowa-2020-rally-speech-transcript-2019-3.

5. Simon van Zulyen-Wood, "When Did Everyone Become a Socialist?" *Intelligencer*, March 3, 2019, https://nymag.com/intelligencer/2019/03/socialism-and-young-socialists.html; Andy Gregory, "More than a Third of Millennials Approve of Communism, YouGov Poll Indicates," *The Independent*, November 7, 2019, https://www.independent.co.uk/news/world/americas/us-politics/communism-millennials-capitalism-socialism-bernie-sanders-cold-war-yougov-a9188116.html; Chris Cillizza, "Bernie Sanders Could Actually Win This Thing," CNN, January 7, 2020, https://www.cnn.com/2020/01/07/politics/bernie-sanders-joe-biden-2020-democratic-primary/index.html; Jason Riley, "Opinion: Be Prepared for President Sanders," *Wall Street Journal*, January 7, 2020, https://www.wsj.com/articles/be-prepared-for-president-sanders-11578441912; Luke Savage, "The Media Is Waking Up to Possible Bernie Victory: Get Bread for the Backlash," *Jacobin*, January 8 2020, https://www.jacobinmag.com/2020/01/media-bernie-sanders-backlash-coverage-2020.

6. V. I. Lenin, *The Collapse of the Second International*, 1915, https://www.marxists.org/archive/lenin/works/1915/csi/index.htm; Lenin, *A Characterisation of Economic Romanticists: Sismondi and Our Native Sismondists*, 1897, https://www.marxists.org/archive/lenin/works/1897/econroman/index.htm. Hereafter cited as *Sismondi*.

7. Cf. Mark Fisher, *Capitalist Realism: Is There No Alternative?* (Ropley: Zer0 Books, 2009).

8. Slavoj Žižek, *Revolution at the Gates: Selected Writings of Lenin from 1917* (London and New York: Verso, 2002), 11; J. Moufawad-Paul, *Continuity and Rupture: Philosophy in the Maoist Terrain* (Ropley: Zer0 Books, 2016); Lenin, "'Left-Wing' Communism: An Infantile Disorder," 1920, https://www.marxists.org/archive/lenin/works/1920/lwc/.

9. Lorenzo Chisea, "Lenin and the Transitional-Revolutionary State," in *The Future of the State*, ed. Artemy Magun (Lanham, MD: Rowman and Littlefield, 2020); Lenin, "Can the Bolsheviks Retain State Power," 1917, https://www.marxists.org/archive/lenin/works/1917/oct/01.htm.

10. Louis Althusser, "Lenin Before Hegel," in *Lenin and Philosophy and Other Essays*, trans. Ben Brewster (New York: Monthly Review, 2001), 73; Yuri Tyanov, "The Vocabulary of Lenin-the-Polemicist," ed. and trans. Saussy et al., unpublished ms, 1924; Friedrich Nietzsche, *Twilight of the Idols*, trans. Richard Polt (Indianapolis: Hackett, 1997).

11. Lars T. Lih, *Lenin Rediscovered: What Is to Be Done? In Context* (Chicago: Haymarket, 2008), 5.

12. Ibid.; Raymond Williams, *The Long Revolution* (Cardigan: Parthian, 2011); Lenin, "Can the Bolsheviks Retain State Power?"

13. Michael Löwy and Robert Sayre, *Romanticism Against the Tide of Modernity*, trans. Catherine Porter (Durham: Duke University Press, 2001), 313.

14. Richard Swedberg, "Lenin's critique of Narodnik Sociology," *Critical Sociology* 8, no. 4 (1979): 53.

15. Karl Marx, *Economic and Philosophic Manuscripts of 1844*, https://www.marxists.org/archive/marx/works/1844/manuscripts/preface.htm.

16. Fisher, *Capitalist Realism*; Prokop, "Read Bernie Sanders," 215; Lenin, *Sismondi*.

17. Zizek, *Revolution at the Gates*, 197.

18. Marx and Engels, *Communist Manifesto*, 38, 40, 36.

19. Ibid., 38.

20. Karl Marx, "Wage Labour and Capital," 1847, https://www.marxists.org/archive/marx/works/1847/wage-labour/.

21. Marx and Engels, *Communist Manifesto*, 39, 43.

22. Jonathan Crary, *24/7: Late Capitalism and the Ends of Sleep* (London and New York: Verso, 2014); Marx, "Wage Labour and Capital"; Eric Santner, *The Weight of All Flesh: On the Subject-Matter of Political Economy* (Oxford: Oxford University Press, 2015); Jacques Lacan, *Encore: The Seminar of Jacques Lacan: Book XX*, ed. Miller, trans. Fink, Encore edition (New York: Norton, 2000), 3.

23. Lenin, *The Left Narodniks*, 1914, https://www.marxists.org/archive/lenin/works/1914/may/14.htm.

24. Lenin, *Sismondi*.

25. Erik Olin Wright, *How to Be an Anti-capitalist in the 21st Century* (London and New York: Verso, 2019), 52.

26. Fredric Jameson, "The End of Temporality," *Critical Inquiry* 29, no. 4 (Summer 2003): 695–718.

27. Lenin, *Sismondi*.

28. Jacques Derrida, *Specters of Marx, The State of the Debt, the Work of Mourning and the New International*, trans. Kamuf (New York: Routledge, 1994).

29. Lenin, *Sismondi*.

30. Ibid.

31. Christian Sorace and William Hurst, "China's Phantom Urbanisation and the Pathology of Ghost Cities," *Journal of Contemporary Asia* 46, no. 2 (2016): 304–22.

32. Compare with a hashtag on Twitter #EveryBillionaireIsAPolicyFailure.

33. Lenin, *Sismondi*.

34. James C. Scott, *Two Cheers for Anarchism: Six Easy Pieces on Autonomy, Dignity, and Meaningful Work and Play* (Princeton: Princeton University Press, 2014), 85.

35. Timothy Mitchell, "Everyday Metaphors of Power," *Theory and Society* 19, no. 5 (1990): 547–77.

36. Lenin, *Sismondi*.

37. João Biehl, *Vita: Life in a Zone of Social Abandonment* (Berkeley: University of California Press, 2013); Tania Murray Li, "To Make Live or Let Die? Rural Dispossession and the Protection of Surplus Populations," *Antipode* 41 (2010): 66–93; Achille Mbembe, *Necropolitics* (Durham: Duke University Press, 2019), 12.

38. Lenin, *Sismondi*.

39. Robert Pollin, "The 'Reserve Army of Labor' and the 'Natural Rate of Unemployment': Can Marx, Kalecki, Friedman, and Wall Street All Be Wrong?" *Review of Radical Political Economics* 30, no. 3 (1998): 1–13.

40. Endnotes 2: Misery and the Value Form (2010): 30; Endnotes 4: Unity in Separation (2015): 277.

41. Robert Kurz, "The Crisis of Exchange Value: Science as Productivity, Productive Labor, and Capitalist Reproduction," in *Marxism and the Critique of Value*, ed. Larsen et al., 53–54 (Chicago: MCM', 2014).

42. Anselm Jappe, *The Writing on the Wall* (Charlotte: Zero Books, 2017), 26.

43. Kurz, 54; Jappe, 26.

44. Jodi Dean, *The Communist Horizon* (London and New York: Verso, 2018).

45. Lenin, "Can the Bolsheviks Retain State Power?"

Bibliography

Althusser, Louis. "Lenin before Hegel." In *Lenin and Philosophy and Other Essays*. Translated by Ben Brewster. New York: Monthly Review Press, 2001.

Bernes, Jasper. "Logistics, Counterlogistics, and the Communist Prospect." *Endnotes* 3 (2013). https://endnotes.org.uk/issues/3.

Bernie Sanders 2020 Campaign. nd. "The Green New Deal." Bernie Sanders—Official Campaign Website. nd. https://berniesanders.com/en/issues/green-new-deal/.

Biehl, João. *Vita: Life in a Zone of Social Abandonment.* Berkeley: University of California Press, 2013.

Carter, Joe. 2018. "We Are All New Deal Socialists Now." Acton Institute PowerBlog. July 26, 2018. https://blog.acton.org/archives/102909-we-are-all-new-deal-socialists-now.html.

Chisea, Lorenzo. "Lenin and the Transitional-Revolutionary State." In *The Future of the State*, edited by Artemy Magun. Lanham, MD: Rowman and Littlefield, 2020.

Choi, David. "Read Bernie Sanders' Full Speech from His First Iowa 2020 Campaign Rally." *Business Insider.* March 8, 2019. https://www.businessinsider.com/bernie-sanders-iowa-2020-rally-speech-transcript-2019-3.

Crary, Jonathan. 24/7: *Late Capitalism and the Ends of Sleep.* London and New York, Verso: 2014.

Dean, Jodi. *The Communist Horizon.* London and New York, Verso: 2018.

Derrida, Jacques. *Specters of Marx, The State of the Debt, the Work of Mourning and the New International.* Translated by Peggy Kamuf. New York: Routledge, 1994.

Endnotes. *Endnotes 2: Misery and the Value Form* (2010). https://endnotes.org.uk/issues/2.

———. *Endnotes 4: Unity in Separation* (2015). https://endnotes.org.uk/issues/4.

Fisher, Mark. *Capitalist Realism: Is There No Alternative?* Winchester, UK: Zero Books, 2009.

Friedman, Milton. 1965. "The Economy: We Are All Keynesians Now." *Time*, December 31, 1965. http://content.time.com/time/magazine/article/0,9171,842353,00.html.

Geraghty, Jim. "Help National Review Eradicate the Socialist Zombie Resurgence." *National Review* (blog). May 8, 2019. https://www.nationalreview.com/2019/05/spring-webathon-help-fight-socialist-resurgence/.

Gregory, Andy. "More than a Third of Millennials Approve of Communism, YouGov Poll Indicates." *The Independent.* November 7, 2019. https://www.independent.co.uk/news/world/americas/us-politics/communism-millennials-capitalism-socialism-bernie-sanders-cold-war-yougov-a9188116.html.

HC Deb. "Bill 329 Second Reading—Hansard." 1887. https://hansard.parliament.uk/Commons/1887-08-11/debates/1303be15-41f0-4657-a623-de06d290c5a5/Bill329SecondReading?highlight=%22we%20are%20all%20socialists%20now%22#contribution-d7f562e6-8ee5-4a16-923e-29ae39fd1657.

Jameson, Frederic. "The End of Temporality." *Critical Inquiry* 29, no. 4 (Summer 2003): 695–718.

Jappe, Anselm. *The Writing on the Wall.* Charlotte, NC: Zero Books, 2017.

Jeong, Seongjin. "Lenin's Economics: A Marxian Critique." In *Revitalizing Marxist Theory for Today's Capitalism*, edited by Paul Zarembka and Radhika Desai,

27:223–54. Research in Political Economy. Emerald Group Publishing Limited, 2011. https://doi.org/10.1108/S0161-7230(2011)0000027010.

Kelsey, Adam. "Bernie Sanders Draws Contrast with Elizabeth Warren: She Says 'She Is a Capitalist through Her Bones.' I'm Not." ABC News. October 13, 2019. https://abcnews.go.com/Politics/bernie-sanders-draws-contrast-elizabeth-warren-capitalist-bones/story?id=66217140.

Kurz, Robert. "The Crisis of Exchange Value: Science as Productivity, Productive Labor, and Capitalist Reproduction." In *Marxism and the Critique of Value*, edited by Neil Larsen, Mathias Nilges, Josh Robinson, and Nicholas Brown, 17–76. Chicago, IL: MCM'. 2014.

Lacan, Jacques. *Encore: The Seminar of Jacques Lacan: Book XX*. Edited by Jacques-Alain Miller. Translated by Bruce Fink. Encore edition. New York: W. W. Norton, 2000.

Lenin, Vladimir Ilyin. *A Characterisation of Economic Romanticists: Sismondi and Our Native Sismondists*, 1897. https://www.marxists.org/archive/lenin/works/1897/econroman/index.htm.

———. *'Can the Bolsheviks Retain State Power?'* 1917. https://www.marxists.org/archive/lenin/works/1917/oct/01.htm.

———. *The Development of Capitalism in Russia*, 1899. https://www.marxists.org/archive/lenin/works/1899/devel/.

———. "Eighth All-Russia Congress of Soviets December 29, 1920." 1920a. https://www.marxists.org/archive/lenin/works/1920/8thcong/index.htm.

———. "'Left-Wing' Communism: An Infantile Disorder." 1920b. https://www.marxists.org/archive/lenin/works/1920/lwc/.

———. *The Left Narodniks*. https://www.marxists.org/archive/lenin/works/1914/may/14.htm.

———. *The Collapse of the Second International*. 1915. https://www.marxists.org/archive/lenin/works/1915/csi/index.htm.

———. *Imperialism, the Highest Stage of Capitalism*, 1916. https://www.marxists.org/archive/lenin/works/1916/imp-hsc/.

———. *The State and Revolution: The Marxist Theory of the State and the Tasks of the Proletariat in Revolution*, 1917. https://www.marxists.org/archive/lenin/works/1917/staterev/.

Levitz, Eric. 2019. "Bernie Sanders Is Right—We're All 'Socialists' Now." Intelligencer. June 13, 2019. https://nymag.com/intelligencer/2019/06/bernie-sanders-socialism-speech-gwu.html.

Li, Tania Murray. "To Make Live or Let Die? Rural Dispossession and the Protection of Surplus Populations." *Antipode* 41 (2010): 66–93.

Lih, Lars T. *Lenin Rediscovered: What Is to Be Done? in Context*. Chicago: Haymarket Books, 2008.

Löwy, Michael, and Robert Sayre. *Romanticism against the Tide of Modernity*. Translated by Catherirne Porter. Durham: Duke University Press, 2001.

Marx, Karl. *Economic and Philosophic Manuscripts of 1844*. https://www.marxists.org/archive/marx/works/1844/manuscripts/preface.htm.
———. *The German Ideology*, 1845. https://www.marxists.org/archive/marx/works/1845/german-ideology/.
———. *Wage, Labour, and Capital*, 1847. https://www.marxists.org/archive/marx/works/1847/wage-labour/.
———, and Friedrich Engels. *Karl Marx and Frederick Engels: Collected Works Vol. 35*. 35th annotated edition. Moscow: International Publishers, 1996.
———. *The Communist Manifesto*. London and New York, Verso: 2012.
Mitchell, Timothy. "Everyday Metaphors of Power." *Theory and Society* 19, No. 5 (1990): 547–77.
Mbembe, Achille. *Necropolitics*. Durham: Duke University Press, 2019.
Moufawad-Paul, J. *Continuity and Rupture: Philosophy in the Maoist Terrain*. Winchester, UK: Zero Books, 2016.
Nietzsche, Friedrich. *Twilight of the Idols*. Translated by Richard Polt. Indianapolis: Hackett, 1997.
Pollin, Robert. "The 'Reserve Army of Labor' and the 'Natural Rate of Unemployment': Can Marx, Kalecki, Friedman, and Wall Street All Be Wrong?" *Review of Radical Political Economics* 30, no. 3 (1998): 1–13. https://doi.org/10.1177/048661349803000301.
Prokop, Andrew. "Read Bernie Sanders's Speech on Democratic Socialism in the United States." Vox, November 19, 2015. https://www.vox.com/2015/11/19/9762028/bernie-sanders-democratic-socialism.
Riley, Jason L. 2020. "Opinion | Be Prepared for President Sanders." *Wall Street Journal*, January 7, 2020, sec. Opinion. https://www.wsj.com/articles/be-prepared-for-president-sanders-11578441912.
Santner, Eric. *The Weight of All Flesh: On the Subject-Matter of Political Economy*. Oxford: Oxford University Press, 2015.
Savage, Luke. "The Media Is Waking Up to a Possible Bernie Victory. Get Ready for the Backlash." *Jacobin*, January 8, 2020. https://jacobinmag.com/2020/01/media-bernie-sanders-backlash-coverage-2020.
Scott, James C. *Two Cheers for Anarchism: Six Easy Pieces on Autonomy, Dignity, and Meaningful Work and Play*. Princeton: Princeton University Press, 2014.
Sorace, Christian, and William Hurst. "China's Phantom Urbanisation and the Pathology of Ghost Cities." *Journal of Contemporary Asia* 46, no. 2 (2016): 304–22.
Swedberg, Richard. "Lenin's Critique of Narodnik Sociology." *Critical Sociology* (1979): 52–55.
Tynanov, Yuri. "The Vocabulary of Lenin-the-Polemicist." Edited and Translated by Haun Saussy, Olga Solovieva, and Yakov Klots. Unpublished 1924.
Webb, Sidney. "Socialism in England." *Publications of the American Economic Association* 4, no. 2 (1889): 7–73.
Williams, Raymond. *The Long Revolution*. Cardigan, UK: Parthian Books, 2011.

Wright, Erik Olin. *How to Be an Anti-capitalist in the 21*[st] *Century*. London and New York: Verso, 2019.

Žižek, Slavoj. *Revolution at the Gates: Selected Writings of Lenin from 1917*. London and New York: Verso, 2002.

Zuylen-Wood, Simon van. "When Did Everyone Become a Socialist?" *Intelligencer*. March 3, 2019. https://nymag.com/intelligencer/2019/03/socialism-and-young-socialists.html.

Chapter 4

Whither the State?

Steve Bannon, the Alt Right, and Lenin's State and Revolution

ALEXANDAR MIHAILOVIC

As I've proudly announced to my friends and family, I am a Leninist of the Right. In elections that count, I vote for the most leftist and the most emphatically anti-white candidates. The crazier the better! Let the majority population groan under the added misery until they react. If they don't, then they fully deserve what they get.

—Paul Gottfried, "America 2034"[1]

Without democracy = without management by people.

"The roots of statist attitudes [*gosudarstvennosti*] in the souls of the workers"? Opportunism and revolutionary social democracy.

—Vladimir Lenin, "Outline for the article 'Toward the Question of the Role of the State'"[2]

While no longer regarded as counterintuitive, the pose of the modern conservative as rebel against the status quo continues to raise eyebrows. In his revised and updated *The Reactionary Mind: Conservatism from Edmund Burke to Donald Trump,* Corey Robin takes particular note of the appropriation of leftist anti-establishment beliefs, as well as rhetorical tactics, by conservative thinkers and movements beginning with the French Revolution. Writing in 1796 with grudging respect, if not modulated admiration, for the Jacobin cause as the worker of geopolitical wonders, Edmund Burke asserted that the only way to "destroy that enemy" was to fashion an approach that bore "some analogy" and resemblance to "the force and spirit which that system exerts."[3] As Robin explains, conservative reactionaries are moved first and foremost by the projects of recovering and restoring what was, rather than preserving and protecting what is.[4] Thus, Supreme Court Associate Justice Antonin Scalia's rigidity on the matter of allowable interpretations of the Constitution—an intransigence that Margot Talbot calls the "jurisprudential equivalent of smashing a guitar on stage"—is not "opposed to his idealism," but rather *is* his idealism.[5] Speaking in the same vein about the reactionary love of shattering expectations and norms, the Irish political commentator Fintan O'Toole has acidly observed that upper-class Brexiteers such as Boris Johnson indulge in a "Tory anarchism" that shares many affinities with "punk nihilism" from Thatcher-era England. Rebellion now becomes the domain of the public-school scions of a "decadent and dilettante political elite," fully expressed by Johnson's often puerile if not violent demeanor, and the deliberately fey yet strangely unembarrassed media maunderings of his pro-Brexit confederate Jacob Rees-Mogg.[6] This is a push for revolution that is driven by the resolutely undemocratic impulse of *droit de seigneur.*

In the contemporary American context, the former Goldman Sachs trader and erstwhile Trump campaign manager Steve Bannon engages in a similar appropriation of leftist affective paradigms. As Joshua Green writes in *Devil's Bargain: Steve Bannon, Donald Trump, and the Storming of the Presidency,* during the spring and summer of 2016 Bannon openly acknowledged the pursuit of "something like the old Marxist dialectical concept of 'heightening the contradictions,' only rather than foment revolution among the proletariat, he was trying to disillusion Clinton's natural base of support."[7] While Bannon claims to have read a book or two, we can safely assume that his contact with Marxism-Leninism is as much through other conservative sources, most likely from the works of American apostates from leftism such as Whittaker Chambers, Sydney Hook, and James Burnham—who, in the *National Review* and other Right-leaning publications, traced their political evolutions during the second half of the twentieth century—as through *State and Revolution,* Lenin's essay quoted most often in the wider non-Russian and nonspecialist readership. For ideologues such as Paul Gottfried in the quotation above, Leninism is a subvariety of the sport of boxing: the "sweet science" of exhausting your opponent through a series of smaller debilitating parries that culminate in a victory. In an interview from 2018 published in the white nationalist journal *American Renaissance*, Gottfried stated that he was "still in theory a Leninist of the Right," while also noting that "in order for this strategy to work, one needs something like a majority or significant minority that can be moved to a counterrevolutionary stance," adding that "Leninism of the Right will provide an effective strategy only if the political system and political establishment are overwhelmed by a catastrophe."[8] There is little doubt that Gottfried, the coiner of the term *alt-right* and former mentor to the neo-Nazi Richard Spencer, is a diligent student of Lenin's life and work. The kinship between Gottfried's cool calculus for victory and Lenin's own knowing embrace of catastrophe and tragedy is close indeed. According to Trotsky, Lenin "conducted systematic and outspoken propaganda against the relief committees" that were created to mitigate the famine of 1891–92 in the Volga region. He believed that famine should be allowed to follow its course natural course: "It's sentimentality to think that a sea of need could be emptied with the teaspoon of philanthropy." Lenin went on to say that the famine would play "the role of a progressive factor" in the eventual fall of Tsarist Russia.[9]

Yet the question persists about the likely superficiality of the alt-Right's appropriation of leftist activist paradigms. Certainly, there can be no question about the deeper furrows tracked by Marxism-Leninism and Trotskyism in the work of academics such as Gottfried, who attended college in the late fifties and early sixties. Gottfried's own extensive publications testify to a critical engagement with Marxist legacies that is more suggestive of Jacob wrestling with the angel than the punch and parry of an actual fight. Indeed, the only branch of Marxism for which Gottfried seems to have no esteem is the work of the Frankfurt School. Such facts mitigate, rather than enhance, the presence of Marxist and Leninist "tactics" in the public pronouncements and political activism of alt-Right figures such as Gottfried's protégé Richard Spencer, and Bannon as the Beast of Breitbart, the "Falstaff in flip-flops" to the Prince Hal figure of the political novice Donald Trump. Unlike Gottfried during his college years at Yeshiva University and prominent neoconservative figures such as Irving Kristol and David Horowitz, figures such as Spencer, Bannon, and Dinesh D'Souza were never drawn to any form of Marxism in the first place; for them, "useful" leftism is, to a significant extent, a matter of trading its content in for its form, its credo for its strategic methods. Turning the Marxist legacy inside out has the effect of extruding its affective core, thereby making it easier to detach. Marx and Engels themselves devoted little space to an actual theory of strategy, limiting themselves to commentaries about the failures and short-lived victories of 1848 and, more than twenty years later, the events surrounding the routing of the Paris Commune. For any theory of tactics within the socialist legacy that the alt-Right would consider adopting, we need to turn to Lenin's life and work. In this essay, we will focus on Bannon as a highly representative example of the alt-Right's engagement with Leninism. As we shall see, the dichotomy of the form and content of Marxism-Leninism ultimately dissolves in Bannon's eccentric lateral burrowing into leftist paradigms. Bannon is powerfully drawn to the negative core of Leninism. For him, Leninism is very much a matter of what the theorist of affect Sara Ahmed characterizes as specific "unhappy affects" in daily life, the deliberate exacerbation of transitions into an unexpected gesture of affirmation: "Unhappiness is not our endpoint. If anything, the experience of being alienated from the affective promise of happy objects gets us somewhere." The unhappy "affect aliens" that Ahmed describes are able to achieve things by "refusing to put bad feelings aside in the hope that we can 'just get along.'"[10] For Bannon, those aliens are the "deplorables": they are members of the white working class who are "left behind" by globalism, which for them is the status quo that they reject. They wear their despair and their exclusion from the "new world order" as badges of honor. As Ahmed might put it, their concern for their "histories of hurt" is "not a backward orientation," because the only possibility for "moving on" from narcissistic injury is to return to the understanding of ourselves as those who have been grievously dispossessed of privilege.[11] Agency, it would seem, may be cultivated from the bitter fruit of disappointment.

As Bannon himself makes a special point of acknowledging, among such "aliens" or refugees of economic globalism we still hear the ornery voices of the male gamers who served as their ideological forebears. The confluence of these two communities—on the one hand, the white "forgotten men" and women who wanted to see America made great again, and the "millions of intense young men (most gamers were men) who disappeared for days or even weeks at a time in alternate realities"—summons forth a disquieting tableau of collapsed time, as if the Russian radical men and women of the 1860s and 1870s become fully contemporaneous with the Bolsheviks who were recognizably their heirs. "[T]hese rootless white guys, who [in the aughts] had enormous power" on message boards for MMORGs (Massive Multiplayer Online Games) such as Wowhead, Allakhazam, and

Thottbot, became for Bannon both the historical vanguard and Pretorian guard of white nationalism.[12] Lenin himself imbibed the heady ramifications of the living in such a time when all rules and expectations seemed to be broken. As he wrote in "The Main Task of our Days" ("*Glavnya zazacha nashikh dnei*") (March 11, 1918), "In just a few months, we have passed through the stages of dealing with the bourgeoisie and the wearing-out of petit-bourgeois illusions, which other countries" took "decades" to accomplish.[13] Bannon's engagement with Leninism is motivated, first and foremost, by his fascination with virtual communities that create their own realities, in what they imagine to be a happy contravention of the administrative state. As superficial as Bannon's understanding of the Marxist-Leninist legacy is, we shall see that his idiosyncratic appropriation of Lenin's militant antistatism draws attention to the distinctive affective character of the first Soviet leader's watershed programmatic essay *State and Revolution* (1917). It is precisely the rhetorical and affect-driven character of Lenin's *State and Revolution*—in which articulated ideals become placeholders, slots, or carefully designed triggers for desired emotive responses, rather than dynamic analytical principles—that makes it possible to ask about Bannon the same question that Corey Robin poses about the legacy of Ayn Rand: "How could such a mediocrity, not just a second-hander but a second-rater" exert a significant influence "on the culture at large?"[14]

First, we need to enter into Ground Zero of Bannon's quasi-Jacobinism, via a statement he made six years ago. In the weeks leading up to the American presidential election, the American historian Ronald Radosh recalled a peculiar conversation he had with Bannon during a Washington, D.C., book party for David Horowitz's *The Black Book of the American Left*, on November 12, 2013. The party was held in Bannon's Georgetown townhouse, which doubled as the headquarters for the Breitbart news service that Bannon had recently taken over. Already in an expansive and puckish mood, Bannon bantered with Radosh in the midst of a motley company that consisted of neoconservative pundits such as Horowitz and Anne Coulter, Republican firebrands such as Senator Ron Johnson from Wisconsin and Representative Louie Gohmert from Texas's 1st congressional district, and reality-TV luminaries such as *Duck Dynasty*'s hirsute Phil Robertson. The gathering anticipated much of the eclectic populism that Bannon would excel in promoting three years later, when Donald Trump chose him to serve as "Chief Strategist" for his presidential campaign: a mix of obscure and fringe talking heads, and crypto-celebrities eager to punch up their street creds within the wider public arena. At roughly the same time two years later, Gohmert would become a fire-breathing purveyor of conspiracy theories about Barack Obama's and Hillary Clinton's commandeering of "deep state" military maneuvers in Texas under the code name "Jade Helmet," and Robertson would be cast as the oracular narrator of Bannon's culture-war documentary *The Torchbearer*. Both in 2013 and afterward, Bannon appeared to see himself as an Aleksandr Parvus–like figure (Helphand) to Donald Trump. Parvus was memorably described as being such to Vladimir Lenin in Aleksandr Solzhenitsyn's novella *Lenin in Zürich*—a text that has occupied a special place of prominence in both the American and Russian canon of conservative Leniniana. In this narrative, which Solzhenitsyn eventually incorporated in his "Red Wheel" cycle of Dos Passos–like novels about Russia's disastrous involvement in World War I and the ten years that followed it, Parvus becomes a physically grotesque figure who spurts "hippopotamus blood" and hardly seems to be human.[15] Taking the lead of *Lenin in Zürich*, in his crudely nationalistic 2017 Russian Television One miniseries *Demon Revoliutsii* the filmmaker Vladimir Khotinenko portrays Parvus as a Mephistopheles without portfolio, a figure who engineers great change while largely working on the periphery of things. As Michael Wolff puts it in his 2018 sensationalistic account *Fire and Fury: Inside the Trump White House*, Bannon was a "marginal, invisible, small-time hustler" reminiscent of a character from an Elmore Leonard novel, who in August 2016 found himself in charge of paving a victory for Trump that went through the white working-class constituencies of Florida, Ohio, Michigan, and Pennsylvania.[16]

We will return to the resonances of Bannon's public persona with both Lenin and his magus benefactor Parvus from *Lenin in Zürich*. In the meantime, let us linger at the book party at the D.C.-based aerie of Breitbart, almost three years to the day of Donald Trump's election. Walking among his guests, Bannon made no secret of being drolly aware of the incongruity of himself as a matchmaker of such dissimilar public actors. An avid follower of internecine squabbles at both ends of the political spectrum, Bannon was well aware of Ronald Radosh's reputation as a liberal centrist academic who had undergone a conversion from the Radical Left of the sixties and early seventies. Demurring from the labels of "populist" and "American nationalist," Bannon proudly proclaimed himself to Radosh as a "Leninist": "Lenin . . . wanted to destroy the state, and that's my goal too. I want to bring everything crashing down, and destroy all of today's establishment."[17] In an attempt to push Radosh's buttons, Bannon went on to call the solidly conservative and largely still identifiably Catholic *National Review* and the libertarian *Weekly Standard* "left-wing magazines" that he also wanted to destroy, given that "no one reads them or cares what they say." Although Bannon has said that he did not recall the conversation, there is certainly much in his demeanor and general outlook that he would seem to share with the Lenin of *State and Revolution*. Like Lenin in that work, Bannon sees himself as a tireless agitator for the formation of a molecular politics. Bannon also seems to share Lenin's view that the theoretical adumbration of tactics is no less important that the advocacy of state dismantlement; he also claims an affinity with Lenin's cultivation of a militantly sectarian activist, one that sees political cousins or allies in the good fight as greater threats than principled enemies. In a characteristic formulation from *State and Revolution,* Lenin called for a break with his fellow socialists Karl Kautsky, Phillip Scheidemann, Georgi Plekhanov, and Emile Vandervelde, "traitors to socialism" who refused to "fight for the complete destruction of the old state machine [with the goal that] the armed proletariat itself *should become the government.*"[18] For Bannon, it would seem that wearing the mask of Leninism is as much a matter of what Susan Sontag would have called a particular style of political will as it is of actual beliefs; it is a public stance that is more the performative expression of a particular life experience, than it is the devout espousal of a beautiful idea.[19]

Yet what is Bannon's personal experience, and what are his beliefs? As Alison Klayman's recent documentary *The Brink* demonstrates, they are more difficult to suss out than one would expect from someone who seems to cultivate the persona of a dissolute and aging frat boy, and stout supporter of unhip white middle-class dowdiness. His faded and frayed double shirts are his body armor, fitted out for the battlefield of a "new" Crusade. On the face of it, Bannon's quip to Radosh would seem to be a characteristic provocation. What could an ultramontane American Catholic who grew up reciting the Latin Tridentine Mass, a reactionary advocate for untrammeled American military and economic supremacy on a global scale—an adherent, among other things, to the notion that Iraq's oil reserves belong to the United States in consequence of "natural law," as the spoils of war—have ideologically in common with Vladimir Lenin, an advocate for a socialism avowed as rigorously Marxian, and a forthright enemy of bourgeois morality, parliamentarian ethics, and a capitalism that was invariably predatory? Certainly, Bannon's preoccupations and essential beliefs would seem to be very distant from what Tony Judt incisively describes as Leninism's "doctrinaire positivism."[20] At best, we may call Bannon's off-the-cuff statement to Radosh as an example of the area where the "far-left and the far-right blur and merge," which the Belgian-American critic Luc Sante regarded as the hallmark of another American eccentric and ideological gadfly, the novelist William S. Burroughs.[21]

There are two different ways of understanding or explaining Bannon's reference to Lenin as a political model. The first is to see it as being of one cloth as the unexpectedly positive assessments of Leninism by other paleoconservatives and radical libertarians. In a well-known interview from May 25, 2001, the Republican strategist and libertarian activist Grover Norquist stated that "I don't want to abolish government; I simply want to reduce it to the size where I can drag it into the bathroom and drown it in the bathtub."[22] Radosh himself and others who have visited Norquist have quizzically taken note of the portrait of Lenin hanging in his home. As Radosh himself recalls from a conversation at Norquist's home twenty years ago, Norquist pointed to the portrait, stating that he shared Lenin's keen interest in dismantling the administrative state.[23] In his memoir of political apostacy *Blinded by the Right: The Conscience of an Ex-Conservative*, David Brock made the following observations about his contact with Norquist in the conservative movement of the nineties:

> There was nothing traditionally conservative in Grover's approach. As I conformed myself to the movement, I was being inculcated into a radical cult that bore none of the positive attributes of classical conservatism—a sense of limits, fair play, Tory civility, and respect for individual freedom. On the contrary, Grover admired the iron dedication of Lenin, whose dictum "Probe with bayonets, looking for weakness" he often quoted, and whose majestic portrait hung in Grover's Washington living room. Grover kept a pet boa constrictor, named after the turn-of-the-century anarchist Lysander Spooner. He fed the snake mice, all of them named David Bonior, the outspoken liberal House whip.[24]

Brock's description of Norquist's admiration for Lenin's pugilistic ruthlessness and affective pose of a political Darwinist serves as something of a mirror image for the other way of making sense of Bannon's profession of temperamental, if not ideological, Leninism at the 2013 book party. Seen from this perspective—and applying Bannon's own characterization of the truculent white populist in the post-Obama era—we would be entirely justified in regarding the first Soviet leader as the original "honey badger."

Quite distinct from its affective thespian dimension, the second way of making sense of Bannon's self-declared Leninism is to see it as an expression of his American conservative Catholic ambivalence about Hayekian free-market purism. We might regard Bannon's comment as being closely aligned to the anarcho-populism of the sailors of the 1921 Kronstadt rebellion, whom Lenin despised for what the historian Paul Avrich insightfully termed a "libertarian socialism" that was inimical to state socialism. It should go without saying that this variety of libertarianism is qualitatively very different from the Koch brothers' brand of unswervingly individualistic libertarianism favored by Norquist in his capacity as founder and continuing chief executive officer of the political action group known as the Americans for Tax Reform. In his now-famous 2014 Skyped-in speech at the Vatican, Bannon makes a distinction that is somewhat unexpected coming from a cultural conservative and former trader at Goldman Sachs, between "enlightened" capitalism on the one hand, and a counterintuitive pairing of the "state capitalism" and the "objectivist school of libertarian capitalism" on the other:

> But there's a strand of capitalism today—two strands of it, that are very disturbing.
> One is state-sponsored capitalism. And that's the capitalism you see in China and Russia. I believe it's what Holy Father [Pope Francis] has seen for most of his life in places like Argentina, where you have this kind of crony capitalism of people that are involved with these military powers-that-be in the government, and it forms a brutal form of capitalism that is really about creating wealth and creating value for a very small subset of people. And it doesn't spread the tremendous value creation throughout broader distribution patterns that were seen really in the twentieth century.
> The second form of capitalism that I feel is almost as disturbing, is what I call the Ayn Rand or the Objectivist School of libertarian capitalism. And, look, I'm a big believer in a lot of libertarianism. I have many many [sic] friends that's a very big part of the conservative movement—whether it's the UKIP movement in England, it's many of the underpinnings of the populist movement in Europe, and particularly in the United States.

In an interview from 2017 with the conservative author Keith Koffler, Bannon bluntly stated that Ayn Rand's Objectivism was the "thing that turned [him] off," reinforcing his belief in the inherent decency and goodness of the "working people." He goes on: "I think Ayn Rand is one of the most dangerous individuals in modern thought," because her glorification of leadership elites is "against human nature, and certainly against all the precepts of the Judeo-Christian West."[25]

If we take away from these statements in 2014 and 2017 Bannon's references to Judeo-Christianity, we are not so far from the buoyant idealism of Lenin's unexpected pronouncement in *State and Revolution* about the goodness that is deeply ingrained in the working people's repressed cultural practices. In the wake of the state withering away, "people will gradually *become accustomed* to observing the elementary rules of social intercourse that have been known for ages and repeated for thousands of years in all copybooks—and to observing them without force, without compulsion, without subordination, *without the special apparatus* for compulsion which is called the state" (emphases in the original).[26] Later in this essay, we will devote particular attention to the deeper contradictions within Lenin's understanding of the withering away of the state, which became more overt in his hostility to labor movements that were independent of the Soviet state. Returning to his 2014 Vatican speech, we hear vivid testimony of Bannon's fuzzy and largely idealistic understanding of grass-roots spirituality as a natural democracy:

> However, that form of capitalism is quite different when you really look at it to what I call the "enlightened capitalism" of the Judeo-Christian West. It is a capitalism that really looks to make people commodities, and to objectify people, and to use them almost—as many of the precepts of Marx—and that is a form of capitalism, particularly to a younger generation [that] they're really finding quite attractive. And if they don't see another alternative, it's going to be an alternative that they gravitate to under this kind of rubric of "personal freedom."[27]

Though counterintuitive at first glance, Bannon's conflation of state capitalism and the unregulated operation of the global marketplace makes complete sense if we regard it from the perspective of the pessimism and apparent antihumanism of his religious upbringing, which segued into sympathy for the views of the American Catholic authoritarian intelligentsia that flourished in the resolutely pro-Franco *National Review* of the seventies, particularly under the influence of the publisher William F. Buckley Jr.'s nephew L. Brent Bozell III. Bannon's professed disdain to Radosh of *National Review* as a "leftist" publication should be taken with a grain of salt. Yet it is important to bear in mind that Bannon gave this speech less than a year after his conversation with Radosh. One almost gets the sense that Bannon is keen upon unmooring Marxism-Leninism from its customary place on the political spectrum. In his comment about one form of capitalism turning "people commodities" and "objectifying" them according to "many of the precepts of Marx," is Bannon wistfully contemplating the possibilities for a Roman Catholic socialism or secularized Catholicism, in the manner of Graham Greene?

Clearly, the answer to this question must be no. Passionate advocacy for autarky and against economic globalism does not, in itself, a socialist make. Furthermore, for his talk about the importance of lifting up "the forgotten man," in his taking over the reins of the Trump campaign Bannon seemed to have forgotten the need for an economic platform. The best that we can say about Bannon's sympathy for aspects of socialism, is that a nuanced understanding of the zealotry of a moral political conversion—the ways in which the tenor, if not the content, of earlier beliefs can fold themselves almost seamlessly into a new belief system—is certainly palpable in his Vatican speech. That public statement is certainly the closest that he has even come to a manifesto or exposition of his worldview. Among other things, Bannon here gives due to Marxism, both as the coin of the political realm and as a referent with at least residually moral value. As someone who straddled the very different professional domains of business and conservative political advocacy, Bannon seems very aware of the schematic character of the free-market moral imagination. As William Kristol once put it to the political scientist Corey Robin, the central problem of American conservatism has always been that it is "so influenced by business culture and by business modes of thinking that it lacks any political imagination, which has always been, I have to say, a property of the left."[28] Bannon also critically points to the two forms of capitalism that Lenin, in his extensions of the Marxist analysis to colonialism, acknowledged as being inimical to the dictatorship of the proletariat: the crony capitalism of the bourgeois national state, and the metastatic global capitalism that respects no national borders. Bannon, like Lenin, recognizes that the two forms of capitalism converge in the creation of colonial empires. In a statement that would not be out of place in Bannon's speech at the Vatican, Lenin argued in his 1916 *Imperialism, the Highest Stage of Capitalism*, that "[m]onopolies, oligarchy, the striving for domination and not for freedom, the exploitation of an increasing number of small or weak nations by a handful of the richest or most powerful nations—all these have given birth to those distinctive characteristics of imperialism which compel us to define it as parasitic or decaying capitalism."[29] It would seem that Bannon argues for a postcolonial nationalism that is not so far removed from the hints in Marx's writing of an "enlightened patriotism which, although quite compatible with a pluralistic internationalism, located the worker's first interests [firmly] within particular national societies."[30] If we substitute "worker" with "white working class," we come very close indeed to Bannon's stated current endeavor, documented by Klayman and others, of creating an international network of white nationalists.

Yet in what sense might a "Judeo-Christian" or enlightened capitalism serve as a counterweight to these two distinct, yet supposedly interwoven strands of free-market economics? Lenin's own paradoxical understanding of the state—as both burden and boon, as a signifier that fluctuates between the categories of organic communities and dictatorship of the proletariat reminiscent of the consensus or "general will" from Rousseau's *Social Contract*—helps us to understand the self-contradicting character of the state in the libertarian formulations of both Bannon and the alt-Right movement as a whole. Like Lenin, Bannon and his confederates are more interested in the redefinition and reconfiguration of the state, than they are in its wholesale abolition. The claims for abolishing the state are, first and foremost, rhetorically useful, the honey spread along the rim of the goblet containing what Plato, in his dialogue *Phaedrus*, characterizes as the bitter draught of truth.

One of the least commented-upon aspects of *State and Revolution* is the riddle of its intended audience. Already on the title page of its first, and pseudonymous, edition, we see an essay title that is seldom acknowledged in its entirety: *State and Revolution. The Marxist Theory of the State, and the Tasks of the Proletariat in the Revolution.* The unwieldiness of the full title would seem to have little in common with the recent Lenin biographer Victor Sebestyen's biting characterization of Lenin's style of argumentation, in person as well as on paper: "He used a battering ram rather than a rapier, but in his finest work he can be powerfully convincing in his reason, logic, and intellectual force, albeit often from a fundamentally flawed premise."[31] From this perspective, the second segment of the title would seem to hide behind a mask of dry scholarly assessment that is highly uncharacteristic of Lenin, perhaps even suggesting that this particular essay is written from a pedantic and relatively nonpartisan specialist by the pseudonym of N. Lenin. Though the publisher of "Life and Knowledge" was known to be Marxist, its catalogue had a surprising political and literary breadth (including children's literature and translations of the work of "bourgeois" socialists such as August Bebel) that certainly would have been inconceivable ten years later. We need, therefore, to bear in mind the ways in which the venue of essay's publication influenced the possibly heterodox way that it was received by its audience.

The full title of the essay is, in regard, highly significant. The phrase *The Marxist Theory of the State*, following *State and Revolution*, opens up a range of possibilities about the goals of the essay. *Uchenie [lit., "teaching"] Marksizma* could alternatively point to the essay's meta-pedagogical intent, as a text that instructs members of the cadre in the art of teaching others. Nowhere in *State and Revolution* do we get a sense of the institutional identity of the proletarian dictatorship, or of the practical mechanisms that bring about the necessary collapse of the bourgeois state. Several scholars have come to the conclusion that Lenin's brief description of the proletarian dictatorship as operating in the manner of a post office is largely a metaphorical afterthought.[32] Unlike almost all of his other written work, Lenin here seems somewhat unconcerned with the logical consistency of his terms. At one point of the essay, he states that the correct understanding of Engels's coining of the phrase "withering away from the state" (from his *Anti-Dühring: Herr Eugen Dühring's Revolution in Science*) is that the "bourgeois state does not 'wither away' but is '*eradicated*' by the proletariat in the course of a revolution," for it is the "proletarian revolution or semi-state [that] withers away after this revolution." At another point, he asserts with a near-Thomistic opacity that "a state which is withering away may be called a nonpolitical state at a certain stage of its withering away"; later yet, that as a "special machine for suppression, the 'state' is still necessary," only this is now a transitional state, and is no longer a state in the proper sense."[33] "Democracy," while remaining an essentially pejorative category that is consistent with its occurrence in Lenin's other works, also ends up passing through a gauntlet of inconsistent and borderline interchangeable usage with other terms. In this case, the conceptual rigor is undermined by an apparent attempt to locate "democracy" within the desired extinction of the bourgeois state: "The elimination of the state also involves the abolition of democracy," and conversely, "The withering away of the state means the withering away of democracy"; "Communism alone is capable of providing a truly complete democracy, and the more complete it is the more quickly will it become unnecessary and wither away by itself."[34] The essay effectively ends, unfinished, at its most important moment, when Lenin needs to speak about the education of people after the withering away of the state. We can almost see Lenin throwing up his hands, having exhausted his vocabulary for speaking about the unnamable: "And then the door will be opened wide for the transition from the first stage of communist society towards its highest phase, and simultaneously towards the complete withering away of the state."[35] Among other things, *State and Revolution* is a surprisingly intimate statement, a performance of political rhetoric with almost haptic qualities.

We can easily imagine Bannon's attraction to an essay such as this, which pelts its readers with dramatic narrative subroutines without clarifying their significance in relation to one another. Taking note of the teeming logical inconsistencies within Bannon's own politics, George Steinmetz and Julie Hell conclude that his understanding of empire is one "driven by a political logic, not an economic one—therefore, in Bannon's view, a nonimperialist empire."[36] The paucity of clearly defined analytical paradigms for "state" and "dictatorship" in *State and Revolution* forces us to consider the possibility that this, his most well-known longer work, may in fact be his least theoretical, which may explain Bannon's own seeming fascination with its pseudo-anarchism. Lenin asserts that in the full victory of the proletariat we see a society that is "no longer the state in the proper sense [*chto uzhe ne est' sobstvenno gosudarstvo*]." He also bluffly asserts that the "withering away [*otmiranie*] of the state" would be an event that is accompanied by the triumph of a diffuse centralism among the citizens of the revolutionary society.[37] In the essay, Lenin takes particular pains to underscore that the absence of the state would result in greater centralization, and that Marx himself was opposed to Federalist models of government, while also being a resolute "centralist." In a highly representative passage from *State and Revolution,* Lenin tautologically argues that "[t]here is no retreat whatever from centralism in [Marx's] quoted observations, and only people suffused with philistine 'superstitious belief' in the state can mistake the destruction of bourgeois state machine for the elimination of capitalism!"[38] This is not writing that is meant to convince or explain; among other things, the audience of the text is already clearly positioned as sharing the author's opinions. As we see here and in many other moments of *State and Revolution,* the author is providing his readers with an inventory of memorably stentorian talking points, rather than a series of devastating analytical rebuttals. How do you spread the word about the new doctrine (*uchenie*) of the vanished State? Just have these formulaic statements at hand, and you'll be fine. *State and Revolution* has a strong scholastic bent, while also manifesting the flavor of a face-to-face demonstration of—or a master class in—evangelizing lectureship. The turns of phrase "properly speaking [*sobstvenno*]" and "in the proper sense [*v sobstvennom smysle etogo slova*]" occur several times throughout the essay, often precisely at moments when theoretical issues need to be clarified and explained, rather than airily dismissed with a chatty verbal tic. Here, Lenin is not interested in convincing his audience of the sound sense of Bolshevik socialism, of its moral rightness. Rather, he is saying: let me show you the language that *signals*, rather than actually embodies, a deeper reasoning; once you assimilate that language, you will come to understand tactics.

In *State and Revolution*, the formula "the withering away of the state" therefore functions more as a totemic object, than as a concept whose ontology is denoted by the operation of its dynamically moving parts. The proper way to understand its significance is as an affective touchstone, rather than a potent heuristic paradigm. The "affect theory" developed by academics such as Lauren Berlant, Sara Ahmed, and Lee Edelman proves to be surprisingly helpful in untangling the skein of anticipated reader responses to *State and Revolution* and goes a long way in explaining the paradox of its conceptual untidiness not undercutting its rhetorical power. As Ahmed explains:

> Anticipations of what an object gives us are also expectations of what we should be given. How is it that we come to expect so much? After all, expectations can make things seem disappointing. If we arrive at objects with an expectation of how we will be affected by them, then this affects how they affect us, even in the moment that they fail to live up to our expectations. Happiness is an expectation of what follows, where the expectation differentiates between things, whether or not they exist as objects in the present.[39]

Ahmed's discussion of affective politics as a sequence of responses triggered by disparate objects—what Lauren Berlant describes in her characterization of ostensible failures of Trump's initial presidential campaign in 2012 as the "wing-flapping [of the fabled butterfly] that sets off revolutions"[40]—helps us to understand why someone such as Bannon, who "produces" aggregated sound bites rather than expressions of a coherent politics, is attracted to the particular treatment of antistatism that we find in Lenin's 1917 essay. In his varied reading during his downtime while serving in the Navy, Bannon might have been struck by this description of Lenin in Solzhenitsyn's *Lenin in Zürich*, which enjoyed considerable popularity among the American conservative intelligentsia of the seventies. Solzhenitsyn portrays a Lenin in 1916 as hopelessly tongue-tied and ineloquent, and vainly struggling to explain dialectical materialism to Fritz Platten, the secretary of the Swiss Socialist Party who helped organize Lenin's return to Petrograd via the sealed train car from Zürich: "Platten's brow became convulsed, his eyes strained and bewildered. How difficult, how terribly difficult it is to master the lofty science of socialism! These grandiose formulas somehow refuse to fit in with your poor limited experience. War is a fraud, and neutrality is a fraud, so neutrality is just as bad as war?" Platten soon finds himself appealing with "a side glance at [his] comrades, who clearly also show that they don't understand it all." Briefly switching to the emphatic voice of a second-person storyteller, the narrator writes that "you are ashamed to admit that you don't [understand], so you pretend [*delaesh' vid*]" that you do.[41] In Solzhenitsyn's novel, this moment is a demonstration of how *not* to reach your audience. Conversion is accomplished through deliberate confusion, not appealing to the audience's sense of logic or even justice. As the nineteenth-century Tory and legal theorist Walter Bagehot explained conservative epistemology, truth is "a succession of perpetual oscillations, like the negative and positive signs of an alternate series, in which you were constantly more or less denying and affirming the same proposition."[42] At this point of Solzhenitsyn's novel, Lenin has yet to learn this hard lesson about the necessarily cruel art of persuasion.

From this perspective, we can hardly be surprised that Bannon is clearly taken with the various conservative biographical accounts of Lenin (such as Robert Conquest's short and hostile 1972 biography, which Bannon possibly read) as a ruthless attack dog and nasty political operator, a "honey badger who don't take no shit," rather than the ineffectual Ciceronian sage that he perceives himself to be early in Solzhenitsyn's novel, prior to his pivotal meeting with Parvus in Berne.[43] In a text from the Cold War that served as foundational for sympathetic American conservative interpretations of Lenin, the encounter with Parvus shakes Lenin's customary confidence and breezy disdain for ideological rivals, while also giving him the laser-like focus to abandon internecine squabbles for the larger realm of well-financed political action. As Lenin ruefully reflects at one point of his Faustian conversation with Parvus, he always came up short in when it came to getting things done. "Everything else, he could manage. But the one thing he couldn't do was to bring *that moment* [R. *priblizit' **tot moment** (emphasis in original)*] any closer," whereas Parvus, "with his millions," connections in port cities, gun-running, and deft assistance in the seizure of the Petrograd Putilov weapons factory, was endowed precisely with that skill.[44]

There is certainly much about Bannon's characterization of his relations with Trump during the presidential campaign that suggests a rotation of three different archetypes between the two men: of the young, fiercely polemical yet scholastic Lenin prior to his European exile, of Parvus the well-connected provocateur, and the post-exile Lenin who represented something of a synthesis of the first two archetypes. One highly representative assessment of Lenin's vituperative rather than enlightenment mode of political suasion comes from Moishe Olgin, his former comrade-in-arms in Petrograd. "He does not reply to an opponent: he vivisects them. . . . [He] is derisive. He ridicules his opponent. He castigates him. He makes you feel that his victim is an ignoramus, a fool, a presumptuous non-entity. You are swept up by the power of his apparent logic. You are overwhelmed by his intellectual passion."[45] As Olgin himself ruefully acknowledged—not surprisingly, he and Lenin eventually had an acrimonious falling-out over political matters—logic is often quite palpably beside the point in such language. Like the vituperative Lenin portrayed in these accounts, Bannon attempts to squeeze dissimilar and occasionally conflicting observations into what he imagines to be a formula for political victory. Yet what Bannon also evinces is a jumbled assemblage of melodramatic views that strongly suggests that he sees himself and Trump as *doppelgängers* of each other, as well as something very much like Parvus and Lenin from Solzhenitsyn's narrative. Especially prominent among these views are the contempt for his fellow fringe agitators (extending both to the *National Review* coterie of "establishment" conservatives, cited earlier, and to the white supremacist and neo-Nazi Richard Spenser, whom Bannon dismissed as a "goober" and a "freak"),[46] his admiration of plutocratic influencing, and his love of the public spectacle of thuggish behavior. Following Lenin's behavioral lead as imagined in the conservative canon, this requires some bluster, much fibbing, and passing over in silence of obvious inconsistencies—if not blatant lapses—in reasoning, what Steinmetz and Hell characterize as a deliberate "politics of chaos and incoherence."[47]

In his responses to the programs of Kerensky, Kautsky, and Plekhanov, Lenin invariably favored disinhibited obloquy over vigorous deconstructive polemic. Among other things, he categorically dismissed all those figures as guilty of philistinism (*meshchanstvo*), ignorance, and otiose parliamentarianism, as if their views were more deserving of verbal assault than engaged rebuttal. In *State and Revolution,* this language of unleashed invective readily lends itself to a slurry of pejorative nomenclature that is signaled by ellipses and trailing abbreviations, as if Kautsky et al. are simply placeholders for a roiling mass of political incoherence and all-around foolishness that is unworthy of any thorough categorization. The essay was, after all, a call to arms rather than an attempt at suasion. As Lenin himself put it in his postscript to the first edition of the essay, "It is more pleasant and useful to undertake the 'experience of revolution' than to write about it."[48]

Certainly, this guiding principle informs what we sense about the essay's target audience, as consisting of what Robert Service calls the "avid followers" rather than any big-tent coalition of social democrats.[49] Service takes note of the curious expository style of Lenin's *State and Revolution*, which at times seems almost "languid" in its repeated use of incomplete inventories of the political errors of others. In characterizing his opponents, Lenin often "appends a carefree 'etcetera'"—in the Russian text, *i t. d.* or, with pointed rhetorical extravagance, *i t. d. i t. p.* [lit., "and so on, and so forth"]—"for the benefit of his readers."[50] It is not at all a stretch to say that Bannon's journalistic mentor Andrew Breitbart engaged in a similar strategy of rhetorical shorthand that was deceptively chatty and slack. A few days after the death of Ted Kennedy, Breitbart called the Massachusetts senator "a villain," "a prick," and "a duplicitous bastard," adding that "I'm more than willing to go off decorum to ensure that THIS MAN is not beatified." As in the case of Lenin's style of inflammatory language, these insults serve as nothing more than the highlighting of a particular node among a network of assumptions, analogous to the identification of a poisonous mushroom. What is such a toxic organism, if not the external body of a deeper root system that consists, in this instance, of the deceased man's cowardly and de facto homicidal behavior at Chappaquiddick, his political corruption, his academic dishonesty in college, etc.? Taking a lead from Breitbart, Bannon himself was open in his admiration for Trump's thuggish demeanor at his debate with Hilary Clinton: "You have to have a certain psychological construct to harass Hillary Clinton by inviting her husband's accusers to the first presidential debate," he was a "classic honey badger—he crushed her."[51] In such garrulous statements, Breibart and Bannon evoke Lenin's own expository stratagem of critique through truncated or abbreviated invective. The target audience is already firmly on your side, and in your corner—all you need to do is to nudge its network of trembling mental associations into a frenetic overdrive.

What does Bannon's style of contestation have in common with Lenin's, and in what ways does the libertarian and alt-Right's disgust with pluralism emerge as a close counterpart to Lenin's self-aware performance of politically sectarian rage in *State and Revolution*? At the very least, there are affinities between Lenin's characterization, in *State and Revolution*, of "equality" as a diffuse structure that is made gravitationally possible by the equal valences of the citizens who inhabit it, and what Jan-Werner Müller calls the "anti-politics" of the populist Right,[52] its glorification of "direct" communication or representation over the malign factionalism of pluralist political systems. But more significant here is what Ruth Wodak identifies as the alt-Right's gossipy "fictionalization of politics," of rendering all politics into a series of theatrical affective prompts, rather than a vigorous dialogue of different views.[53] As Wodak explains it, this form of propaganda is composed of scripts, a series of jabs or directorial prompts, rather than moments of dialogic engagement. Bannon seems to imagine that Lenin favored this kind of politicized sociality, in which affect is deliberately and artificially driven by the "drama of decision."[54] What matters most here is, as Lauren Berlant explains, the high affective drama of "remaining in attachment" to an object—in this case, in an antagonistic one to another person.[55] What does that person "signal"? Or put in another way, what is the affect that "they" (or the images of them) communicate to us?

Bannon has no interest in the Marxist essence of Lenin's written work. What animates him is an appreciation of Lenin as the philosopher of political contestation. In this regard, Bannon has surprising affinities with Louis Althusser, another idiosyncratic Catholic appropriator of Lenin. Above all, Althusser was interested in Lenin as a theorist of materialist unfolding, rather than Lenin as an appropriator of Hegel's historical idealism. As Althusser explains in his controversial 1969 essay "Lenin before Hegel," for Lenin "it is absolutely essential (as he had learnt simply from a thorough-going reading of *Capital*) *to suppress every origin and every subject, and to say:* what is absolute is *the process without a subject,* both in reality and in scientific knowledge (emphasis in original)."[56] It is highly unlikely that Bannon, steeped as he is in the ephemeral culture of the smashmouth sound bite, is at all aware of Althusser's understanding of Lenin as an apostle of developing socialism, of an unfolding perfectibility that recalls Thomist as well as Marxian categories. Yet what Bannon and Althusser undoubtedly share is an avowed interest in what Lauren Berlant identifies as an understanding of any given historical moment as a "visceral moment" in which "corporeal, intimate, and political performances of adjustment" create a "shared atmosphere." Like the physical environment in the Anthropocene, the presence of multiple human actors inevitably transforms that atmosphere, whose new chemical composition becomes, in Berlant's formulation, an object "theory-in-practice of how a world works."[57] The ephemerality of political culture—of a politics without resolution or end, reveling in its own incoherence—is at the center of Bannon's appropriation of Lenin. This is truly the politics in which the "affective structure remains," after the subject has left the building.[58] In the case of Bannon's fond yet selective evocation of Lenin, the great architect of Soviet socialism had never set foot in the building in the first place.

Notes

1. Paul Gottfried, "America in 2034." *American Renaissance*, https://www.amren.com/news/2014/06/america-in-2034-2/.

2. V. I. Lenin, *Polnoe sobranie sochinenii. T. 33: Gosudarstvo i revoliutsiia.* 5th Edition (Moscow: Izd. Politicheskoi literatury, 1977), 339. The translation is mine.

3. Quoted in Corey Robin, *Conservatism from Edmund Burke to Donald Trump* (Oxford: Oxford University Press, 2018), 47.

4. Ibid., 51, 56.

5. Ibid., 223, 226.

6. Fintan O'Toole, *Heroic Failure: Brexit and the Politics of Pain* (London: Apollo Books, 2018), 127, 134.

7. Joshua Green, *Devil's Bargain: Steve Bannon, Donald Trump, and the Storming of the White House* (New York: Penguin Press, 2017), 159.

8. Hubert Collins, "Not a Prophet in His Own Land" [Interview with Paul Gottfried], *American Renaissance*, April 27, 2018, https://www.amren.com/features/2018/04/not-a-prophet-in-his-own-land/.

9. Victor Sebestyen, *Lenin: The Man, the Dictator, and the Master of Terror* (New York: Pantheon Books, 2017), 70–71.

10. Sara Ahmed, "Happy Objects," in *The Affect Theory Reader*, ed. Melissa Gregg and Gregory J. Seigworth (Durham: Duke Univ. Press, 2010), 50.

11. Ibid.

12. Green, 145.

13. V. I. Lenin, *Polnoe sobranie sochinenii. T. 36* 5th Ed. (Moscow: Izd. Politicheskoi literatury, 1977), 78–79. The translation is mine.

14. Robin, 186.

15. Alexander Solzhenitsyn, *Lenin in Zürich*, trans. H. T. Willetts (New York: Farrar, Straus and Giroux, 1976), 116.

16. Michael Wolff, *Fire and Fury: Inside the Trump White House* (New York: Henry Holt, 2018), 60.

17. Ronald Radosh, "Steve Bannon, Trump's Top Guy, Told Me He Was a Leninist," *The Daily Beast*, August 22, 2016, https://www.thedailybeast.com/steve-bannon-trumps-top-guy-told-me-he-was-a-leninist.

18. Lenin, *The State and Revolution*, trans. Robert Service (Penguin, 1992), 107; emphasis in the original.

19. "Without the personal experience, if one is looking in from the outside, [the performative demeanor of the sixties radicals] does look messy and almost pointless." Susan Sontag, "What's Happening in America" (1966), in *Essays of the Sixties and Seventies* (New York: Library of America, 2013), 458.

20. Tony Judt, *Reappraisals: Reflections on the Forgotten Twentieth Century* (New York: Penguin Books, 2008), 109.

21. Luc Sante, "Invisible Man," *New York Review of Books*, May 10, 1984. https://www.nybooks.com/articles/1984/05/10/the-invisible-man/.

22. Interview from May 25, 2001, https://www.npr.org/templates/story/story.php?storyId=1123439.

23. Phone interview with Ronald Radosh, June 29, 2019.

24. David Brock, *Blinded by the Right: The Conscience of an Ex-Conservative* (New York: Broadway Books, 2003), 361.

25. Keith Koffler, *Bannon: Always the Rebel* (Washington, DC: Regnery, 2017), 95–96.

26. Lenin, *The State and Revolution*, 80; emphases in the original.

27. J. Lester Feder, "This Is How Steve Bannon Sees the Entire World," November 16, 2016, https://www.buzzfeednews.com/article/lesterfeder/this-is-how-steve-bannon-sees-the-entire-world#.ylO3kAedo; Steven Bannon. Module 3–Should Christians impose limits on wealth creation? https://www.youtube.com/watch?time_continue=159&v=FWXScQaZ2uI.

28. Robin, 202.

29. V. I. Lenin, *Selected Works: Volume 1* (Moscow: Progress Publishers, 1963), 764.

30. Erica Benner, *Really Existing Nationalisms: A Post-Communist View from Marx and Engels* (Oxford: Clarendon Press, 1995), 106–107.

31. Sebestyen, 73.

32. See Christopher Read, *Lenin: A Revolutionary Life* (London: Routledge, 2005), 166–67, 171, 214; James L. White, *Lenin: The Practice and Theory of Revolution* (New York: Palgrave, 2001), 156–57.

33. Lenin, *The State and Revolution*, 57, 81.

34. Ibid., 73, 81.

35. Ibid., 93.

36. Julia Hell and George Steinmetz, "A Period of 'Wild and Fierce Fanaticism': Theo-Political Militarism, and the Crisis of US Hegemony," *American Journal of Cultural Sociology* 5, no. 3 (October 2017): 387.

37. Lenin, *The State and Revolution*, 38.
38. Ibid., 48.
39. Ahmed, 41.
40. Quoted in Hua Hsu, "The Feeling When: What Affect Theory Teaches about the New Age of Anxiety," *New Yorker*, March 25, 2019, 62.
41. Aleksandr Solzhenitsyn, *Lenin in Zürich*, trans. H. T. Willets (New York: Farrar, Straus and Giroux, 1975), 44. Russian text: *Lenin v Tsiurikhe* (Paris: YMCA Press, 1975), 37.
42. Quoted in Robin, 240.
43. The phrase about the ferocity of the Honey Badger has become a well-known meme among the far right. One of the most insightful explanations of this meme comes from the unexpected place of Tamsin Shaw's review of a 2016 production of *Othello* at the New York Theatre Workshop: "In this reading . . . [Daniel] Craig's Iago calls to mind above all the 'honey badger' that has become the mascot for the white-supremacist far right. A popular YouTube video, 'The Crazy, Nastyass Honey Badger,' shows this small creature display a viciousness, fearlessness, and recklessness unparalleled in the animal kingdom, attacking a huge cobra, diving into a beehive to eat the larvae in spite of being stung all over. The video's narrator coined the phrase that Steve Bannon and Breitbart news have taken for their motto: 'Honey badger don't give a shit.' This is a choice, this not giving a shit. It is the voluptuous enjoyment that Nietzsche described. It is the freedom and exhilaration of moral insensibility." Tamsin Shaw, "The Iago Problem," *NYR Daily*, December 14, 2016, https://www.nybooks.com/daily/2016/12/14/iago-problem-choosing-evil-othello/.
44. *Lenin v Tsiurikhe*, 153.
45. Sebestyen, 83.
46. Joshua Green, "Inside the Secret, Strange, Origins of Steve Bannon's Nationalist Fantasia," *Vanity Fair*, July 17, 2017), https://www.vanityfair.com/news/2017/07/the-strange-origins-of-steve-bannons-nationalist-fantasia.
47. Hell and Steinmetz, 388.
48. Lenin, *State and Revolution*, 111.
49. Service, xxi.
50. Ibid., xxiv.
51. Green, 90, 219.
52. Jan-Werner Müller, *What Is Populism?* (Philadelphia: University of Pennsylvania Press, 2016), 35–36.
53. Ruth Wodak, *The Politics of Fear: What Right-Wing Populist Discourses Mean* (London: SAGE, 2015), 12.
54. Lauren Berlant and Lee Edelman, *Sex, or the Unbearable* (Durham: Duke University Press, 2014), 95.
55. Ibid., 14.
56. Louis Althusser, *Lenin and Philosophy and Other Essays* (New York: NYU Press, 2011), 82.

57. Lauren Berlant, *Cruel Optimism* (Durham: Duke University Press, 2011), 16.

58. Ibid., 81.

Bibliography

Ahmed, Sara. "Happy Objects." In *The Affect Theory Reader*, ed. Melissa Gregg and Gregory J. Seigworth, 29–51. Durham,: Duke University Press, 2010.

Althusser, Louis. *Lenin and Philosophy and Other Essays*. New York: NYU Press, 2011).

Bannon, Steven. "Module 3–Should Christians impose limits on wealth creation?" https://www.youtube.com/watch?time_continue=159&v=FWXScQaZ2uI.

Berlant, Lauren. *Cruel Optimism*. Durham: Duke University Press, 2011.

———, and Lee Edelman. *Sex, or the Unbearable*. Durham: Duke University Press, 2014.

Benner, Erica. *Really Existing Nationalisms: A Post-Communist View from Marx and Engels*. Oxford: Clarendon Press, 1995.

Brock, David. *Blinded by the Right: The Conscience of an Ex-Conservative*. New York: Broadway Books, 2003.

Collins, Hubert. "Not a Prophet in His Own Land" [Interview with Paul Gottfried], *American Renaissance*, April 27, 2018, https://www.amren.com/features/2018/04/not-a-prophet-in-his-own-land/.

Feder, J. Lester. "This is How Steve Bannon Sees the Entire World," November 16, 2016, https://www.buzzfeednews.com/article/lesterfeder/this-is-how-steve-bannon-sees-the-entire-world#.ylO3kAedo.

Gottfried, Paul. "America in 2034." *American Renaissance*, https://www.amren.com/news/2014/06/america-in-2034-2/.

Green, Joshua. *Devil's Bargain: Steve Bannon, Donald Trump, and the Storming of the White House*. New York: Penguin Press, 2017.

———. "Inside the Secret, Strange, Origins of Steve Bannon's Nationalist Fantasia," *Vanity Fair*, July 17, 2017, https://www.vanityfair.com/news/2017/07/the-strange-origins-of-steve-bannons-nationalist-fantasia.

Hell, Julia, and George Steinmetz. "A Period of 'Wild and Fierce Fanaticism': Theo-Political Militarism, and the Crisis of US Hegemony." *American Journal of Cultural Sociology* 5, no. 3 (October 2017): 373–91.

Hsu, Hua. "The Feeling When: What Affect Theory Teaches about the New Age of Anxiety," *New Yorker*, March 25, 2019: 58–64.

Judt, Tony. *Reappraisals: Reflections on the Forgotten Twentieth Century*. New York: Penguin Books, 2008.

Koffler, Keith. *Bannon: Always the Rebel*. Washington, DC: Regnery, 2017.

Lenin, V. I. *Selected Works: Volume 1*. Moscow: Progress Publishers, 1963.

———. *The State and Revolution*, trans. Robert Service. London: Penguin, 1992.

———. *Polnoe sobranie sochinenii. T. 36: Gosudarstvo i revoliutsiia.* 5th Edition. Moscow: Izd. Politicheskoi literatury, 1977.

Müller, Jan-Werner. *What Is Populism?* Philadelphia: University of Pennsylvania Press, 2016.

O'Toole, Fintan. *Heroic Failure: Brexit and the Politics of Pain.* London: Apollo Books, 2018.

Radosh, Ronald. "Steve Bannon, Trump's Top Guy, Told Me He Was a Leninist." *The Daily Beast,* August 22, 2016, https://www.thedailybeast.com/steve-bannon-trumps-top-guy-told-me-he-was-a-leninist.

Read, Christopher. *Lenin: A Revolutionary Life.* London: Routledge, 2005.

Robin, Corey. *Conservatism from Edmund Burke to Donald Trump.* Expanded and Revised. New York: Oxford University Press, 2018.

Sante, Luc. "Invisible Man," *New York Review of Books,* May 10, 1984, https://www.nybooks.com/articles/1984/05/10/the-invisible-man/.

Sebestyen, Victor. *Lenin: The Man, the Dictator, and the Master of Terror.* New York: Pantheon Books, 2017.

Service, Robert. "Introduction." In V. I. Lenin, *The State and Revolution,* trans. Robert Service. London: Penguin, 1992.

Shaw, Tamsin. "The Iago Problem," *NYR Daily,* December 14, 2016, https://www.nybooks.com/daily/2016/12/14/iago-problem-choosing-evil-othello/.

Solzhenitsyn, Aleksandr. *Lenin v Tsiurikhe.* Paris: YMCA Press, 1975.

———. *Lenin in Zürich.* Trans. H. T. Willets. New York: Farrar, Straus and Giroux, 1975.

Sontag, Susan. "What's Happening in America" (1966). In *Essays of the Sixties and Seventies.* New York: Library of America, 2013.

White, James L. *Lenin: The Practice and Theory of Revolution.* New York: Palgrave, 2001.

Wodak, Ruth. *The Politics of Fear: What Right-Wing Populist Discourses Mean.* London. SAGE, 2015.

Wolff, Michael. *Fire and Fury: Inside the Trump White House.* New York: Henry Holt.

Chapter 5

Saving the Vanguard

The Contemporary Relevance of Lenin's Military Metaphor

DANIEL EGAN

The victory of the October Revolution and the subsequent development of the Soviet Union confirmed for many Marxists the validity of what came to be known as "Leninism." However, this model was subjected to considerable criticism from a wide range of Marxists (council communists, autonomists, post-Marxists, Marxist feminists, etc.), criticism that later appeared to be substantiated by the collapse of the USSR and Soviet Marxism between 1989–1991. Post-2008, during the era that can be defined as the Left's remobilization, there has been a renewed effort to free Lenin from the straightjacket of "Leninism" and to understand his relevance for contemporary revolutionary struggles.[1] This chapter examines a core element of Lenin's revolutionary practice: his concept of the vanguard party. More specifically, I explore Lenin's use of the metaphor of a vanguard, a term that has specific meanings associated with the military and war, in his analysis of the party. In doing so I reject the association of Lenin with "vanguardism," a concept emerging from the Left critique of Soviet Marxism. Although "vanguardism" was seen by a considerable portion of the Left as a concrete expression of all that was problematic about Soviet Marxism, which has come to be defined as (1) the organization of a relatively small core of committed revolutionaries in a disciplined, highly centralized political party, and (2) the subordination of working class self-organization to this party. I argue that rejecting the vanguard metaphor altogether comes with considerable costs. In the end, the revolutionary self-organization of the oppressed classes requires the existence of a vanguard. Without such a vanguard, various political activities and struggles will remain fragmented and defensive in nature, incapable of bringing forth revolutionary changes. To reject the necessity of a vanguard because of the history of twentieth-century Leninism is to adopt, however unintentionally, a fetishized understanding of the party—one that, as I demonstrate, Lenin himself argued against.[2] Contemporary revolutionary struggles must embrace and make use of Lenin's theory of the vanguard as a set of *functions* rather than a specific organizational *form*. Revolutionary movements must rescue Lenin's complex, dialectical understanding of the vanguard from its "Leninist" heritage if they are to have any hope of advancing toward an authentic socialist future.

Marxism and Military Metaphors

Metaphors are more than simply a stylistic flourish, a literary device created by the author to connect two seemingly unrelated phenomena. They cannot be understood "as mere ornamentation, as a quirk of individual style, or employing the figurativity where theory cannot express itself clearly." Instead, "the function of metaphor is to develop and even implement the function of theory."[3] In the context of revolutionary theory and revolutionary movements, metaphors reflect a particular set of background assumptions—assumptions regarding the historical and structural conditions out of which such a movement emerges, relevant forms of organization, strategy and tactics, and so on—which serve as the foundation for revolutionary praxis. Such metaphors are simultaneously an objective and subjective reality. On the one hand, the objective boundaries of potential metaphors are set by the mode of production, the history of a specific social formation, and the balance of forces within that social formation. At the same time, in order for these metaphors to serve as a resource for revolutionary praxis they must be understandable not only by those who make use of them directly but also by the broader masses of exploited and oppressed peoples in a particular social formation.

Given this, the ultimate test of a particular configuration of metaphors is practice. Do subordinate classes recognize their lived experience of exploitation and oppression in these metaphors? Do they make use of these metaphors as they engage in political activity? How are these metaphors reflected in the forms of organization, the strategic goals, and the tactical innovations that emerge from this activity? In the end, does the political activity associated with a particular configuration of metaphors result in victory or defeat for the subordinate classes?

The use of military metaphors has been a consistent feature of Marxist theory since its origins. Military metaphors were significant for Marx and Engels given the role played by the dialectic in their analysis of capitalism and the possibilities for socialism. Conflict was an inherent feature of all social phenomena, they argued, so conflict was necessarily the driving force for the development of socialism. Capitalism contained within itself the seeds of its own negation: the contradictions of capital accumulation created structural opportunities in the form of recurrent crises as well as the revolutionary agent—the proletariat—whose conscious activity would ultimately lead to socialism. Socialism would not arrive as the generalized outcome of utopian experiments in cooperation at the community or organizational level (such as Robert Owen's New Lanark and New Harmony or the Rochdale Society of Equitable Pioneers) that would provide proof of the possibility for a peaceful, evolutionary transformation toward a more rational and equitable social system. Instead, Marx and Engels's scientific, dialectical understanding of capitalism revealed that socialism would emerge from an objective historical process of conflict between classes with fundamentally contradictory interests; this would be a protracted and bitter conflict in which the terrain of struggle—the capitalist labor process, the state, bourgeois ideology—was particularly hostile to the working class. If, as Engels noted, force "is the midwife of every old society which is pregnant with the new . . . the instrument by the aid of which social development forces its way through and shatters the dead, fossilized, political forms,"[4] then military metaphors are not simply appropriate for understanding class struggle but an essential resource for the development of a revolutionary praxis.

For Marx and Engels, the bourgeoisie and proletariat were "two great hostile camps" engaged "in a constant battle"—one in which the communists possessed "the advantage of clearly understanding the line of march, the conditions, and the ultimate general results of the proletarian movement." They described the factory system as one in which workers "are organized like soldiers. As privates of the industrial army they are placed under the command of a perfect hierarchy of officers and sergeants."[5] Elsewhere, in the first volume of *Capital*, Marx described an "industrial army of workmen under the command of a capitalist [which] requires, like a real army, officers (managers) and N.C.O.s (foremen, overseers), who command during the labor process in the name of capital." The centralization of labor within the factory creates a new, collective productive power "[j]ust as the offensive power of a squadron of cavalry, or the defensive power of an infantry regiment, is essentially different from the sum of the offensive or defensive powers of the individual soldiers taken separately." The factory creates "a barrack-like discipline," and the atrocious working conditions to which workers are subjected in the factory "[produces a] list of those killed and wounded in the industrial battle." Those workers who are deemed to be surplus continue to play an important role in capitalist accumulation as a "disposable industrial reserve army."[6] In the *Manifesto*, Marx and Engels had already insisted that the contradictory nature of capitalism ensures that "not only has the bourgeoisie forged the weapons that bring death to itself; it has also called into existence the men who are to wield those weapons—the modern working class—the proletarians." The struggle against capital, Marx argued, must "not be exclusively absorbed in these unavoidable guerilla fights incessantly springing up from the never ceasing encroachments of capital or changes of the market. . . . Instead of the *conservative* motto: '*A fair day's wage for a fair day's work!*' they ought to inscribe on their banner the *revolutionary* watchword: '*Abolition of the wages system!.*'"[7]

Hostile camps fighting a constant battle, the bourgeoisie organized the proletariat in factories as an industrial army as hierarchical as any military, while the communists among them followed along their own line of march, forging the working class-for-itself into a great historical weapon that must be wielded judiciously. For Marx and Engels, military metaphors were an appropriate and useful resource for the development of a revolutionary praxis. There is thus nothing particularly unique about Lenin's use of military metaphors in his writings. However, with the exception of Gramsci and his concepts of war of maneuver and war of position there is no other Marxist for whom military metaphors played such a significant role as Lenin.[8] This is most clearly illustrated in his theory of the vanguard party.

What Is a Vanguard?

Before I address how Lenin made use of the vanguard metaphor, I would like to examine the military context from which it originates. To do so, I make use here of the work of Antoine Henri Jomini and Carl von Clausewitz, two of the principal military theorists of the nineteenth century, to outline a military definition of vanguard that would have been familiar to Lenin. Their relevance for Lenin came indirectly through their influence, particularly Jomini's, on Marx and Engels and more directly through Lenin's own reading on the art of warfare.[9] According to Jomini and Clausewitz, a vanguard, or advanced guard, is a unit of a larger military force that marches ahead of that force in order to conduct reconnaissance of the terrain and the size, quality, and disposition of enemy forces: it is "capable of forming correct ideas as to the enemy's movements and of giving an accurate account of them to the general, thus enabling him to make his plans understandingly."[10] In so doing, the vanguard is able to determine the line of march most likely to accomplish the military force's goal, whether that be direct engagement with the enemy (e.g., identifying the point in the enemy's forces against which the assault is most likely to succeed) or retreat to avoid such an engagement and provide time and space for the military force to rebuild with the goal of ultimately returning to the offensive. In Clausewitz's words,

> Any force that is not completely ready for battle needs an advance guard to detect and reconnoiter the enemy's approach before he comes into view. After all, a troop's range of vision does not usually extend much beyond it range of fire. How unfortunate it would be if our eyes could see no further than our arms can reach!

Clausewitz identified two other functions for the vanguard: (1) the vanguard "will become the rear guard should the line of march be reversed," thereby protecting the withdrawal of the main force, and (2) "[w]hen the troops are in billets or in camp, the advanced guard takes the form of an extended line of lightly held pickets—the outposts."[11]

There is nothing particularly "modern" about the concept of an advanced guard and the functions it performs. What distinguishes the modern vanguard from advanced guards in previous historical periods is the specialized nature of the former. Clausewitz suggested that the dramatic increase in the size and complexity of, and dramatic changes in tactics employed by, military forces in the Napoleonic era required the use of a strong and permanent advance guard:

> Nowadays an army is no longer led into battle as a compact whole and by word of command alone, in order to settle the score more or less by dint of skill and bravery, like a large-scale duel. Today the peculiarities of the terrain and the general circumstances are

taken more into account. The battle is composed of a number of different parts. What used to be a simple decision has become a complex plan, and the word of command has turned into lengthy dispositions, based on time-tables and other data.[12]

Such a strong and permanent force "should be composed of light troops of all arms" (including dragoons, horse artillery, and irregular cavalry), some sappers and pontoniers, and a topographical officer, with "some of the *élite* troops of the army as a main body."[13]

Based on this overview, we can identify some characteristics that are and are not associated with the military vanguard: (1) a vanguard is a specialized unit or a set of units *within* but *at a distance from* a larger military force possessing a particular set of skills and resources necessary for it to perform specific functions; (2) given the configuration of forces making up the vanguard, it is clear that the vanguard is *not intended to engage the enemy on its own*. The vanguard must be far enough ahead of the main military force to perform its functions, but not so far ahead that it loses contact with that force; and (3) while the vanguard is a specialized body within the main military force, the vanguard *does not exercise command* of that force. It *directs* or *leads* by virtue of its concrete analysis of the enemy's forces and the terrain on which they are distributed, as well as by virtue of its evaluation of the most opportune point and direction of attack or the safest path of retreat.

Lenin's Use of "Vanguard"

Lenin made extensive use of the vanguard metaphor throughout his writings, applying it to multiple levels of analysis within the revolutionary movement in Russia. In the first place, and most fundamentally, Lenin applied the vanguard metaphor to the proletariat as a class. In the struggle against autocracy and for the bourgeois-democratic revolution, the proletariat was "the *vanguard fighter* for political liberty and for democratic institutions," the "vanguard fighter for democracy," "the people's fighting vanguard."[14] The proletariat occupied the position of vanguard for a number of reasons. In the context of the bourgeois-democratic revolution, Lenin argued that the bourgeoisie's commitment to that revolution was limited within certain boundaries consistent with creating and reproducing their class power; in other words, the bourgeoisie was likely to call a halt to the democratic revolution in midstream. At the same time, the specific character of late–nineteenth-century Russian capitalism was defined by the presence of a relatively small and dependent bourgeoisie, one that lacked the political capacity to lead the bourgeois-democratic revolution. The proletariat, on the other hand, in order to fulfill its mission of socialist revolution, required the most expansive form of democracy within which to develop the theoretical and organizational tools necessary for such a revolution. In addition, although the Russian working class was relatively small, its strategic location within the heart of the capitalist labor process and its high degree of concentration in the major urban centers gave it a political capacity out of proportion to its numbers. The way in which the conditions of existence of the Russian working class made it a particularly significant actor in the bourgeois-democratic revolution also explains why the peasantry, while committed to such a revolution as the means by which feudal relations could be overthrown, could not take a leadership role in this revolution; in contrast to the concentration of the proletariat, the localized and personalized relations characteristic of the feudal mode of production made it difficult for the peasantry to organize itself for revolution. It was essential, Lenin argued, that the proletariat-as-vanguard preserve its autonomy within the broader democratic movement, for it was this autonomy that allowed the proletariat to march ahead of the movement and thereby perform its vanguard functions in the first place:

> [T]he *merging* of the democratic activities of the working class with the democratic aspirations of other classes and groups would *weaken* the democratic movement, would *weaken* the political struggle, would make it less determined, less consistent, more likely to compromise. On the other hand, if the working class *stands out* as the vanguard fighter for democratic institutions, this will *strengthen* the democratic movement, will *strengthen* the struggle for political liberty, because the working class will *spur on* all the other democratic and political opposition elements, will push the liberals towards the political radicals, will push the radicals towards an irrevocable rupture with the whole of the political and social structure of present society.[15]

With the transition from bourgeois-democratic revolution to socialist revolution, the vanguard role of the proletariat was confirmed:

> The proletarian revolution is impossible without the sympathy and support of the overwhelming majority of the working people for their vanguard—the proletariat. . . . The class struggle waged by the proletariat for the sympathy and support of the majority of the working people does not end with the conquest of political power by the proletariat. *After* the conquest of power this struggle continues, but in *other* forms.[16]

While the support of the peasantry was essential to ensure the success of socialist revolution, its interests did not make such support inevitable; indeed, it was likely that a substantial portion of the peasantry, particularly the middle and rich peasants, their demand for land satisfied by the democratic revolution, would balk at going over to the socialist revolution. The poor peasants would have to be won over to socialist revolution by the one class objectively committed to that revolution—the proletariat.

Second, in addition to seeing the proletariat as the vanguard of the toiling classes in both the bourgeois-democratic and socialist revolutions, Lenin also applied the vanguard metaphor to the politically conscious element within the proletariat that identified with social democracy. In the years prior to the October Revolution, Lenin saw the Social Democrats as "the ideological vanguard of the proletariat" and asserted that the "politically conscious, advanced section of the class . . . is its vanguard."[17] The party became the particular organizational form through which the advanced workers could undertake their vanguard functions:

> [T]he advanced contingent, the organisation, must carry on all its activity among the masses, drawing from the masses all the best forces without any exception, at every step verifying carefully and objectively whether contact with the masses is being maintained and whether it is a live contact. In this way, and only in this way, does the advanced contingent train and enlighten the masses, expressing *their* interests, teaching them organisation and directing *all* the activities of the masses along the path of conscious class politics.[18]

The necessity of the party, Lenin argued, came from the fact that the spontaneous activity of the working class "represents nothing more nor less than consciousness in an *embryonic form*." This consciousness is embryonic as a result of the thorough penetration of bourgeois ideology throughout all aspects of social life, and even if we acknowledge the contradictory nature of this ideology it is still much stronger than its socialist counterpart: "[B]ourgeois ideology is far older in origin than socialist ideology . . . it is more fully developed . . . and it has at its disposal *immeasurably* more means of dissemination."[19] Lenin's famous statement in *What Is to Be Done?* that class consciousness must come from outside the working class, hence the need for a party grounded in revolutionary theory, is best understood not as a call for a party that *imposes* socialist ideology onto the working class but rather one that makes possible the full development of the embryonic consciousness of the proletariat.

Third, Lenin also made use of the vanguard metaphor in his discussion of soviets. The soviets first emerged during the 1905 Revolution and then again in 1917 as an expression of working-class consciousness and self-organization. Lenin thought that they constituted the means by which the working masses could wield power in the midst of a socialist revolution and following the defeat of the bourgeoisie and its allies in that revolution. As "an organizational form for the vanguard, i.e., for the most class-conscious, most energetic and most progressive section of the oppressed classes, the workers and peasants," Lenin argued, soviets were "an apparatus by means of which the vanguard of the *oppressed* classes can elevate, train, educate, and lead *the entire vast mass* of these classes, which has up to now stood completely outside of political life and history."[20]

> Soviets were also the best mass organization of the vanguard of the working people, i.e., the proletariat engaged in large-scale industry, which enables it to lead the vast mass of the exploited, to draw them into independent political life, to educate them politically by their own experience; therefore for the first time a start is made by the *entire* population in learning the art of administration, and in beginning to administer[21]

While the soviets had been conceptualized by Lenin as a form of social self-management by the workers and poor peasants, best expressed through his discussion of the Commune-state in *State and Revolution*, the subsequent devastation of civil war, imperialist invasion, and famine ensured that the party-form of the vanguard metaphor became relatively more important in the years immediately following the October Revolution. Lenin argued that the working class itself could no longer exercise power and perform its vanguard functions and that "it is only the advanced section of the working class, its vanguard, that is capable of leading the country." In this historical conjuncture, the Communist Party, as "the class-conscious vanguard of the working class" and "the revolutionary vanguard of the proletariat," was identified as the vanguard of the dictatorship of the proletariat:

> [O]nly the political party of the working class, i.e., the Communist Party, is capable of uniting, training and organising a vanguard of the proletariat and of the whole mass of the working people ... and of guiding all the united activities of the whole of the proletariat, i.e., of leading it politically, and through it, the whole mass of the working people. Without this the dictatorship of the proletariat is impossible.[22]

The multiple ways in which Lenin used the vanguard metaphor are not mutually exclusive, but rather express the dialectical nature of the relationship between class and party. An important feature of Lenin's analysis of this dialectic was his argument that the vanguard party should not be a mass party. The law of uneven development, he argued, applied just as much to the proletariat as to capitalism in its totality.[23] Although capital accumulation is predicated on the extraction of surplus value from a class possessing formal ownership of its labor power, that class does not necessarily experience this process of exploitation in a uniform way, nor does the development of a class consciousness recognizing the nature of this exploitation and the historical role of the proletariat in abolishing exploitation occur in a uniform manner; Lenin, for example, noted that "the metalworkers are the *vanguard* of the entire Russian proletariat." Lenin made a similar point with regard to the vanguard role taken on by the Party in the years following the October Revolution:

> [T]he Party, shall we say, absorbs the vanguard of the proletariat, and this vanguard exercises the dictatorship of the proletariat. . . . [T]he dictatorship of the proletariat cannot be exercised through an organisation embracing the whole of that class, because in all capitalist countries (and not only over here, in one of the most backward) the proletariat is still so divided, so degraded, and so corrupted in parts (by imperialism in some countries) that an organisation taking in the whole proletariat cannot directly exercise proletarian dictatorship. It can be exercised only by a vanguard that has absorbed the revolutionary energy of the class.

For this reason, if the party is to serve its vanguard functions it must restrict its membership to only the most class-conscious, most committed members of the working class. This is most famously reflected in Lenin's assertion that, in the period of intense repression that forced it to operate underground, the party must consist of "*professional* revolutionaries," but it is also expressed in his acknowledging the necessity for the periodic culling of Party membership, a process which was especially important following the October Revolution and the seizure of state power. Such purges, he argued, were essential to ensure that Party members were up to the specific tasks required of it at each historical juncture, which "will make [the Party] a vanguard that is more strongly bound up with the class, more capable of leading it to victory amidst a mass of difficulties and dangers."[24]

Just as in war, therefore, where the vanguard is a specially trained element of a much larger force and must be a certain distance ahead of that main force in order to perform its functions successfully, for Lenin there could be no conflation of party and class. At the same time, however, a vanguard which runs too far ahead of the main force is likely to lose communication with that force and thus fail to perform its functions successfully:

> One of the greatest and most serious dangers that confront the numerically small Communist Party which, as the vanguard of the working class, is guiding a vast country in the process of transition to socialism (for the time being without the direct support of the more advanced countries), is isolation from the masses, the danger that the vanguard may run too far ahead and fail to "straighten out the line," fail to maintain firm contact with the whole army of labor, i.e., with the overwhelming majority of workers and peasants. Without an alliance with non-Communists in the most diverse spheres of activity there can be no question of any successful communist construction.[25]

The risks associated with a vanguard that runs too far ahead of its main force go beyond simply interfering with or losing altogether its ability to perform its functions. Vanguards are not meant to take on the enemy's main force on their own, and so a vanguard that has run too far ahead of its main force runs the risk of being destroyed should it come into contact with the enemy's main force:

> Victory cannot be won with the vanguard alone. To throw the vanguard alone into the decisive battle, before the whole class, before the broad masses have taken up a position either of direct support of the vanguard, or at least of benevolent neutrality

towards it and one in which they cannot possibly support the enemy, would be not merely folly but a crime.[26]

It is in this context that Lenin argued consistently that the Party must always maintain organic connections to the proletariat.

It was the weakness of these organic connections that helped to explain why, in 1917, the July Days did not present an opportunity for a successful insurrection, as the Bolsheviks "still lacked the support of the class which is the vanguard of the revolution"; by September of that year, Lenin argued, the Bolsheviks had "the following of the majority of a *class*, the vanguard of the revolution, the vanguard of the people, which is capable of carrying the masses with it."[27] With the successful seizure of state power in the October Revolution, Lenin was especially concerned that the enthusiasm for socialist revolution among the workers and poor peasants not outpace the concrete tasks of the vanguard that had to, albeit reluctantly, make compromises necessary to consolidate Soviet power. There were, he argued, moments in which strategic retreat was necessary in order to rest and rebuild exhausted political forces with the goal of eventually returning to the strategic offensive. In contrast, for example, to those who opposed the Brest-Litovsk Treaty ending Russia's participation in World War I and who instead advocated for the initiation of revolutionary war, Lenin recognized that the peasantry, which made up the bulk of a newly emerging Red Army, would not fight such a war. Pursuing such a war thus threatened to undermine the essential task of winning the support of the peasantry for the consolidation of the new Soviet state. A similar concern lay behind Lenin's introduction of the New Economic Policy. Lenin recognized that the policies of war communism, particularly the forced requisition of grain, while deemed a necessity in the context of the extreme conditions of the Civil War, would turn the peasantry against the revolution if they were to continue after the end of that war; this was in contrast to those such as Bukharin, who saw war communism as expressing a fundamentally socialist form of economic organization. In each case, Lenin understood that to pursue "maximum" socialist policies before the mass of working people were fully prepared and committed to taking on such tasks would threaten the very existence of socialist Russia.

Finally, it should be noted briefly that a vanguard that lags behind the main force is no vanguard at all. Lenin was highly critical of those moments in the revolutionary struggle in which the Party was "lagging behind the spontaneous awakening of the masses."[28] In the midst of the 1905 Revolution, for example, a revolution that caught the RSDLP by surprise, Lenin called for a reorganization of the Party with special attention paid to rejuvenating its links with the proletariat:

> Our Party has stagnated while working underground. As a delegate to the Third Congress rightly said, it has been suffocating underground during the last few years. The "underground" is breaking up. Forward, then, more boldly; take up the new weapon, distribute it among new people, extend your bases, rally all the worker Social-Democrats round yourselves, incorporate them in the ranks of the Party organizations by hundreds and thousands. Let their delegates put new life into the ranks of our central bodies, let the fresh spirit of young revolutionary Russia pour in through them. . . . It will give us fresh young forces rising from the very depths of the only genuinely and thoroughly revolutionary class, the class which has won half freedom for Russia and will win full freedom for her, the class which will lead her through freedom to socialism![29]

The risk associated with what Lenin called "*tail-ism*,"[30] was that, by failing to provide a sufficiently strong and cohesive form of leadership, it provided an opening for petty-bourgeois forces—in the context of the bourgeois-democratic revolution—and counterrevolutionary forces—in the context of the socialist revolution—to win over elements of the proletariat and its allied forces and thus undermine the revolutionary project.

In employing the vanguard metaphor to both class and party while at the same time maintaining a distinction between the two, Lenin offered a complex dialectical analysis of the class-party relationship:

> Victory over capitalism calls for proper relations between the leading (Communist) party, the revolutionary class (the proletariat) and the masses, i.e., the entire body of the toilers and the exploited. Only the Communist Party, if it is really the vanguard of the revolutionary class, if it really comprises all the finest representatives of that class, if it consists of fully conscious and staunch Communists who have been educated and steeled by the experience of a persistent revolutionary struggle, and if it has succeeded in linking itself inseparably with the whole life of its class and, through it, with the whole mass of the exploited, and in completely winning the confidence of this class and this

mass—only such a party is capable of leading the proletariat in a final, most ruthless and decisive struggle against all the forces of capitalism. On the other hand, it is only under the leadership of such a party that the proletariat is capable of displaying the full might of its revolutionary onslaught, and of overcoming the inevitable apathy and occasional resistance of that small minority, the labor aristocracy, who have been corrupted by capitalism, the old trade union and co-operative leaders, etc.—only then will it be capable of displaying its full might, which, because of the very economic structure of capitalist society, is infinitely greater than its proportion of the population.[31]

Both class—that is, the proletariat—and party are vanguards, but the vanguard nature of each is dependent upon the emergence of an organic relationship between the two. Without such a relationship, neither can accomplish its historically defined mission.[32]

Can the Vanguard Be Saved?

Contrary to Lenin's dialectical use of the metaphor, in subsequent debates "vanguardism" has come to be associated with rigid or doctrinaire ideas of the Party exercising leadership over the people, dictating to the proletariat itself the "line of march." The origins of "vanguardism" lie not in Lenin's revolutionary praxis but in the leadership struggles within the Communist Party of the Soviet Union following Lenin's death. This is not to say that Lenin did not make statements that lent themselves to what became known as "vanguardism"; I argue that when he did so he qualified them in ways that undermine such an interpretation. When, for example, he responded following the 1905 Revolution to critics who attacked the conception of the party offered in *What Is to Be Done?*—that is, one that comes closest to the "vanguardist" model—Lenin wrote:

> [Their] basic mistake . . . is to treat the pamphlet apart from its connection with the concrete historical situation of a definite, *and now long past* [my emphasis], period in the development of our Party. . . . *What Is to Be Done?* is a summary of *Iskra* tactics and *Iskra* organizational policy in 1901 and 1902. Precisely a "*summary*," no more and no less.[33]

Later on, in developing the terms of admission to the Communist International presented to its Second Congress in 1920, Lenin argued:

> The Communist parties can perform their duty only if they are organized in a most centralized manner, are marked by an iron discipline bordering on military discipline, and have strong and authoritative party centers invested with wide powers and enjoying the unanimous confidence of the membership.

This argument, however, was presented as relevant "*[i]n this period of acute civil war* [my emphasis]."[34] In other words, Lenin's argument concerning centralization and military-style discipline was not a statement of principle but rather one grounded in the needs of a specific historical conjuncture. Lenin's refusal to fetishize organizational form was in stark contrast to the drive toward "bolshevization" of communist parties by the Communist International beginning at its Fifth Congress in 1924 as well as the affirmation of "socialism in one country" by the Russian Communist Party around the same time—that is, shortly after Lenin's death—that enshrined "vanguardism" as an essential component of what came to be known as "Leninism." This process was in fact a negation of Lenin's fundamentally democratic organizational principles.[35]

If Lenin's concept of the vanguard is to be meaningful in contemporary revolutionary struggles, it must first be freed from Soviet Marxism's "Leninism." First, an authentically Leninist perspective rejects self-proclaimed vanguards.[36] Just like a vanguard in its original military sense, which is a constituent element of a much larger force rather than an autonomous force acting on its own, a political vanguard must emerge organically from the subordinate classes and must constantly demonstrate through its actions that it is deserving of this label:

> It is not enough to call ourselves the "vanguard," the advanced contingent; we must act in such a way that *all* the other contingents recognise and are obliged to admit that we are marching in the vanguard.[37]

The emergence of a vanguard organization must be seen more as a process rather than an event, a process characterized by trial and error, victories and defeats over the course of protracted struggles. Second, an authentically Leninist perspective affirms that the vanguard nature of such an organization can be understood only within a specific balance of forces and a specific historical conjuncture. Lenin's admonition to the Fourth Congress of the Communist International that the organizational rules introduced at the Third Congress were "almost entirely Russian" and that "if by way of exception some foreigner does understand it, he cannot carry it out" is a powerful affirmation that there cannot be one particular organizational form of the vanguard relevant for all situations.[38]

In this context, it may be more fruitful to think of the vanguard more as a set of functions essential for the success of a revolutionary movement than a specific organizational form to be taken by that movement.[39] First, given the uneven development of class consciousness, the vanguard serves an undeniable educational function.[40] It is the means by which the subordinate classes can place their everyday struggles in a structural and historical context—to understand the terrain of struggle, as it were—and develop a sense of their own collective power. Second, the vanguard brings together a diversity of struggles and thereby allows for them to share experiences and draw lessons regarding strategy, tactics, and organization that are relevant both for specific struggles as well as for the broader revolutionary process. Finally, in light of the uneven development of revolutionary struggles, one essential function of the vanguard is to ensure a degree of continuity from one period of revolutionary activity to the next. The vanguard keeps the memory of historical struggles alive during periods in which the masses, either out of exhaustion, disillusionment, or fear of repression, pull back from the revolutionary process—in other words, the vanguard ensures that a revolutionary movement's retreat is orderly and preserves its ability to fight another day. It is the mechanism through which those past struggles can be evaluated critically and a reservoir of resources—strategic and tactical, organizational, symbolic, etc.—necessary for the next wave of mass struggles can be established.

These vanguard functions are especially important in the context of post-2008 struggles, which despite their intensification in recent years remain constrained by a lack of a broad, cohesive strategic framework. This is due, in part, to the challenges inherent in bringing together a diverse range of struggles at the level of a specific social formation, much less a global level. It is also due to a hard turn toward spontaneity following the collapse of the USSR by a considerable segment of the global Left, a shift that rejected the party form of organization as necessarily authoritarian.[41] While this perspective has some valuable insights—in particular the recognition of the diversity of movements and organizational forms associated with revolutionary struggles—it fails to recognize that these struggles, by themselves, will have at best *tactical* significance within a specific social formation or within the capitalist world system in its totality and, in the end, can be no more than *defensive* in nature. If these struggles are to take the *offensive*—that is, if they are to be fought on terms that are advantageous not to capital but to the mass movements of workers and the oppressed—there must be some way of bringing these diverse struggles together in a coherent manner. The vanguard would then be needed to evaluate the strengths and weaknesses of the enemy at specific moments in time and space, to best determine the line of attack, and to decide how these attacks should be organized. Conceptualizing the vanguard as a set of *functions* rather than a specific organizational *form* thus allows us to avoid the anti-Leninist tendency to fetishize organization, a costly error which led the international communist movement in the previous century to be mired in a substitutionist trap in which the calcified party came to speak on behalf of a politically demobilized class. At the same time, Lenin's theory of the vanguard allows us to develop the strategic unity necessary for the organized offensive against capital.

In highlighting the specifically military nature of the vanguard metaphor, it is clear that the longstanding "spontaneity versus organization" debate obscures what is in fact a dialectical relationship between the two. There can be no doubt that the prospects for revolution in the post-2008 era dictate an acknowledgment of the wide variety of social struggles, both in content and form, that characterize both specific social formations as well as the world capitalist system. At the same time, it has become increasingly clear that the necessity for some conscious strategic articulation—materially, organizationally, symbolically—of these diverse struggles calls for a "new political instrument" or "a party of a different type."[42] The purpose of such an organization is not to impose specific strategies, tactics, and organizational forms on popular struggles, but rather to facilitate their autonomous development and initiative; far from being an obstacle to the diversity and creativity of popular movements from below, the party is their very condition of success. By providing a space in which popular struggles can learn from each other, coordinate their activities, and move beyond a partial, localist understanding of politics to a more global one, the party is the concrete expression of the central role of *strategy* in revolutionary politics. "Rather than a single line of march in this asymmetrical warfare against capital," however, such a strategy is characterized by "guerrilla units functioning under a general line and understanding the need for unity in struggle for major battles."[43] The specific forms this new type of a party takes cannot be dictated in advance, but will be a function of the specific conditions of struggle out of which they emerge.

In the end, the revolutionary self-organization of the subordinate classes requires the existence of a vanguard. In the absence of such a vanguard, the political activity of the subordinate classes will remain fragmented and defensive in nature and thus incapable of achieving revolutionary social transformation. In contrast to the sterile "vanguardism" of twentieth-century "Leninism," however, an authentic revolutionary vanguard is not "a timeless elite but . . . the shock troops or front line of a mass movement" and thus cannot exist independently of that mass movement.[44] Lenin's uncompromising analysis of this dialectic between the vanguard and the mass movements of the subordinate classes is indispensable to contemporary revolutionary struggles.

Notes

1. See Tamás Krausz, *Recontructing Lenin: An Intellectual Biography* (New York: Monthly Review, 2015); Lars T. Lih, *Lenin Rediscovered: "What Is to Be Done?" In Context* (Chicago: Haymarket, 2008); August H. Nimtz, *Lenin's Electoral Strategy from Marx and Engels Through the Revolution of 1905. The Ballot, the Streets—or Both* (New York: Palgrave Macmillian, 2014); Nimtz, *Lenin's Electoral Strategy From 1907 to the October Revolution of 1917: The Ballot, the Streets—or Both* (New York: Palgrave Macmillian, 2014); and Alan Shandro, *Lenin and the Logic of Hegemony* (Chicago: Haymarket, 2015). This includes new editions of previously published works such as Neil Harding, *Lenin's Political Thought and Practice in the Democratic and Socialist Revolutions* (Chicago: Haymarket, 2009); Paul Le Blanc, *Lenin and the Revolutionary Party* (Chicago: Haymarket, 2015); and Marcel Liebman, *Leninism under Lenin* (Chicago: Haymarket, 2017).

2. It is characteristic of the sterile debate of "organization versus spontaneity" that has long plagued the world revolutionary movement.

3. Lev Kreft, "The Function of Metaphor in Marx's Theory," *Vestnik IMS* 1 (1988): 115–22, 118, and 116.

4. Friedrich Engels, *Anti-Dühring: Herr Eugen Dühring's Revolution in Science* (New York: International, 1939), 303.

5. Karl Marx and Friedrich Engels, *The Communist Manifesto* (New York: International, 1948), 9, 18, 22, 16.

6. Marx, *Capital*, Volume 1 (New York: Penguin, 1976), 450, 443, 549, 552, 784.

7. Marx, *Value, Price, and Profit* (New York: International, 1935), 61.

8. On Gramsci's wars of maneuver and position, see Daniel Egan, *The Dialectic of Position and Maneuver: Understanding Gramsci's Military Metaphor* (Chicago: Haymarket, 2017).

9. Azar Gat, "Clausewitz and the Marxists: Yet Another Look," *Journal of Contemporary History* 27 (1992): 363–82. N. K. Krupskaya, *Reminiscences of Lenin* (New York: International, 1979). In this regard, Lenin is known primarily for his 1915 reading of *On War*. See Donald E. Davis and Walter S. G. Kohn, "Lenin's 'Notebook on Clausewitz,'" *Soviet Armed Forces Review Annual* (Gulf Breeze, FL: Academic International Press, 1977), 188–229; and Jacob W. Kipp, "Lenin and Clausewitz: The Militarization of Marxism, 1914–1921," *Military Affairs*, October 1985, 184–91. More generally, in referring to Lenin Trotsky noted that "[m]ilitary stratagems always appealed to him." Leon Trotsky, *On Lenin* (Chicago: Haymarket, 2017), 265.

10. Antoine Henri Jomini, *The Art of War* (Westport, CT: Greenwood, 1977), 239.

11. Carl von Clausewitz, *On War*, ed. and trans. Michael Howard and Peter Paret (Princeton: Princeton University Press, 1984), 302.

12. Ibid., 303.

13. Jomini, *Art of War*, 239.

14. V. I. Lenin, "The Tasks of the Russian Social-Democrats," *Collected Works*, Vol. 2 (Moscow: Progress, 1961), 323–51, 336; *What Is to Be Done?* (New York: International, 1969), 78; "Revolution and Counter-Revolution," *Collected Works*, Vol. 13 (Moscow: Progress, 1962), 114–22, 120.

15. Lenin, "Tasks of the Russian Social-Democrats," 336.

16. Lenin, "Greetings to Italian, French, and German Communists," *Collected Works*, Vol. 30 (Moscow: Progress, 1965), 52–62, 60.

17. Lenin, "Revolution and Counter-Revolution," 115; "How Vera Zasulich Demolishes Liquidationism," *Collected Works*, Vol. 19 (Moscow: Progress, 1963), 394–416, 406.

18. Lenin, "How Vera Zasulich," 409.

19. Lenin, *What Is to Be Done?* 31, 42.

20. Lenin, "Can the Bolsheviks Retain State Power," *Collected Works*, Vol. 26 (Moscow: Progress, 1964), 87–136, 103–104.

21. Lenin, *The Immediate Tasks of the Soviet Government* (Moscow: Progress, 1970), 36.

22. Lenin, "Eighth All-Russia Conference of the R.S.D.L.P. (B.), Political Report of the Central Committee," *Collected Works*, Vol. 30, 170–88, 186; "The Role and Functions of the Trade Unions Under the New Economic Policy," *Collected Works*, Vol. 33, 184–96, 190; "Theses on the Fundamental Tasks of the Second Congress of the Third International," *Collected Works*, Vol. 31 (Moscow: Progress, 1966), 184–201, 185; "Tenth Congress of the R.C.P. (B.), 'Preliminary Draft Resolution

of the Tenth Congress of the R.C.P. on the Syndicalist and Anarchist Deviation in Our Party," *Collected Works*, Vol. 32 (Moscow: Progress, 1965,) 245–48, 246.

23. Ernest Mandel, "The Leninist Theory of Organization: Its Relevance for Today," in *Revolutionary Marxism and Social Reality in the 20th Century*, ed. Bloom, 77–127 (Atlantic Highland, NJ: Humanities Press, 1994); Mandel, "Vanguard Parties," in Bloom, 60–76.

24. Lenin, "Material on the Conflict Within the Social-Democratic Duma Group," *Collected Works*, Vol. 19, 458–74, 465; "The Trade Unions, the Present Situation, and Trotsky's Mistakes," *Collected Works*, Vol. 32, 19–42, 20–21; *What Is to Be Done?*, 107; and "Purging the Party," *Collected Works*, Vol. 33, 39–41, 40.

25. Lenin, "Role and Function of the Trade Unions Under the NEP," 192

26. Lenin, *Immediate Tasks of the Soviet Government*, 73–74.

27. Lenin, "Marxism and Insurrection," *Collected Works*, Vol. 26 (Moscow: Progress, 1964) 22–27, 23, 24.

28. Lenin, *What Is to Be Done?*, 127.

29. Lenin, "The Reorganization of the Party," *Collected Works*, Vol. 10 (Moscow: Progress, 1962), 29–39, 32–33.

30. Lenin, *What Is to Be Done?*, 52.

31. Lenin, "Theses on the Fundamental Tasks of the Second Congress of the Third International," 187–88.

32. Even when Lenin made use of other metaphors that on their face clash with the vanguard metaphor, they were tempered by his dialectical understanding of the relationship between class and party. For example, at times he referred to the party as a "'general staff'" (Lenin, "Letter to Iskra," *Collected Works*, Vol. 7 [Moscow: Progress, 1961], 114–17, 117), a metaphor implying command and thus closer to what came to known as "vanguardism," but he then qualified this metaphor in a way that allows us to reject such an interpretation: this "general staff" is one requiring "the *good* and *conscious* will of an army that follows and *at the same time directs* [my emphasis] its general staff" (ibid., 117). This is a "general staff" that *leads* but does not *command*, a situation consistent with the understanding of "vanguard" advanced here.

33. Lenin, "Preface to the Collection *Twelve Years*," *Collected Works*, Vol. 13, 94–113, 101–102.

34. Lenin, "The Terms of Admission into the Communist International," *Collected Works*, Vol. 31, 206–11, 210.

35. Paul Le Blanc, *Lenin and the Revolutionary Party* (Chicago: Haymarket, 2015). Liebman, *Leninism under Lenin*. Lenin's concept of democratic centralism, the critique of which is central to many Left arguments against "Leninism," was in fact developed after the 1905 Revolution to ensure that higher-level Party bodies were fully accountable to lower-level ones and to provide for full freedom for discussion and criticism within the boundaries articulated by the Party program as approved by

the Party Congress. As such, it was "part of a polemic against *too much* centralism, *too tight* an organizational structure and *too little* democracy" [emphasis added]: Paul Kellogg, "Leninism: It's Not What You Think," *Socialist Studies* 2 (2009): 41–63, 49.

36. Eagleton expresses this point in a slightly different manner: "elites are self-perpetuating whereas vanguards are self-abolishing": Terry Eagleton, "Lenin in the Postmodern Age," in *Lenin Reloaded: Toward a Politics of Truth*, ed. Budgen et al. (Durham: Duke University Press, 2007), 42–58, 47.

37. Lenin, *What Is to Be Done?*, 83.

38. Lenin, "Five Years of the Russian Revolution and the Prospects of the World Revolution," *Collected Works*, Vol. 33, 418–32, 430.

39. Mandel, "Leninist Theory of Organization."

40. For an analysis of Lenin's educational metaphors, especially the "test," see Derek Ford, this volume.

41. Michael Hardt and Antonio Negri, *Multitude* (New York: Penguin, 2005) and *Assembly* (New York: Oxford University Press, 2017). John Holloway, *Change The World Without Taking Power: The Meaning of Revolution Today* (London: Pluto, 2002). Ernesto Laclau and Chantal Mouffe, *Hegemony and Socialist Strategy* (New York: Verso, 1985).

42. Marta Harnecker, *Rebuilding the Left* (London: Zed, 2007), 83. Michael A. Leibowitz, *The Socialist Alternative: Real Human Development* (New York: Monthly Review, 2010), 161.

43. Harnecker, 162.

44. Eagleton, "Lenin in the Postmodern Age," 49.

Bibliography

von Clausewitz, Carl. *On War*. Edited and translated by Michael Howard and Peter Paret. Princeton: Princeton University Press, 1984.

Davis, Donald E., and Walter S. G. Kohn. "Lenin's 'Notebook on Clausewitz.'" In *Soviet Armed Forces Review Annual*, 188–229. Gulf Breeze, FL: Academic International Press, 1977.

Eagleton, Terry. "Lenin in the Postmodern Age." In *Lenin Reloaded: Toward a Politics of Truth*, edited by Sebastian Budgen, Stathis Kouvelakis and Slavoj Žižek, 42–58. Durham: Duke University Press, 2007.

Egan, Daniel. *The Dialectic of Position and Maneuver: Understanding Gramsci's Military Metaphor*. Chicago: Haymarket Books, 2017.

Engels, Frederick. *Anti-Dühring: Herr Eugen Dühring's Revolution in Science*. New York: International Publishers, 1939.

Gat, Azar. "Clausewitz and the Marxists: Yet Another Look." *Journal of Contemporary History* 27 (1992): 363–82.

Harding, Neil. *Lenin's Political Thought: Theory and Practice in the Democratic and Socialist Revolutions*. Chicago: Haymarket Books, 2009.

Hardt, Michael, and Antonio Negri. *Multitude*. New York: Penguin Books, 2005.

———. *Assembly*. New York: Oxford University Press, 2017.

Harnecker, Marta. *Rebuilding the Left*. London: Zed Books, 2007.

Holloway, John. *Change The World Without Taking Power: The Meaning of Revolution Today*. London: Pluto Press, 2002.

Jomini, Antoine Henri. *The Art of War*. Westport, CT: Greenwood Press, 1977.

Kellogg, Paul. "Leninism: It's Not What You Think." *Socialist Studies*, no. 2 (2009): 41–63.

Kipp, Jacob. W. "Lenin and Clausewitz: The Militarization of Marxism, 1914–1921." *Military Affairs* Oct (1985): 184–91.

Krausz, Tamás. *Reconstructing Lenin: An Intellectual Biography*. New York: Monthly Review Press, 2015.

Kreft, Lev. "The Function of Metaphor in Marx's Theory." *Vestnik IMS* 1 (1988): 115–22.

Krupskaya, N. K. *Reminiscences of Lenin*. New York: International Publishers, 1979.

Laclau, Ernesto, and Chantal Mouffe. *Hegemony and Socialist Strategy*. New York: Verso, 1985.

Le Blanc, Paul. *Lenin and the Revolutionary Party*. Chicago: Haymarket Books, 2015.

Lebowitz, Michael A. *The Socialist Alternative: Real Human Development*. New York: Monthly Review Press, 2010.

Lenin, V. I. *"Left-Wing" Communism: An Infantile Disorder*. New York: International Publishers, 1940.

———. *State and Revolution*. New York: International Publishers, 1943.

———. "The Tasks of the Russian Social-Democrats." In *Collected Works*, Volume 2, 323–51. Moscow: Progress Publishers, 1960.

———. "Letter to *Iskra*." In *Collected Works*, Vol. 7, 114–17. Moscow: Progress Publishers, 1961.

———. "The Reorganization of the Party." In *Collected Works*, Volume 10, 29–39. Moscow: Progress Publishers, 1962a.

———. "Preface to the Collection *Twelve Years*." In *Collected Works*, Volume 13, 94–113. Moscow: Progress Publishers, 1962b.

———. "Revolution and Counter-Revolution." In *Collected Works*, Volume 13, 114–22. Moscow: Progress Publishers, 1962c.

———. "On the Road." In *Collected Works*, Volume 15, 345–55. Moscow: Progress Publishers, 1963a.

———. "How Vera Zasulich Demolishes Liquidationism." In *Collected Works*, Volume 19, 394–416. Moscow: Progress Publishers, 1963b.

———. "Material on the Conflict within the Social-Democratic Duma Group." In *Collected Works*, Volume 19, 458–74. Moscow: Progress Publishers, 1963c.

———. "Marxism and Insurrection." In *Collected Works*, Volume 26, 22–27. Moscow: Progress Publishers, 1964a.
———. "Can the Bolsheviks Retain State Power?" In *Collected Works*, Volume 26, 87–136. Moscow: Progress Publishers, 1964b.
———. "Greetings to Italian, French, and German Communists." In *Collected Works*, Volume 30, 52–62. Moscow: Progress Publishers, 1965a.
———. "Eighth All-Russia Conference of the R.S.D.L.P. (B.), Political Report of the Central Committee." In *Collected Works*, Volume 30, 170–88. Moscow: Progress Publishers, 1965b.
———. "The Trade Unions, the Present Situation, and Trotsky's Mistakes." In *Collected Works*, Volume 32, 19–42. Moscow: Progress Publishers, 1965c.
———. "Tenth Congress of the R.C.P. (B.), "Preliminary Draft Resolution of the Tenth Congress of the R.C.P. on the Syndicalist and Anarchist Deviation in Our Party." In *Collected Works*, Volume 32, 245–48. Moscow: Progress Publishers, 1965d.
———. "Purging the Party." In *Collected Works*, Volume 33, 39–41. Moscow: Progress Publishers, 1965e.
———. "The Role and Functions of the Trade Unions under the New Economic Policy." In *Collected Works*, Volume 33, 184–96. Moscow: Progress Publishers, 1965f.
———. "Five Years of the Russian Revolution and the Prospects of the World Revolution." In *Collected Works*, Volume 33, 418–32. Moscow: Progress Publishers, 1965g.
———. "Theses on the Fundamental Tasks of the Second Congress of the Third International." In *Collected Works*, Volume 31, 184–201. Moscow: Progress Publishers, 1966a.
———. "The Terms of Admission into the Communist International." In *Collected Works*, Volume 31, 206–11. Moscow: Progress Publishers, 1966b.
———. *What Is to Be Done?* New York: International Publishers, 1969.
———. *The Immediate Tasks of the Soviet Government*. Moscow: Progress Publishers, 1970.
Liebman, Marcel. *Leninism under Lenin*. Chicago: Haymarket Books, 2017.
Lih, Lars T. *Lenin Rediscovered: "What Is To Be Done?" in Context*. Chicago: Haymarket Books, 2008.
Mandel, Ernest. "The Leninist Theory of Organization: Its Relevance for Today." In *Revolutionary Marxism and Social Reality in the 20th Century*, edited by Steve Bloom, 77–127. Atlantic Highlands, NJ: Humanities Press, 1994a.
———. "Vanguard Parties." In *Revolutionary Marxism and Social Reality in the 20th Century*, edited by Steve Bloom, 60–76. Atlantic Highlands, NJ: Humanities Press, 1994b.
Marx, Karl. *Value, Price, and Profit*. New York: International Publishers, 1935.

———. *Capital*, Volume I. New York: Penguin Books, 1976.
———, and Frederick Engels. *The Communist Manifesto*. New York: International Publishers, 1948.
Nimtz, August H. *Lenin's Electoral Strategy from Marx and Engels Through the Revolution of 1905: The Ballot, the Streets—or Both*. New York: Palgrave Macmillan, 2014a.
———. *Lenin's Electoral Strategy From 1907 to the October Revolution of 1917: The Ballot, the Streets—or Both*. New York: Palgrave Macmillan, 2014b.
Shandro, Alan. *Lenin and the Logic of Hegemony*. Chicago: Haymarket Books, 2015.
Trotsky, Leon. *On Lenin*. Chicago: Haymarket Books, 2017.

PART II

CENTERING THE BLACK LENINIST TRADITION

PART II

CENTERING THE BLACK FEMINIST TRADITION

Chapter 6

Elaborations of Leninism

Self-Determination and the Tradition of Radical Blackness

CHARISSE BURDEN-STELLY

On Stretching Leninism:
The Tradition of Radical Blackness and Racial Capitalism

According to the revolutionary psychiatrist and freedom fighter Frantz Fanon, Marxism required modification when applied to the colonial situation. "In the colonies, the economic substructure is also a superstructure," he analyzed. "The cause is the consequence. You are rich because you are white, you are white because you are rich. This is why Marxist analysis should always be slightly stretched every time we have to do with the colonial problem."[1] He further maintained that racial subjection could not be fully understood apart from capitalist exploitation: "The Negro problem does not resolve itself into a problem of Negroes living among white men but rather of Negroes exploited, enslaved, despised by a colonialist, capitalist society that is only accidentally white."[2] Fanon's corpus of works demonstrates that only through a rigorous analysis, trenchant critique, and vehement rejection of both racial *and* class antagonism can global conditions of dehumanization be upended. Following Fanon and drawing on Vladimir I. Lenin's *The Socialist Revolution and the Right to Self-Determination (Theses)*,[3] this chapter examines intellectual production in what I call the Tradition of Radical

Blackness that "stretched" Leninism by centering the exploitation, domination, and oppression of African-descended peoples. Lenin's position in this seminal work on self-determination, the national question, imperialism, and war extended the ideas of Karl Marx into the epoch of imperialism. In turn, twentieth-century radical Black thinkers updated and refashioned Leninism to theorize, analyze, and challenge what Cedric Robinson coined "racial capitalism."[4]

The Tradition of Radical Blackness can be understood as Black anti-capitalist thought and activism rooted in and attendant to local, national, and global anti-black political economies. This tradition theorizes Blackness as a special relationship to the capitalist mode of production; considers intraracial class conflict and antagonism; and strives for the eventual overthrow of racial capitalism. Informed by and engaged with real-world struggles, it encompasses African descendants' multivalent and persistent antisystemic and counterhegemonic challenges to material and discursive processes and practices that sustain exploitation, exclusion, dispossession, and domination rooted in racial and gender hierarchies. As such, it is systematically targeted, often through discourses of anticommunism, by statist and imperial authorities as extremism, authoritarianism, and/or terrorism to rationalize the use of extraordinary force, violence, and exception. Such an expansive tradition necessarily constitutes real and significant ideological, analytical, and conceptual differences, disagreements, and antipathies; however, these contradictions and antagonisms demonstrate the heterogeneous and complicated ways that freedom fighters from Esther V. Cooper to C. L. R. James, Claudia Jones to Kwame Nkrumah, struggled against Euro-American racial capitalism.

It is important to note that the Tradition of Radical Blackness is distinct from Cedric Robinson's "Black radical tradition," which emphasizes culturally encoded challenges to the racial and nationalist foundations of international capitalism.[5] As Robin D. G. Kelley argues, Robinson sought to "rewrit[e] the history of the West from ancient times to the mid-twentieth century, scrutinizing the idea that Marx's categories of class can be universally applied outside of Europe." Robinson believed that, instead of a radical rupture from feudalism in the Marxist sense, capitalism was a continuation of European feudalism's racialism that developed into an international system of exaggerated difference predicated upon slavery, imperialism, genocide, and violence. He posited that intra-European ethnonationalism transformed into even more pernicious forms of subjugation of non-Europeans as capitalism spread throughout the world. As such, the Black radical tradition names the "rebellions and expressions" of African descendants meant to challenge this system that, according to Robinson, Marxism misrecognizes through its universalization of European realities.[6] On his view, racialization is the transhistorical and structuring feature of international economic and social relations. As such, the most robust and significant Black radical challenges to exploitation and exclusion emanate from endogenous Black and African metaphysics and cultural forms.

By contrast, the Tradition of Radical Blackness conceptualizes racialization, especially its enunciation of antiblackness, as imbricated with the capitalist mode of production, understood as a unique world-historical formation in which both Blackness and radicalism inexorably threaten property relations, divisions of labor, and hierarchical economic relations that constitute the modern world system. Thus, attention to critical political economy, the capitalist foundations of racialization, and the discursive strategies that maintain and reproduce racial subjection are paramount.

My definition of racial capitalism likewise borrows, but is distinct, from that of Robinson, who conceives of racial capitalism as the continuation of "the social, cultural, political, and ideological complexes of European feudalisms"—that is, its "racial, tribal, linguistic, and regional" antagonisms—into the capitalist form that is unique primarily in its extension into "the larger tapestry of the modern world's political and economic relations."[7] In other words, the distinction between feudalism and capitalism is in the latter's internationalization of "the increasingly uneven character of development among European peoples themselves and the world beyond"; in the need to produce new historical agents and opportunities for accumulation; and in consolidation of race as the preeminent "rationalization for the domination, exploitation, and/or extermination of non-'Europeans.'"[8] Contradistinctively, I draw on Black communist and socialist thought to define racial capitalism as a historically discrete global political economic system of racial hierarchy and perpetual war constituting white supremacist accumulation, dependent extraction, imperial expropriation, labor superexploitation, and (neo)colonial absorption of capital risk.[9] In what follows, I will elaborate upon each of my formulation's constitutive terms.

Racial hierarchy is endemic to racial capitalism because, as historian Gerald Horne asserts, from the seventeenth century onward it was the ideological glue that held together disparate European nations and peoples and functioned as the rationalization for the confiscation of resources, land, and labor from those on the darker side of the color line.[10] As Walter Rodney reasoned, the enslavement of African peoples created the material conditions for colonialism, imperialism, and capitalist expansion, and these processes of domination inevitably led to the ordering of races based on discourses of superiority and inferiority.[11] Likewise, according to political theorist Adom Getachew, racial hierarchy "designates . . . processes of integration and interaction that produce unevenly distributed rights, obligations, and burdens." The "structural and embedded processes" and "institutional arrangements" of unequal integration, she continues, "create the international conditions of ongoing imperial [racial capitalist] domination."[12]

War and militarism facilitate the endless drive for profit by perpetually constructing threats, primarily in the racialized world, against which to defend progress, prosperity, freedom, and security. Likewise, the manufacturing of conflict facilitates and legitimates the mobilization of extraordinary violence to cheaply expropriate untold resources that make possible prosperity and privilege in the Global North. Moreover, the ruling elite and labor aristocracy in imperialist countries wage perpetual war to defend their way of life and standard of living against the racialized majority who, because they would benefit most from the redistribution of the world's wealth and resources, represent a perpetual threat to it.

White supremacist accumulation denotes the genocidal, violent, and rapacious processes of accumulation by dispossession, in conjunction with the unscrupulous, dishonest, and unethical practices, reserved for peoples and countries deemed racially inferior.

Dependent extraction entails the coercive removal or withdrawal of vital means of subsistence, such as liquidity and currency, by imperial powers, made possible by relations of economic dependence that transfer surplus value from underdeveloped nations to overdeveloped ones and turn weaker nations into extensions of foreign capitalist imperatives.

Imperial expropriation designates the seizure and confiscation of land, assets, material resources, property, bodies, etc.—what philosopher Nancy Fraser dubs "*confiscation-cum-conscription-into-accumulation*"[13]—set to work by international relations and regimes rooted in racially ordered imperialism.

Labor superexploitation can be understood as an economic relationship in which the intensity, form, and racial basis of exploitation differs little from slavery. Its effects are so extreme that it pushes racialized, particularly Black, labor effectively "below the level of sheer physical subsistence." Superexploitation constitutes a combination of direct exploitation, outright robbery, physical violence, legal coercion, and perpetual indebtedness. It stifles "the free economic and cultural development" of the Black masses "through racist persecution as a basic condition for maintaining" virtual enslavement.[14]

Finally, (neo)colonial absorption of capital risk describes the processes by which declining rate of profit and investment risk are largely externalized to and absorbed by nations, citizens, peasants, and workers whose position at the bottom of the national and international racial hierarchies renders them vulnerable to, and unable to defend against, such imposition.

Anticapitalists in the Tradition of Radical Blackness militantly opposed racial capitalism as I have defined it here. In doing so, they "stretched" Leninist concepts to illuminate the racialized brutality constituting their systemic realities. For radical Black thinkers, Leninism was far from a dogma to be mechanically applied; rather, it was an opening to a more finely tuned materialist analysis of anti-Black formations sutured to capitalist (super) exploitation.

Imperialism and the Tradition of Radical Blackness: Lenin and Du Bois on World War I

The related but distinct analyses of World War I offered by Lenin and W. E. B. Du Bois demonstrate how the Tradition of Radical Blackness nuances and revises Leninism. In "The Proletarian Revolution and the Renegade Kautsky," Lenin wrote the following about World War I: "The imperialist war of 1914–1918 is a war between two groups of the imperialist bourgeoisie for the division of the world, for the division of booty, and for the appraisal for the plunder and strangulation of small nations. This was the appraisal of the impending war given in the Basel Manifesto of 1912, and it has been confirmed by the facts."[15] This analysis is remarkably similar to that of Du Bois in "The African Roots of War," written in 1915.[16] Du Bois's articulation, however, is distinct in that racism, white supremacy, and the plunder of Africa feature prominently. For Du Bois, as Berlin sought its place in the sun and aimed to displace London in particular, the imperialist rivalry for the booty on offer *in Africa* drove the conflict. Both men agreed that World War I was a function of capitalism's historical development: "The war is not a product of the evil will of rapacious capitalists," Lenin argued, "although it is undoubtedly being fought *only* in their interests and they alone are being enriched by bit. The war is a product of half a century of development of world capitalism and of billions of threads and connections."[17] However, Du Bois expanded Lenin's conception by critiquing the anti-African foundations of capitalist expansion. He held that the struggle to the death during the Great War for African resources and labor had begun to "pay dividends" centuries earlier through the enslavement of African peoples, the subsequent conflation of color and inferiority, and the reduction of what was routinely referred to as the "Dark Continent" to a space of backwardness ideally suited for dispossession.

Regarding the winners and losers of World War I, Lenin assessed: "The present war is, on the part of both groups of the belligerent powers, an imperialist war, i.e., one waged by the capitalists for the division of the profits obtained from world domination, for markets for finance (banking) capital, for the subjugation of the weaker nationalities, etc."[18] Du Bois concurred that "with the waning possibility of Big Fortune . . . at home, arose more magnificently the dream of exploitation abroad," but he added the caveat that, by the twentieth century, white *labor* also sought to share in the "golden stream" of racialized expropriation. This "democratic despotism" allowed for the white working class to "share the spoil of exploiting 'chinks and niggers,'" which implicated not simply the ruling class but "the nation; a new democratic nation composed of united capital and labor"[19] that perpetuated racial capitalism across class lines. While Lenin claimed, "Each day of war enriches the financial and industrial bourgeoisie and impoverishes and saps the strength of the proletariat and peasantry of all the belligerents, as well as the neutral countries,"[20] Du Bois noted that the disrespect and dehumanization of the racialized toilers and peasants in the plundered colonies actually *mitigated* the exploitation and impoverishment of the white working class in imperial countries. This superexploitation allowed white workers to get a share, however pitiful, of "wealth, power, and luxury . . . on a scale the world never saw before"[21] and to benefit from the "new wealth" accumulated from the "darker nations of the world" through cross-class consent "for governance by white folk and economic subjection to them"—a consensus solidified through the doctrine of "the natural inferiority of most men to the few."[22]

Furthermore, while Du Bois affirmed Lenin's contention that "[i]t is *impossible* to slip out of the imperialist war and achieve a democratic, non-coercive peace without overthrowing the power of capital and transferring state power to *another* class, the proletariat,"[23] the former elaborated: "Our duty is clear. Racial slander must go. Racial prejudice will follow." He continued, "The domination of one people by another without the other's consent, be the subject people black or white, must stop. The doctrine of forcible economic expansion over subject peoples must go." In other words, the dictatorship of the proletariat must also be committed to the complete eradication of racial hierarchy; the latter did not automatically follow from the former. For Du Bois, then, it was not simply the proletariat, but also the darker peoples and nations of the world, who would challenge racial capitalism and its constitutive technologies of imperialism, colonialism, and war. This included Japan, China, India, and Egypt, in addition to "the twenty-five million grandchildren of the European slave trade . . . and first of all the ten million black folk in the United States."[24]

Du Bois's analysis of the roots of imperialism in exploitation and oppression falling along the color line is indicative of the capacious conceptual and political terrain inhered in the Tradition of Radical Blackness. In the period during and after World War I, Black radical thinkers engaged in a robust internationalist critique of the forces and structures of racial capitalism, in various configurations of struggle with, within, and sometimes in contention with, the organized socialist left. The example of Black Americans living under the rule of extreme U.S. racism, and its manifold technologies of repression and subjection, animated national and global debates about national oppression throughout the period. The conceptual apparatus of "self-determination" was one of the crucial terrains of theorization and ideological struggle. As Lenin often insisted, self-determination was a bourgeois ideal, but it was precisely imperialism's inability to grant it to the nations it oppressed that made it an important issue for Marxists. As the post-Versailles world coalesced around re-entrenched colonial oppression, so too did the conditions of Black national oppression intensify. Different theorists and political actors picked up and developed Leninist positions on self-determination and national oppression. In many cases, those immersed in the Tradition of Radical Blackness "stretched" the Leninist doctrine of self-determination with conceptual frameworks that merged with, but also predated and exceeded, orthodox "Marxist" theoretical language. The remainder of this chapter explores how diverse anticapitalist thinkers creatively employed concepts of self-determination in analyzing the material conditions at the intersection of Black national oppression and capitalist exploitation. In doing so, this essay excavates the ways that practitioners in the Tradition of Radical Blackness mobilize and transform revolutionary theory by centering the exploitation, domination, and oppression of African-descended peoples.

The Socialist Revolution and the Right to Self-Determination in the Tradition of Radical Blackness

In the midst of the Great War, Lenin published *The Socialist Revolution and the Right to Self-Determination (Theses)*, drafted between January and February 1916, which included nine theses:

1. Imperialism, Socialism, and the Liberation of Oppressed Nations
2. The Socialist Revolution and the Struggle for Democracy
3. The Meaning of the Right to Self-Determination and Its Relation to Federation
4. The Proletarian-Revolutionary Presentation of the Question of the Self-Determination of Nations
5. Marxism and Proudhonism on the National Question
6. Three Types of Countries in Relation to Self-Determination of Nations
7. Social-Chauvinism and Self-Determination of Nations
8. The Concrete Task of the Proletariat in the Immediate Future
9. The Attitude of Russian and Polish Social-Democracy and the Second International to Self-Determination[25]

Throughout the theses, Lenin meticulously theorized self-determination as an essential aspect of the struggle against capitalism and the realization of international socialism. In doing so, he rejected national chauvinism, support for World War I, arguments that self-determination and secession were impractical in the framework of capitalism, and failure to support federation as one step in the path to socialism. Those purporting to be socialists who supported such positions, he fumed, were "committing treachery to socialism" and behaving like "lackeys of the blood-and-mud-stained imperialist monarchies and the imperialist bourgeoisie."[26] The spirit of the theses, which were written in the context of imperialism—the highest stage of capitalism—monopolization, worsening material conditions for the majority of workers, the growth of militarism and war, and what Lenin perceived to be the overall sharpening of class antagonism,[27] animates the Tradition of Radical Blackness between World War I and the Cold War. This is not least because, throughout the twentieth century, such conditions, though distinctive in their appearance, continued to permeate the capitalist world system. However, through their engagements with *racial* capitalism and its particularly oppressive effects on African descendants, Black communists, socialists, and independent Marxists alike directly and indirectly reworked, specified, and modified Lenin's theses.

Harry Haywood

In the first thesis, Lenin writes: "Victorious socialism must achieve complete democracy and, consequently not only bring about the complete equality of nations, but also give effect to the right of oppressed nations to self-determination, *i.e.,* the right to free political secession. . . . Socialist Parties [must] prove . . . that they will free the enslaved nations and establish relations with them on the basis of a free union—and a free union is a lying phrase without right to secession."[28] Lenin would later acknowledge that, though he lacked "concrete information" about the situation of African Americans they undoubtedly fell under the purview of the National Question.[29] The long-time communist Harry Haywood was arguably the most vehement and protracted defender of the national character of Black oppression in the "Black Belt" of the United States. Drawing on Lenin's ideas in the theses and other writings, Haywood argued that the "Negro question" was a national question given the special suffering of African American people, the history of trans-Atlantic enslavement, and the failure of the Civil War to completely overthrow the feudal order in the U.S. South. Internally colonized under the yoke of capitalist imperialism, they were superexploited as racialized persons; subjugated as toilers and workers; imprisoned in plantation systems in the South through sharecropping, tenancy, and land dispossession; and extremely marginalized in the textile and other industries. Likewise, the Black masses occupied the worst forms of employment, endured the most dangerous and unhealthy work conditions, were paid unequal wages or went unpaid, and lacked even the most basic civil rights. As Haywood explained: "[T]he stifling effects of the race factor are most strikingly illustrated by the drastic differences in the economic and cultural status of Negroes and whites . . . Beyond all doubt, the oppression of the Negro, which is the basis of the degradation of the 'poor whites,' is of separate character demanding a special approach."[30] In other words, their condition was not a result of discrimination, but rather of national oppression.

In constituting the Negro question as a national question Haywood, like Lenin, was working in a world-revolutionary framework with capitalist exploitation and imperialism at the center. For example, Haywood characterized the relationship between Northern absentee corporate and financial entities and the Black Belt as "industrial imperialism" that included the financing of Southern plantations by Eastern banks' credit systems; the control of the majority of coalfields in the South by capitalist families like the

Mellons, Fords, and Rockefellers; and Northern financial institutions owning the natural gas and electric companies in the South.[31] However, Haywood augmented Lenin to underscore the "revolutionary strength of the Negro liberation movement" in throwing off the fetters of racial capitalism.[32] In his 1930 position paper "Against Bourgeois-Liberal Distortions of Leninism on the Negro Question in the United States," Haywood—reminiscent of Lenin's excoriation of Karl Kautsky's deviationism in "The Proletarian Revolution and the Renegade Kautsky"—took chauvinist white communists and Black communists such as Otto Huiswoud to task for their opportunism and revisionism. Referencing the reduction of the condition of U.S. Blacks to a function of racial discrimination, Haywood chided:

> The Bolshevik exiom [sic] that there is no difference in substance between open opportunism and opportunism covered by "left" phrases . . . [is] represented respectively by the chauvinist tendencies among white comrades and the "left" social democratic tendencies among Negroes. The chauvinist tendencies in the Party are rooted in a deep lack of faith in the Negro masses . . . which finds its political expression in an under-estimation of the liberation struggles of the Negroes. The proponents of this position consider the Negro movement not as an ally of the proletariat, not as a movement to be utilized in the interest of strengthening the class struggle of the latter, but as a factor detracting from pure proletarian class struggle, as something contradictory to the struggle. . . . On the other hand, the "leftism" among Negro comrades is a complete capitulation before the chauvinist position.[33]

Such a position, he argued, misrecognized that the struggle in the Black Belt was for *self-determination* and *national independence*.[34]

The "energetic" racist ideologies and policies in the United States, Haywood explained, resulted from the fact that Blacks and whites were not territorially separated as was the case in Africa and the West Indies. The ultimate aim of this racial superstructure was to conceal the class policies of the bourgeoisie which inhered in the national oppression and the super-exploitation of subject peoples, namely, Black people. In addition, "The epoch of imperialism . . . the political superstructure of which, according to Lenin, 'is a return from democracy to political reaction' reflects a similar retrogression in the realms of ideology." In the U.S. context, "further fusion of finance capital with remnants of the pre-capitalist form in Southern agriculture, which takes place in this period, is accompanied by a corresponding unity in the field of ideology."[35] Nonetheless, in the final analysis, the national character of Black oppression was rooted not in ideology, but in the difference in economic and cultural development between Blacks and whites and in imperial efforts to violently preclude the economic and cultural development of Black people. Such efforts aided in the perpetuation of Black superexploitation in Southern agriculture and in unskilled industry. Given this objective reality, the Black struggle was fundamentally a revolutionary struggle against *national oppression* and for the right to self-determination in the Black Belt.[36]

In using the condition of African Americans as the basis of his analysis, Haywood elaborated upon Leninism not only to explain the historical, material, and ideological development of racism in the United States in relationship to capitalist exploitation and imperialism—thus offering a theory of *racial* capitalism—but also to illuminate the struggle for Black liberation in the United States as an essential aspect of global proletarian revolution.

Doxey Wilkerson

Doxey Wilkerson was a Black radical who left his teaching position at Howard University in 1943 to become a "professional revolutionary" and to join the Communist Party USA. A theorist of, and activist against, racial capitalism, he, like Harry Haywood, applied Leninism to the special plight of African descendants. His 1944 pamphlet *The Negro People and the Communists*, in which he theorized the relationship between democracy, socialism, antifascism, and Black liberation in the context of World War II, resonated with Lenin's position on World War I. For example, in "Resolution on the War," published in *Pravda* in 1917, Lenin wrote, "It is *impossible* to slip out of the imperialist war and achieve a democratic, non-coercive peace without overthrowing the power of capital and transferring state power to *another* class, the proletariat."[37] Likewise, Wilkerson analyzed that a "powerful clique of American pro-fascists and imperialists" were mobilizing against the Tehran conference and its negotiations for peace in an attempt to prolong the war. This capitalist cabal, he continued, was attempting to "establish an oppressive fascist regime" in the United States to overturn the gains made by labor and African Americans, to preserve monopoly capitalism, and to crush the progressive masses at home and abroad. In doing so, they were aiming to emulate Hitler's "conquest of foreign markets through military aggression."[38] By emphasizing how monopoly capitalists were embracing fascism to undermine peace and prolong war in an effort to expand their overseas markets, Wilkerson fitted Lenin's analysis to the historical realities of World War II.

Both Lenin, in the context of World War I, and Wilkerson, in the context of World War II, believed that democracy was instrumental to beating back the forces of capitalist imperialism. In the second thesis of *The Socialist Revolution and the Right to Self-Determination,* Lenin wrote, "[J]ust as socialism cannot be victorious unless it introduces complete democracy, so the proletariat will be unable to prepare for victory over the bourgeoisie unless it wages a many-sided consistent and revolutionary struggle for democracy."[39] Focusing his attention on African Americans, Wilkerson argued that a durable peace could only be secured if this group was "brought quickly into the democratic national front." Because "the basic interests of the Negro and the nation as a whole" were inextricably linked, the realization of democracy necessarily entailed a struggle against *racism*.[40] Democratic rights for Black people, especially civil rights and job opportunities, Wilkerson enjoined, were instrumental to influencing not only the outcome of the war, but also the redistribution of wealth and resources thereafter. At the same time, the broader struggle for price control, rent control, abolition of the poll tax, the fullest use of war-manpower, and the election of a pro-Tehran Congress and president would help to ensure Black democratic participation.[41] Here, Wilkerson built upon Leninism to argue for democracy as a class-based *and* race-based imperative. Struggle on both of these fronts was essential to the eradication of racial capitalism, imperialism, and war.

Kwame Nkrumah

The ideas of Kwame Nkrumah, the father of continental Pan-Africanism, about a United States of Africa resonate with Lenin's position on federation expressed in his third thesis. Indeed, Nkrumah drew heavily on Lenin's writings, not least *Imperialism: The Highest State of Capitalism,* which influenced his equally important *Neo-Colonialism: The Highest Stage of Imperialism.* On federation, Lenin explained, "The aim of socialism is not only to abolish the present division of mankind into small states and all national isolation; not only to bring the nations close to each other, but also to merge them. And in order to achieve this aim we must . . . demand the liberation of the oppressed nations, not only in general, nebulous phrases, not in empty declamations . . . but in a clearly and precisely formulated political programme."[42] Lenin believed that national self-determination was essential to upending capitalism and that federalism, especially as an alternative to forcible subjection, was an acceptable path to democratic centralism.[43] Nkrumah took a similar position in his vision of a liberated and united Africa. As Adom Getachew explains, federation was an attempt to fix, spatially and institutionally, the indirect domination of former colonies by colonizing countries; to rectify the distortions of postcolonial sovereignty that resulted from international hierarchy and economic dependence; and to achieve economic and political redistribution.[44] Nkrumah believed that the liberation of individual African states was a prerequisite for freeing the masses from international and domestic capitalist imposition and for adopting socialism, which would unite the continent as a whole.

To promote federation, Nkrumah convened the Conference of Independent African States on April 15, 1958, for the eight African nations that were independent at the time. He sought to develop a coordinated program of trade, mutual cultural and educational cooperation, and support for liberation struggles throughout the continent. The conference also took a firm stance against colonialism, racialism, and imperialism.[45] Further, Nkrumah updated Lenin's critique of national division and isolation to condemn the arbitrary colonial bifurcation of the continent by the Sahara Desert, which undermined African unity. Moreover, given his belief in the unification of not just nations, but also African *people*, including trade unions, youth organizations, cooperative movements, against neocolonialism and imperialism, Nkrumah convened the All African Peoples Conference in December 1958. There, he stressed the interrelated necessities of national liberation, continental unity, and socialist transformation. The objectives outlined at the conference, in their focus on the needs of postcolonial Africa, particularized Leninism to African objectives. Participants emphasized an assault on colonialism and imperialism with Africans as the primary agents; the use of both peaceful means and force, depending upon the historical and material specificities of each country; coordinated efforts to achieve independence and freedom from Western powers; and rejection of racialism, especially South African apartheid and U.S. Jim Crow. Based on these principles, Nkrumah, borrowing from and innovating upon Lenin, strove doggedly toward the federation of African states; his efforts, though not fully successful, resulted in the formation of the Organization of African Unity in 1963.[46]

JAMES FORD

In his fourth and fifth theses, Lenin insisted that oppressed nations had the right to both self-determination and secession, and that the revolutionary proletariat in each country had the obligation to support "the colonies and

[the] nations that 'its own' nation oppresse[d]." Further, Marx's conceptions of internationalism and socialism, he explained, were predicated on the reality that "no nation can be free if it oppresses other nations . . . it was only in this way that Marx was able to urge the bringing together of the nations, not by force, but on the basis of a free union of the proletarians of all countries."[47] In thesis six he was even more direct, insisting that

> [s]ocialists must not only demand the unconditional and immediate liberation of the colonies without compensation—and this demand in its political expression signifies nothing more or less than the recognition of the right to self-determination—but must render determined support to the more revolutionary elements in the bourgeois-democratic movements for national liberation in these countries and assist their rebellion—and if need be, their revolutionary war—*against* the imperialist powers that oppress them.[48]

In *The Negro in a Soviet America*, co-authored with James S. Allen,[49] the prodigious Black Communist James W. Ford focused on the Black Belt in the U.S. South to concretize Lenin's position on self-determination in the United States. Ford argued that the upending of U.S. racial capitalism required the rebellion of the "oppressed nation" in the Black Belt. This "land revolution," precipitated by the oppressed Black national minority, required the support and participation of the "hundreds of thousands of white share-croppers and poor farmers" who were also subjected to the plantation and credit systems. Such collaboration, however, was only possible if whites abandoned their race prejudice and ideas of white superiority.[50] Extending beyond Lenin's demand that socialists support colonial and national liberation, Ford argued that the white working class must also "realize that the main responsibility for establishing working class unity rested upon their shoulders" and acknowledge that "for centuries the Negro people ha[d] been oppressed by white nations," which had led to a "deep distrust of all whites" among Black workers. As such, white workers must "figh[t] for Negro rights, figh[t] against race prejudice, [and] insis[t] upon equal treatment in all places for Negroes" so that Black toilers could begin to rely upon whites as comrades.[51] Here, the struggle against racism generally, and antiblackness particularly, was an essential part of the U.S. proletariat's demand for national liberation.

Further, while, like Lenin, Ford argued that as an oppressed nation, the "Negro revolution for land and freedom" in the U.S. South was an important *ally*—that is, secondary struggle—to the international proletarian revolution, his focus on U.S. racial capitalism gave Black liberation much more weight. He argued that it was the oppressed Black nation that would do the most to expropriate U.S. capitalists, for these reasons: First, "the power of the landlords and capitalists [was] threatened most of all in the Black Belt."[52] Second, only through the overthrow of the Old South and the establishment of a Black-led revolutionary government would Black *and* white laborers enjoy real freedom.[53] Finally, the realization of socialism in the United States would be fundamentally tested by whether the Black Belt republic was free to choose between federation with and separation from its former oppressor. To the latter point, Ford echoed Lenin in his insistence that "the free union of peoples on the basis of equality is possible only through free choice arrived by the majority of the people";[54] thus, a prerequisite for socialist society in the United States was respect for—and defense of—Black self-determination.

Sojourners for Truth and Justice

Lenin's seventh and eighth theses stress the necessity, in the "advanced countries," of struggle against chauvinism and nationalism, the rejection of participation in the imperialist war in "defense of the fatherland," and distinction between imperial violence and revolutionary violence.[55] The activism of the antiwar, anti-imperialist, and antiracist group, the Sojourners for Truth and Justice (STJ), founded in September 1951 by a national cadre of U.S. radical Black women, applied all of these principles, in the context of the Cold War, to the realities of Black Americans—especially triply exploited Black women. As the radical journalist and STJ founding member Charlotta Bass argued, independence from Great Britain in 1776 had yet to result in freedom for 15,000,000 African Americans, who "continued down the road of second-class citizenship." And, she added, "other American minorities who because of their alien background or national idiosyncrasies" were treated little better.[56] Here, she conveyed that in the United States, chauvinism, nationalism, and "defense of the fatherland" amounted to racial repression and marginalization. Thus, STJ militated against chauvinism in the form of anti-Black racism, nationalism in the form of anticommunism, imperialist war in Korea, and imperial violence against racialized people in the United States and throughout the world. The group sought to rally and organize Black women, wives, widows, and mothers to defend Black leaders who were being systematically victimized by the state, "legally lynched," imprisoned, hounded by U.S. authorities, and subjected to police terrorism.[57] They also condemned the loss of their sons in imperialist wars and the U.S. war machine's use of Black men to kill other oppressed peoples on behalf of the "fatherland" that systematically devalued and disregarded Black life.

In response, STJ organized a sojourn to the Department of Justice in Washington, D.C., from September 29 to October 1, 1951, during which they protested the national oppression of Black men, manifested in their subjection to lynching, beating, shooting, and structural unemployment. STJ also supported the revolutionary violence of "colored peoples" in Korea and elsewhere waged against U.S. imperialism. In 1952, the group continued its struggle at a conference for members on the Eastern seaboard. They rebuked U.S. chauvinism, nationalism, and imperialist war that sent their husbands, brothers, and sons abroad to undermine self-determination and reproduce national oppression; that appropriated astronomical sums "for the destruction and enslavement of other peoples," but that provided "no protection to the homes and persons of Negro citizens"; and that "refuse[d] passports to Americans who speak the truth."[58] Moreover, STJ expanded Leninism by specifying the ways that chauvinism, nationalism, "defense of the fatherland," and imperialism particularly affected the oppressed Black nation: it led to racialized terrorism, such as the bombing murder of Harry and Harriet Moore on Christmas Day 1951; state terrorism, like the wrongful conviction of the Martinsville Seven and Willie McGee; and imperial terrorism, like the draft of Black men into an unjust and unnecessary war.[59]

STJ added a critical element to Leninism in their analysis of anticommunism as a method of undermining self-determination by targeting and silencing those who rejected racial capitalism, imperialism, and warmongering. According to Esther V. Cooper Jackson, a Black Communist and comrade to many of the STJ founders, "The war drive of the rulers of America and their assault on civil liberties led to increased attacks upon Negro leaders and the Negro people as a whole. It matters not whether they are Communists, non-Communists or anti-Communists, Negro leaders are being persecuted as 'dangerous subversives,' threatened, jailed, deported, lynched." This anticommunist violence menaced not only African Americans, but also anyone who held ideas that were deemed "foreign" by the "thought police" and therefore dangerous. Anticommunism, as a particularly pernicious enunciation of U.S. nationalism, chauvinism, and imperialism, Jackson conveyed, was rooted in the government's "traditional two-facedness," which "indulge[d] in loud proclamations about democracy, equality and freedom and at the same time reveal[ed] in life a picture of great privilege and riches for the few owners of the national wealth and a miserable existence of poverty, ignorance and want for the millions." This was true "[e]specially in the South [where] the Negro people face[d] disenfranchisement, segregation, and Jim Crow."[60]

Furthermore, in their challenge to military buildup, aggression against other nations, and the Korean War, STJ provided an alternative political strategy to Black Cold War liberals[61]—"the rather avowed servants of the bourgeoisie"—who supported U.S. "imperialism and concentration [as] progressive."[62] The radical Pan-Africanist STJ founder Eslanda Robeson, for example, excoriated "[a]ppropriating billions of dollars for arms, making military treaties with Canada and South American countries, actually fighting wars, with money, men and guns in Greece, China, Indonesia and Indo-China, and fighting what we call a Cold War in Russia." As such, she asserted, a third party—namely the Progressive Party—was needed to upend U.S. imperial warmongering.[63]

STJ took up the task to "educate the masses," especially triply exploited Black women, "in the revolutionary spirit" promoted by Lenin, and supported the "freedom [of] *all* oppressed nations (*i.e.*, the right to self-determination),"[64] which included Blacks in the United States struggling against national oppression, Koreans struggling against the U.S. war machine, and all subject nations and racialized people suffering under the yoke of imperialism.

CLAUDIA JONES

In his final thesis, Lenin describes how the formal recognition of the right to self-determination of nations at the International Socialist Congress convened in London in 1896 needed to be updated to reference:

1. The urgency of self-determination under imperialism

2. The politically conditional nature and class content of demands for political democracy

3. The necessity of distinguishing between concrete tasks of those in oppressing and those in oppressed nations

4. The hypocritical recognition of self-determination by opportunists

5. The identity of chauvinists who fail to champion freedom of secession for colonies and nations oppressed by "their own" nations

6. The "necessity of subordinating the struggle for this demand, as well as for all the fundamental demands of political democracy, to the immediate revolutionary mass struggle for the overthrow of the bourgeois governments and for the achievement of socialism."

These supplements helped to guard against "involuntary support [for] the most dangerous chauvinism and opportunism of the Great Power nations."[65] In a similar fashion, and with similar points in mind, Claudia Jones drew upon the condition of the oppressed Black nation in the United States to defend self-determination and to excoriate deviationism. She argued that increasing political repression of African Americans by the government required an updating of and recommitment to the Black Belt's right to self-determination. In the context of encroaching U.S. fascism, the attack of "Big Business" on gains made in industry by Black workers during World War II, and the increase in lynching and other antiblack attacks, it was important to reemphasize the struggle for civil rights as one step toward the realization of Black liberation from *national* oppression.[66] Here, following Lenin, she argued for the urgent need for self-determination in the Black Belt given the extant realities of U.S. imperialism.

In the 1930s, Jones reminded, the Communist position on the Negro question as a special question that required a systematic struggle against white supremacy and white chauvinism and as a national question that theorized U.S. Blacks as oppressed by imperial forces, put the CPUSA at the forefront of the struggle against racial capitalism.[67] However, much like the Polish Social-Democrats during World War I, Earl Browder offered up a revisionist position in 1944—one that distorted the teachings of Lenin who, in 1913, made "a *direct* reference to the Negro people as an *oppressed nation*."[68] Browder contended that U.S. Blacks desired full integration into U.S. society, not separation.[69] Jones held that Browder's main fallacy was his conflation of separation with self-determination. On the contrary, she corrected, a rigorous understanding of the historical and material conditions of U.S. Blacks showed that "integration [could not] be considered a substitute for the right to self-determination," that "National liberation [was] not synonymous with integration," and that "the two concepts [were not] mutually exclusive."[70] Here, akin to Lenin, Jones insisted upon an understanding of the *politically conditional* nature and class content of demands for political democracy—in this case, integration. Additionally, Jones demonstrated that

Browder's failure to champion the right of the Black Belt to self-determination amounted to national chauvinism.

Just as Lenin insisted on clarity between the concrete tasks of those in oppressing versus those in oppressed nations, so too did Jones distinguish between Black people in the North whose objective reality was that of a racial minority in the oppressing nation, and those in the Black Belt who were an oppressed nation. For Blacks in the North, whose "problems [were] akin to those of an oppressed national minority," the fight was for *equal rights* and was primarily being waged by the presence of a large and growing Black proletariat that provided the critical link between the broader working class and the toilers in the Black Belt. In the latter, by contrast the struggle was for *emancipation*—to wipe out the economic, political, and social survival of slavery and to enforce equal rights through the exercise of the right to self-determination. Self-determination, though, did not exclude "the struggle for partial demands" that aided "the class struggle against exploitation."[71] Furthermore, Jones argued, the objective reality of workers in the Black Belt demonstrated that they desired self-determination, that they abhorred their superexploited status under Jim Crow, and that the ideology of white supremacy denied them full freedom and equality. Failure to acknowledge this reality was to deny the obligation of the working class to struggle for conditions in which Blacks could make their own choice regarding national liberation.[72] In the final analysis, Jones clarified, what distinguished Leninists from "reactionary Social-Democrats"—like those Lenin condemned in his ninth thesis—was precisely the latter's rejection, in the name of internationalism, of the right of oppressed peoples to self-determination.

Jones, expanding and updating Lenin, defended self-determination in the Black Belt as a guiding principle, as a recognition of the concrete stage of the Black liberation movement at the time, and as the basis for building a strong Black and white worker's alliance. "The goal of national self-determination," she averred, "should serve as a beacon to the day-to-day struggles for Negro rights and should serve to hasten the realization of the right to self-determination."[73]

Lenin and Black Liberation

Scholars operating in the Tradition of Radical Blackness, including W. E. B. Du Bois, Claudia Jones, Kwame Nkrumah, and Eslanda Robeson, revised, refashioned, and remade Leninism to theorize and analyze the structural and material realities of those racialized as Black in Africa, the United States, the Caribbean, and throughout the diaspora. By centering the conditions, dilemmas, and lived experiences of those on the darkest side of the color line, they offered a fundamental challenge to racial capitalism, a racist and war-bound global system of white supremacist accumulation, dependent extraction, imperial expropriation, and labor superexploitation. These thinkers worked with and beyond Leninism to innovate ways to understand the racialized contours of issues ranging from self-determination to federation. Elaborations of Leninism in the Tradition of Radical Blackness remain exceedingly relevant to explaining the ubiquity, reproduction, and durability of race and class antagonisms and the manifold catastrophes wrought by the endurance of imperialism and racial capitalism.

Notes

1. Frantz Fanon, *The Wretched of the Earth* (New York: Penguin Book, 1963), 30–31.
2. Frantz Fanon, *Black Skin, White Masks* (New York: Grove Press, 1967), 202.
3. Vladimir I. Lenin, "The Socialist Revolution and the Right to Self-Determination (Theses)," in *Lenin on the National and Colonial Questions: Three Articles* (Peking: Foreign Languages Press, 1967).
4. Cedric Robinson, *Black Marxism: The Making of the Black Radical Tradition* (London: Zed Books, 1983).
5. Ibid.
6. Robin D. G. Kelley, "What Did Cedric Robinson Mean by Racial Capitalism?" *Boston Review*, January 12, 2017, http://bostonreview.net/race/robin-d-g-kelley-what-did-cedric-robinson-mean-racial-capitalism.
7. Robinson, *Black Marxism*, 10.
8. Ibid., 26–27.
9. For my explication of the U.S. mode of racial capitalism, see Charisse Burden-Stelly, "Modern U.S. Racial Capitalism: Some Theoretical Insights," *Monthly Review* 72, no. 3 (July–August 2020): https://monthlyreview.org/2020/07/01/modern-u-s-racial-capitalism/.
10. Gerald Horne, *The Apocalypse of Settler Colonialism: The Roots of Slavery, White Supremacy and Capitalism in North America and the Caribbean in the 17th Century* (New York: Monthly Review Press, 2018).
11. Walter Rodney, *How Europe Underdeveloped Africa* (London: Bogle-L'Ouverture Publications, 1972).
12. Adom Getachew, *Worldmaking after Empire: The Rise and Fall of Self-Determination* (Princeton: Princeton University Press, 2019), 32–33.

13. Nancy Fraser, "Expropriation and Exploitation in Racialized Capitalism," *Critical Historical Studies* 3, no. 1 (Spring 2016): 166–67.
14. Harry Haywood, *Negro Liberation* (Chicago: Liberator Press, 1976), 37, 139.
15. Vladimir I. Lenin, "The Proletarian Revolution and the Renegade Kautsky," in *Lenin: Selected Works in Three Volumes, July 1918 to March 1923*, vol. 3 (New York: International Publishers, 1967), 92.
16. W. E. B. Du Bois, "The African Roots of War," *The Atlantic Monthly* 115 (May 1915): 707–14.
17. Vladimir I. Lenin, "The Task of the Proletariat in Our Revolution," in *Lenin: Selected Works in Three Volumes, March 1917 to June 1918*, vol. 2 (New York: International Publishers, 1967), 32.
18. Vladimir I. Lenin, "Resolution on the War," in *Lenin: Selected Works in Three Volumes, July 1918 to March 1923*, vol. 3 (New York: International Publishers, 1967), 90.
19. Du Bois, "African Roots of War," 709.
20. Lenin, "Resolution on the War," 90.
21. Du Bois, "African Roots of War," 709.
22. Ibid., 709–10.
23. Lenin, "The Task of the Proletariat," 32.
24. Du Bois, "African Roots of War," 714.
25. Lenin, "The Socialist Revolution," 1–19.
26. Ibid., 2, 16.
27. Ibid., 1–2.
28. Ibid., 2.
29. Ibid., 21.
30. Haywood, *Negro Liberation*, 46–48.
31. Ibid., 55–59.
32. Harry Haywood, "Against Bourgeois-Liberal Distortions of Leninism on the Negro Question in the United States," *The Communist* (August 1930), 694.
33. Ibid., 695.
34. Ibid., 694.
35. Ibid., 699.
36. Ibid., 701.
37. Lenin, "Resolution on the War," 32.
38. Doxey Wilkerson, *The Negro People and the Communists* (New York: Workers Library Publishers, 1944), 11.
39. Lenin, "The Socialist Revolution," 2.
40. Wilkerson, *The Negro People*, 13–14.
41. Ibid., 17.
42. Lenin, "The Socialist Revolution," 6.
43. Ibid.

44. Getachew, *Worldmaking after Empire*, 108, 113, 141.
45. Kwame Nkrumah, *Revolutionary Path* (London: Panaf Books, 1967), 125–29.
46. Ibid., 130–31.
47. Lenin, "The Socialist Revolution," 10.
48. Ibid., 13.
49. James W. Ford and James S. Allen, *The Negro in a Soviet America* (New York: Workers Library Publishers, 1935).
50. Ibid., 25–26.
51. Ibid., 30.
52. Ibid., 29.
53. Ibid., 26.
54. Ibid., 32.
55. Lenin, "The Socialist Revolution," 13–16.
56. Charlotta A. Bass, "The 1950 Congressional Campaign," in *Forty Years: Memoirs from the Pages of a Newspaper* (Los Angeles: Charlotta A. Bass, 1960), 174.
57. 58. "Digest of Proceedings [1951]," box 13, folder 5, Louise Thompson Patterson Papers (869), Stuart A. Rose Manuscript, Archives, and Rare Books Library, Emory University [LTP papers hereafter]. Also see Keith Gilyard, *Louise Thompson Patterson: A Life of Struggle for Justice* (Durham: Duke University Press, 2017), 162–81.
59. "Our Cup Runneth Over: Statement Issued by the Sojourners for Truth and Justice, Relative to the Murder by Bombing of Mr. and Mrs. Harry T. Moore of Mims Florida [1951]," box 13, folder 2, LTP Papers.
60. Esther Cooper Jackson, *This Is My Husband: Fighter for His People, Political Refugee* (Brooklyn: National Committee to Defend Negro Leadership, 1953), 32–34.
61. See Charisse Burden-Stelly, "Black Cold War Liberalism as an Agency Reduction Formation during the Late 1940s and Early 1950s," *International Journal of Africana Studies* 19, no. 2 (2018): 77–130.
62. Lenin, "The Socialist Revolution," 14.
63. 3. Barbara Ransby, *Eslanda: The Large and Unconventional Life of Mrs. Paul Robeson* (New Haven: Yale University Press, 2013).
64. Lenin, "The Socialist Revolution," 15.
65. Ibid., 18–19.
66. Claudia Jones, "On the Right to Self-Determination for the Negro People in the Black Belt," in *Claudia Jones: Beyond Containment* (Boulder: Lynne Rienner, 2011), 60–61.
67. Ibid., 62.
68. Ibid., 64.
69. Ibid., 65.
70. Ibid., 66.
71. Ibid., 66–67.

72. Ibid., 67–68.
73. Ibid., 70.

Bibliography

Bass, Charlotta A. *Forty Years: Memoirs from the Pages of a Newspaper.* Los Angeles: Charlotta A. Bass, 1960.

Burden-Stelly, Charisse. "Black Cold War Liberalism as an Agency Reduction Formation during the Late 1940s and Early 1950s." *International Journal of Africana Studies* 19, no. 2 (2018): 77–130.

———. "Modern U.S. Racial Capitalism: Some Theoretical Insights." *Monthly Review* 72, no. 3 (July–August 2020). https://monthlyreview.org/2020/07/01/modern-u-s-racial-capitalism/.

Davies, Carole Boyce, ed. *Claudia Jones: Beyond Containment.* Boulder: Lynne Rienner, 2011).

"Digest of Proceedings [1951]." Box 13, folder 5, Louise Thompson Patterson Papers (869), Stuart A. Rose Manuscript, Archives, and Rare Books Library, Emory University.

Du Bois, W. E. B. "The African Roots of War." *The Atlantic Monthly* 115 (May 1915): 707–14.

Fanon, Frantz. *The Wretched of the Earth.* New York: Penguin Book, 1963.

———. *Black Skin, White Masks.* New York: Grove Press, 1967.

Ford, James W., and James S. Allen. *The Negro in a Soviet America.* New York: Workers Library, 1935.

Fraser, Nancy. "Expropriation and Exploitation in Racialized Capitalism." *Critical Historical Studies* 3, no. 1 (Spring 2016): 163–78.

Getachew, Adom. *Worldmaking after Empire: The Rise and Fall of Self-Determination.* Princeton: Princeton University Press, 2019.

Gilyard, Keith. *Louise Thompson Patterson: A Life of Struggle for Justice.* Durham: Duke University Press, 2017.

Haywood, Harry. "Against Bourgeois-Liberal Distortions of Leninism on the Negro Question in the United States." *The Communist* (August 1930): 694–712.

———. *Negro Liberation.* Chicago: Liberator Press, 1976.

Horne, Gerald. *The Apocalypse of Settler Colonialism: The Roots of Slavery, White Supremacy and Capitalism in North America and the Caribbean in the 17th Century.* New York: Monthly Review Press, 2018.

Jackson, Esther Cooper. *This Is My Husband: Fighter for His People, Political Refugee.* Brooklyn: National Committee to Defend Negro Leadership, 1953.

Kelley, Robin D. G. "What Did Cedric Robinson Mean by Racial Capitalism?" *Boston Review,* January 12, 2017. http://bostonreview.net/race/robin-d-g-kelley-what-did-cedric-robinson-mean-racial-capitalism.

Lenin, Vladimir I. *Lenin: Selected Works in Three Volumes, March 1917 to June 1918*, vol. 2. New York: International Publishers, 1967).
———. *Lenin: Selected Works in Three Volumes, July 1918 to March 1923*, vol. 3. New York: International Publishers, 1967.
———. *Lenin on the National and Colonial Questions: Three Articles*. Peking: Foreign Languages Press, 1967.
McDuffie, Erik. *Sojourning for Freedom: Black Women, American Communism, and the Making of Black Left Feminism*. Durham: Duke University Press, 2011.
Nkrumah, Kwame. *Revolutionary Path*. London: Panaf Books, 1967.
"Our Cup Runneth Over: Statement Issued by the Sojourners for Truth and Justice, Relative to the Murder by Bombing of Mr. and Mrs. Harry T. Moore of Mims Florida [1951]." Box 13, folder 2, Louise Thompson Patterson Papers (869), Stuart A. Rose Manuscript, Archives, and Rare Books Library, Emory University.
Ransby, Barbara. *Eslanda: The Large and Unconventional Life of Mrs. Paul Robeson*. New Haven: Yale University Press, 2013.
Robinson, Cedric, *Black Marxism: The Making of the Black Radical Tradition*. London: Zed Books, 1983.
Rodney, Walter. *How Europe Underdeveloped Africa*. London: Bogle-L'Ouverture Publications, 1972.
Wilkerson, Doxey. *The Negro People and the Communists*. New York: Workers Library Publishers, 1944.

Chapter 7

Black Leninist Internationalism

The Anticolonial Center

ROBERT R. MACLEAN

Black Marxism in the Mid-twentieth Century

In Mike Davis's recent essay collection *Old Gods, New Enigmas: Marx's Lost Theory*, he notes in passing that around 1968, when he became active in communist reading groups in Southern California, almost no one in that circle of radicals had much more than a passing knowledge of Marx and Marxism, let alone Leninist revolutionary theory. The problem was not confined to the upstart "New" leftists. In fact, "[t]he *only* member of the L.A. Party,[1] young or old, who seemed to have a serious understanding of Marx, and indeed was reading the *Werke* in German, was Angela Davis, and she was fighting too many important battles to have time to tutor the rest of us" (emphasis added). Davis had only months earlier returned from Frankfurt, having told her planned dissertation advisor, Theodor W. Adorno, that political events in the United States made it necessary for her to go back there. The "furiously burning" 1965 rebellions in the Watts neighborhood in Los Angeles and across the country made it clear that a "new Black militancy" was on the move and Davis could see it clearly even from Germany. "Everywhere there were upheavals," she writes in her *Autobiography*, composed of organized groups "formed to defend the special interests of

Black people." Upon her return from Frankfurt, she continued her studies at the University of California San Diego with Herbert Marcuse, while being at the same time involved in the Black Panther Party, CPUSA, and the Che-Lumumba Club (a communist youth organization in Los Angeles). It was true that Davis at the time was too engaged in Black struggle to bring her other, mostly white comrades up to speed on the philosophical matters of Marxism and Leninism. However, Mike Davis's remark about Angela Davis's philosophical and political expertise, well known and justly celebrated in leftist circles, points toward a possible and quite dramatic reframing of the historiography of the Left, and not just in the United States, but in the imperialist core more generally.[2]

This chapter argues that there is a moment of Black Leninism that to a certain extent spans, and gives contours to, the short twentieth century.[3] The mid-twentieth century is defined by the struggles (over, for, and against) Black Leninism. The centrality of Black liberatory struggle to histories of socialist agitation, on the one hand, and anti-imperialist geopolitical struggle, on the other, is, however, significantly obscured by the "libidinal economy," the affective and ideological contours, of anti-Black racism.[4] In the academic discipline of history, for example, the long history of Black struggles for liberation, meticulously charted decades earlier by such luminaries as Ida B. Wells-Barnet, W. E. B. Du Bois, and C. L. R. James, among many others, only became conceptually available to the broader (white) field after the tumult and fury of the revolutionary wave, or "Second Reconstruction," of the 1960s and 1970s. Moreover, U.S. political culture is organized around massive amnesiac constructions that work to erase the reality of historical rupture and struggle and replace it with a mythology of democratic fulfillment and transcendence. Thus, it should be no surprise that the "centrality," the place of prominence of Black Leninist struggle against imperialism in twentieth-century history, has been most often relegated to a subterranean current, to the background, the barely audible rhythm that nonetheless sets the pace, and the terms, of revolutionary optimism the world over. On the other hand, moments where Black Leninism—the revolutionary assault on imperialism's entire "racial-economic" structure—was made especially explicit have suffered from active and passive erasure. For example, the "We Charge Genocide" campaign Black communists brought to the UN in its early years laid bare the contradiction between the rhetorical idealism of the new U.S.-led world order and its structural reliance on obscene and brutal violence. It is no wonder that it rarely appears prominently in "mainstream" narratives of U.S. inclusive democratic expansion. One of the most prominent examples of the juncture I refer to as Black Leninism is the debate over the Black Belt thesis, which I will discuss later in this chapter. That debate animated ideological struggle within the CPUSA for decades and its abandonment is a key event for later debates among communists about the party's alleged "revisionism."

Black Leninists agreed that there will be no escape from racism and a repeatedly resurgent doctrine of white supremacy without a revolutionary solution that would involve overcoming imperialism in the capitalist core and in the colonies. To put a fine point on it, this is not because racism is a useful technology for capitalists seeking to divide the working class—although that is true. It's because racism, colonialism, and national oppression are integral features of capitalism, especially exacerbated under conditions of imperialism, which in Leninist terms designates a global system for inter-bourgeois competition over resources, markets, and trade routes. As a thesis and a program, Black Leninism is therefore a *re*statement of the subject of Black communism that insists on the historiographic and conceptual overlap of mid-century Black struggle and Marxism-Leninism. It also insists that this juncture, in turn, is central to the historiography of twentieth-century communism. (Put simply, one cannot understand "Leninism" without appreciating the centrality of Black anticolonial struggle and the liberation struggles of all oppressed nations.)

Mainstream historiography (or what professional historians call "the discipline") has only quite recently begun to take up the problematic of capitalism's relation to slavery, racial formation, and state racism.[5] They are more than a half-century behind Black radical historians such as W. E. B. Du Bois or Walter Rodney. In *Black Reconstruction* (1935), Du Bois demonstrated that the enslaved were indeed workers in class society, whose properly revolutionary activity was the impetus behind emancipation, and the experiment in multiracial democracy that briefly followed (i.e., Reconstruction). In later works, Du Bois deepened his exploration of what he himself had defined as a much younger man as his century's problematic (or perhaps its "primary contradiction"), the global color line. In *The World and Africa*, Du Bois articulated the structural link between the poverty and dispossession of Africa's material and human resources and the wealth of the capitalist world system, busy reconstructing itself in the 1940s. Historians and critics of "whiteness" rediscovered Du Bois's thesis that racism offered its beneficiaries a "psychological wage" back in the 1990s.[6] The distorting power of racism in the formation of social classes in the United States has been much appreciated, then and since. Another trend or line of thought takes up Du Bois's suggestion that the oppressed Black working class was or is a revolutionary class, an idea that had animated the "anti-revisionist" U.S. Communist movement in the 1970s.[7] We arguably inherit, therefore, one well-traveled problematic of Du Bois's, and another that has been largely forgotten. The first maps well onto the anxiously reiterated age-old question of "American" (exceptionalist) historiography—Why is there no socialism in the United States?—and offers a pat answer: the racism of the white workers combined with the super-exploitation of Black workers divides and demoralizes the multinational working class, robbing the proletariat of organizational unity and the assumption of solidarity. A well-known story, and a tragically true characterization—that nonetheless remains stuck within a U.S. exceptionalist narrative frame.[8]

The "forgotten" problematic is an internationalist one, but it is not "the international" or "global" as such. The latter is a difficult concept to think with, in part because of a tendency to map the "one world" planetary imagination of post-1990 "globalization" onto previous eras. For Marxist-Leninists and anticolonial revolutionaries in the mid-twentieth century, in a fundamental sense there was neither one world, nor three, but two: the racist imperialist "world order," imposed on the planet by ceaseless waves of violence, and the revolutionary-socialist struggle to liberate humanity, which was *concentrated* in the so-called peripheral or colonial world but *immanent* throughout capitalist-imperialist society. The analyses pursued by Black Leninists such as Du Bois (who wrote openly as a socialist in the 1940s and later joined the CPUSA) shared this important assumption, that colonialism and racism (often couched in language of "bigotry" and "chauvinism") were central to and pervasive within metropolitan societies, and that colonized nations were a "central" and inevitable aspect of capitalism as such.

In the first instance, the framework I am calling "Black Leninist" appreciates the extent to which capitalism's global system is indebted to Africans both by way of the slave trade, which was instrumental in developing the financial architecture of commodity capitalism, and the continuing hyper-exploitation, and active *underdevelopment* (Rodney), of the resources and peoples of Africa. As captives, arrivants, and migrants, Black peoples have occupied and pervaded imperialist societies for centuries. Black people—who are in a way produced by systems of racial oppression, classification, and "marking"[9]—are central to the history of capitalism, but peculiarly so in that commodification of Black embodied labor, the objectification of Black personhood, was a functional "step" or "stage" in the theorization and material formation of commodities and commodity rule. In commodity ("imperialist") societies, Black people become the signifiers of commodification per se. From the beginning, Black peoples, natally alienated, nevertheless more or less immediately took up the collective struggle to smash capitalism, at first in its nascent, brutal, or "primitive" form. One of the great Black Leninists, C. L. R. James, devoted significant study to chronicling and interpreting the unending tenacious and desperate resistance that always and everywhere accompanied enslavement.[10]

This chapter takes note of the simple fact, complexly obscured by the compounded effects of anti-Blackness and anticommunism, that during the revolutionary "short century" between 1917 and 1989 it was antiracist and anti-imperialist solidarity that most often propelled revolutionary upsurges and mass participation in political life. A comprehensive account of Black Leninists would not be confined to the African continent and the Atlantic-American diaspora, but would necessarily include all those Black Communists who traveled to and worked alongside comrades in Asia or Europe, all those immigrants, temporary migrants, and displaced persons, refugees, and deportees who took up residence in the various metropoles, but also indeed all those theorists of Marxism-Leninism who took up the Black struggle for liberation as a central object of theoretical reflection. On all continents Marxist-Leninists, in perpetually shifting alliances or feuds with other progressive sectors, pursued policies of proletarian internationalism and articulated visions of Black liberation revising and updating, in turn, Marxist and Leninist theories. In the United States, the Bolshevik Revolution almost immediately helped spur the coalescing of the African Black Brotherhood (in 1919), which would become the nucleus that theorized the CPUSA's official policy (after 1928) of the Black Belt and Black National Liberation. For midcentury Leninism, the Black struggle for liberation in both hemispheres was inseparable from the fight against imperialism. This fact made international working-class solidarity with Black American freedom fighters a more profound issue than one of Soviet "propaganda victories" or "embarrassing" the U.S. bid for global leadership. Black revolutionaries received expressions of solidarity across the world during the "long black freedom movement" or "Second Reconstruction," which like the first one was in reality a sustained revolutionary upsurge of an oppressed people. The political horizon for the Black Leninist century was the total destruction of white supremacy, not as an attitude or a cultural bias, but as the institutional apparatus of the world economy, and racial capitalism, not as a special form or distortion of capitalism, but as the form in which real world capitalism in fact took shape and place.[11]

Toward a Definition of "Black Leninism"

"Black Leninism" names a mid-twentieth-century configuration of Black struggle—the conjuncture where the multicentury history of Black struggle aligns and articulates with the organized Marxist Left in the wake of the October Revolution of 1917. It is a struggle that is at once a struggle for the liberation of peoples of African descent; a struggle to dismantle or destroy racist social systems and racist societies; and a struggle over, against, and beyond the terrain of a prematurely predicated *humanity*. Black struggle has always been an oceanic, planetary, or global struggle, but we can mark or periodize phases of how the *necessary internationalism* of Black national liberation struggles has been articulated.[12] The middle of the twentieth century in particular witnessed the emergence of a profound "tricontinental" formation of Black revolutionaries, artists, intellectuals, and workers who analyzed the cataclysms of late colonial Europe as deeply rooted in (or routed through) the violent expropriations of imperialism's own practices.[13] The middle of the twentieth century, especially what Domenico Losurdo refers to as the "Second Thirty Years War" (i.e., World Wars I and II), was from Europe's self-referential perspective a unique catastrophe, but from the historical perspective of the oppressed nations the same catastrophe appears as the rebounding violence of colonialism itself "coming home to roost," in Malcolm X's memorable formulation.[14] The oppressed nations had in actual fact been laboratories for the genocidal techniques of total war, not least in Tulsa, Oklahoma, in 1921, where white supremacist terrorists bombed the Black business district from the air among a "riot" of bloodletting. A similar incident helped radicalize the young Harry Haywood, the future CPUSA militant and chief formulator of the Party's Black Belt Thesis. Freshly returned from the carnage of World War I, Haywood found himself in 1919 in the midst of a pitched battle against white terrorists on the streets of Chicago, veterans and others preparing ambush positions with machine guns and rifles to try to protect the Black neighborhoods from sustained assaults.[15] In fact, the "Red Summer" of 1919 was characterized by violent unrest across the United States, not only in Chicago, as anti-Black racism and antiradicalism merged, as they so often do, and produced violent white mobs akin to the pogromists familiar in central Europe. Where the quotidian indignities and "discursive" or "epistemic" violence of colonial domination erupted into the "total" violence of armed conflict, that "color line" or threshold was for Haywood a qualitative turning point, shaping a lifetime of struggle against racial capitalism, which for Haywood was manifested by the white supremacists he faced down. As Haywood later reflected, "It came to me then that I had been fighting the wrong war. The Germans weren't the enemy—the enemy was right here."[16]

So, the period 1917–1989 witnessed a profound confluence of Black struggle against racism—not of the residual South, but of the U.S. state qua leader of global imperialism—as part and parcel of a planetary struggle against colonial white supremacy. However profound these global debates and revolutionary movements became between the 1920s and 1970s, they did not, however, inaugurate the internationalism of Black liberation struggle—rather, that character of black struggle was there from the beginning, and manifested in the long and bloody history of revolts against enslavement—whether instigated in castle, mine, or factory; organized on board ships or transmitted in coded, ritualized form through ring shouts, drum signals, or, later on, work songs and spirituals; the organized black political formation wherever it manifested was a conspiracy across boundaries of language, culture, religion, and region—precisely those putatively "stable" continuities that ground nationality as a concept.[17]

Therefore, how we interpret "nationality" will be crucial going forward. For Cedric Robinson—among many others—it is on the theorization of nationality that black critical theory must part ways with Marxism. For Robinson, not only did Marxists misconstrue or misrecognize Black Nationalism as petit-bourgeois, but their alleged hostility to Black National formation was materially destructive under the weight of late–twentieth-century racial capitalism: "The charades of neocolonialism and race relations have worn thin," he points out (prophetically, from the worn-out days of our time): "In the metropoles, imprisonment, the stupor of drugs, the use of lethal force by public authorities and private citizens, and the more petty humiliations of racial discrimination have become epidemic."[18] Robinson's famous conclusion presents a dilemma: his analysis points to a "civilizational" incompatibility between "Marxist" socialism and Black radicalism—one that however intractable *may yet be overcome,* but only in a distant future:

> It is not the province of one people to be the solution or the problem. But a civilization maddened by its own perverse assumptions and contradictions is loose in the world. A Black radical tradition formed in opposition to that civilization and conscious of itself is one part of the solution. Whether the other

oppositions generated from within Western society and without will mature remains problematical. But for now we must be as one. (318)

The final line is ambiguous, but is usually interpreted as a call for racial and Black national solidarity across ideological lines. Robinson's provisional, rather than strategic, nationalism extends de facto into the present, four decades later. The Left is divided, notionally, between two allegedly asymmetric currents: (1) a white-dominated class-first social democratic electoralism in various states of "alliance" and divergence from (2) a "social justice"–oriented "radical liberal" formation that emphasizes "wokeness," that is, correct language regarding racism and sexism. The latter current tends to claim pro-Black cultural formulations as its own, to the point of hyperbolizing the white American penchant for acquiring an identity by way of adopting (mimicking) Black speech. Meanwhile, actual Black people who want to organize politically are faced with a (at least) triple dilemma: the severe and often murderous pressure of the state, the general unreliability of white liberal-minded Americans too stuck in various racial fantasies to be of any use, but also theorizations of Black nationhood as organically distinct and separate from the class dynamics of American (or any capitalist) society as a whole. Robinson's call to close ranks in the face of entrenched anti-Black racism is among other things a practical political adaptation to these conditions.

Robinson's excavation of a Black radicalism separate from the sojourns of European socialism is, in other words, partially a postmortem on an era of dashed revolutionary hopes. In the United States particularly, by the early 1980s it was beyond clear the progressive tide had ebbed; conditions for the Black working class were rapidly worsening; as is usually the case in U.S. history, white liberals and radicals had retreated from radical antiracist struggle. By contrast the mid-century moment of Black Leninism was first of all marked by a buoyant faith in the international working class to find the political unity necessary to smash the structures of its planetary oppression. The point is not to decide retroactively who was right or wrong in their assessment of the balance of forces, but to engage more deeply with a formation that eschewed the fatalism common to our contemporary politics.

In the mid-twentieth century, Marxists-Leninists theorized Black peoples' predicament in the United States as one of national oppression—meaning that the U.S. bourgeois-imperialist state maximized its profits in part by way of the superexploitation of Black peoples. The oppression of Black people, therefore, could not be neatly separated from the exploitative machinery of U.S. imperialism per se. Naming a configuration of "Black Leninism" works to restate the Black radical currents of the middle twentieth century, the radically internationalist and anti-imperialist character of which was and is often summarized as "Pan-African," as at the same time a struggle to resituate and retheorize the revolutionary subject of Marxism.

Turning now to a working definition of Leninism, which is often reduced in bourgeois and even some "leftist" discourses to a focus on the seizure of state power as such, I will suggest five major characteristics that distinguish it. *First,* the party—not the party as an organizational form as such, which was ubiquitous in the socialist and proletarian movement of Lenin's time, but the model of the party as vanguard—a military metaphor (see Egan in this volume) that positions the "professional revolutionaries" of the most "advanced" elements of the proletariat in an advance position, scouting terrain for the progressive masses. *Second,* "Leninism" is inseparable from the strategic analysis of imperialism. The analysis itself is not unique to Lenin (who famously borrowed his definition in part from the English liberal J. A. Hobson): what is, arguably, uniquely Leninist is the strategy of "revolutionary defeatism," whereby it is the duty of socialists to work for and promote the defeat of their own national bourgeoisie in imperialist conflict. *Third,* Lenin liked to say that the "soul" of Marxism was the "concrete analysis of concrete conditions," which in the context of imperialism's world system meant that no particular or local struggle could be understood without fitting it into the planetary fight against the international bourgeoisie as a whole. *Fourth* the role of nationality and national self-determination: for Leninism, nationalism (like all entities coming under a dialectical materialist analysis) splits into two: the conflict between bourgeois nationalism and proletarian internationalism is expressed in the division of the world between oppressor and oppressed nationalities. In other words, nationalism is not a singular quality, or "spirit," that can be measured from country to country or "people" to "people"; it is neither, *pace* Benedict Anderson, an emergent technology within modernity as such. Rather, for Leninists, nationalism is itself divided by class struggle: bourgeois nationalists contradictorily proclaim the equality of all nations (nations "compete" on the global "marketplace") and manifest the most extreme jingoism and chauvinism ("our" "nation" is "best"); *proletarian internationalism,* in fierce opposition to bourgeois nationalism, articulates not only the alliance of working classes across national boundaries but also the revolutionary necessity of liberating oppressed nationalities. For some "nations" are rendered "permanently" subordinate within the modern world system: the Irish, for example, developed national consciousness under the specific, concrete conditions of English *national* oppression.[19] Strategically, this meant that the national liberation struggles of oppressed peoples have a progressive character in the planetary fight against imperialism. *Finally,* Leninism insists on the "dictatorship of the proletariat" (or what is otherwise known as "proletarian democracy") as the *sine qua non* of Marxism: even the bourgeois political economists recognized class struggle as the motor of history, but Lenin's theory of the state requires a transitional moment (which may indeed last a long time) of a workers' state for the proletariat to wield power in order for the state to begin the process of withering away (see Zanotti in this volume).

From the Black Panther Party, to Amilcar Cabral's successful fight against Portuguese colonialism, to Thomas Sankara and the revolutionary struggle in Burkina Faso, to Walter Rodney's engagement with Tanzanian African socialism and his pan-Caribbean political leadership, to the organizing and agitation among West Indian migrants to London by the important militant and theorist Claudia Jones, indeed to diverse revolutionary movements mobilizing tens of millions across Africa, the Caribbean, and the Americas—Black Leninists shared a political/strategic and broad theoretical framework. They adopted a Marxist-Leninist framework not because of some fetishization of the Soviet Union, but because of an agreement with and commitment to the outlines of the anti-imperialist analysis and the model for fostering social revolution first sketched by the Bolsheviks. They also broadly agreed with Lenin's own insistent conception of Marxism as something wholly other than a dogma or codicil to be rigidly applied to local situations. For Lenin and the broad current of revolutionary thought and practice that sought Black liberation through social revolution, Marxism was a method of concrete analysis. Thus, in each case there is not a dogmatic adherence to Marxism-Leninism, but its use to develop concrete analyses of concrete political-economic configurations. For instance, Claudia Jones's thesis of the "super-exploitation" of Black women, that Black women in the United States faced a "triple oppression" that emerges out of class relations (rather than being their epiphenomenon), has had an enduring and transformative impact on communist theorization of "race and gender." In facing down Portuguese colonialism across disparate nations and cultures of Africa, Cabral found that he had to discard certain of the classical categories of Marxist analysis. For Cabral, the colonial so-called petite bourgeoisie, unlike the European version, had no hope of transforming into a national bourgeoisie. Under the conditions of colonial domination and national oppression, the comprador classes in the colony were doomed to stagnancy or perpetual decline. Cabral urged, therefore, the conscious choice of class suicide: the so-called colonial petit bourgeois could never achieve bourgeois independence, but it could help overthrow colonialism by liquidating itself in struggle. A distinctive feature of Cabral's African revolutionary struggle was that it succeeded not only in gaining national independence, it sparked an anticolonial and antifascist revolution in the metropole itself. The last of the European colonies in Africa gained independence in a process that also overthrew Portuguese fascism, which Cabral, assassinated in 1973, pointed the way toward though he did not live to witness it. More well-known, at least among Americanists, are the ideological twists and turns of the Black Panther Party as it coalesced and tenaciously defended itself against the assaults of the U.S. state. Interpreting how the ideological production of the Panthers did or did not relate to "Leninism" is a complex issue beyond the scope of this chapter, but the Panthers likewise looked to Marx and Lenin (and Mao and Ho and Fidel) as part and parcel of a living tradition of revolutionary theory, not a recipe, program, or codicil. Later in this chapter we will see how, in Black Panther revolutionary study, "reading Lenin" is neither academic nor casuistic, but immediately transformative.[20]

We can appreciate the materialist approach shared by Black Leninists by looking in more detail at how one of the intellectual and political giants of mid-century Black Leninism characterized it. In 1975, five years before his assassination by car bomb, Guyanese historian and activist Walter Rodney addressed a crowd of young activists in New York. Some were Marxists, others not, and many were infused with the oppositional spirit of Black Power: the question on the agenda was whether Marxism had any relevance to the Black struggle for liberation. Was it true that Marxism was a "European" theory that was not applicable beyond the boundaries of intra-European social and class struggle? Rather than directly answering, Rodney insisted that American activists and intellectuals pay attention to the actual history of how Marxism had been taken up by revolutionary movements, especially in Africa. Marxism, he asserted, was being discussed on every continent—everywhere the oppressed found in Marxist theory emancipatory tools, and in doing so, revolutionaries were not simply "applying" Marxism to colonial situations. Rather, Rodney insisted in the best tradition of historical materialism, Marxism (and Leninism) was an analytical and organizational *method*: there were no fixed categories in Marxism.[21]

Rodney was speaking at what we in retrospect can see as the "tail end" of a historical process of Black liberation across multiple continents that explicitly named itself Marxist-Leninist. In 1975, there still existed a prominent New Communist movement in the United States in which multiple, often conflicting, political formations identified themselves as Maoists, Third Worldists, and/or antirevisionist Marxist-Leninists. It was only into the 1980s, during the era of Reagan's "rollback" and covert wars that imperialism became successful in overturning Marxist revolutions in the third world—Burkina Faso, Grenada, and elsewhere. The endless present, now at a profound historical break, that we call neoliberalism—its major theories and institutional edifices were already being emplaced, and the whole world could recognize the coup against Chilean antifascist, socialist President Salvador Allende on September 11, 1973, that installed the murderous dictator Pinochet as an experiment in regime change and the management of populations, an attempt at a forceful reorganization of the governmentality of capital—an experiment that would be repeated, ad infinitum, over the next forty years, across the world. But in 1975 its victory was not assured, it was not accomplished—that only took place (if at all) in the aftermath of the global crises of 1989–91, during which the USSR disintegrated, and communism was defeated—allegedly, in the discourses of the triumphant victors, for all time.

What Is This Black in Black Leninism? Time and Place in Mid-Century Black Liberation

The Black British Marxist theoretician Stuart Hall asked a question in 1992 that was bound to become famous, a key articulation of developing black critical theory in the academy. "What is this Black in 'Black Popular Culture,'" he asked, and by way of Gramsci, provided a detailed and virtuosic answer: the essay articulated a warning that, absent a materialist analysis, to rely on a metaphysics of racial being was a constant danger. Nevertheless, Hall showed blackness to be an affirmative project of cultural politics and poetics. Taking his lead, this section will explore how a grounded materialist analysis of blackness is necessary to analyze the concrete projects of mid-century Black Leninists. It will also try to justify the essay title's invocation of blackness (for Marxists, for the Left) as not a particularistic or identitarian subdivision but a primary modality of mid-century internationalism.

So why say Black *Leninism,* why assign mid-century Black revolutionary struggle to this proper name in particular? Where even communism might be given a hearing, "Leninism" can be a divisive epithet. One can easily collate and designate a genre of mid-century struggle called "Black Communism," so why insist on a relation, if not fidelity, to *Leninism* as a particular operational configuration of struggle? The gesture here is to invite struggle and contestation. To designate a formation of Black Communism is no doubt accurate, but it might be too easily assimilated into the stances of reinterpretation, problematization, deconstruction, etc. What the chapter aims at is not to highlight a particular tendency or subgenre of communism, nor to propose a model for a twenty-first-century antiracist communism, nor, if it can be avoided, to take sides in the (quite often arcane) debates among complex and highly advanced (in the triple sense of sophisticated, overdetermined, and getting on in years) intellectual projects that, in many ways, have sustained the Left over the last century. Saying "Leninism" is a way of *repeating* communism, calling for its repetition even in its reiteration, opening communism again to political symbolization, and finally to assert its inevitable return. The proper name "Lenin," finally, is not the name for a "Master," for a sage or prophet whose words should be kept under glass and followed religiously. To say that a political configuration called Black Leninist internationalism was a prominent current of mid-century struggle is a trenchant reminder that in the twentieth century some Marxist mass movements overthrew states, and others sought the liberation of the vast majority of the world *by way of* the overthrow of the remaining bourgeois-imperialist states. However rude its repetition might appear, the legacy of Black Leninism is in part an incisive reminder that liberation, for the vast majority, *still depends* on the revolutionary transformation of imperialism as a world system of exploitation.[22]

That the "colored peoples of the world," to use the famous phrase from W. E. B. Du Bois, are and have always been the vast majority of humanity is, first of all, an undeniable fact whose presence, secondly, has been and still is denied systematically in the most basic shared assumptions that structure U.S. (and UK, France, etc.) political culture. America continues to be animated by a racialized common sense whose power depends on not speaking its name. The realpolitik of American civic discourse represses its own content, its imagined future: constructing an armored preserve for the rich while psychologically preparing for the liquidation of the vast majority of humanity: the people Fanon called "the wretched of the earth," victims of the most brutal extractive primitive accumulation, in antagonism to the comprador bourgeoisies of their own country. As the climate crisis, and capitalism's inability to mitigate its effects, combines with ruthless exploitation and militarism, we are moving toward an eliminationist logic that operates on a racial basis on the condition that we do not say so.

Thus, we return to the central question of this section: What is invoked by, what racial analysis underpins, the nomination of Black Leninism? Here, I won't speak of the overlapping, arguably diasporic, histories of *African* America, but rather of the singular history of *Black* America. Which is to say that this thing called America, I mean the continent, the hemisphere, is and has been, from the beginning, in addition to whatever else it has been, also, Black; from the moment something like an American social or conceptual or discursive formation can be said to have existed, it was already Black—meaning that Black people were physically present, of course, people we moderns would "recognize" as Black, but also that conceptually America's (repetitively erased and constantly disavowed) Blackness cannot be disentangled. Put more simply, an America that transcends race—an unquestioned faith that sustains U.S. civic discourse—is an impossibility since "America" itself is a racial project. But never a singular project, and never unopposed.

Now, to speak of America as a hemispheric antagonism between racial projects, to speak so encompassingly, let's say, should be taken with a grain of salt. Is there not an arrogance of presumption to declare, from within an Anglophone and Anglocentric discourse, to speak on behalf of the multilingual—and we are speaking here not only of the great imperial linguistic formations that pattern and divide "America" into Franco-, Luso-, and Hispanic "groups" who remain off the radar for Anglocentrism's imperial soundscape, but also of the thousands of languages dispersed and disintegrated by the same imperial processes that have scarred the hemisphere with the linguistic traces of unceasing imperialist warfare; is there not some fatal politics of representation that cannot be tarried with? Without going into the many important debates about the subaltern's capacity for speech, the theorist's capacity for hearing, or, to summarize, the global division of labor within intellectual production, I can only say that my aim in pointing to America's ineradicable Blackness is not to represent the (Black) peoples of the hemisphere, nor to universalize in the sense of homogeneity, but rather to shift strategically the dynamics of majoritarian and minoritarian forces, to set in sharp relief the unexamined illusions that pervade U.S., and more generally *imperialist,* civic life and historiography.

Angela and the White Comrades: Unrealized Universality and the Materiality of Theory

In a productive contradiction, the vantage point of the U.S./UK/etc. Left often relegates Black revolutionary activity to a tangential, symbolic, or "merely" affective, even reductively identitarian position. Consider, for instance, Mike Davis's complimentary reference to Angela Davis: while he himself is full of praise for the philosopher, his rhetorical address nonetheless reveals something of the ideological coordinates by which the (white) Left persistently misunderstands its relation to anti-imperialist political imperatives. Angela Davis's expertise is affirmed beyond doubt: she is patently more "advanced" in her study of Marxism than the other comrades, who struggle by themselves to catch up, to overcome their backwardness. The thought of Angela Davis tutoring these fledgling radicals is unthinkable, however, in deference to the importance of her engaged political work. A fantasy of Angela Davis's access to Marxism—if only she could bring up her white peers—blocks or represses the obvious question: Was the "white Left" able to recognize the priority of the struggle for Black self-determination, that the oppression of Black people formed a primary contradiction in the U.S. empire? Mike Davis's insight that the "white Left" required the tutelage of committed Black Marxist theorists—those who materially advance, through study and struggle, Black self-determination—is correct, but its articulation relies on a fantasy that obscures the ideological fault lines in the "white Left" during the long Black freedom movement.

What's foreclosed in the fantasy of Angela Davis perhaps not being too busy to educate her non-Black comrades is the possibility that they could help, could join in her struggle. Why is it beyond question that the non-Black comrades might prioritize, first and foremost, their material activity in support of Black revolution? Why is her work so obviously separate from theirs? Is it not in contradiction to the imperatives of proletarian internationalism that later motivated global expressions of solidarity for Angela once she became the target of the U.S. government, to sustain, however tacitly, the bourgeois (segregationist) fiction of racial "communities" acting in isolation or competition? We can only answer these questions if we take seriously the implications of (the centrality of) Black Leninism: that is, the indispensable quality of Black struggle and self-determination to the overthrow of capitalism in the era of imperialism.

Memoirists of the period (especially those who do not share Mike Davis's fidelity to Marxism or the people's movement as such) often portray Black resistance to white support as a one-way street, that it was Black mistrust, whether understandable, excessively emotional, or petit-bourgeois, that prevented more disciplined engagement. This too is a fantasy, an egregious one—for it not only conceals the actual practical involvement and solidarity of white revolutionaries, not just the white racism that was and is palpable at times on the Left but also that the communist movement itself was at the time suffering from severe fractures on this precise question, the Party's theorization of Black struggle in its relation to prospects for revolution in the United States. In other words, white racism is commonly understood as the reason (or at least a principle one) for the collapse of the communist movement in the United States. Of course, this is true, but it would be a mistake to understand racism, in this instance as much as any other, only in terms of psychological "attitudes" or exclusion from majoritarian institutions and spaces—what midcentury communists referred to as "racial chauvinism" was not limited to individual biases, but was also the conceptual and ideological failure to see the struggle for Black self-determination in the United States and the struggle against imperialism qua global capitalism as unified struggles.

The most prominent Black Leninist formation in the United States, at the time and certainly in historiographical attention, was the Black Panther Party. Angela Davis recounts, in her autobiography, that a short while after returning to the United States she found herself immersed in the Black Panther Party's political education programs, reading Lenin in a radically different context. "When we read Lenin's State and Revolution," she writes,

> there were sisters and brothers in the class whose public school education had not even allowed them to learn how to read. Some of them told me how they stayed with the book for many painful hours, often using the dictionary to discover the meaning of scores of words on one page, until finally they could grasp the significance of what Lenin was saying. When they explained, for the benefit of the other members of the class, what they had gotten out of their reading, it was clear that they knew it all—they had understood Lenin on a far more elemental level than any professor of social science. (192)

To draw the obvious contrast: the style of communist pedagogy described here differs radically from what we imagined above, Angela Davis schooling the "white Left." If we say, echoing Lenin, that the latter is "backward," what we cannot mean is that they needed to have gone and studied with Adorno (or Marcuse). One of Lenin's key contributions was to emphasize the "backwardness" of the context from which he was writing, namely, late imperial Russia. Relentlessly, he insisted that conditions in Russia could not be measured against those in the central imperialist/capitalist countries, including arguing in the 1890s that the introduction of capitalism in the countryside would be a progressive development. That Russia's development was (not just uneven but) "backward" in the context of world capitalism was a crucial insight in organizing Bolshevik revolutionary cadres. It also became a key putative component of the influence of "Leninism" on anticolonial revolutionaries, for the Russian Revolution demonstrated, against the assumptions of Marx and Engels and the European socialist movement generally, that imperialism could be countered most effectively in its "backwaters," where it was organizationally and institutionally weakest. For white U.S. leftists at mid-century, it was not their society but their movement, their (aspiring) "vanguard," that was backward, in multiple senses: it largely failed to move the masses of workers toward class consciousness and solidarity; it was unable effectively to purge its ranks of chauvinists; it could not properly counter the state's efforts at infiltration and provocation; while it made ceaseless appeals to Black, colonized, and racialized workers, these did not for the most part produce militant mass organizations or cadre growth, nor offset the appeal of nationalist groups: the prominence of the latter is arguably a key indicator or symptom of the failure of the (white) U.S. Left to overcome its "chauvinism," or to use a later idiom, its "investment" in "whiteness."[23]

Nevertheless, what we can perceive in Davis's example is not only the gulf separating the quasi- and semi-academic (white) Left from Black revolutionary struggle, but also the liberatory desire that animates the latter. In the example of reading Lenin with the Black Panther Party—reading Lenin simultaneously as part and parcel of the development of both literacy and political technique—is revealed the universality of revolutionary theory and struggle. Outside of academic—and *also* outside the para-academic, civil society, etc.—contexts, the fact that theory can take on material actuality starts to become palpable. The vaunted high points of Black radical history—Black Panther Party community political education projects—hide in plain sight the explosive power of theory in the hands of the masses of (Black) people.[24]

The same contradiction, between the impotence of "hegemonic" critical theory in civil society and the material power of revolutionary theory in the hands of the oppressed masses, can be appreciated by turning to a person who was arguably at the time the *second* most advanced Marxist theorist in California and likely the United States as a whole: George Jackson. Jackson became imprisoned in 1960 as a teenaged petty criminal and had no formal education. For holding up a gas station, he was given an "indeterminate" sentence, which became a practical life sentence. By the end of the decade, he was the Black Panther Party's leading theoretician and wrote cogently on the application of Lenin and other revolutionary theorists to the struggle for liberation in the United States and especially in the prison system. He did this with a shockingly limited access to textual resources and wrote much of his theoretical output on a plastic typewriter. As was and is common in U.S. prisons, he was subjected to extended solitary confinement as punishment, some of that time in open-air cages. In his letters and writings he described the prison's sadistic tortures, its corruptions and obscenities and plots. At the time of his death he had ninety-nine books in his cell: his access to Lenin's thought was limited and he mostly had to rely on secondary sources or anthologies. The fact that his theoretical development was so acute and sophisticated under these conditions suggests something of the universal pertinence of revolutionary theory in the Leninist vein.

In his theoretical work, especially *Blood in My Eye*, a major work published posthumously, Jackson attempted a clear-eyed confrontation with the "fascist" character of the U.S. racial state and social system. He also excavated Leninist revolutionary theory's relevance to the predicament of America's oppressed masses, insisting over and again on the international character of the struggles raging in U.S. ghettos and prisons. Following Mao Zedong in particular, Jackson advocated a prolonged people's war against the U.S. government. Echoing Engels, he insisted that "People's War is not polite or proper. . . . People's War is improvisation and more improvisation."[25] Following Fanon, he appreciated the importance of state violence in imposing colonial conditions and recognized that the development of revolutionary class consciousness was hindered absent a militarily powerful revolutionary movement that could offer real protection for oppressed peoples. Like Lenin, Jackson always framed his struggle as a planetary struggle of oppressed peoples against imperialism. In *Left-Wing Communism* and other texts, Lenin characterized the newly formed workers' state as engaged in unrelenting war with the international bourgeoisie. For Jackson likewise, the latest sadistic technique of brutality introduced by the "pigs"—prison guards—was but a material manifestation of the real global struggle that the Black Panther Party shared with the National Liberation Front, and other military forces opposing the U.S. empire.

Jackson is a quintessential Leninist not only because he persistently advocated for proletarian revolution (although that is so), but because he conceived of his own struggle, which was one of life and death within a small enclosed space, as part and parcel of a planetary transition that was open to scientific, materialist analysis. From his cell, Jackson could reevaluate the history of the U.S. state and social system without illusion, and realize that as a racial dictatorship, its history was linked to and coeval with other forms of fascism. Prison lays power relations bare—on that, most would agree. But for Jackson, the effect was not to narrow his vision to the demoralizing and undignified intrusions of the state onto his person, but to evince a stark and penetrating analysis of the prison as a legible manifestation of white supremacist global governance. It is such a perspective, I am arguing in part, that allows for and warrants the designation "Leninist": an uncompromisingly revolutionary stance toward "local" political questions, such as the fate of one particular nation-state:

> We must accept the eventuality of bringing the USA to its knees; accept the closing off of critical sections of the city streets, soldiers everywhere, tommy guns pointed at stomach level, smoke curling black against the daylight sky, the smell of cordite, house-to-house searches, doors being kicked down, the commonness of death. . . . We simply stop allowing ourselves to be hunted and do some stalking of our own; their secret police aren't really too secret at all. (55)

As Lenin insisted in *State and Revolution*, a materialist idea of the state sees it as *nothing* more than "special bodies of armed men, prisons, etc."[26] From George Jackson's vantage point of being completely controlled by this apparatus, he concluded optimistically that its overthrow was nigh. The latter, moreover, was a prerequisite for the realization of a true universality, one where Black people were in fact free to live.

What does it mean to point, then, to the unrealized universality of (Leninist) revolutionary theory? For one thing, it serves to remind us that whatever one thinks of the heroic scenario of the proletariat's role in history, its alleged mission to abolish first the capitalist system and then all class distinctions as such (creating a proletarian state and then "withering" it into nonexistence),[27] it is a theoretical terrain open to the future—and *not* one that restricts understanding of class struggle to the point of production.[28] Second, perhaps more pointedly, it reminds us that for Lenin and revolutionary theorists of the twentieth century broadly, imperialism was the name for the planetary system into which capitalism had developed, not a policy of this or that country. Imperialism was, and is, inseparable from the division of the planet into oppressor and oppressed nationalities: liberation from national oppression thus cannot come without a confrontation with imperialism qua global system. Third, and most pointedly still, it insists that there can be no talk of universality as if it were a settled accomplishment: we cannot talk as if humanity is not still "divided." Put more simply, "humanity" itself is (has always been) the name for a false, presumptive (white supremacist) operationalization of "universality," the latter having been foreclosed by the racial dynamics of capitalism's own development. Finally, we cannot understand Black Leninism without understanding its never-ending confrontation with white supremacist counterrevolutionary forces, without understanding Blackness as premature death, without the dialectical relations of the "unrealized" and universal. White supremacist state violence is not an ancillary condition of capitalism—it cannot be explained away in a footnote as in contradiction to this or that philosopher's appeal to the universal condition of humanity. On the contrary, the "universal" as we have come to inherit it is not just drenched in blood, but irredeemably constricted by its emergence from *within* the racial partitioning of humanity. Only a revolutionary break with the white supremacist racial states that continue to govern the imperialist system can allow for the realization of a true universality.

If we take together the examples of two mid-century comrades, Angela Davis and George Jackson, it couldn't be clearer: the Black claim to universal emancipation elicits state violence. Liberation for Black people means liberation from the U.S. empire, which is why the latter designates so many state resources to the global and local maintenance of white supremacy. The violence unleashed against Jackson and whosoever invoked his name to assert the "humanity" of the imprisoned (at Attica and so on); the state's determined effort to try Davis for her life—such examples must be appreciated in the context of a truly planetary operational field (U.S. support for Rhodesia, its proxy wars to prop up apartheid Southern Africa, etc.).

Quite simply, the history of Black Leninism suggests that the putative universals we have come to anticipate, such as "humanity" or emancipation per se or theory for that matter, require a thoroughgoing and radical reconstruction, rather than to be "decentered" amid a pluralism of incommensurate forms of life. After the apparent contraction of Black liberation struggles in the late 1970s, the (temporary) end of the long Black freedom movement, there was much academic hand-wringing about whether and to what degree Marxist theory does or can attend to Black liberation, to a universality constituted by Black people: does it not throw Marxism, or Leninism, as "European" theories, into epistemological crisis, or push them uncomfortably into a different ontological terrain? On the contrary, I have argued in this section that it is only by way of Black critique of putative universals do we arrive at the truly universal implications (realizable in the future) of the Leninist ambition to overthrow imperialism as the world system. Moreover, critiques of the presumptive universality of (white, European) theory are necessary to the revival of revolutionary theory per se—not as an idealist, academic language game, but as a material force that grips and bolsters the multinational working class. The final section will examine one particular example of a policy oriented toward a revolutionary transformation within the heart of imperialism—the Black Belt Thesis.

The Black Belt and "American History": Toward a Revival of Revolutionary Answers

Put simply, the Black Belt Thesis posits the problem of racism and white supremacy in the United States as part and parcel of imperialism as a global system. That is, the predicament of Black Americans was linked profoundly to the struggle of peoples everywhere against colonial oppression. The Black Belt Thesis proposed that we think of the contiguous, majority-Black counties that stretch across the U.S. South from the outskirts of Washington, D.C., to New Orleans, as the territory constituting Black people as an *oppressed nation* within the territory of the United States. Black people are not the only oppressed nation within U.S. territory: many indigenous nations are also directly colonized, and constitute oppressed nations within the United States' "prison house."[29] When it was formulated in 1928, the huge majority of Black people in the United States lived on the contiguous territory of the Black Belt. Today, even after the migration of millions of workers to Northern cities, deliberate racist gerrymandering, and the influx of millions of non-Black workers to the "Sunbelt," there remains a Black-majority contiguous area. Even as the course of the twentieth century made Black territory of most U.S. urban centers, the Black Belt remains as a contiguous territory across many states. The Black Belt is primarily a *theoretical* intervention: it says that Black people in the United States are in fact members of an oppressed nation (rather than an ethnic minority, for instance).

On a practical level, one must appreciate the nuances of the Leninist approach to nationality. The right of self-determination, as Lenin theorized it in the 1910s, did nothing to dictate the final settlement(s) of territory, sovereignty, and so on. Lenin and others analogized it to the right of divorce: that women had the right to sue for divorce (as they did for the first time in Revolutionary Russia) did not mean that all would do so. Therefore, that there *is* a Black Belt does not force a principled Marxist to advocate for its independence from the United States. Rather, its existence demonstrates that there *is* an oppressed nation within the United States, one that can and must have the right to self-determination.

It was Harry Haywood who formulated the Black Belt Thesis and the Party's espousal of Black self-determination as an answer to what communists called, in their jargon, the National question. At first, Haywood, like most communists, rejected the idea that there was a territorial basis for Black Nationality. Yet his experience of the powerful resonance that movements such as Marcus Garvey's had among the oppressed Black masses, along with his study of the dynamics of colonial oppression globally, including an extended sojourn studying and working in the USSR, convinced him of the need for communists to declare the Black Belt the home of an oppressed nationality, and to defend the right of Black people to self-determination. Haywood worked closely with Soviet theoreticians—for a time he was basically alone in his position among the delegation of American communists—and absorbed voluminous information about how Soviet nationality policies had played out during the Revolution and consolidation of the Soviet workers' state. For Haywood, the oppression of Black Americans was so tangible, so immediate, that it was alienating for it to be assimilated into the Soviets' general theory about national conflict. Over time, however, Haywood came to appreciate that the alternative—Black oppression codified merely as "racial discrimination"—had only one political solution: integration on white terms. Preeminent for Haywood, however, was the liberation of Black people on their own terms: to him, the Black Belt nationality policy did that. In short, it was whether in the United States Black people were denied self-determination, or simply equal rights under the law, that was at stake. Even more, in his time in the USSR, Haywood came to appreciate that the oppression of Black people in the United States was neither exceptional nor sui generis; it was not a "national" predicament in the sense, so often repeated demagogically, of anti-Black racism as a moral test of the American character. On the contrary, the most militant and uncompromising position against white racism, Haywood concluded, was one that eschewed the sentimental cast of Black and white Americans as occluded compatriots. In short, Haywood's sojourn in the USSR convinced him that U.S. social realities had to be analyzed in *internationalist*, rather than *exceptionalist*, terms: throughout his struggle for the Black Belt thesis within the CPUSA, Haywood insisted that the Black Belt was a manifestation of a consistently revolutionary and internationalist perspective.

Even today, many writers and publications, including some that call themselves socialist, will refer to the Black Belt Thesis as a crude, mechanical imposition from Moscow that had little to no appeal to Black workers in the United States. This is simply not true. As developed by Haywood and his close comrades, the Black Belt Thesis was a vehicle for the recruitment of thousands of sharecroppers and other poor Black people in the Deep South.[30] It was also inseparable from the actual organizing successes the CPUSA experienced in the 1930s, such as the international spotlight put on the case of the Scottsboro boys.[31] Nevertheless, it was regarded by some leadership cadres as incompatible with the Party's emphasis on multinational unity, and as obstructing the class conscious solidarity of Black and white workers. By the 1950s, the Party abandoned the thesis entirely, in favor of the view that capitalist development would itself bring Black and white workers closer together over time. Discouraged, and down but not out, Haywood would go on to be an instrumental player in constituting a New Communist movement to fight against what he regarded as the CPUSA's capitulation to "revisionism."

Haywood leaves us with a useful motto, that given the actuality of revolutionary theory—its mobilization as a tool of struggle by the masses, independent of academic or civil society debatecraft—the central theoretical questions facing attempts to diagnose the stagnation and rebirth of history cannot be resolved abstractly; the answers will only emerge by way of struggle. As Haywood writes:

> Just as the ruling class ideology of white supremacy had its influences on white comrades, it was not unusual that Black comrades would similarly be affected by petty bourgeois nationalist ideology. These moods and sentiments were expressed in feelings of distrust of white comrades, in skepticism about the possibility of winning white workers to active support in the struggle for Black rights, and in the attitude that nothing could be accomplished until white chauvinism was completely eliminated. This latter was particularly dangerous because it failed to understand that white chauvinism could only be broken down in the process of struggle.[32]

Haywood's significant contribution to the debates animating the CPUSA in the late 1950s about the viability of the Black Belt thesis was forcefully to insist that the *real* question that underlay the debates was whether the problem of Black oppression would be answered by a *revolutionary* solution, or by one that made revisionist capitulations to white supremacy. In other words, for Haywood, to abandon the Black Belt thesis was akin to the "revisionist" thesis of peaceful coexistence with imperialism: it posited a "peaceful coexistence" with white racists and bigots, and ultimately the U.S. state, that was contrary to the goal of revolutionary transformation. Beyond the still relevant questions of demography, migration, the dispersal of sovereignty, and the relation of territorial contiguity to national formation, what the Black Belt thesis indicates is that U.S. history remains open to the future: it remains possible to imagine revolutionary reconfigurations of the settled geopolitical reality of the American empire. Haywood pointed out that his rhetorical opponents depended on a more or less clearly articulated prognosis (or desire) that an integrated U.S. nation-state was on the practical horizon. In so doing, they not only misunderstood the nature of Black oppression: they were unprepared for the revolutionary upsurge of Black people that Haywood (correctly) anticipated on the near-term horizon. Today, as Black people are again on the move, the question for any newly reconstituted Left is: can Marxists, or revolutionaries in general, remain open to a future that truly reconfigures U.S. imperialism, that smashes the machinery of state violence, and that holds open a space for the liberatory movements of (and toward) Black sovereignty? This kind of question will only be answered in the process of struggle: this chapter's contribution is to suggest that the mid-century centrality of anticolonial Black Leninism offers a usable past for that struggle's militants.

Whatever their many differences, Black Leninists agree that there will be no solution to racism and a repeatedly resurgent doctrine of white supremacy without overcoming capitalism and the capitalist state. What was true a century ago remains true: the oppression of Black people cannot be easily separated, either from planetary patterns of racial and neocolonial subjugation, nor from the operation of imperialist capitalism at its very core. For the strategists of the CPUSA and the Comintern, Black struggle in the United States was the "Achilles heel" of the American Empire, and although it might appear at first glance that the prospects for a renewal of "Black Leninism" are bleak, the actual struggles on the ground, and the links that activists make across time and space, between, to use a famous example, Ferguson and Palestine, are part of a process of reconstituting the *continuity* of Black anticapitalist struggle. Despite the literal wars waged on Black activists by the U.S. government, this tradition of struggle is ineradicable. What it calls on us to do is militantly struggle against "white chauvinism" wherever we find it, lend our support to the as yet unrealized *right to self-determination* of Black people everywhere, and commit to constructing a fighting organization of the multinational working class.

Notes

1. I.e., the Los Angeles branch of the Communist Party of the United States of America (CPUSA).

2. Mike Davis, *Old Gods, New Enigmas: Marx's Lost Theory* (Verso, 2018), xi. Angela Y. Davis, *Angela Davis: An Autobiography* (International Publishers, 1974/1988), 144.

3. Normally periodized, and punctuated, between the revolutionary years of 1917 and 1979.

4. Frank Wilderson III, *Red, White, and Black: Cinema and the Structures of U.S. Antagonisms* (Durham: Duke University Press, 2010). Wilderson credits Jared Sexton for a definition of "libidinal economy": "Jared Sexton describes libidinal economy as 'the economy, or distribution and arrangement, of desire and identification (their condensation and displacement), and the complex relationship between sexuality and the unconscious.' Needless to say, libidinal economy functions variously across scales and is as 'objective' as political economy. Importantly, it is linked not only to forms of attraction, affection and alliance, but also to aggression, destruction, and the violence of lethal consumption. He emphasizes that it is 'the whole structure of psychic and emotional life,' something more than, but inclusive of or traversed by, what Gramsci and other marxists call a 'structure of feeling'; it is 'a dispensation of energies, concerns, points of attention, anxieties, pleasures, appetites, revulsions, and phobias capable of both great mobility and tenacious fixation'" (9). My contention here is not over whether anti-Blackness is an ontology, nor tracking the relation between "marxism" and the theoretical field of "Afro-Pessimism." Rather, I am pointing to the mid-twentieth century as a period in which a wide variety of political actors believed deeply in the potential of a revolutionary rupture with and smashing of the material apparatus of anti-Black racism, that Black liberationist struggles and Marxist-Leninist revolutionary agitation not only overlapped but were seen as necessarily linked. Moreover, it was widely assumed then that anti-Black racism in the U.S. domestic scene was inseparable from other forms of colonial violence, and was in fact a profound manifestation of imperialism, the (temporary, but prolonged) victory of "racial capitalism" as a global economic order. In other words, to overthrow imperialism was to overturn the U.S. field of racial antagonism, and vice versa.

5. For instance, see Edward E. Baptist, *The Half Has Never Been Told: Slavery and the Making of American Capitalism* (New York: Basic, 2016); Sven Beckert, *Empire of Cotton: A Global History* (New York: Vintage, 2015); and Walter Johnson, *River of Dark Dreams: Slavery and Empire in the Cotton Kingdom* (Cambridge:

Harvard University Press, 2017). Johnson's earlier work traced the slave market's commodification of bodies and labor power, *Soul by Soul: Life Inside the Antebellum Slave Market* (Cambridge, Harvard University Press, 2001). See also Diana Ramey Berry, *The Price for Their Pound of Flesh: The Value of the Enslaved, from Womb to Grave, in the Building of a Nation* (Boston: Beacon, 2017).

6. W. E. B. Du Bois, *Black Reconstruction in America, 1860–1880* (New York: Free Press, 1998 [1935, 1962]; Du Bois, *The World and Africa* (New York: International Publishers, 1979 [1947]. David R. Roediger, *The Wages of Whiteness: Race and the Making of the American Working Class* (New York: Verso, 1991).

7. In the context of Marxism-Leninism, "revisionism" has a specific meaning distinct from its ordinary usage. A "revisionist" originally and basically refers to a "Marxist" who believes capitalism can be reformed, that socialism can be arrived at through gradual policy changes rather than mass organization and revolution. In the decades after 1956, it was often used (including by Mao and other Chinese communists) to refer directly to the USSR, especially its attempt to achieve "peaceful co-existence" with imperialism. More generally, it can refer to any concession or allowance to "bourgeois forces" in the class struggle. In the 1960s and 1970s there was a flourishing of "antirevisionist" communist organizations in the United States and elsewhere. This was in part a response to fractures in the CPUSA (many members were expelled or left the party during the 1950s). In the United States specifically there were intense line struggles over the proper conceptualization of how racial oppression and class exploitation should be theorized together.

8. Unless by "socialism" one refers to a post-Blair Labour Party, or the Center-Left bankers' social club that tends to run France, then the failure/defeat of the U.S. working classes looks less like an exceptional story than a common feature of imperialist (or "bribed") working classes. This dynamic, furthermore, was in Lenin's writing a constituent feature of imperialism per se. For an example, see *Proletarian Revolution and The Renegade Kautsky*, where Lenin characteristically refers to the way in which a joint stock company commonly known as "England and France" manipulates political forces in peripheral countries.

9. Thomas C. Holt, "Marking: Race, Race-Making, and the Writing of History," *American Historical Review* 100, no. 1 (Feb. 1995): 1–20.

10. C. L. R. James, *A History of Pan-African Revolt* (Oakland: PM, 2012 [1938; 1969]). James's thesis, in part, is that there was only one successful slave revolt, the Haitian Revolution; the rest were heroic but brutally crushed failures. In stark contrast to Du Bois, he is compelled to read the U.S. Civil War in the traditional "Marxist" way, against Karl Marx himself, who James notes regarded the war as "the greatest event of the age": for James, the Civil War was the culmination of a gradual economic transformation, and emancipation was in the final analysis the victory of the industrial bourgeoisie rather than that of the enslaved. Three years earlier, Du Bois, in *Black Reconstruction*, had by contrast depicted formal or legal emancipation as the inevitable outcome of the world's greatest "general strike"

whereby the enslaved workers had risen up and literally smashed the slave empire's means of production.

11. The term *racial capitalism* is from Cedric Robinson, whose *Black Marxism* argues that European race-thinking and national chauvinism predate and shape profoundly capitalism's emergence. He focuses on Du Bois, James, and Richard Wright as Black radical thinkers who represent and draw on an organic intellectual tradition that is distinct from and more expansive than Marxism, which Robinson portrays as irredeemably Eurocentric.

12. The material conditions of capture and confinement arguably make internationalism a necessary feature of Black national liberation in a particular or unique way. Africans from dozens of different cultures and several major, and distinct, language groups were forced to cohabitate, collaborate, and conspire. Thus, from the beginning Black national formation in the Americas was a practical exercise in "international" solidarity.

13. The perspective this anti-imperial formation developed on the world in crisis, during and after World War II, was summed up precisely by Aimé Césaire, whose *Discourse on Colonialism* pointed out that fascism was the turning inward of the limitless violence projected onto the colonies. That this is unrecognizable as such, for Europeans, reflects the distorted quality of even the most basic truisms and categories of (white) social analysis. For Césaire, one might say, the most sedimented and encrusted unities—hu/man or "nation," for instance—have been imposed from without, and in the wake of Europe's self-destruction are open to radical question. "Tricontinental" refers to a conference held in Cuba in 1966 that articulated revolutionary solidarity among freedom fighters in Latin America, Africa, and Asia.

14. For Losurdo's analysis see especially *War and Revolution*. It is noteworthy that each of the dominant powers after the war developed a civic religion around its unique pain and sacrifice: the American Greatest Generation dominates middle-brow sentiment despite the U.S.'s low casualties and relatively minor contribution to the defeat of the Nazis; the English fetishize their meager cross-class unity; every Frenchman fought in the Resistance; and no one suffered more than the Russians.

15. According to Haywood, one carload of white invaders was gunned down by a Browning machine gun in an elevated position. "Among them were several Chicago police officers—'off duty,' of course." Haywood, *A Black Communist in the Freedom Struggle: The Life of Harry Haywood*. Ed. Gwendolyn Midlo Hall (Minneapolis: University of Minnesota Press, 2012), 72.

16. Ibid., 3.

17. For historian Michael Gomez, to take but one example from a massive literature, Black American nationality was a more or less conscious fusion of preexisting nationalities: wherever captured Africans found themselves, they were speaking different languages and inhabiting different cosmologies. In struggle against their confinement and exploitation—a struggle to survive, or to die well—captive Africans by necessity created a syncretic national consciousness that synthesized what was

translatable among them and aestheticized what wasn't. See *Exchanging Our Country Marks: The Transformation of African Identities in the Colonial and Antebellum South* (Chapel Hill: University of North Carolina Press, 1998).

18. Cedric Robinson, *Black Marxism: The Making of the Black Radical Tradition* (Chapel Hill and London: University of North Carolina Press, 2000 [1983]), 318.

19. A useful collection of Lenin's writings on the subject can be found in V. I. Lenin, *National Liberation, Socialism, and Imperialism: Selected Writings* (New York: International Publishers, 1968).

20. See Carole Boyce Davies, *Left of Karl Marx: The Political Life of Black Communist Claudia Jones* (Durham: Duke University Press, 2008). For Cabral, see the collection of his speeches and writing in *Unity and Struggle* (New York and London: Monthly Review Press, 1979).

21. Walter Rodney, "Marxism and National Liberation," speech given at Queens College, N.Y. Available at https://www.marxists.org/subject/africa/rodney-walter/works/marxismandafrica.htm.

22. One might say that the "zero level" or "kernel" of "Leninism" as a political stance is a profound belief in the necessity and *actuality* of social revolution. In his own life and work, Lenin was deeply consistent in praising, analyzing, and exhorting the "really existing" peoples' movements to grow, test their strength, and seize power wherever possible. This is contrary to some predominant characterizations of Lenin as elevating the party apparatus above the workers out of concern regarding the latter's insufficient class consciousness. In fact, this view is not textually substantiated, as Lars Lih has copiously demonstrated in *Lenin Rediscovered*. Lih, in that work as well as in a revealing concise biography, shows that throughout his life Lenin demonstrated an unwavering fidelity to the working class's ability to organize and govern society. The *sine qua non* of Leninism, therefore, is arguably a desire for *the working class to become the ruling class* in society, that is, what Lenin himself insisted was Marxism's central problematic, *the dictatorship of the proletariat* (in other words, proletarian democracy). In short, Leninism is a word for a faith that social revolution, "people power," really can (despite appearances) transform society and chart an exit from capitalism as a world system. If you think of Paul Robeson celebrating the harmony of the world's many peoples in the American crossroads even as he was persecuted by the U.S. government, the dogged persistence with which Harry Haywood insisted on a *revolutionary* solution to Black oppression, the repeated insistence of the Black Panther Party that revolution could and would occur, Claudia Jones's disciplined and regular Party work even under the conditions of state repression and alienation, and so on, it is arguable that Black Leninists, especially in the putatively "crazy" belief they shared that the United States could be transformed by revolution, were the *most faithful* to Lenin's own faith (in the working masses).

23. Today, in the aftermath of a half-century of neoliberal strip-mining of the mildly social democratic or "welfare" state, one can appreciate the "backwardness"

of the United States in particular and the imperialist countries generally in a blunt, "vulgar" materialist sense. "Outsourcing" of manufacturing and "globalization" of supply chains has left a "really existing" United States that has a nonexistent social safety net, entrenched poverty, deep racialized divisions, and almost no manufacturing capacity to speak of. Its military capacity gives it the illusion of international strength, but the state is extremely brittle and liable to fracture in the face of any serious crisis, such as we are witnessing in 2020, the year of the coronavirus epidemic.

24. This point is made in a different context by Robin D. G. Kelley's landmark study *Hammer and Hoe: Alabama Communists during the Great Depression* (Chapel Hill: University of North Carolina Press, 1990).

25. George L. Jackson, *Blood in My Eye* (Baltimore: Black Classic Press, 1990), 41.

26. Lenin, *The State and Revolution: The Marxist Theory of the State and the Tasks of the Proletariat in the Revolution*, collected in Robert C. Tucker, ed. *The Lenin Anthology* (New York: Norton: 1975). For the relevant passages see especially 315–16.

27. See Zanotti, this volume.

28. For a reconstruction of Marx and Engels' thinking on the heterogeneity of class struggle, see Domenico Losurdo, *Class Struggle: A Political and Philosophical History*, trans. Gregory Elliott (London: Palgrave Macmillan, 2016).

29. Late imperial Russia was nicknamed "the prison-house of nations" because Great Russians ruled over many Baltic, Eastern European, and Central Asian captive nations. That Russia and America cannot be usefully compared is one of C. L. R. James's complaints against Haywood, but from today's vantage point modern America looks very much like a twenty-first-century "prison-house of nations," especially if we take real decolonization (i.e., transfers of land) to be a serious possibility. Moreover, the United States as a political entity greatly exceeds the "continental" imaginary and thus includes many more colonized nations: Guam, Puerto Rico, etc.

30. Kelley, *Hammer and Hoe*.

31. Publicizing the case of the "Scottsboro boys," who were put on trial under a dubious rape charge, was a major project of the CPUSA in the early 1930s.

32. Harry Haywood, *Black Bolshevik: Autobiography of an Afro-American Communist* (New York: Liberator, 1978), 430.

Bibliography

Baptist, Edward E. *The Half Has Never Been Told: Slavery and the Making of American Capitalism*. New York: Basic, 2016.

Berry, Diana Ramey. *The Price for Their Pound of Flesh: The Value of the Enslaved, from Womb to Grave, in the Building of a Nation*. Boston: Beacon, 2017.

Cabral, Amilcar. *Unity and Struggle*. New York and London: Monthly Review Press, 1979.

Césaire, Aimé. *Discourse on Colonialism.* Translated by Joan Pinkham. New York: Monthly Review, 2001.

Davies, Carole Boyce. *Left of Karl Marx: The Political Life of Black Communist Claudia Jones.* Durham: Duke University Press, 2008.

Davis, Angela Y. *Angela Davis: An Autobiography.* New York: International Publishers, 1988 [1974].

Davis, Mike. *Old Gods and New Enigmas: Marx's Lost Theory.* New York: Verso, 2018.

Gomez, Michael A. *Exchanging Our Country Marks: The Transformation of African Identities in the Colonial and Antebellum South.* Chapel Hill: University of North Carolina Press, 1998.

Haywood, Harry. *Black Bolshevik: Autobiography of an Afro-American Communist.* New York: Liberator, 1978.

———. *A Black Communist in the Freedom Struggle: The Life of Harry Haywood.* Edited by Gwendolyn Midlo Hall. Minneapolis: University of Minnesota Press, 2012.

Holt, Thomas C. "Marking: Race, Race-Making, and the Writing of History." *American Historical Review* 100, no. 1 (February 1995): 1–20.

Jackson, George L. *Blood in My Eye.* Baltimore: Black Classic Press, 1990.

James, C. L. R. *A History of Pan-African Revolt.* Oakland: PM, 2012 [1938; 1969].

Johnson, Walter. *River of Dark Dreams: Slavery and Empire in the Cotton Kingdom.* Cambridge: Harvard University Press, 2017.

———. *Soul by Soul: Life Inside the Antebellum Slave Market.* Cambridge: Harvard University Press, 2001.

Kelley, Robin D. G. *Hammer and Hoe: Alabama Communists during the Great Depression.* Chapel Hill: University of North Carolina Press, 1990.

Lenin, V. I. *The Lenin Anthology.* Edited by Robert C. Tucker. New York: Norton, 1975.

———. *National Liberation, Socialism, and Imperialism: Selected Writings.* New York: International Publishers, 1968.

Lih, Lars T. *Lenin.* London: Reaktion, 2011.

———. *Lenin Rediscovered: What Is to Be Done? in Context.* Chicago: Haymarket, 2008.

Losurdo, Domenico. *Class Struggle: A Political and Philosophical History.* Translated by Gregory Elliott. London: Palgrave Macmillan, 2016.

———. *War and Revolution: Rethinking the Twentieth Century.* Translated by Gregory Elliott. New York: Verso, 2015.

Robinson, Cedric. *Black Marxism: The Making of the Black Radical Tradition.* London and Chapel Hill: University of North Carolina Press, 2000 [1983].

Rodney, Walter. "Marxism and Africa," speech given at Queens College, NY, 1975. https://www.marxists.org/subject/africa/rodney-walter/works/marxismandafrica.htm.

Chapter 8

Lenin and East African Marxism
Abdul Rahman Mohamed Babu and Dani Wadada Nabudere

ZEYAD EL NABOLSY

Introduction: A Response to the Charge of Eurocentrism

With the contemporary global resurgence of interest in Marxism, including its Marxist-Leninist form(s), as a theoretical framework that can orient contemporary struggles against capitalism and its attendant depredations, it has become even more urgent to address some of the key criticisms that were leveled at Marx, Engels, and Lenin when they came to be treated as "dead dogs" towards the end of the twentieth century.[1] One key criticism was the charge that alleged that Marxism as such, including its Marxist-Leninist form(s), was and is irredeemably Eurocentric in character. While there have been attempts to counter such charges by excavating and reframing Marx's writings on the "non-Western world," this essay proposes to take another approach toward the charge of Eurocentrism in relation to Marxism (and Marxism-Leninism in particular).[2] One should take seriously Salah M. Hassan's methodological insight that an adequate response to the charge of Eurocentrism in relation to Marxism must take into consideration the ways in which Marxism was adopted, adapted, and refined by "Third World

Marxists."[3] This essay proposes to contribute to responses to the charge of Eurocentrism, by taking seriously the theoretical contributions of two African Marxists to the development of Marxism-Leninism. The focus is on Marxism-Leninism because it is primarily in this form that Marxism came to play an important role in the anticolonial and anti-neocolonial struggles on the African continent.[4] The question of "influence" is treated in a manner that demonstrates that African Marxists were never mere passive "adopters" of Marxism-Leninism. Thus, while it is true that they were influenced by Marx, Engels, and Lenin in specifiable ways, they also contributed to the development and refinement of Marxism-Leninism, through the formulation of insights that are of contemporary relevance both in relation to the African continent and beyond. This essay shows the specific ways in which two prominent East African Marxists, namely Abdul Rahman Mohamed Babu (1924–1996) and Dani Wadada Nabudere (1932–2011) were both deeply influenced by Lenin and made important contributions to Marxism-Leninism.

Babu was born and grew up in Zanzibar, where he came to play an important role in the anticolonial movement. In 1964, he attained the position of foreign minister in the revolutionary government headed by Abeid Karume, which was formed after the Zanzibar Revolution.[5] His revolutionary Marxism was seen as a threat by U.S. officials, who attempted to neutralize what they perceived to be his attempt to turn Zanzibar into an "African Cuba" by engineering the unification of Zanzibar with Tanganyika in April 1964.[6] Babu's critical attitude, formulated from a Marxist standpoint, towards Julius K. Nyerere's "African socialism" led to tensions between them. Eventually, Babu was imprisoned by Nyerere's Tanzanian government from 1972 to 1978.[7] In 1979, Babu left Tanzania to teach in the United States, and in 1984 he moved to London. In exile, he continued his quest to develop a version of Marxism that was suitable to conditions in East Africa through contributions to journals such as *The Journal of African Marxists*, *Review of African Political Economy*, and *Africa World Review*.[8] He also served as an adviser to progressive movements from Eritrea, Uganda, Ethiopia, and Rwanda.[9]

Nabudere, despite his stature as a key figure in African Marxism and an important revolutionary figure in Uganda's political history, has been described by some of his friends as "not very well known outside the circle of people who crossed his path."[10] Nabudere was active in the Ugandan struggle against British colonialism as a member of the executive committee of the United Kingdom Uganda Students Association. Nabudere was also a member of the youth wing of the Uganda People's Congress, although he was expelled and then accused of organizing a "communist plot," and eventually he was arrested in 1969.[11] Nabudere would later be released and would work for Idi Amin's government, until he became disenchanted and left in 1972 to Dar es Salaam where he participated in the famous Dar es Salaam debates.[12] These debates had to do in part with the assessment of Tanzanian "African socialism" from a Marxist standpoint. Nabudere would also go on to play an important role in the founding of the Uganda National Liberation Front (UNLF) which came into power in April 1979. After the overthrow of the UNLF in May 1980, the UNLF, which was renamed UNLF (Anti-Dictatorship), with Nabudere as a leading figure, launched a brief armed struggle. Nabudere would eventually leave to teach in Denmark in 1982, where he continued writing works on Marxist political economy. By the mid-1990s Nabudere was back in Uganda, where he eventually founded the Marcus Garvey Pan-African Institute (later to become a university).[13]

Both Babu and Nabudere were preoccupied with the formulation of a Marxist-Leninist critique of the theory and practice of "African socialism" as developed by Julius K. Nyerere. They also both contributed to the Dar es Salaam debates.[14] This essay seeks to demonstrate the relevance of Marxism-Leninism to anticolonial and anti-neocolonial struggles in East Africa by focusing on two aspects of Lenin's thought which were influential on the theoretical outlooks of Babu and Nabudere. The first aspect is Lenin's theory of imperialism and his account of the significance of national liberation struggles in light of this theory. The second aspect is Lenin's critique of the Narodniks in Russia. Furthermore, the essay demonstrates how Babu, through adopting Lenin's understanding of national struggles against imperialism as part of the global struggle against capitalism, was able to provide a theoretical basis for the endorsement of Pan-Africanism from a Marxist-Leninist standpoint, by arguing that Pan-Africanism is the expression of African nationalism vis-à-vis a racialized imperialism. This essay also shows how criticisms from the proponents of African socialism to the effect that Marxism was a foreign ideological import into Africa were met by Babu and Nabudere through a Leninist analysis of the class basis of African socialism, and through a critique of the view of African history that was endorsed by proponents of African socialism, a critique that was consciously modeled on Lenin's critique of the Narodniks' view of Russian history. In sum, Marxism-Leninism was not merely adopted in East Africa; it was also further refined and developed.

The Significance of Lenin's Theory of Imperialism for East African Marxism

In order to understand the historical significance of Lenin's theory of imperialism for Marxists in Africa in general and East Africa in particular, we should note that Lenin posited imperialism as the noncontingent outcome of the logic of accumulation of the capitalist mode of production in its monopolistic phase (characterized by the dominance of finance capital, i.e., the merged capital of the big monopolistic banks with the capital of the monopolistic industrialists).[15] This theory allowed Marxists in the colonies and neocolonies to identify ties between national liberation struggles and the struggle against capitalism. Lenin, insofar as he had argued that imperialism, and the "territorial division of the whole world among the biggest capitalist powers" that is associated with it,[16] was not a policy that the ruling classes of the capitalist powers could choose to pursue or not to pursue, as Karl Kautsky had claimed,[17] was essentially arguing that for the colonized or semicolonized peoples of the world the struggle for self-determination cannot come apart from the struggle against monopoly capital. In other words, the successful pursuit of the struggle against monopoly capital may not be a sufficient condition for the emancipation of African peoples, but it is nonetheless a necessary one. Lenin himself was clear that the triumph of socialism was a necessary condition for overcoming national and racial oppression, but he never claimed that it was sufficient: "To abolish national oppression a foundation is necessary, namely, socialist production; but on this foundation a democratically organized state, a democratic army, etc., must *also* be built. By transforming capitalism into socialism, the proletariat creates the *possibility* for complete abolition of national oppression; this possibility will become *reality* 'only'—'only'—when complete democracy is introduced in all spheres, including the fixing of state boundaries in accordance with the 'sympathies' of the population and including complete freedom of secession."[18]

Moreover, Lenin's theory emphasized the significance of colonies, semicolonies, and what we would call neocolonies for the accumulation of capital in the so-called advanced capitalist countries. This was important, because it allowed East African Marxists such as Nabudere and Babu to argue that contrary to prevalent discourse (and this discourse is still prevalent today), the "Global South" (if I may use this anachronism) was not and is not marginal to the processes of capitalist accumulation in the advanced countries. They argued that the problem of African countries was not that they are not integrated enough into the global economy. In fact, the problem is that they are too integrated into the world economy in the wrong way. As Babu puts it: "It is clear that foreign investment is the cause and not a solution, to our economic backwardness."[19] The issue for Babu is that African economies are export-oriented and internally disarticulated (i.e., lacking complementarity between different sectors of their national economies, i.e., agricultural production does not serve the needs of industrial development in most African countries, insofar as agricultural production remains oriented toward the cultivation of cash crops for export): "Our economies are rendered always responsive only to what the Western world is prepared to buy and sell, and hardly responsive to our internal development needs."[20] Thus, in postindependence East African countries, the agricultural sector insofar as it was geared toward the production of crops that could be exported was articulated with the industrial sectors of Europe, the United States, and Japan, and not with local industrial sectors.[21]

Babu and Nabudere understood Lenin's theory of imperialism as suggesting that while racism was a factor in the "Scramble for Africa" (1881–1914), one should not attempt to explain it solely or even primarily in terms of racism.[22] Instead, one should understand it primarily in terms of the economic requirements of monopoly capitalists, even if one must recognize that racism informed the manner in which control over African resources was exerted, namely, direct colonial control.[23] This was significant for them (and especially for Babu) because it gave them a vantage point from which to criticize those whom they referred to "as petty-bourgeois intellectuals," who attempted to provide explanations of societal phenomena and intersocietal interactions from a *purely racial standpoint* in a manner that obscured the managerial role of many of the ruling African elites in facilitating the continued exploitation of the African continent.[24]

It is important to recognize that Babu and Nabudere were not satisfied with simply adopting Lenin's theory of imperialism and "applying" it to the African context. They were also interested in updating it and defending it from the objections that had been raised against it. For example, in response to the objection that Lenin overstated the importance of overseas investment to the accumulation of capital in the imperialist centers, and that this is shown by the fact that "the major part of the direct investments of the major capitalist countries takes place amongst themselves," Nabudere answers that "such profitable investment in the imperialist countries is dependent on the investments in the Third World neo-colonies, since production in the center is dependent on raw materials from these countries."[25] In other words,

Nabudere points out that it is not simply a matter of the value of capital exports, because other factors come into consideration, such as the potential future use of resources and cutting off potential competitors from supplies of raw materials.[26] It is interesting to note that some contemporary theorists who think of themselves as working within the Marxist tradition continue to raise this objection against Lenin's theory of imperialism, without being at all aware that Nabudere had responded to this objection.[27] One way in which Eurocentrism has been detrimental to the development of Marxist theory is that it has hindered the diffusion of important theoretical advances that have been made by Marxists in the Global South/Third World. The "rediscovery of imperialism" by the Western Left,[28] should be accompanied by the rediscovery of the theories of imperialism that were developed by Third World Marxists.

Moreover, Nabudere makes an original contribution to Marxist political economy insofar as he updates and extends the argument Lenin made in *Imperialism: The Highest Stage of Capitalism*. In this text, Lenin starts out from the fact of the existence of monopolies as a response to the crisis of 1873, and the consolidation of cartels by 1903.[29] Lenin then notes that Marx (at a time when free competition was the rule rather than the exception) had argued that free competition leads to the formation of monopolies.[30] However, Lenin does not provide a rigorous argument that connects imperialism with Marx's account of the workings of capitalism in *Capital*, and specifically he does not explicitly connect imperialism with Marx's account of the tendency of the rate of profit to fall in chapter 13 of the third volume of *Capital*.[31] This is what Nabudere sets out to do in his *The Political Economy of Imperialism*.[32] Nabudere, following Marx, argues that the tendency of the rate of profit to fall is a function of the increase of the rate of constant capital in relation to variable capital, assuming that the rate of surplus value (the intensity of the exploitation of labor) remains constant.[33] Nabudere argues that this tendency explains the rise of monopolies and imperialism: "The tendency of the rate of profit to fall at home could only be reversed by increased supplies of cheap raw and auxiliary materials, expanding markets, and lower wages, which implied an intensification of the exploitation of labor."[34]

I have used the word *neocolonies* deliberately in my description of Lenin's theory of imperialism, even though Lenin himself did not employ this term (instead, he referred to "colonial" and "semi-colonial" peoples, and of course, he published his book in 1917, before the post–World War II period and the end of the direct colonial rule in Africa and Asia). However, the important thing to note is that *Lenin's definition of imperialism does not imply that imperialism always involves direct political control* (by "direct political control," I mean a form of control that takes the form of direct annexation, the carrying out of a mandate, or the establishment of a protectorate). Lenin himself warned against the possibility that imperialist states when confronted by a rising tide of nationalism might resort to "creating, under the guise of politically independent states, states which are wholly dependent upon them economically, financially and militarily."[35] He also argued that "[f]inance capital is such a great, such a decisive, you might say, force in all economic and in all international relations, that it is capable of subjecting and actually does subject, to itself even states enjoying the fullest political independence."[36] However, this does not mean that independence is insignificant or that it is not worth fighting for political independence given the dominance of finance capital over the global economy, because there is greater room for maneuver when a hitherto colonized society has attained juridical sovereignty.[37] Moreover, if one argues that one should not struggle for political independence given the domination of finance capital over the global economy, because under such conditions independence is only achievable in a mutilated form, then one must also commit oneself to the claim that one should abandon all other demands of political democracy, since, as Lenin pointed out, all the other demands of democracy can only be achieved in a mutilated form under the dominance of finance capital.[38]

Moreover, it is important to recognize that the fact that imperialism implies control and not always occupation or colonization (occupation and colonization being only two possible modes of control that are resorted to under certain historical circumstances) does not imply that imperialism is not "in general, a striving towards violence and reaction."[39] For the recognition of the juridical sovereignty of former colonial states does not imply that they are not vulnerable to the use of organized violence by former colonizing powers under various pretexts (e.g., intervention on humanitarian grounds and so on). For example, we can point to the various military coups that have been orchestrated by the French state in its former African colonies since the 1960s: coups in the Central African Republic, Mali, Chad, Niger, Benin, Burkina Faso, Cote d'Ivoire, and Togo.[40]

If we look at the five features that Lenin took to be the essential characteristics of imperialism: (1) the creation of monopolies, (2) the merging of bank capital with industrial capital (finance capital), (3) the increased importance of the exporting of capital as opposed to the exporting of commodities, (4) "formation of international monopolist capitalist associations which share the world among themselves," and (5) the "territorial division of the whole world among the biggest capitalist powers,"[41] we can note that strictly speaking those five conditions can obtain without there being direct colonial rule. As Walter Rodney put it: "Imperialism is essentially an economic phenomenon, and it does not necessarily lead to direct political control or colonization."[42] The fifth characteristic should not be understood in terms of direct political rule per se, but rather in terms of the ability of the biggest capitalist powers to acquire the raw materials that they need and to carve up markets and secure investment opportunities.

This point is important because it allowed East African Marxist theorists such as Babu and Nabudere to make a conceptual distinction between colonialism and neocolonialism on the one hand, and imperialism on the other hand. Colonialism (involving direct political control) is only one way in which imperialism takes form. Depending on historical conditions, imperialism can also take the form of neocolonialism (whereby the juridical sovereignty of a specific territory is recognized, but mechanisms are implemented that allow for the exploitation of its raw materials and its cheap labor reserves, etc.). Imperialism is a genus, of which colonialism (of the kind that was manifested in the "Scramble for Africa" for example) is a species. This conceptual distinction allows Babu to argue in his *African Socialism or Socialist Africa?* that "direct colonialism is not suited to the post-war [WWII] economic needs of imperialism. Colonies could not have supported the enormous debts which are currently being contracted by the neo-colonies, because ultimately the responsibility for such heavy financial burdens would have fallen on the colonial power itself."[43] In fact, Babu takes the well-known Leninist remark that "politics is the most concentrated expression of economics"[44] and creatively applies it to the situation of the formerly colonized countries in order to argue that the actualization of the right to self-determination (insofar as it requires more than the attainment of juridical sovereignty) requires the transformation of the economic structures of the formerly colonized countries.[45] Babu emphasizes this point when he notes that there can be no solution to the problem of underdevelopment by way of shifting trading partners (i.e., trading with the socialist bloc), without transforming the internal structure of the inherited colonial economies.[46]

The Justification of Pan-Africanism from a Marxist-Leninist Standpoint

Lenin's theory of imperialism as the highest stage of capitalism led him to emphasize the significance of national liberation struggles from a Marxist standpoint. As Horace B. Davis has noted, prior to Lenin's interventions on the significance of the "national" and "colonial" questions, the principle of the right to national self-determination had not been formally recognized by Marxists (Davis 1967).[47] In fact, some prominent Marxists such as Rosa Luxemburg had opposed the formal recognition of the right to national self-determination.[48] Lenin, on the other hand, was uncompromising in his recognition of the right to national self-determination (including the right to form independent national states). As Nabudere puts it, "The Bolsheviks widened the scope of the national question from the limited question of combating national oppression in Europe to the general question of emancipating oppressed peoples, colonies and semi-colonies from imperialism in general."[49] This extension of the scope of the national question was based on Lenin's recognition of the importance of supporting the struggles of an oppressed nation seeking self-determination, even if that nation did not have a significant industrial proletariat and even if its struggle for liberation was led by its bourgeoisie.[50] As Lenin put it in his polemic with Luxemburg: "If the bourgeoisie of the oppressed nation fights against the oppressing one, we are always, in every case, and more resolutely than anyone else, *in favor*; for we are the staunchest and most consistent enemies of oppression"; he also argued that "the bourgeois nationalism of *every* oppressed nation has a general democratic content which is directed *against* oppression, and it is this content that we support *unconditionally.*"[51]

Babu draws on this characterization of nationalism in the colonies and neocolonies in order to argue that Pan-Africanism insofar as it represents a nationalism that is hostile to imperialism is a progressive nationalism that must be supported and cultivated by African Marxist-Leninists and other Marxist-Leninists.[52] Babu refines Lenin's approach by arguing that due to the fact that the African nation-states that came into being with independence were the result of various compromises between different imperialist powers, and "had been artificially created without regard for homogeneous ethnic, cultural, or even (in some cases) linguistic identity,"[53] expressions of African nationalism should not be exclusively sought at the level of the African nation-state.[54] Instead, Babu argues, expressions of African nationalism should be sought in Pan-Africanism:[55] "African nationalism and Pan-Africanism are one and the same thing."[56] Furthermore, he suggests that Pan-Africanism is a more reliable vehicle for bringing about what he calls the "African Revolution" (perhaps in a nod to Fanon) than the nation-state.[57]

Babu also makes a conceptual distinction between "cultural" Pan-Africanism and "political" Pan-Africanism. He does not explicitly favor one over the other, regarding them as complementary forms.[58] However, he does note that these two forms have historically been distributed unevenly across Africa and the African diaspora. In particular, he argues that the cultural form of Pan-Africanism "is more common in the Diaspora where Africans are a minority," whereas on the African continent "the political tendency is more common."[59] In conceiving of Pan-Africanism as the most developed form of African nationalism, Babu made an important contribution to Marxist-Leninist theories of nationalism. If we look at Stalin's famous definition of nationalism (and of nations), which he advanced in his influential *Marxism and the National Question* (1913), we will notice that it does not provide a foundation for conceiving of Africans and members of the African diaspora as members of one nation.[60] Stalin defines the nation as "a historically evolved, stable community of language, territory, economic life, and psychological make-up manifested in a community of culture."[61] It is significant to note that Stalin thought that the nonexistence of any single one of these features was a sufficient reason for not characterizing a given set of people as a nation.[62]

This definition is problematic, however, from the standpoint of somebody who is attempting to articulate the theoretical foundations of Pan-Africanism as the most developed form of African nationalism. For it is clear that, to take just one of the aforementioned elements, Africans and the members of the African diaspora are not united by a stable community of language, nor, given the historical fact of uneven development on the African continent, can one say that all Africans have historically shared the same form of economic life. Moreover, Babu does not believe that "there is a community of culture" among Africans and people of African descent in the diaspora. As he puts it: "There is no single 'African culture' any more than there is a single Asiatic, Europe[an] or Latin American culture."[63] Instead, Babu argues that "it is the common history of oppression and its modern manifestations and the common struggle against them. This is the foundation on which the theory and practice of Pan-Africanism is based."[64] In other words, Pan-Africanism is understood by Babu to be a nationalist movement that responds to the depredations of racialized capitalism (or perhaps more accurately, capitalism as such) in its imperialist stage of development. If classical Marxist theorists in Europe maintained that capitalism (in its developed phase) creates its own gravediggers by creating an industrial proletariat, Babu argues that capitalism (in its imperialist monopoly finance phase) creates its own gravediggers by creating a common history of oppression that allows Africans and peoples of African descent to act as a collective historical subject that will play an essential role in bringing about imperialism's demise.

African Socialism as African Narodism

The claim that Marxism-Leninism is Eurocentric and not suited to the interpretation of social reality in other parts of the world is not new. On the African continent, this claim was advanced by adherents of a rival ideological framework and guiding theory for development, namely, "African socialism," during the 1960s and 1970s.[65] The theory of African socialism, in particular the version developed by Julius K. Nyerere, the first president of Tanzania,[66] maintained that the development of African countries is "dependent on the rehabilitation, reactivation, and modernization of pre-colonial communalism, which imparted to the continent a unique humanity based on classless and conflict-resolving communal relations."[67] Nyerere proposed that the foundation of African socialism lies in the extended family and used the Swahili term *Ujamaa* (meaning "familyhood") to refer to African socialism.[68] *Ujamaa* was thus seen as an indigenous framework that was more suitable for African conditions than Marxism-Leninism. Nyerere proposed that "traditionally we [Africans] lived as families, with individuals supporting each other and helping each other on terms of equality" based on communal ownership of land.[69] He argued that insofar as this was true, "traditional African society was a socialist society."[70] At times, Nyerere suggested that there were no real social classes in Tanzania and that, consequently, it did not make any sense to adopt a theory that emphasizes the role of class struggle in bringing about structural social transformations.[71]

Babu and Nabudere devoted significant efforts to the criticism of "African Socialism." Babu interpreted Nyerere's doctrine as a form of African Narodism, based on a conception of development that aims to protect the peasantry's communal village systems from the corrosive influences associated with the expansion of capitalist relations of production.[72] Babu drew explicitly on Lenin's critique of the Narodniks in Russia, (and especially the "old Narodniks" of the 1860s and 1870s who argued that there could be noncapitalist socialist development in Russia based on the traditions of village communes, and who were regarded by Lenin as being more principled and consistent than their epigones). In his *The Economic Content of Narodism and the Criticism of It in Mr. Struve's Book* (1895), Lenin had characterized Narodism in the following terms: "The essence of Narodism is that it represents the producers' interests from the standpoint of the small producer, the petty bourgeois."[73] In thinking that development was possible on the basis of the protection of the small and middling peasantry (and the undermining of the accumulation and concentration of land in the hands of rich peasants), Nyerere, his East African Marxist critics suggested, essentially formulated a theory of socialism that in reality represented the interests of the small-commodity producers.[74] Babu explicitly characterizes the defenders of African socialism as petty-bourgeois intellectuals, that is to say, intellectuals who represent the point of view of the small commodity producer: "By looking backward, our petty bourgeois intellectuals idealize our backwardness, for example communal life."[75]

One of the fundamental issues that was the subject of dispute between Lenin and the Narodniks, namely, the characterization of life in the village communes of the peasantry, therefore resurfaces in the dispute between East African Marxist-Leninists on the one hand and proponents of African socialism on the other. Both the Narodniks and Nyerere thought that the values of the peasants who lived in village communes should be preserved. Lenin, on the other hand, argued that the development of capitalist relations of production in the countryside is positive insofar as it tears "the peasant from the patriarchal, semi-feudal family, from the stupefying conditions of village life."[76] Likewise, Babu and Nabudere maintain that capitalism plays a progressive role at a certain point in its development and that there is something essentially incoherent about the attempt to bring about socialism while attempting to preserve or resuscitate "social values corresponding to a pre-feudal mode of production [the village commune]" (Babu 1981, xv).[77] It is important to recognize that the dispute is not about the "moral character" of the peasantry. Instead, the main issue is whether one can bring about a socialist transformation of society without at the same time bringing about a transformation in the outlook of peasants through the transformation of the objective socioeconomic structures that condition that outlook.

For both Lenin and Babu (as well as Nabudere), socialism in the Marxist theoretical framework presupposes the emergence of the modern individual subject, and this modern individual subject is the product of capitalist relations of production that historically play a progressive role insofar as they emancipate the individual from various ties of personal dependency that encumber the individual in precapitalist societies. Lenin is quite clear on this point: "It was capitalism alone that created the conditions which made possible this protest of the individual."[78] Similarly, Babu recognizes that the concept of the individual as the bearer of rights (prior to the specification of any duties) is a modern concept that came to be with the rise of capitalism.[79] This view of the individual as the product of capitalism was also adhered to by Marx and Engels.[80] Babu therefore maintains that a Marxist position that deals with its subject matter objectively does not allow one to uncritically romanticize the past. In fact, a Marxist must point out that "to idealize the 'equality' or 'right,' 'freedom' or 'democracy' of that past is to play right into the hands of our imperialist oppressors; it is to idealize tyranny and oppression."[81] A Marxist should also be able to point out to their opponent that the individual protest, based on the moral conscience of a subject that can think of itself as standing outside its given social context, which their opponent is engaged in by comparing the oppressive conditions of the capitalist present with the purportedly idyllic life of precapitalist societies, is itself the product of capitalist relations of production.[82]

Babu makes an explicit analogy between those who claimed that Marxism was not suitable for conditions in Asia and Africa and those who advanced the same claim in relation to Russia pre-1917.[83] Babu's key point is that *the claim to uniqueness is not itself unique*. As Nabudere also points out, it is the product of underdevelopment in the neocolonial world, which leads the petty bourgeoisie there to abandon the arena of political and economic struggle against imperialism and to attempt to wage a struggle exclusively in the cultural field. "Neocolonial culture as expressed in the writings of the neo-colonial intellectual reflected this depressed culture. Appeal to the past instead of the future dominated so-called 'Black culture,' 'Arab culture' or 'Asian culture'. This reflected generally backward conditions in the neocolony."[84] Thus, underlying the claims to uniqueness was in fact a more or less uniform condition of underdevelopment and domination by finance capital.[85]

This does not imply that the cultural sphere is an unimportant arena for struggle against imperialism. Nabudere's point is that it is a mistake to wage a struggle against imperialism *solely* through cultural contestations, especially when "African culture" is presented in monolithic terms, thereby obscuring the fact that "culture is a class product. There is no such thing as human culture devoid of class bias."[86] Nabudere argues that given the dominance of finance capital, to claim that there is something uniquely African is to underemphasize the manner in which Africa has been successfully (from the point of view of imperialist exploiters) integrated into the capitalist world system: "There is nothing uniquely African in an era where finance capital has united all the peoples of the world under its rule. An African proletariat is no less international than an Asian one or a European one. They are all exploited by the same monopolies, the same class, the same capital, only in different measure. There can therefore be no different general solution to the problem of imperialist exploitation."[87]

This is not to say that Nabudere and Babu were opposed to the development of a concrete analysis of specific sociohistorical situations and contexts. However, they made a conceptual distinction between the demands for a concrete analysis of specific historical contexts and claims that uphold what Olúfẹ́mi Táíwò has described as the "metaphysics of difference," that is, the thesis that there is an essential difference in kind between Black African peoples and other peoples.[88] For instance, some of the proponents of African socialism argued that there is something uniquely African in the manner in which individuals support one another in African communities, namely, the claim that "traditional" African societies were historically socialist societies.[89] Babu does not deny the existence of strong bonds of solidarity in many African societies at various points in African history. However, he argues that such bonds of solidarity were a characteristic of all human societies that were at a similar level with respect to the development of their productive forces: "The qualities which our petty-bourgeois intellectuals describe as essentially African are really human qualities which find expression when a community is at a certain level of productive capacity. When a community does not have the capacity to produce social surplus, there is simply no means of becoming unequal."[90] The emergence of individuals capable of asserting themselves in relation to their communities in a manner that can undermine communal ties of solidarity is thus contingent upon the existence of sufficient levels of surplus that would allow for the emergence of inequality. Babu's point is that when we adopt a historical materialist approach to the study of African history, we do not need to rely on "the metaphysics of difference" in order to explain African realities. By contrast, fidelity to the realities of African societies is compatible with denying that there is anything uniquely African that requires a specifically African theory that expresses a specifically "African culture" understood in essentialist ahistorical terms.[91] As Babu puts it, "In Africa, as everywhere else, survival entailed exploitation and class struggle; the greater the development of productive-forces, the sharper the struggle."[92] A true historical materialist approach to African history, Babu asserts, would undermine the thesis that there is something uniquely African that sets African history apart from the rest of human history. Moreover, we should add that it has been pointed out by some scholars that the concept of "traditional" African societies that was employed by proponents of African socialism was, at least in part, derived from colonialist anthropology.[93]

In contrast to proponents of African socialism who asserted that there might be a path toward the construction of socialism on the African continent through political projects that rejected class struggle,[94] Babu and Nabudere argued that such approaches were inadequate even if they were carried out in good faith. They criticized the thesis that there was no class-based stratification in African societies before the advent of colonialism. Babu argued that different social formations have existed throughout African history, including tributary empires: "Since Africa, like the rest of the world, is subject to uneven development, it is not difficult to find, from its very rich past, evidence of various levels of social development."[95] In his historical account of the colonization of East Africa by the British and the Germans, Nabudere points out that many societies in East Africa were characterized by the existence of an aristocratic ruling class, for example, in areas such as "Buganda, Bunyoro, Ankole, Kigezi, Toro, Buhaya and Barwanda-Burundi."[96] In sum, Babu and Nabudere were able to successfully draw on Lenin's thought in order to counter claims that Marxism was an essentially foreign theoretical framework that was being foisted onto Africans. More importantly, these East African Marxists were able to make important contributions to Marxist-Leninist theory by refining and developing the Marxist-Leninist research program in African contexts.

A Concluding Methodological Plea

Returning to this essay's opening remarks on the need to come to terms with the charge of Eurocentrism that has been leveled at Marxism-Leninism, the success or failure of this essay should be judged not in relation to whether it has adequately answered the question: Is Marxism-Leninism Eurocentric? For it is obvious that a fully adequate answer to this question would require a much longer discussion. Instead, the success or failure of this essay should be judged in relation to whether it has adequately answered the following question: With what must the attempt to respond to the charge of Eurocentrism begin? The answer offered in this essay is that it must begin by a serious and critical examination of the writings of those intellectuals in the "Third World" (or the "Global South," in current parlance), who have found Marxism-Leninism to be a useful theoretical framework in their anticolonial and anti-neocolonial struggles.[97] Methodologically speaking, it must be recognized that it is absurd for Marxist-Leninists (or Marxists in general) in the Western world to attempt to grapple with the charge of Eurocentrism, while at the same time continuing to systematically ignore the intellectual contributions of Marxist intellectuals from the "Third World."[98] For example, it is only by engaging in a serious critical study of the work that has been produced by Marxist theoreticians from the African continent, that any progress can be made regarding questions such as whether historical materialism is an adequate theoretical framework for studying the history of African social formations. When viewed from the perspective of the rich intellectual history of Marxism in the Third World, the specter of Eurocentrism appears rather old and frail.

Notes

I wish to thank Afifa Ltifi, Charisse Burden-Stelly, the editors of this volume, and two anonymous reviewers for their insightful comments on earlier versions of this manuscript.

1. In 1873, Marx famously remarked that it had become fashionable to treat Hegel as a "dead dog" and he vehemently criticized this superficial treatment of Hegel; Karl Marx, *Capital, Vol. 1*, trans. Ben Fowkes (London: Penguin Books, 1990), 102. This very same fate also befell Marx, Engels, Lenin, and other Marxist thinkers towards the end of the twentieth century.

2. For an attempt to counter the charge of Eurocentrism that has been leveled at Marx by excavating his relatively unknown writings on the "non-Western world," see Kevin Anderson, *Marx at the Margins: On Nationalism, Ethnicity, and Non-Western Societies* (Chicago: University of Chicago Press, 2010). For an attempt that focuses on Marx's scattered references to the African continent, see Stefan Kalmring and Andreas Nowak, "Viewing Africa with Marx: Remarks on Marx's Fragmented Engagement with the African Continent," *Science & Society* 81, no. 3 (2017): 331–47.

3. Salah M. Hassan, *How to Liberate Marx from His Eurocentrism: Notes on African/Black Marxism* (Berlin: Hatje Cantz Verlag, 2012), 4–7.

4. Badawi Riad 'Abd al Sami'a, *Al-Ard we al- 'ansuryia fe Itihad Janub Ifriqyiah* [*Land and Racism in the Union of South Africa*] (Cairo: Matba'at Dar al-Kutub we al-Wathaeq al-Qumyia be al-Qahira, 2014), 268. Also see, James Morris Blaut, "Evaluating Imperialism," *Science & Society* 61, no. 3 (1997): 382–93, and James Morris Blaut, "Marxism and Eurocentric Diffusionism," in *The Political Economy of Imperialism: Critical Appraisals*, ed. Ronald H. Chilcote (New York: Rowman and Littlefield, 2000): 127–40.

5. For a biographical overview of Babu's life, see Amrit Wilson, "Abdul Rahman Mohamed Babu: Politician, Scholar and Revolutionary," *The Journal of Pan African Studies* 1, no. 9 (2007): 10–24. For a periodization of Babu's political activities by one of his friends, see Samir Amin, "The First Babu Memorial Lecture," *Review of African Political Economy* 25, no. 77 (1998): 475–84.

6. For a full account of this episode, see Amrit Wilson, *The Threat of Liberation: Imperialism and Revolution in Zanzibar* (London: Pluto Press, 2013).

7. Seth M. Markle, "Brother Malcolm, Comrade Babu: Black Internationalism and the Politics of Friendship," *Biography* 36, no. 3 (2013): 540–67.

8. Wilson, *The Threat of Liberation*, 97.

9. Wilson, "Abdul Rahman Mohamed Babu," 15.

10. Yash Tandon, "Dani Wadada Nabudere, 1932–2011: An Uncompromising Revolutionary," *Review of African Political Economy* 39, no. 132 (2012): 335.

11. Ibid.

12. For a critical overview of the debates, see, Omwony Ojwok, "Review of the Debate on Imperialism, State, Class, and the National Question, University of Dar es Salaam, 1976–1977," *Utafiti: Journal of the Faculty of Arts and Social Science, University of Dar es Salaam* 2, no. 2 (1977): 371–89.

13. For more biographical information on Nabudere see the obituary by David Simon 2012, "Remembering Dani Wadada Nabudere," *Review of African Political Economy* 39, no. 132 (2012): 343–44.

14. Abdul Rahman Mohamed Babu, "Introduction," in *The University of Dar es Salaam Debate on Class, State, and Imperialism*, ed. Yash Tandon (Dar es Salaam: Tanzania Publishing House, 1982), 1–12; Dani Nabudere, "Imperialism, State, Class, and Race: A Critique of Issa Shivji's *Class Struggles in Tanzania*," in ibid., 55–67; Dani Nabudere, "A Caricature of Marxism-Leninism (A Reply to Karim Hirji)," in ibid., 83–127; Dani Nabudere, "A Reply to Mamdani and Bhagat," in ibid., 133–47.

15. Vladimir I. Lenin, "Imperialism: The Highest Stage of Capitalism," in *Imperialism and War: Classic Writings by V. I. Lenin and Nikolai Bukharin*, ed. Phil Gasper (Chicago: Haymarket Books 2017 [1917]), 101–102. Note that "imperialism" can also be used to characterize, for example, the Portuguese expansion into the Indian Ocean and the East African coast from the sixteenth century onward. However, this kind of imperialism was based on mercantilist accumulation techniques, that is, it was based on the accumulation of "surplus products" as opposed to "surplus value"; see Dani Nabudere, *Imperialism in East Africa. Volume 1: Imperialism and Exploitation* (London: Zed Press, 1981), 6. In other words, it is clear that there is a sense in which imperialism has always been an important feature of the capitalist world system. However, it is important to differentiate between different forms of imperialism, namely, mercantilist imperialism, "free-trade" imperialism, and monopoly capital imperialism. In this chapter I will be using the term *imperialism* to refer to the latter form of imperialism.

16. Lenin, "Imperialism," 102.

17. Karl Kautsky, "Imperialism," in *Discovering Imperialism: Social Democracy to World War I*, ed. and trans. Richard B. Day and Daniel Gaido (Chicago: Haymarket Books, 2012 [1914]), 753–74.

18. Vladimir I. Lenin, "The Right of Nations to Self-Determination," in *The Right of Nations to Self-Determination: Selected Writings by V. I. Lenin* (New York: International Publishers, 1951 [1915]), 90.

19. Abdul Rahman Mohamed Babu, "Postscript to *How Europe Underdeveloped Africa*," in *The Future that Works: Selected Writings of A.M. Babu*, ed. Salma Babu and Amrit Wilson (Asmara, Eritrea/ Trenton, NJ: Africa World Press, 2002 [1971]), 4.

20. Ibid., 5.

21. Dani Nabudere, *Imperialism in East Africa. Volume 1: Imperialism and Exploitation* (London: Zed Press, 1981), 129.

22. Abdul Rahman Mohamed Babu, *African Socialism or Socialist Africa?* (London: Zed Press, 1981), 102. Dani Nabudere, *Imperialism in East Africa. Volume 1*, 21.

23. Walter Rodney, *How Europe Underdeveloped Africa* (Washington, DC: Howard University Press, 1982 [1972]), 141.

24. Abdul Rahman Mohamed Babu, *African Socialism or Socialist Africa?* (London: Zed Press, 1981), 102–103. Babu's position on the issue of racism and the analysis of its underlying socioeconomic causes is evident in his approach to politics in Zanzibar on the eve of the revolution of 1964. Babu's Umma Party was the only political party in Zanzibar that did not recruit on a racial basis, and it was the most multiracial party on Zanzibar's political scene. In fact, Babu was able to convince some of the "Arabs" that their class interests aligned with the revolution against the sultan's regime, and some of the "Arabs" who joined the Umma Party ended up fighting against the sultan. Walaa' Saber Al Busati, *Afariqah we Arab fe Thawrat Zanjibar 1964* [Africans and Arabs in the Zanzibar Revolution of 1964] (Cairo: Maktebat Gezirat al-Ward, 2016), 153–58. See also, Wilson, *The Threat of Liberation*, 42.

25. Dani Nabudere, *The Political Economy of Imperialism: Its Theoretical and Polemical Treatment from Mercantilist to Multilateral Imperialism* (London: Zed Press, 1978), 190.

26. Ibid., 218.

27. For examples see, David McNally, "Understanding Imperialism: Old and New Dominion," *Against the Current* 117 (July–August 2005): https://www.marxists.org/history/etol/newspape/atc/255.html; Costas Lapavitsas, *Profiting without Producing: How Finance Exploits Us All* (London: Verso, 2013), 66.

28. John Bellamy Foster, "The Rediscovery of Imperialism," *Monthly Review* 54, no. 6 (2002): 1–16.

29. Lenin, "Imperialism," 42.

30. Ibid., 40–41.

31. Karl Marx, *Capital, Vol. III* (New York: International Publishers, 1967 [1894]), 212. Lenin did of course discuss Marx's account of the tendency of the rate of profit to fall in various other contexts, for example, in Vladimir I. Lenin, "Karl Marx," in *Introduction to Marx, Engels, Marxism (Articles by V. I. Lenin)* (New York: International Publishers, 1987 [1915]), 79. However, Lenin did not explicitly discuss it in his *Imperialism*.

32. Ojwok, "Review of the Debate," 377.

33. Nabudere, *The Political Economy of Imperialism*, 59.

34. Ibid., 77.

35. Vladimir I. Lenin, "Preliminary Draft of Theses on the National and Colonial Questions (For the Second Congress of the Communist International)," in *Lenin on the National and Colonial Questions: Three Articles* (Beijing: Foreign Language Press, 1967 [1920]), 28.

36. Lenin, "Imperialism," 96.

37. Vladimir I. Lenin, "The Socialist Revolution and the Right of Nations to Self-Determination (Theses)," in *The Right of Nations to Self-Determination: Selected Writings by V.I. Lenin* (New York: International Publishers, 1951 [1916b]), 74.

38. Vladimir I. Lenin, "The Discussion of Self-Determination Summed Up," In ibid., 75.

39. Lenin, "Imperialism," 104.

40. Demba Moussa Dembélé, "New Forms of Exploitation of Africa by Monopoly Capitalism: From Lenin's Imperialism to the Imperialism of the Triad in the 21st Century," in *Lenin's Imperialism in the 21st Century*, ed. Antonio A. Tujan Jr. (Manila: Institute of Political Economy, 2017), 50.

41. Lenin, "Imperialism," 102.

42. Rodney, *How Europe*, 157.

43. Babu, *African Socialism*, 48.

44. CPSU, "On the Question of the Trade Unions and their Organization," in *Resolutions and Decisions of the Communist Party of the Soviet Union, Volume 2: The Early Soviet Period, 1917–1929*, ed. Richard Gregor (Toronto: The University of Toronto Press, 1974 [1920]), 101.

45. Babu, *African Socialism*, 40.

46. Ibid.

47. Horace B. Davis, "Lenin and Nationalism: The Redirection of the Marxist Theory of Nationalism, 1903–1907," *Science & Society* 31, no. 2 (1967): 164–85.

48. Ibid., 164.

49. Dani Nabudere, *Imperialism in East Africa. Volume 2: Imperialism and Integration* (London: Zed Press, 1982d), 32.

50. James Morris Blaut, "Evaluating Imperialism," 386. James Morris Blaut, "Marxism and Eurocentric Diffusionism,"134. For a defense of the importance of the "national question" today, see Max Ajl, *A People's Green New Deal* (London: Pluto Press, 2021), 146–62.

51. Lenin, "The Right of Nations to Self-Determination," 24–25.

52. Abdul Rahman Mohamed Babu, "Pan-Africanism and the New World Order," in *The Future that Works: Selected Writings of A. M. Babu*, ed. Salma Babu and Amrit Wilson (Asmara, Eritrea/ Trenton, NJ: Africa World Press, 2002 [1994]), 98. It was Babu who was most concerned with providing a Marxist-Leninist account of Pan-Africanism, since Nabudere, unlike Babu, believed (at least in the early 1980s) that "the nation state is today the most revolutionary instrument in the majority of the countries of the world . . . for redressing the uneven development that has been exacerbated by imperialism"; Nabudere, *Imperialism in East Africa. Volume 1*, 181.

Babu, on the other hand, was a staunch advocate for Pan-Africanism throughout his life and he "was the driving force behind the 7th Pan African Congress held at Kampala in April 1994"; Wilson, "Abdul Rahman Mohamed Babu," 22. Babu was also instrumental in presenting Black radical struggles in the United States to an African audience; Seth M. Markle, *A Motorcycle on Hell Run: Tanzania, Black Power, and the Uncertain Future of Pan-Africanism, 1964–1974* (East Lansing: Michigan State University, 2017), 60. However, while Nabudere was not as interested in issues of race during the 1970s and 1980s, it should be noted that by the 1990s he came to show greater interest in Pan-Africanism; Tandon, "Dani Wadada Nabudere," 335–41. For a critique of the absence of race as a category of analysis in Nabudere's *The Political Economy of Imperialism*, see Corinna Mullen, "Insurgent Theory in Times of Crisis: Dani Wadada Nabudere's *The Political Economy of Imperialism*," *Liberated Texts*, May 2, 2021, https://liberatedtexts.com/reviews/insurgent-theory-in-times-of-crisis-dani-wadada-nabuderes-the-political-economy-of-imperialism/. In Nabudere's later work, we can detect a kind of autocritique of his earlier approach. Since he seems to indicate that the political economy perspectives of the 1970s and 1980s did not sufficiently emphasize problems of culture and cultural identity (including, one assumes, racial identity); Dani Nabudere, *Archie Mafeje: Scholar, Activist, and Thinker* (Pretoria: Africa Institute of South Africa, 2007), 34.

53. Babu, *African Socialism*, 101.

54. Babu claims that this situation is uniquely African: "The problem of nation states as an accidental offshoot of imperialist aggression was a uniquely African experience" Babu, *African Socialism*, 101. However, I think that this is not correct. A similar situation occurred in the "Arab World," specifically in the Levant or "Greater Syria region," see Nazih N. Ayubi, *Over-stating the Arab State: Politics and Society in the Middle East* (London/ New York: I. B. Tauris, 1995). In this sense, one can say that Pan-Africanism and Pan-Arabism emerged in response to structurally analogous (at a sufficient level of abstraction) circumstances. Babu limits the general applicability of his analysis of Pan-Africanism and its conditions of emergence in a way that is not justified.

55. Babu seems to have believed that ethnicity was inadequate as a basis for African nationalism because of the manner in which states in Africa were constituted in a way that cut across ethnic lines. However, it is not clear why one should not seek to construct multinational or multiethnic states, which, moreover, are the norm throughout the world.

56. Babu, "Pan-Africanism and the New World Order," 97.

57. Babu, *African Socialism*, 101.

58. Babu, "Pan-Africanism and the New World Order," 96–97.

59. Babu sees the political form of Pan-Africanism as more universalist in its orientation insofar as "it includes North Africans as an essential part of Pan Africa and as an essential part of Pan-African struggle"; Babu, "Pan-Africanism and the New World Order," 97. In general, one can say that Babu was a staunch critic of

the division of Africa into North Africa and Africa "proper" (Africa south of the Saharan desert): "Our enemy, therefore, is anyone who wants to disrupt that unity. In their attempt to divide Africa the imperialists tried to classify us into two groups. Africans North of the Sahara and Africans South of the Sahara. The creation of the All African People's Conference [held in Accra, Ghana [in 1958] dealt a decisive blow to this imperialist scheme"; Babu, "Speech Delivered at the 4th PAFMECA Conference," in *The Future that Works*, 60.

60. I should note that at least theoretically speaking, Lenin seems to have endorsed Stalin's definition, with the caveat that a given set of people must wish to be considered a nation (this voluntarist element is absent from Stalin's definition); Davis, "Lenin and Nationalism," 171. For an example of Lenin's emphasis on this voluntarist element, see e.g., Vladimir I. Lenin, "The Discussion of Self-Determination Summed Up," in *The Right of Nations to Self-Determination*, 89.

61. Joseph Stalin, "Marxism and the National Question," in *Marxism and the National and Colonial Question: A Collection of Articles and Speeches by Joseph Stalin* (Moscow: Foreign Languages Publishing House, 1940 [1913]), 7.

62. Ibid., 7–8.

63. Babu, "Pan-Africanism and the New World Order," 95.

64. Ibid.

65. Kwesi Botchwey, "Marxism and the Analysis of African Reality," *Africa Development/ Afrique et Développement* 2, no. 1 (1977): 9–16.

66. While there have been different forms of African socialism, e.g., the version that was developed by Léopold Sédar Senghor, *On African Socialism*, trans. Mercer Cook (London: Frederick A. Praeger, 1964 [1961]), Nyerere's *Ujamaa* has been described as "the most ambitious and sustained version of African socialism," by Priya Lal, "Maoism in Tanzania: Material Connections and Shared Imaginaries," in *Mao's Little Red Book: A Global History*, ed. Alexander C. Cook (Cambridge: Cambridge University Press, 2014), 99.

67. Robert Fatton, "The Political Ideology of Julius Nyerere: The Structural Implications of 'African Socialism,'" *Studies in International Comparative Development* 20, no. 2 (1985): 4.

68. Paul Bjerk, *Julius Nyerere* (Athens: Ohio University Press, 2017), 58–59.

69. Julius K. Nyerere, "Principles and Development: June 1966," in *Freedom and Socialism [Uhuru na Ujamaa]: A Selection from Writings and Speeches, 1965–1967* (Dar es Salaam: Oxford University Press, 1968 [1966a]), 198.

70. Ibid., 199.

71. Julius K. Nyerere, "Education for Self-Reliance: March 1967," in *Freedom and Socialism [Uhuru na Ujamaa]: A Selection from Writings and Speeches* (Dar es Salaam: Oxford University Press, 1968 [1967a]), 276.

72. Babu, *African Socialism*, xiv–xv; the question of whether Babu was correct in his interpretation of Nyerere's views is beyond the scope of this essay, although I will note that Nyerere also recognized some of the limitations of what he called

"traditional African society." For example, in Julius K. Nyerere, "The Power of Teachers: 27 August 1966," in *Freedom and Socialism [Uhuru na Ujamaa]*, 228. Julius K. Nyerere, "Socialism and Rural Development: September 1967," in ibid., 339.

73. Vladimir I. Lenin, "The Economic Content of Narodism and the Criticism of it in Mr. Struve's Book (The Reflection of Marxism in Bourgeois Literature)," in *V.I. Lenin: Collected Works, Vol. 1: 1893–1894*. Moscow: Progress Publishers, 1960 [1895], 396.

74. Issa G. Shivji, "The Village in Mwalimu's Thought and Political Practice," In *Africa's Liberation: The Legacy of Nyerere*, ed. Chambi Chachage and Annar Cassam (Cape Town/Dakar/ Nairobi: Pambazuka Press, 2010), 123.

75. Babu, *African Socialism*, 53.

76. Lenin, "The Economic Content of Narodism," 414.

77. Babu, *African Socialism*, xv. See also, Abdul Rahman Mohamed Babu, "Letter to Karim Essack," in *The Future that Works: Selected Writings of A.M. Babu*, 277. Nabudere, *The Political Economy of Imperialism*, 67.

78. Lenin, "The Economic Content of Narodism," 415.

79. Babu, *African Socialism*, 172.

80. Karl Marx and Frederick Engels, *The German Ideology* (Amherst, NY: Prometheus Books, 1998), 2. See also Marx, *Capital, Vol. 1*, 173. Marx's understanding of capitalism as relatively progressive insofar as it undermines ties of personal dependence is discussed extensively in Derek Sayer, *Capitalism and Modernity: An Excursus on Marx and Weber* (London: Routledge, 1991), 17–37.

81. Babu, *African Socialism*, 53.

82. This mode of argument essentially mirrors Hegel's critique of Romanticism. For a defense of this claim and for an account of the significance of Hegel's critique of Romanticism for Marxist movements today, see Zeyad el Nabolsy, "*Nasserism and the Impossibility of Innocence*," *International Politics Review* (2021): https://doi.org/10.1057/s41312-021-00105-1.

83. Babu, *African Socialism*, xiii.

84. Dani Nabudere, Essays *on the Theory and Practice of Imperialism* (London: Onyx Press, 1979), 86.

85. In fact, even under Nyerere, Tanzania's educational policies in the 1960s and 1970s were driven by the conditions set by foreign donors, Zeyad el Nabolsy, "African Socialism in Retrospect: Karim Hirji's *The Travails of a Tanzanian Teacher*," *Liberated Texts* (March 23, 2021): https://liberatedtexts.com/reviews/african-socialism-in-retrospect-karim-f-hirjis-the-travails-of-a-tanzanian-teacher/.

86. Nabudere, *Essays on the Theory and Practice of Imperialism*, 85.

87. Ibid., 93.

88. Olúfẹ́mi Táíwò, "Cabral, Culture, Progress, and the Metaphysics of Difference," in *Claim No Easy Victories: The Legacy of Amilcar Cabral*, ed. Firoze Manji and Bill Fletcher Jr. (Dakar and Montreal: CODESRIA and Daraja Press, 2013).

89. See, Priya Lal, "Africa," in *The Bloomsbury Companion to Marx*, ed. Jeff Diamanti et al. (New York: Bloomsbury Academic, 2018), 504; Marion Mushkat, "African Socialism Reappraised and Reconsidered," *Africa: Rivista trimestrale di studi e documentazione dell'Istituto italiano perl'Africa e l'Oriente* 27, no. 2 (1972): 154; Monique A. Bedasse, *Jah Kingdom: Rastafarians, Tanzania, and Pan-Africanism in the Age of Decolonization* (Chapel Hill, NC: The University of North Carolina Press, 2017), 60; Bjerk, *Julius Nyerere*, 59.

90. Babu, *African Socialism*, 57. For example, many of the features that have been claimed to be uniquely African were found in rural communities in nineteenth-century Russia, as is evident from Dimitrii Ivanovich Rostislavov, *Provincial Russia in the Age of Enlightenment: The Memoir of a Priest's Son*, trans. and ed. Alexander M. Martin (DeKalb: Northern Illinois University Press, 2002), 86–96.

91. For a Cabralian elucidation of this point, see Zeyad El Nabolsy, "Amílcar Cabral's Modernist Philosophy of Culture and Cultural Liberation," *Journal of African Cultural Studies* 32, no. 2 (2020): 237–38.

92. Babu, *African Socialism*, 59.

93. Asli Berkaty, "Negritude and African Socialism: Rhetorical Devices for Overcoming Social Divides," *Third Text* 24, no. 2 (2010): 210.

94. Tomáš František Žák, "Applying the Weapon of Theory: Comparing the Philosophy of Julius Kambarage Nyerere and Kwame Nkrumah," *Journal of African Cultural Studies* 28 no. 2 (2016): 150; Priya Lal, "African Socialism and the Limits of Global Familyhood: Tanzania and the New International Economic Order in Sub-Saharan Africa," *Humanity: An International Journal of Human Rights, Humanitarianism, and Development* 6, no. 1 (2015): 21.

95. Babu, *African Socialism*, 60.

96. Nabudere, *Imperialism in East Africa. Volume 2*, 19. Also see Nabudere, "Imperialism, State, Class and Race," 67. This point was also made by other African defenders of the relevance of Marxism to the analysis of African history, e.g., Botchwey, "Marxism," 14, as well as Kwesi Kwaa Prah, *Jacobus Eliza Johannes Capitein: A Critical Study of an 18th Century African* (Trenton: Africa World Press, 1992), 79–93.

97. For an example of recent work that takes this methodological point seriously (with respect to Marxism in general), see Max Ajl, "Auto-centered Development and Indigenous Technics: Slaheddine el-Amami and Tunisian Delinking," *The Journal of Peasant Studies* 46, no. 6 (2019): 1240–50; and Max Ajl, "Delinking, Food Sovereignty, and Populist Agronomy: Notes on an Intellectual History of the Peasant Path in the Global South," *Review of African Political Economy* 45, no. 155 (2018): 66–70.

98. For a further discussion of this point from the standpoint of African Marxism, see Claude Ake, "The Political Economy Approach: Historical and Explanatory Notes on a Marxian Legacy in Africa," *Africa Development/ Afrique et Développement* 2, no. 1 (1983): 9–16.

Bibliography

'Abd al Sami'a, Badawi Riad. *Al-Ard we al- 'ansuryia fe Itihad Janub Ifriqyiah* [Land and Racism in the Union of South Africa]. Cairo: Matba'at Dar al-Kutub we al-Wathaeq al-Qumyia be al-Qahira, 2014.

Ajl, Max. "Delinking, Food Sovereignty, and Populist Agronomy: Notes on an Intellectual History of the Peasant Path in the Global South." *Review of African Political Economy* 45, no. 155 (2018): 64–84.

———. "Auto-centered Development and Indigenous Technics: Slaheddine el-Amami and Tunisian Delinking," *The Journal of Peasant Studies* 46, no. 6 (2019): 1240–65.

———. *A People's Green New Deal.* London: Pluto Press, 2021.

Ake, Claude. "The Political Economy Approach: Historical and Explanatory Notes on a Marxian Legacy in Africa." *Africa Development/ Afrique et Développement* 2, no. 1 (1983): 9–16.

Al Busati, Walaa' Saber. *Afariqah we Arab fe Thawrat Zanjibar 1964* [Africans and Arabs in the Zanzibar Revolution 1964]. Cairo: Maktebat Gezirat al-Ward, 2016.

Amin, Samir. "The First Babu Memorial Lecture." *Review of African Political Economy* 25, no. 77 (1998): 475–84.

Anderson, Kevin B. *Marx at the Margins: On Nationalism, Ethnicity, and Non-Western Societies.* Chicago: University of Chicago Press, 2010.

Ayubi, Nazih N. *Over-stating the Arab State: Politics and Society in the Middle East.* London and New York: I. B. Tauris, 1995.

Babu, A. M. *African Socialism or Socialist Africa?* London: Zed Press, 1981.

———. "Speech Delivered at the 4th PAFMECA Conference." In *The Future that Works: Selected Writings of A. M. Babu*, edited by Salma Babu and Amrit Wilson, 59–62. Asmara, Eritrea/Trenton, NJ: Africa World Press, 2002. [1958].

———. "Postscript to *How Europe Underdeveloped Africa.*" In *The Future that Works: Selected Writings of A. M. Babu*, edited by Salma Babu and Amrit Wilson, 3–9. Asmara, Eritrea/Trenton, NJ: Africa World Press, 2002 [1971].

———. "Letter to Karim Essack." In *The Future that Works: Selected Writings of A. M. Babu*, edited by Salma Babu and Amrit Wilson, 276–83. Asmara, Eritrea/Trenton, NJ: Africa World Press, 2002. [1982].

———. "Pan-Africanism and the New World Order." In *The Future that Works: Selected Writings of A. M. Babu*, edited by Salma Babu and Amrit Wilson, 94–99. Asmara, Eritrea/Trenton, NJ: Africa World Press, 2002. [1994].

———. "Introduction." In *The University of Dar es Salaam Debate on Class, State, and Imperialism,* edited by Yash Tandon, 1–12. Dar es Salaam: Tanzania Publishing House, 1982.

Bedasse, Monique A. *Jah Kingdom: Rastafarians, Tanzania, and Pan-Africanism in the Age of Decolonization.* Chapel Hill: The University of North Carolina Press, 2017.

Berkaty, Asli. "Negritude and African Socialism: Rhetorical Devices for Overcoming Social Divides." *Third Text* 24, no. 2 (2010): 205–14.

Bjerk, Paul. *Julius Nyerere.* Athens: Ohio University Press. 2017.

Blaut, J. M. "Evaluating Imperialism." *Science & Society* 61, no. 3 (1997): 382–93.

———. "Marxism and Eurocentric Diffusionism." In *The Political Economy of Imperialism: Critical Appraisals*, edited by Ronald H. Chilcote, 127–40. New York: Rowman and Littlefield, 2000.

Botchwey, Kwesi. "Marxism and the Analysis of African Reality." *Africa Development/ Afrique et Développement* 2, no. 1 (1977): 9–16.

CPSU. "On the Question of the Trade Unions and their Organization." In *Resolutions and Decisions of the Communist Party of the Soviet Union, Volume 2: The Early Soviet Period, 1917–1929*, edited by Richard Gregor, 100–104. Toronto: The University of Toronto Press, 1974 [1920].

Davis, Horace B. "Lenin and Nationalism: The Redirection of the Marxist Theory of Nationalism, 1903–1907." *Science & Society* 31, no. 2 (1967): 164–85.

Dembélé, Demba Moussa. "New Forms of Exploitation of Africa by Monopoly Capitalism: From Lenin's Imperialism to the Imperialism of the Triad in the 21st Century." In *Lenin's Imperialism in the 21st Century*, edited by Antonio A. Tujan Jr., 45–58. Manila: Institute of Political Economy, 2017.

El Nabolsy, Zeyad. "Amílcar Cabral's Modernist Philosophy of Culture and Cultural Liberation." *Journal of African Cultural Studies* 32, no. 2 (2020): 231–50.

———. "Nasserism and the Impossibility of Innocence." *International Politics Review* (2021): https://doi.org/10.1057/s41312-021-00105-1.

———. "African Socialism in Retrospect: Karim Hirji's *The Travails of a Tanzanian Teacher*." *Liberated Texts* (March 23, 2021): https://liberatedtexts.com/reviews/african-socialism-in-retrospect-karim-f-hirjis-the-travails-of-a-tanzanian-teacher/.

Fatton, Robert. "The Political Ideology of Julius Nyerere: The Structural Implications of 'African Socialism.'" *Studies in International Comparative Development* 20, no. 2 (1985): 3–24.

Foster, John Bellamy. "The Rediscovery of Imperialism." *Monthly Review* 54, no. 6 (2002): 1–16.

Hassan, Salah M. *How to Liberate Marx from His Eurocentrism: Notes on African/Black Marxism.* Berlin: Hatje Cantz Verlag, 2012.

Kalmring, Stefan, and Andreas Nowak. "Viewing Africa with Marx: Remarks on Marx's Fragmented Engagement with the African Continent." *Science & Society* 81, no. 3 (2017): 331–47.

Kautsky, Karl. "Imperialism." In *Discovering Imperialism: Social Democracy to World War I*, edited and translated by Richard B. Day and Daniel Gaido, 753–74. Chicago: Haymarket Books, 2012 [1914].

Lal, Priya. "Maoism in Tanzania: Material Connections and Shared Imaginaries." In *Mao's Little Red Book: A Global History*, edited by Alexander C. Cook, 96–116. Cambridge: Cambridge University Press, 2014.

———. "African Socialism and the Limits of Global Familyhood: Tanzania and the New International Economic Order in Sub-Saharan Africa." *Humanity: An International Journal of Human Rights, Humanitarianism, and Development* 6, no. 1 (2015): 17–31.

———. "Africa." In *The Bloomsbury Companion to Marx*, edited by Jeff Diamanti et al., 501–507. New York: Bloomsbury Academic, 2018.

Lapavitsas, Costas. *Profiting without Producing: How Finance Exploits Us All*. London: Verso, 2013.

Lenin, V. I. "Karl Marx." In *Introduction to Marx, Engels, Marxism (articles by V. I. Lenin)*, 53–95. New York: International Publishers, 1987 [1915].

———. "The Right of Nations to Self-Determination." In *The Right of Nations to Self-Determination: Selected Writings by V. I. Lenin*, 9–64. New York: International Publishers, 1951 [1915].

———. "The Discussion of Self-Determination Summed Up." In *The Right of Nations to Self-Determination: Selected Writings by V. I. Lenin*, 86–119. New York: International Publishers, 1951 [1916a].

———. "The Socialist Revolution and the Right of Nations to Self-Determination (Theses)." In *The Right of Nations to Self-Determination: Selected Writings by V. I. Lenin*, 73–85. New York: International Publishers, 1951 [1916b].

———. "Imperialism: The Highest Stage of Capitalism." In *Imperialism and War: Classic Writings by V. I. Lenin and Nikolai Bukharin*, edited by Phil Gasper, 23–144. Chicago: Haymarket Books, 2017 [1917].

———. "The Economic Content of Narodism and the Criticism of it in Mr. Struve's Book (The Reflection of Marxism in Bourgeois Literature)." In *V.I. Lenin: Collected Works, Vol. 1: 1893–1894*, 333–508. Moscow: Progress Publishers, 1960 [1895].

———. "Preliminary Draft of Theses on the National and Colonial Questions (For the Second Congress of the Communist International)." In *Lenin on the National and Colonial Questions: Three Articles*, 20–29. Beijing: Foreign Language Press, 1967 [1920].

Markle, Seth M. "Brother Malcolm, Comrade Babu: Black Internationalism and the Politics of Friendship." *Biography* 36, no. 3 (2013): 540–67.

———. *A Motorcycle on Hell Run: Tanzania, Black Power, and the Uncertain Future of Pan-Africanism, 1964–1974*. East Lansing: Michigan State University, 2017.

Marx, Karl. *Capital, Vol. I*. Translated by Ben Fowkes. London: Penguin Books, 1990 [1867].

———. *Capital, Vol. III*. New York: International Publishers, 1967 [1894].

Marx, Karl, and Frederick Engels. *The German Ideology*. Amherst, NY: Prometheus Books, 1998.

McNally, David. "Understanding Imperialism: Old and New Dominion." *Against the Current* 117 (July–August 2005): https://www.marxists.org/history/etol/newspape/atc/255.html.

Mullen, Corinna. "Insurgent Theory in Times of Crisis: Dani Wadada Nabudere's *The Political Economy of Imperialism*." *Liberated Texts*, May 2, 2021, https://liberatedtexts.com/reviews/insurgent-theory-in-times-of-crisis-dani-wadada-nabuderes-the-political-economy-of-imperialism/.

Mushkat, Marion. "African Socialism Reappraised and Reconsidered." *Africa: Rivista trimestrale di studi e documentazione dell'Istituto italiano perl'Africa e l'Oriente* 27, no. 2 (1972): 151–78.

Nabudere, Dan. *The Political Economy of Imperialism: Its Theoretical and Polemical Treatment from Mercantilist to Multilateral Imperialism*. London: Zed Press, 1978.

———. *Essays on the Theory and Practice of Imperialism*. London: Onyx Press, 1979.

———. *Imperialism in East Africa. Volume 1: Imperialism and Exploitation*. London: Zed Press, 1981.

———. "Imperialism, State, Class, and Race: A Critique of Issa Shivji's *Class Struggles in Tanzania*." In *University of Dar es Salaam Debate on Class, State, and Imperialism*, edited by Yash Tandon, 55–67. Dar es Salaam: Tanzania Publishing House, 1982a.

———. "A Caricature of Marxism-Leninism (A Reply to Karim Hirji)." In *The University of Dar es Salaam Debate on Class, State, and Imperialism*, edited by Yash Tandon, 83–127. Dar es Salaam: Tanzania Publishing House, 1982b.

———. "A Reply to Mamdani and Bhagat." In *The University of Dar es Salaam Debate on Class, State, and Imperialism*, edited by Yash Tandon, 133–47. Dar es Salaam: Tanzania Publishing House, 1982c.

———. *Imperialism in East Africa. Volume 2: Imperialism and Integration*. London: Zed Press, 1982d.

———. *Archie Mafeje: Scholar, Activist, and Thinker*. Pretoria: Africa Institute of South Africa, 2007.

Nyerere, Julius K. "Principles and Development: June 1966." In *Freedom and Socialism [Uhuru na Ujamaa]: A Selection from Writings and Speeches, 1965–1967*, 187–206. Dar es Salaam: Oxford University Press, 1968 [1966a].

———. "The Power of Teachers: 27 August 1966." In *Freedom and Socialism [Uhuru na Ujamaa]: A Selection from Writings and Speeches, 1965–1967*, 223–28. Dar es Salaam: Oxford University Press, 1968 [1966b].

———. "Education for Self-Reliance: March 1967." In *Freedom and Socialism [Uhuru na Ujamaa]: A Selection from Writings and Speeches, 1965–1967*, 267–90. Dar es Salaam: Oxford University Press, 1968 [1967a].

———. "Socialism and Rural Development: September 1967." In *Freedom and Socialism [Uhuru na Ujamaa]: A Selection from Writings and Speeches, 1965–1967*, 337–66. Dar es Salaam: Oxford University Press, 1968 [1967b].

Ojwok, Omwony. "Review of the Debate on Imperialism, State, Class, and the National Question, University of Dar es Salaam, 1976–1977." *Utafiti: Journal of the Faculty of Arts and Social Science, University of Dar es Salaam* 2, no. 2 (1977): 371–89.

Prah, Kwesi Kwaa. *Jacobus Eliza Johannes Capitein: A Critical Study of an 18th Century African.* Trenton: Africa World Press, 1992.

Rodney, Walter. *How Europe Underdeveloped Africa.* Washington, DC: Howard University Press, 1982 [1972].

Rostislavov, Dimitrii Ivanovich. *Provincial Russia in the Age of Enlightenment: The Memoir of a Priest's Son.* Translated and edited by Alexander M. Martin. DeKalb: Northern Illinois University Press, 2002.

Sayer, Derek. *Capitalism and Modernity: An Excursus on Marx and Weber.* London: Routledge, 1991.

Senghor, Léopold Sédar. *On African Socialism.* Translated by Mercer Cook. London: Frederick A. Praeger, 1964 [1961].

Shivji, Issa G. "The Village in Mwalimu's Thought and Political Practice." In *Africa's Liberation: The Legacy of Nyerere*, edited by Chambi Chachage and Annar Cassam, 120–33. Cape Town/Dakar/ Nairobi: Pambazuka Press, 2010.

Simon, David. "Remembering Dani Wadada Nabudere." *Review of African Political Economy* 39, no. 132 (2012): 343–44.

Stalin, Joseph. "Marxism and the National Question." In *Marxism and the National and Colonial Question: A Collection of Article and Speeches by Joseph Stalin*, 3–53. Moscow: Foreign Languages Publishing House, 1940 [1913].

Táíwò, Olúfẹ́mi. "Cabral, Culture, Progress, and the Metaphysics of Difference." In *Claim No Easy Victories: The Legacy of Amilcar Cabral*, edited by Firoze Manji and Bill Fletcher Jr., 355–64. Dakar and Montreal: CODESRIA and Daraja Press, 2013.

Tandon, Yash. "Dani Wadada Nabudere, 1932–2011: An Uncompromising Revolutionary." *Review of African Political Economy* 39, no. 132 (2012): 335–41.

Wilson, Amrit. "Abdul Rahman Mohamed Babu: Politician, Scholar and Revolutionary." *The Journal of Pan African Studies* 1, no. 9 (2007): 10–24.

———. *The Threat of Liberation: Imperialism and Revolution in Zanzibar.* London: Pluto Press, 2013.

Žák, Tomáš František. "Applying the Weapon of Theory: Comparing the Philosophy of Julius Kambarage Nyerere and Kwame Nkrumah." *Journal of African Cultural Studies* 28, no. 2 (2016): 147–60.

PART III

THE ACTUALITY OF LENIN'S THEORY

Chapter 9

"Withering Away"

State, Revolution, and Social Objectivity

GIOVANNI ZANOTTI

The "withering away of the state" is one of Lenin's most famous and controversial theses. Criticized from the Right as utopian (since it allegedly postulates a full redemption of human nature) and from the Left as authoritarian (since it maintains the necessity of a state, however transitional, instead of invoking its *immediate* suppression), it touches the deepest layers of Marxist political theory and practice and has never ceased to challenge both of them. In a 1919 lecture, Lenin affirmed that the question of the state "has acquired the greatest importance and has become, one might say, the most burning one, the focus of all present-day political questions and political disputes."[1] After a century, this claim hardly appears to be obsolete. The question of the state has been recently brought back into the limelight within the debate on the crisis of neoliberalism and the subsequent rise of the new nationalistic ultra-Right populist movements. Specifically, the long-established left-wing tradition of cosmopolitanism celebrating "the end of nation-states" as both a positive and an already occurring process[2] is now being opposed in the name of a neostatist Left position, "reclaiming the state" not only as something still pivotal, but also as the proper space for democracy and even class struggle.[3]

From a Leninist perspective, as we shall see, these opposite positions could be easily criticized, for they both abstract from the essential qualitative difference between the state that precedes and the one that follows the revolutionary leap. On the one side, neocosmopolitans consider it possible that a *bourgeois* state "withers away." Neostatists, in turn, attribute to this same bourgeois state thaumaturgical qualities that, according to Lenin, it cannot possess. For Lenin, it is only the postrevolutionary workers' state that is capable of withering away; similarly, and for the same reasons, it is only the postrevolutionary state that can intervene on behalf of workers. These insights, despite their political urgency, would remain fruitless, however, and be exposed in turn to the suspicion of dogmatism, if carried out without a prior discussion of the *theoretical* issues implicit in Lenin's thesis. I will address some of these issues in what follows, hoping that such preliminary examination will also provide a better basis for a future *historical* discussion of the problem of the state—namely, of what has changed and what has remained the same since Lenin's own historical experience of "bourgeois states."

In the first part of this chapter, I will briefly present the withering-away thesis in its basic conceptual structure and point out some of the most difficult problems that Lenin's own formulation of this thesis leaves open from the point of view of the theory of the state. I will then take a step back and move to the debate on the theoretical framework of Marx's critique of political economy itself. I will summarize the innovative conception of capital as a "social objectivity" as it has been developed in the context of the German "New Marx Reading," indicate its conceptual bases, and emphasize some of its consequences for political theory. Finally, I will reexamine the withering-away thesis—including the concept of revolution implied by it—in light of these consequences and, while amending it (by removing some of the mechanistic residues still present in Lenin), I will defend its fundamental correctness and actuality.[4]

Lenin and the "Two States"

State and Revolution was written between August and September 1917. Famously, its main theoretical contribution consists in the transformation of a remark from Engels's *Anti-Dühring*—a passing one, although other, similar statements are to be found in Engels's writings—into the systematic cornerstone of a doctrine of social revolution.[5] In 1878, Engels wrote:

> The first act by virtue of which the state really constitutes itself as the representative of the whole of society—the taking possession of the means of production in the name of society—this is, at the same time, its last independent act as a state. State interference in social relations becomes, in one domain after another, superfluous, and then dies out of itself [*schläft ein*: literally, it "falls asleep"]; the government of persons is replaced by the administration of things, and by the conduct of processes of production. The state is not "abolished." *It withers away* [*stirbt ab*].[6]

This well-known and infinitely debated passage summarizes the main elements of a conception of the state that, although formulated by Engels, may probably be at least partially extended to Marx, who had read and approved the *Anti-Dühring*.[7] According to this conception, the state is, in every imaginable form (including democracy), a "particular repressive force," an "organ of society above society," a false universality which, by the very fact of becoming autonomous as a separated body opposed to the particulars, reveals itself as a particular on its own.[8] Therefore, the state is essentially an instrument of domination, which ultimately means: economic class domination. Its existence is coextensive with the existence of social antagonism. This implies—as Lenin insists from the beginning—that under no circumstances can the state fulfill the function that ideology ascribes to it, namely, that of providing a positive resolution for conflicts between classes. The state is not a reconciliation, but rather an expression and a result of the conflict *inasmuch as it is objectively irreconcilable*. This equally implies, moreover, that not even a social revolution can immediately bring about the disappearance of the state. The latter will continue to exist, at least in the so-called transition period, to the exact extent to which its performances will be made necessary by the presence of residual antagonisms (in other words, by the necessity of repressing the bourgeois reaction). And it will exist precisely as a "dictatorship" of one class over the other, as a "systematic and organized violence," according to the general definition of *any* state.[9]

Hence the contrast, explicit in Engels's passage, between the abstract idea of an "abolition" of the state and a new, curious image, which was destined to an unexpected fortune, namely, that of the "withering away" (*Absterben*) of the state.[10] This expression is supposed to mean something like a progressive becoming-superfluous. As Lenin claims: "The expression 'the state *withers away*' is very well-chosen, for it indicates both the gradual and the spontaneous nature of the process.[11] That is to say, in no conceivable situation will the conflict end by decree, which means at the same time: neither with a single strike (hence, "gradual") nor by an act of will (hence, "spontaneous"). Yet, conversely, it is not unthinkable that the conflict might vanish in a different way. It has been frequently noticed that Lenin's political polemic possesses a peculiarly twofold character, that it is always possible, so to speak, to see the issue at hand from both sides—the anti-anarchist side or the anti-opportunist one—where one or another prevails according to contingent urgencies. Such a double-faced nature is already present in Marx and Engels, but becomes structurally evident in Lenin and is particularly transparent in *State and Revolution*. This is probably because its theoretical foundation lies precisely in the complexity of such a concept as "withering away." Against the anarchists, the state cannot be abolished; against the opportunists, it must be possible to overcome it.[12]

And yet, Lenin's specific contribution in *State and Revolution* consists in the introduction of a further distinction. At the level of political theory—and that is the crucial point—this amounts to a sort of *duplication of the concept of state*. If the reformists of the Second International tended to interpret Engels's passage in the sense of a linear path, situating the "withering away" in the present, as if it were a process already in progress, Lenin brings the moment of discontinuity back to the foreground by objecting: the state must wither away, yes, but *which state*? The present, "bourgeois" state is organic to class antagonism; therefore, it shares that tendency to self-reproduction, that inertia and circularity that are intrinsic to domination in general (in Adorno's words, its being "always-the-same"). The bourgeois state cannot "wither away." Rather, the withering away concerns *another*, "proletarian" state, which must be posited *ex novo*, after smashing the former. If, on the one side, the anti-anarchist polemic defends not simply the use of the state in the present with tactical goals, but also the necessity of a postrevolutionary transitional state (the "dictatorship of the proletariat"), the anti-opportunist polemic, on the other side, ultimately results in the thesis of a qualitative difference between a state that *cannot* and one that *can* wither away. "Revolution" precisely consists in this "passage from one kind of state to another."[13] Thus, the "abolition," as opposed to the "withering away," reappears with regard to the first state. The voluntarist moment of the "decision," as an active rational position, keeps playing a double role in the strategy, first as the smashing of the bourgeois state and then as the institution of the proletarian one. The bourgeois state can only be abolished, not wither away; the proletarian state can only wither away, not be abolished (Figure 9.1).

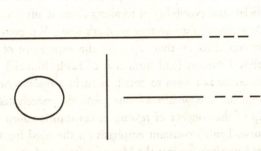

Figure 9.1. The upper line represents the classic bourgeois idea of the state as something eternal. The middle one symbolizes the opportunist attempt to come to terms with the letter of Engels's passage, while at same time conceiving the "withering away" as a spontaneous result of reformist politics. The position defended by Lenin as "orthodox" is represented by the lower drawing, where a clear break (revolution) separates the self-perpetuating bourgeois state from a future state, defined by its *capacity* for withering away.

So far, Lenin's argument. As is well known, the events following the October Revolution forced Lenin himself to the famous "two steps back," also—and especially—with regard to the problem of the state.[14] Thereafter, the thesis of the state's withering away shared the twentieth-century vicissitudes of the labor movement. De facto set aside by Stalin on both the practical and the theoretical level, it has continued to live a sort of underground life in certain currents of Western Marxism.[15] More recently, as I have mentioned in the introduction, the idea of a "withering away of the state" is beginning to be discussed anew—mostly as a polemical target—following the structural crisis of the neoliberal globalization process.[16] Apart from the changes in historical context, however, the withering-away thesis undoubtedly presents many problems already on the theoretical level. I will consider two of them in particular.

First, the duality of bourgeois and proletarian state, on which the whole argument depends, is all but obvious. What allows such duplication? Even if one accepts every other premise of Lenin's, why would it not be enough to argue for a change in the political orientation of a single state, rather than speaking of two different states? Lenin seems to take a cue from Marx's analysis of the Paris Commune, which "was no longer a state in the proper sense of the word," and considers a series of strictly institutional implications for the new political body.[17] Examples of such are: replacement of the permanent police and army with a popular militia; abolishment of the division of powers and transformation of the executive into a parliamentary commission; eligibility of all public officials and possibility of recalling them at any time; and limitation of their remuneration to an average worker's wage. Yet, even if one abstracts from the obvious distance that separates the experience of the Commune from our political context (and from that of Lenin himself), these measures, although radical, do not seem to entail, as such, a *replacement* of the existing state, but only its *transformation*—one perfectly conceivable, in particular, with the help of the concept of *reform*, as constitutionalism would have it.

Of course, Lenin's constant emphasis on the need for a violent revolution is directed precisely against the idea of reform and the gradualism that it might entail (but that, as we shall see, it does *not* necessarily entail). In fact it seems that, for Lenin, the question of violence is the real point at stake in his emphasis on the necessary break between "two states." Once again, however, moral and political problems inherent in the idea of a violent revolution aside, its discussion appears to belong to a different and more contingent register of theory. The question of each state's identity—and thus, of the meaning of an alleged transition from "one state" to "another"—is independent from the question of whether violence is required for its transformation (or replacement).[18]

It should be noted, in this regard, that a state's identity is a function, first and foremost, of its territorial determination. The most radical revolution, in a given country, might very well replace the "bourgeois state" with a deeply different "proletarian state"; both, however, will have at least in common the fact of being, before and after the revolution, the state *of that country*. This is because a state's identity is guaranteed simply by the existence *of other states*—a point always curiously undertheorized (although not ignored in its practical effects) by both Lenin and Marxism in general. Lenin's insistence on *discontinuity* thus appears to be incomplete at the very least. It seems to be essentially driven by the urge to establish a logical and temporal divide, a qualitative leap between a "before" and an "after" whose meaning, however, is not fully determined.

The second problem concerns the very concept of "withering away of the state," which seems to imply a complete and necessary disappearance of social conflict. The objections that have been raised against this concept can roughly be reduced to two, namely: the objection of *utopianism*, since it does not take into account the anthropological persistence of general (not socially specific) interhuman conflicts; and the objection of *mechanicism*, since it seems to view both social revolution and (especially) its outcome as deterministically unavoidable processes. On this last point, in fact, Lenin casts no doubts. He claims, for example: "According to Marx, the proletariat needs only a state that is withering away, i.e., a state constituted so that it begins to wither away immediately *and cannot but wither away.*"[19] Countless analogous formulations can be found in the text. They sound unquestionably problematic today, in light of the critique that evolutionary determinism has been submitted to by the most diverse currents of Western Marxism since Lenin's times. It might be possible, however, to fully accept this second objection and then attempt to reformulate the withering-away thesis in such a way as to remove, at the same time, the (undeniable) determinism and the (alleged) utopianism of Lenin's position. It is the strategy I will pursue in the following paragraphs, while also trying to come to terms with the first problem—that of the meaning of the "two states."

In order to do so, I will provisionally set aside Lenin's theory of state and, instead, focus on the debate on the critique of political economy, namely, the theory concerning the specifically capitalist mode of production. I will lay out some essential elements of Adorno's reading of Marx's *Capital* that have been developed in the context of the so-called New Marx Reading (*Neue Marx-Lektüre*). Specifically, I will focus on the idea of capitalist relations of production as a *social objectivity*.[20]

The Concept of Social Objectivity

The phrase "social objectivity" (*gesellschaftliche Objektivität*) appears only sporadically in Adorno's sociological writings; however, the *concept* that it refers to is pivotal to his interpretation of capitalist modernity.[21] For Adorno, "society" in the full sense of the word is only modern society, in which the "relationships between men . . . have grown increasingly independent of them, opaque, now standing off against human beings like some different substance."[22] These relationships are *social*, since they are constantly produced and reproduced by social agents, usually in an unconscious form, through the process of commodity exchange. For this same reason, they can always, in principle, be abolished by social agents as well. The thesis of the structural specificity and, therefore, historical contingency and superability of the capitalist mode of production is founded precisely upon its social character.

At the same time, however, these relationships are *objective*, since they impose themselves upon the same individuals who produce them, as a given system of material conditionings and limitations, which necessarily follow from the dynamic laws inherent in the value-form. While this is a seemingly obvious thesis for any reader of Marx, it has far-reaching theoretical consequences. They depend on how one determines the exact meaning of such "objectivity." Indeed, the phrase "social objectivity"—or rather, "social objectivities," in the plural (*gesellschaftliche Gegenständlichkeiten*)—is also used, for example, by the late Georg Lukács, but in a quite different sense, which is much closer to what he had called "form of objectivity" in *History and Class Consciousness*.[23] For Lukács, a specific "(social) objectivity" is the common configuration that both the objects and the prevailing modes of thinking take in any given society (in capitalistic societies, it is the commodity-form).[24] This concept refers back to Wilhelm Dilthey's idea of *culture* as a formally specified, organic totality. In Lukács, it aims, among other things, at overcoming the mechanical character of the unilateral structure/superstructure causal determination as it had been traditionally conceived. Today's widespread definition of capitalism as "a form of life"[25] shares a similar intention, and so does every theory that somehow tries to solve the structure/superstructure problem through a more or less defined idea of interaction. Adorno's concept of social objectivity, however, is radically different from these efforts.[26]

First, "objectivity" in Adorno's sense is not a transhistorical category, but appears solely within the capitalist mode of production. Notably, it would be absent in a postcapitalist society, and so would *necessity* and *legality* in the peculiarly *social* sense that the two terms possess in this context. Even more importantly, though, capital is, so to speak, demythologized in this perspective, inasmuch as it is reduced to *mere* material objectivity. The basic idea is that capital is not a *form* common to both subject and object, but rather an objective *limit* to the subjective action—one, of course, that *then* forces subjectivity into determinate forms.[27] This allows one to maintain a—negative—primacy of the objectivity without reducing, in a deterministic sense, the exteriority of the subjective moment (that is, ultimately, of the *productive forces*) to the objective relations of production. To put it in simpler terms: *within capitalism*, the economic structure indeed determines the superstructure, but it does not "produce" subjectivity any more than a system of channels "produces" the water which then, based on its constraints, takes a determinate shape.

In short: contrary to the opinion of many, capital *is not a subject*.[28] It has neither "agency" nor formal-spiritual nature, it is no "essence," "principle," or "source of meaning"—not even a broken one. Nor does it reproduce itself automatically, for it needs the only true subjects, that is, concrete individuals. Nevertheless, it *determines* the actions of concrete individuals within more or less wide limits, thereby being continuously reproduced. It is *effective* and, indeed, preponderant, without being subjective, since it is not an acting force, but a *structural legality*[29] (Figure 9.2).

This legality, as is shown in the first chapters of *Capital*'s first volume, originates from the immediately private, and only mediately social, character of labor—that is, in the peculiar mediation established by commodity

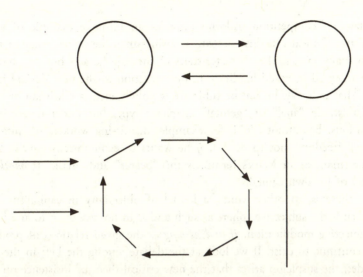

Figure 9.2. The first drawing represents the "holistic" conception of structure and superstructure in terms of formal analogy and mutual determination. The second one, by contrast, illustrates the theory of social objectivity (the relations of production) as the "different substance" (Adorno), i.e., as clearly distinct in essence from living subjective agencies (the forces of production), not really "acting" upon them, but rather *blocking* their free development and, thereby, forcing them into a specific (circular, self-perpetuating) movement.

exchange. The exchange laws establish class domination as an *impersonal*, that is to say, *objectively mediated domination* (*sachlich vermittelte Herrschaft*). According to Stefano Breda, there are two possible interpretations of this concept of Marx's. For a weak (and prevalent) reading, capitalist domination is ultimately personal, but is disguised as a *seemingly* impersonal one by the objective *appearance* of exchange-based relations, for the veil of formal freedom and equality conceals brute power and actual exploitation. For a strong reading, on the contrary, *really objectified* relations dominate over *all* social agents—including the capitalists—by setting clear limits to their individual actions in advance.[30] This, of course, does not eliminate the class character of the relations of production, nor the subjective interests related to it. However, it is *everyone's* obedience to the laws of capital that also generates—among other consequences—the reproduction of the privileges of a few.[31]

Central to the objectification process is the mechanism of *competition*, which, in this reading of *Capital*, is essential to any capitalist system (and so is the need for cyclical crises).[32] According to Marx, the constraints deriving from capitalist relations are imposed upon capitalists themselves through the laws of competition. Adorno provides an intuitive example of what "objectivity" means in this context. A businessman, he writes, "may or may not actually possess the character-traits of the role he acts but . . . having once accepted it, could hardly from one situation to the next deviate from it."[33] That is to say, he can be subjectively enlightened, a Christian or even a Marxist, an "anal" or "genital" character type, but under determinate conditions, he cannot avoid, for example, dismissing workers (despite his "formal freedom" not to do so), *if* he wants to economically survive as a businessman, or in Marx's terms, as the "bearer" and "mask" (*Charaktermaske*) of his own capital.[34]

There is, in other words, a kernel of objectivity in capitalism that transcends the subjective sphere as such and is in no way open to any form of subjective modification, *if and as long as* the given relations of production continue to exist. If we look at the debate among the Left in the last decades, the suspicion arises that the new critical theories' insistence on the subjective dimension—be it in the form of Habermas's intersubjectivity or of the poststructuralist affirmation of difference—may be partially explained as a Freudian repression of social objectivity, in the very historical phase in which its constraints reappear as ever more binding once again. Against this forgetfulness, as early as 1971, Cesare Luporini already warned that the theoretical essence of historical materialism consists in the *irreducibility* of relations of production to "intersubjective and interpersonal relationships."[35]

The transcendence of objectivity, in fact, does not only concern individual subjects, but also collective ones. Namely, it limits the scope of possible political intervention. This is because social objectivity is, above all, a *system*—an overall structural connection. Marx's critique of political economy is precisely the explanation of connections between different phenomenal forms of the capitalist relations of production—commodity, money, surplus value, capital, credit, and so on. These forms appear to be reciprocally independent to the empirical consciousness (and to bourgeois political economy), while actually belonging together. One cannot exist without all the others. This mutual interdependence had already been the theoretical ground for Marx's critique of the "utopian socialists" of his time (Proudhon, Owen), inasmuch as they attempted to think a generalized commodity exchange without capital accumulation or even without money. Today, similar arguments could be employed to object to the widespread image of a "healthy" market economy without "financial excrescences," but also to question, for example, the objective feasibility of redistributive policies during an accumulation crisis—the necessary, implicit presupposition of any gradualist program.

The "possibilities" and "impossibilities" whose range is thus defined by the system of social objectivity—this is the essential point—are *logical-structural* ones, and thereby, qualitatively different from *political* ones, that is, possibilities and impossibilities that are each time determined by the contingent balance of power between social agents. The very concept of such "balance of power" (or "power relations"), although important in its own right, must therefore be relativized as to its political scope. Actually, the idea of a "shift in the balance of power" is sometimes used (especially in neo-Gramscian contexts)[36] as an all-powerful conceptual tool, capable of making *any* political scenario conceivable in principle. Anything might be done, provided that the "balance of power" is favorable enough, and, in particular, there would be no contradiction in pursuing radical goals through a gradualist practice (since the balance of power could be gradually and indefinitely shifted in favor of the lower classes).

By contrast, according to the theory of social objectivity, *not* everything depends on the balance of power, since not everything is open to the decision of any individual or collective subject—not even of the entire capitalist class. The change in the balance of power can certainly permit transformations within certain limits; and, at a higher level, it can create the conditions for abolishing social objectivity as a whole. However, it cannot break its internal connections. A *and* B (commodity and surplus value, capital and imperialism . . .) can be suppressed together, but no subjective will, as powerful as it may be, can make it possible to have A *without* B. The balance of power, in other words, is determined by class *struggle,* but struggles take place between subjects, and capital, not being a subject, is not one of the poles of a struggle. One struggles against capitalists, but not, strictly speaking, against capital. In itself, capital can only exist or be suppressed, even if its suppression necessarily presupposes a political struggle between collective *subjects,* namely, the classes. Of course, capital can *always* be suppressed, and in this sense, the impossibilities are always *conditioned* impossibilities—objectivity is social, not natural. Necessary in its internal structure, the capitalist mode of production is contingent as a whole. To stress its systemic coherence, therefore, by no way means to deny the effectiveness of class struggle, or even the "autonomy of the political" in Mario Tronti's sense.[37] On the contrary, such autonomy always exists in principle. It is not, however, an *indeterminate* autonomy, for it is conditioned in turn by the existence of structural—that is to say, essentially nonpolitical—connections. Not everything is possible, or rather: everything is possible, but *under certain conditions*.

The concept of social objectivity thus throws light on another central dilemma of the Marxist tradition, that is, the tension between determinism and voluntarism, between the need for scientific certainty and the irreducible contingency of praxis. In fact, it is precisely the impersonal character of capitalist relations that makes them *knowable* in the most rigorous scientific sense—for their connections are logically necessary. At the same time, though, the scope of such knowledge is thus limited in two ways. First, the knowledge of capital is not the general science of history, but only of a specific social form. Second, it is not the science of the entire social-historical world, but only of its *objective* side, and precisely as something negative, that is, a limit to the subjects' (actual) freedom. There are no "laws of history," but a socially specific necessity, which can be overcome. And there is no scientific politics. There are, indeed, scientific *grounds* for politics, which, however, are merely negative. They are *the science of what is impossible* in a given context, that is, of the conditions that must be met, the limits that must be removed in order for a certain accomplishment to be simply *possible*. These limits vary considerably in different historical situations, but they always ultimately refer back to the existence of social objectivity as a system. This is the meaning of Breda's thesis that the concept of social objectivity grounds at the same time, and for the same reasons, the *scientific* and the *revolutionary* character of the theory.[38]

Toward a Disenchanted Concept of Revolution

If these are the premises, then the consequences for the theory of state, and especially for the withering-away thesis, are already given, too. The "bourgeois state" in Lenin's sense is the one whose normal functioning is mediated and conditioned by the existence of social objectivity. The "proletarian state" is the one whose performances are free from such specific limitation, *without anything else being ascribable to it in advance except for this negative determination*. In principle, both can be even identical as for their institutional architecture, and the transition from one to another can be well understood as a transformation rather than a replacement, thus preserving the identity that is essential to any given state. This transformation, moreover, is perfectly conceivable as carried out by constitutional/parliamentary means ("reforms").

And yet, the systemic nature of social objectivity allows one to maintain, at the same time, the fundamental relation of *discontinuity* pivotal to Lenin's theory, which thus receives a more defined conceptual place. The qualitative leap between "before" and "after" continues to exist in spite of every possible concession to a "reformist" path, because social objectivity either exists as a system or does not exist at all. In other words, the concept of social objectivity makes it possible to dissociate the problem of legal revolution from the problem of gradualism. Social objectivity may well be abolished through reform (i.e., in a nonviolent way), but under no imaginable circumstance could it be abolished bit by bit.

It has been argued, notably, that Lenin's position, while being somewhat reasonable in his own time, has been rendered obsolete by new theoretical and practical tools that would allow contemporary states to attain Lenin's goals by different means, namely constitutionalism and Keynesianism. Both would have made states much more plastic and dynamic, by increasing their capacity for internal evolution on one side, and, on the other, by extending the scope of their activity from pure repression to providing social welfare and crisis management.[39] To this objection, it should be answered: constitutionalism maybe, but not Keynesianism. Their respective dimensions are different. On the one hand, the problem of the *transformation* of the state actually assigns some philosophical centrality to the concept of "constitutional reform." On the other hand, however, the gradualism that defines the essence of any "Keynesian" politics lies entirely upstream or, in another sense, entirely downstream of that very transformation. It cannot cross it. In other words: gradualism, while constituting an important dimension of political emancipation, can only belong to processes that either prepare or follow the *break* to which the suppression of social objectivity is necessarily tied. The construction of the political *conditions* for this break is certainly gradual, and so is, thereafter, the unfolding of liberated potentialities. The break as such, however, cannot but have a punctual character.[40]

Lenin's idea of the "two states" is therefore rescued as well, albeit in a new sense. I will give only one example of its practical relevance—one that is politically strategic today. In the current debate on immigration, it is sometimes argued that even a progressive politics, in order to avoid falling into wishful thinking, must assume something like the Hegelian "point of view of the whole"—namely of the state—which necessarily implies, among other things, the need for a certain migratory flow regulation. This is true in some sense (abstracting from any instrumental use of this issue), but precisely here Lenin's question becomes pertinent again: *Which state*? The present one has its material capacity to accept immigrants distorted by the relations of production, due not only to the unequal distribution of wealth, but also to the structural limitation of possible economic growth that those relations entail. A (much) higher acceptance capacity, therefore, would be actually possible based on the already existing level of the productive forces, only in a "different state," i.e., a systematically different political organization of social production. Hence the irrationality—and political regressiveness—of any affirmative identification with the limitations imposed by the *present* state. Similar examples could be easily multiplied.

If the need for *discontinuity* thus grounds the withering-away thesis upon the critique of political economy, on the other side, the moment of *continuity* between the "two states"—say, the anti-anarchist side of Lenin's polemic—reveals the centrality of the theory of state for the theory of social change. The suppression of social objectivity defines the transformation of the state, but, conversely, the state is the central dimension of such suppression, as Lenin had correctly acknowledged. In other words, the suppression—of which the socialization of production is a necessary, although not sufficient condition—is essentially a political act. Strictly speaking, this means that a communist society cannot be *built*. If anything, it is made possible. What can be actually built, planned, *posited* by an act of (collective) rational will is the socialist state. And the identity of a given state even through its deepest transformation is the middle term that makes the transition from one to the other condition conceivable—"withering away" as *self*-overcoming.

Finally, the concept of *revolution* is preserved, but at the same time, as one might say, "disenchanted" (in the Weberian sense). It is not a necessary process; rather, it entails the suppression of necessity as such. Neither is it an instant of sudden redemption. The passage is not from historical to messianic time, but "only" from the impossible to the possible—the removal of an obstacle. Thus, the concept of "withering away" itself is redefined. The proletarian state "cannot but wither away," Lenin says, whereas it must be claimed instead: the proletarian state *can* wither away, while the bourgeois state *cannot*—and this is the very *definition* of bourgeois and proletarian state. The objection of utopianism is, in fact, the accusation of secularizing the theological ideal of a full eschatological salvation of human nature. However, the "utopia" of the withering away is not thought as positively given, but in a negative sense, as an opening of possibilities whose development and outcome is in principle indeterminable. This indeterminacy, on the other side, draws its meaning and depth from the very concrete *determinacy*—in both senses of the word—of current relationships. The future "it can" loses its evanescence—everything is abstractly conceivable—inasmuch as it relies on the reality of the present "it cannot" (Figure 9.3).

To the withering-away thesis it is normally objected that even in a communist society conflicts can occur between individual or collective economic agents. Of course—but they *can* also not occur, while in the present condition, they *cannot but* occur. In a society free from the capitalism-induced constraints to human activity, new tools might be invented

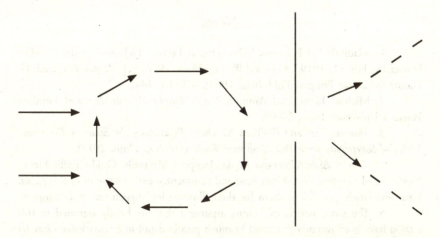

Figure 9.3. The (revolutionary) break of the barrier constituted by social objectivity frees the productive forces from their circular movement of expansion-crisis and exploitation. Therefore, the future possibilities do not remain fully abstract, but are somehow determined—what could be made *actually possible* is something that *already exists* as a repressed tendency. At the same time, however, their further development remains indeterminate. The dotted line represents the ultimate unpredictability of the postrevolutionary scenario.

and employed to reduce and mitigate conflicts, moving toward the vanishing point of their complete disappearance—through political, analytical, pedagogic work, and so on. Today, however, such *work*, like any productive force, is necessarily inhibited by the relations of production.[41] In this sense, Adorno claims: "The trouble is not that free men do radical evil . . . ; the trouble is that as yet there is no world in which . . . men would no longer *need* to be evil."[42] The thesis of the perfectibility of human nature is obvious in a certain sense, that is, if it means that human nature, like everything else, is material, and *labor* can be applied to it; in another sense, as a positive idea of perfection, it is literally undecidable. The *compulsion* to deny it, though, can be positively deduced as a socially necessary illusion, namely, as a reflection of the circularity with which the given relations perpetuate themselves. The inertia of nature is a social image of the block. Its rejection, far from being "utopian," has become an immediate imperative today. In a historical moment in which the tangles of social objectivity shrink once again, letting ever smaller possibilities pass through, the withering-away thesis gains new actuality as well.

Notes

1. Vladimir Ilyich Lenin, "The State. A Lecture Delivered at the Sverdlov University. July 11, 1919," *Collected Works, Volume 29: March–August 1919*, ed. G. Hanna (Moscow: Progress Publishers, 1965), 470–88, 484.

2. Michael Hardt and Antonio Negri, *Empire* (Cambridge and London: Harvard University Press, 2000).

3. Thomas Fazi and William Mitchell, *Reclaiming the State: A Progressive Vision of Sovereignty for a Post-Neoliberal World* (London: Pluto, 2017).

4. Yasmin Afshar, Stefano Breda, Iacopo Chiaravalli, Guido Frilli, Henry Pickford and Manfred Posani have read and commented earlier versions of this paper. I am immensely grateful to them for their illuminating suggestions and critiques.

5. The same aspects of Lenin's argument that are briefly outlined in this section have been recently discussed in much greater detail in a remarkable essay by Lorenzo Chiesa, who persuasively shows how, "for Lenin, 'communism' and 'state' "— as well as "state" and "revolution"—"are far from being incompatible concepts" and need, on the contrary, "to be articulated dialectically," Chiesa, "Lenin and the State of Revolution," *Crisis and Critique* 4, no. 2 (2017): 107–31, 108–109. Chiesa, in particular, identifies this specifically *dialectical* element of Lenin's view with his idea of "a state that increasingly withers away *thanks* to its strengthening" (ibid., 109; emphasis in the original). I also agree with Chiesa on both the essential correctness and the residual tensions in Lenin's interpretation of Marx's and Engels's claims about the state—a point, however, that I cannot further develop here. For a useful overall introduction to *State and Revolution*, see also Todd Chretien, "A Beginner's Guide to State and Revolution," in Lenin, *State and Revolution: The Marxist Theory of the State and the Tasks of the Proletariat in the Revolution*, ed. Chretien (Chicago: Haymarket, 2014), 1–31.

6. Translation altered by G. Z. (in the original one the aside in the first sentence is missing, and both "*schläft ein*" and "*stirbt ab*" are translated as "dies out"). The passage is quoted from a part of *Anti-Dühring. Herr Eugen Dühring's Revolution in Science* (1878), which is mostly known as section three of the pamphlet *Socialism: Utopian and Scientific*, published by Engels in 1880. The full text of *Anti-Dühring* is available online: https://www.marxists.org/archive/marx/works/1877/anti-duhring/index.htm. Accessed July 3, 2019.

7. Lenin himself does, in fact, trace it to Marx.

8. This is quite a classical critical scheme in Marxism. It first appears in the young Marx who, in turn, takes it up from the young Hegel's polemic against Fichte. See G. W. F. Hegel, *Faith and Knowledge*, trans. W. Cerf and H. S. Harris (Albany: State University of New York Press, 1977), and Karl Marx, *Critique of Hegel's Philosophy of Right*, trans. O'Malley (Oxford: Oxford, 1978).

9. In the same sense, Chiesa correctly claims that, for both Marx (in his *Critique of the Gotha Programme*) and Lenin, *right* necessarily implies violence and

inequality, and therefore, "right as such is at bottom 'bourgeois right.'" Chiesa, "Lenin and the State of Revolution," 116.

10. See in particular Lenin, *State and Revolution*, ch. 1.4.

11. Ibid., 127.

12. Lenin's position, however, at least in this phase, is not of perfect equidistance between the two sides. After claiming that the withering-away thesis is directed against both opportunists and anarchists, he nevertheless emphasizes that "Engels puts in the forefront that conclusion, drawn from the proposition that 'the state withers away,' which is directed against the opportunists." Ibid., 54. In the manuscript *Marxism and the State*, which was propaedeutic to the writing of *State and Revolution*, the disagreement with the opportunists is traced back to "more profound, more permanent truths" as compared to the disagreement with the anarchists.

13. Chiesa, 110.

14. See Chretien, "Beginner's Guide," 29–31.

15. Stalin's liquidation of the withering-away thesis as historically overcome during the Eighteenth Congress of the PCUS in 1939 is usefully reconstructed in the introduction to the Italian edition of *State and Revolution*, Valentino Gerratana, "Introduzione," V. I. Lenin, *Stato e rivoluzione* (Roma: Editori Riuniti, 1970), 7–16.

16. In this context, the phrase is often quoted with no reference to Lenin and confused with an expression of the anarchist—or even the alleged neoliberal—hostility to any form of state. See, for example, Fazi and Mitchell, *Reclaiming the State*, 8, 95–96, 101.

17. Lenin, *State and Revolution*, 122.

18. Yet another interpretation of Lenin's distinction might focus on the material substance of the state, the "proletarian state" being the one in which workers "really have" the power. But, again, why should this considered as "another" state and not as the proletarian appropriation of the already existing one?

19. Lenin, *State and Revolution*, 61; emphasis added.

20. See Helmut Reichelt, "Kritische Theorie als Programm einer neuen Marx-Lektüre," https://www.ca-ira.net/verlag/leseproben/reichelt-neue-marx-lektuere_lp-1/, 2013, accessed December 10, 2019; Tommaso Redolfi Riva, "Teoria critica della società? Critica dell'economia politica. Adorno, Backhaus, Marx," http://www.consecutio.org/2013/10/teoria-critica-della-societa-critica-delleconomia-politica-in-adorno-backhaus-marx/, 2013, accessed December 10, 2019; Stefano Breda, "Sachlich vermittelte Herrschaft und gesellschftliche Objektivität. Zur Bedeutung der Marxschen Kritik der politischen Ökonomie für eine Theorie emanzipatorischer Praxis," in *Radikale Philosophie und Kritik der Politik. Festschrift für F. O. Wolf zum 75. Geburtstag*, ed. M. Rahlwes, T. Rudnick, and N. Tzanakis Papadakis (Münster: Westfälisches Dampfboot, 2019), 52–63. Moishe Postone, *Time, Labor, and Social Domination: A Reinterpretation of Marx's Critical Theory* (New York: Cambridge, 1993) is also an essential reference, although based on a partially independent set of assumptions. See also Giovanni Zanotti, "La psyché démodée. Psychanalyse et

objectivité sociale chez Adorno," *META: Research in Hermeneutics, Phenomenology, and Practical Philosophy* VI/1 (2014): 67–97 for an elaboration of Adorno's concept of social objectivity. On Adorno's overall critique of political economy, see especially Dirk Braunstein, *Adornos Kritik der politischen Ökonomie* (Bielefeld: transcript Verlag, 2015). For a discussion of Adorno's own attitude toward Lenin, see Lars Quadfasel, "Adornos Leninismus. Kritische Theorie und das Problem der Avantgarde," https://jungle.world/artikel/2013/21/adornos-leninismus, 2013, accessed December 10, 2019.

21. Its first occurrence is probably in Adorno, "Sociology and Psychology (Part 1)," trans. I. Wohlfarth, *New Left Review* 46 (1967): 67–80, 77: "For the rest, the manifest or repressed instinctual moment exists within social objectivity [*in der gesellschaftlichen Objektivität*] only as a component, that of need, which has today become wholly a function of profit interests." Translation altered by G. Z. (orig.: "the manifest or repressed instinctual moment finds expression only in the form of needs, which have today become . . . ," where precisely the passage on social objectivity is removed).

22. Adorno, "Society," trans. F. Jameson, *Salmagundi* 3 (1969): 144–53, 147.

23. See, respectively, for example, Georg Lukács, *The Ontology of Social Being 3. Labour*, trans. D. Fernbach (London: The Merlin Press, 1980), 117; *History and Class Consciousness: Studies in Marxist Dialectics*, trans. R. Livingstone (Cambridge, Mass.: The MIT Press, 1972), 13.

24. In a similar sense, Moishe Postone, while acutely emphasizing the impersonal and objective character of capital, also speaks of "forms of social objectivity and subjectivity," Postone, *Time, Labor, and Social Domination*, especially 5, 37, 72–77, 170, 218–25, 322, thus apparently reaffirming the priority of a formal-analogical model over a material-functional one, in line with his understanding of capital as a subject-object (see note 28).

25. Rahel Jaeggi, *Critique of Forms of Life*, trans. C. Cronin (Cambridge: Harvard University Press, 2018).

26. The conclusions that I will draw from this concept are not always explicit in Adorno, and are sometimes even contradicted by the letter of his texts. Rather, they should serve as a further development of Adorno's basic insight, as it has been actually carried out in part by the authors within the "New Marx Reading" debate, especially by Breda. Most of what follows is based either on Breda's already published writings or on conversations I have had with him and is related to a common research in progress into the theory of social objectivity.

27. There is no need, therefore, to deny that a structural analogy exists in capitalist societies between the value/commodity form and subjective "forms of rationality" (identity-thinking, legal, religious, psychological concepts . . .), as authors such as Alfred Sohn-Rethel and Adorno himself (but also Marx and Lukács) have convincingly shown. The point, however, is that such "superstructural" forms are not on the same plane as social objectivity—not because one "produces" the other, but in the very concrete sense that even a complete (subjective) overcoming of the

former would not, per se, in the least touch the material limitations posed by the latter to individual and collective action (see below). This is precisely the aspect that the phrase "social objectivity" stresses, as compared, for example, to the closely related concept of "second nature." It is also an important and often neglected part of what Adorno means by "object's preponderance," a concept that has not only a positive side—the transcendence of the object's determinations to identity-thinking—but also a negative one—the blocking of subjective possibilities by *social* objectivity. This is especially clear in the late Adorno's critique of Lukács's "idealistic" emphasis on reification, "itself . . . the reflexive form of false objectivity" and, thus, a mere "epiphenomenon." "The trouble is with the conditions that condemn mankind to impotence and apathy and would yet be changeable by human action; it is not primarily with people and with the way conditions appear to people," Adorno, *Negative Dialectics,* trans. E. B. Ashton (London and New York: Routledge, 2004), 190. In the same passage, Adorno also explicitly vindicates the greater importance of Marx's *Capital* against the "present popularity" of his earlier writings on alienation and distinguishes the double meaning of the "object's preponderance": namely, "as a product of criticism" and as "its extant caricature, its distortion by the merchandise character." See also ibid., 194, on the "obverse form" of the object's preponderance. On Adorno's concept of blocked possibility, see Iain Macdonald, *What Would Be Different: Figures of Possibility in Adorno* (Stanford: Stanford University Press, 2019).

28. The most direct reference here is Postone's emphasis on capital as a "self-moving substance" or "automatic subject" (granted, two expressions of Marx's), or even as *the* "historical Subject in the Hegelian sense," *Time, Labor, and Social Domination,* 75. Here, it seems to me that a confusion arises between what capital *is* and what it *necessarily appears* to be. However, Postone's view on this specific point is shared, quite paradoxically, by a great part of the current that he criticizes as "traditional Marxism," which similarly conceives the "economic structure" (with its internal "objective" dialectic of capital and labor) as a causally preponderant *agency* in a more or less deterministic way, thus simply replacing the universal subject-object of idealism with mythological "laws of history" and/or nature. In both cases, capital or economic structure is anthropomorphized. Postone—whose analyses are otherwise of the greatest importance for the theory of social objectivity—sometimes seems to believe that substituting—if one might say so—a good with an evil God is enough to fulfill the task of disenchanting Hegel's *Geist.*

29. This view obviously owes much to Althusser's concept of "structural causality," whose limit, however, consists in denying *any* place to subjectivity as a nonstructural agency in history, thereby conceiving productive forces on the model of the relations of production, whereas both Hegelian and positivist Marxists conceive the latter on the model of the former (see note 28).

30. On this point, see also Postone, *Time, Labor, and Social Domination,* 3–7, 78, 214.

31. Breda, "Sachlich vermittelte Herrschaft und gesellschftliche Objektivität," 53–54.

32. Contrary to Friedrich Pollock's influential thesis that both competition and the objective need for crisis have been overcome by "state capitalism," in "State Capitalism: Its Possibilities and Limitations," *The Essential Frankfurt School Reader*, ed. A. Arato and E. Gebhardt (New York: Continuum, 1990), 71–94.

33. Adorno, "Sociology and Psychology," 75.

34. Karl Marx, *Capital: A Critique of Political Economy. Volume One*, trans. B. Fowkes (London: Penguin, 1976), 92, 179.

35. Cesare Luporini, "Introduzione," in K. Marx and F. Engels, *L'ideologia tedesca*, trans. F. Codino (Roma: Editori Riuniti, 1971), XI–LXXXVIII, LXXXV. Lukács, on the contrary, had explicitly stated that Marx "reduc[es] the objectivity of the social institutions so hostile to men to relations between men" (Lukács, *History and Class Consciousness*, 49), thus highlighting only one side of the problem.

36. See, for example, the articulation between "hegemony," "contingency," and "power relations" that lies at the heart of Laclau and Mouffe's "radical-democratic" project, Ernesto Laclau and Chantal Mouffe, *Hegemony and Socialist Strategy. Towards a Radical Democratic Politics*, 2nd ed. (London and New York: Verso, 2001), vii–xix.

37. See, for example, Mario Tronti, "The Political," trans. M. Mandarini, https://www.viewpointmag.com/2014/09/02/the-political-1979/, 1979, accessed December 10, 2019.

38. Breda 2019, 55.

39. It is the attitude that Chretien defines as "the 'things have changed' interpretation," already attributing some versions of it to Bernstein and Kautsky. For a brilliant case about the combination of constitutionalism and Keynesianism, see Luigi Cavallaro, *Lo Stato dei diritti. Politica economica e rivoluzione passiva in Occidente* (Napoli: La Scuola di Pitagora, 2013). Fazi and Mitchell also base their "post-neoliberal" vindication of the state on similar premises.

40. This does not mean, of course, that it cannot itself occur through a process with a duration in time—this would in turn remythologize revolution as a messianic "instant." It does mean, rather, that revolution breaks the continuity in the range of political possibilities in such a way as to mark a crucial divide between *two qualitatively different* types of "gradualism."

41. This interpretation of the classic Marxist idea of an "unfettering of the productive forces" presupposes a qualitative and—so to speak—minimal definition of the productive forces themselves, which are conceived here simply as the actually existing capacities to transform the world in order to satisfy human desires. On the contrary, a merely quantitative notion of the productive forces—as an ever-growing tendency to industrialization—has been generating dreadful equivocations in many past currents of Western Marxism. Even the capacity to transform nature in order to make human labor dispensable is a productive force that needs to be "unfettered." "Productivism" in the current sense is, therefore, just a particular expression of the "fettering of the productive forces."

42. Adorno, *Negative Dialectics*, 218–19; emphasis added.

Bibliography

Adorno, Theodor W. "Sociology and Psychology (Part 1)." Translated by I. Wohlfarth. *New Left Review* 46 (1967): 67–80.

———. "Society." Translated by F. Jameson. *Salmagundi* 3 (1969): 144–53.

———. *Negative Dialectics*. Translated by E. B. Ashton. London and New York: Routledge, 2004.

Braunstein, Dirk. *Adornos Kritik der politischen Ökonomie*. Bielefeld: transcript Verlag, 2015.

Breda, Stefano. *Sachlich vermittelte Herrschaft und gesellschftliche Objektivität. Zur Bedeutung der Marxschen Kritik der politischen Ökonomie für eine Theorie emanzipatorischer Praxis*. In *Radikale Philosophie und Kritik der Politik. Festschrift für F. O. Wolf zum 75. Geburtstag*, edited by M. Rahlwes, T. Rudnick, and N. Tzanakis Papadakis, 52–63. Münster: Westfälisches Dampfboot, 2019.

Cavallaro, Luigi. *Lo Stato dei diritti. Politica economica e rivoluzione passiva in Occidente*. Napoli: La Scuola di Pitagora, 2013.

Chiesa, Lorenzo. "Lenin and the State of Revolution." *Crisis & Critique* 4, no. 2 (2017): 107–31.

Chretien, Todd. *A Beginner's Guide to State and Revolution*. In V. I. Lenin, *State and Revolution*, 1–34. Chicago: Haymarket Books, 2004.

Engels, Friedrich. *Socialism: Utopian and Scientific*. Translated by E. Burns. In *The Marx-Engels Reader*, 2nd edition, edited by R. C. Tucker, 683–717. New York and London: W. W. Norton, 1978.

Fazi, Thomas, and William Mitchell. *Reclaiming the State. A Progressive Vision of Sovereignty for a Post-Neoliberal World*. London: Pluto Press, 2017.

Gerratana, Valentino. *Introduzione*. In V. I. Lenin, *Stato e rivoluzione*. Roma: Editori Riuniti, 7–52, 1970.

Hardt, Michael, and Antonio Negri. *Empire*. Cambridge and London: Harvard University Press, 2000.

Hegel, Georg Wilhelm Friedrich. *Faith and Knowledge*. Translated by W. Cerf and H. S. Harris. Albany: State University of New York Press, 1977.

Jaeggi, Rahel. *Critique of Forms of Life*. Translated by C. Cronin. Cambridge: Harvard University Press, 2018.

Laclau, Ernesto, and Chantal Mouffe. *Hegemony and Socialist Strategy. Towards a Radical Democratic Politics*. 2nd ed. London and New York: Verso, 2001.

Lenin, Vladimir Ilyich. *The State. A Lecture Delivered at the Sverdlov University. July 11, 1919*. In *Collected Works. Volume 29: March–August 1919*, edited by G. Hanna, 470–88. Moscow: Progress Publishers, 1965.

———. *State and Revolution. The Marxist Theory of the State and the Tasks of the Proletariat in the Revolution*. Edited by T. Chretien. Chicago: Haymarket Books, 2014.

Lukács, Georg. *History and Class Consciousness. Studies in Marxist Dialectics.* Translated by R. Livingstone. Cambridge: The MIT Press, 1972.

———. *The Ontology of Social Being 3. Labour.* Translated by D. Fernbach. London: The Merlin Press, 1980.

Luporini, Cesare. *Introduzione.* In K. Marx and F. Engels, *L'ideologia tedesca,* translated by F. Codino. Roma: Editori Riuniti, XI–LXXXVIII, 1971.

Macdonald, Iain. *What Would Be Different. Figures of Possibilities in Adorno.* Stanford: Stanford University Press, 2019.

Marx, Karl. *Critique of Hegel's Philosophy of Right.* Translated by J. O'Malley. Oxford: Oxford University Press, 1970.

———. *Capital. A Critique of Political Economy. Volume One.* Translated by B. Fowkes. London: Penguin Books, 1976.

Polloch, Friedrich. *State Capitalism. Its Possibilities and Limitations.* In *The Essential Frankfurt School Reader,* edited by A. Arato and E. Gebhardt, 71–94. New York: Continuum, 1990.

Postone, Moishe. *Time, Labor, and Social Domination. A Reinterpretation of Marx's Critical Theory.* New York: Cambridge University Press, 1993.

Quadfasel, Lars. *Adornos Leninismus. Kritische Theorie und das Problem der Avantgarde.* https://jungle.world/artikel/2013/21/adornos-leninismus. 2013. Accessed December 10, 2019.

Redolfi Riva, Tommaso. *Teoria critica della società? Critica dell'economia politica. Adorno, Backhaus, Marx.* http://www.consecutio.org/2013/10/teoria-critica-della-societa-critica-delleconomia-politica-in-adorno-backhaus-marx/. 2013. Accessed December 10, 2019.

Reichelt, Helmut. *Kritische Theorie als Programm einer neuen Marx-Lektüre.* https://www.ca-ira.net/verlag/leseproben/reichelt-neue-marx-lektuere_lp-1/. 2013. Accessed December 10, 2019.

Tronti, Mario. *The Political.* Translated by M. Mandarini. https://www.viewpointmag.com/2014/09/02/the-political-1979/. 2013. Accessed December 10, 2019.

Zanotti, Giovanni. "La psyché démodée. Psychanalyse et objectivité sociale chez Adorno." *META. Research in Hermeneutics, Phenomenology, and Practical Philosophy* VI/1 (2013): 67–97.

Chapter 10

Lenin and the Materialist Critique of Law

CAMILA VERGARA

Given the growing perception that the liberal rule of law does not protect individuals from domination, it seems necessary to revisit Vladimir Lenin's critical assessment of the emancipatory role of law within a capitalist system of production in which workers are in a relation of dependence. Despite Lenin's important critical contributions to the study of law, much of the scholarship on Lenin neglects his focus on the law in favor of his analysis of the state, and the few who have analyzed his texts dealing with the law favor his work written after the 1917 Revolution.[1] This focus on Lenin's postrevolutionary work makes the study of his legal analysis especially challenging given Lenin's departure from his approach to law after coming into power. As Jane Burbank has argued, Lenin, post-1917, appears to have embraced the courts as true organs of proletarians and peasants, seeing the disciplinary role of the judiciary as emancipatory, the most effective way to educate workers into their new revolutionary role. According to Burbank, Lenin's analysis after he began wielding state power turned "instrumentalist and statist," using the law and the courts to defend "the interests of the socialist state, the workers' state, even when this meant disciplining the workers."[2]

This chapter aims to fill the gap in scholarship on Lenin's legal theory by presenting an analysis of his critique of law in his early, prerevolutionary writings. From a materialist legal perspective that takes into account power struggles as well as patterns of domination and resistance in the making and application of the law,[3] it will primarily analyze two essays in which Lenin engages with the problem of law: *Explanation of the Law on Fines Imposed on Factory Workers* (1895) and *The New Factory Law* (1897). These two essays are significant not only because they are Lenin's first essays dealing directly with law, but also because they contend specifically with *labor* laws—the most pro-proletarian of all laws as they explicitly regulate labor relations to protect workers against the arbitrary power of employers. At the moment when labor relations were being codified in Russia, Lenin's insights exposed labor law as the legalization of exploitation that deepens the dependence of workers not only on individual employers but also on the system of production as a whole. The legal codification of labor relations that rest on unequal bargaining power brings about a new form of *public* exploitation, in which domination is exerted not only through the power of the employer, but also by the police and the administrative and juridical branches of the state that act as enforcers of the law. Lenin argues that the law, even allegedly "proletarian law" designed to protect workers, "will always be partial to the capitalist employers, because the latter will always succeed in devising ruses for evading the law."[4] And even if pro-worker laws were to be free from loopholes and find adequate enforcement, the formal equality guaranteed by the law ends up benefiting the powerful, who have the resources to cleverly use the law to assert their power. Even if rights belong "alike to the factory owner and the worker," the protection of workers, concludes Lenin, "is merely a paper one."[5]

By analyzing labor regulations, the conjuncture in which they arose, and the consequences of their enforcement or lack thereof, Lenin shows precisely the mechanisms through which abuse by employers was enabled by regulation, while protection of workers was disabled by the lack of redress procedures. While ambiguity and omission in the language of the law allowed for loopholes through which the powerful were able to circumvent legality, the lack of mechanisms for workers to exert oversight and get reparations left the meager protections afforded by the laws without proper enforcement. Viewed through Lenin's critical materialist lens, even provisions designed to improve working conditions and empower workers should not be considered emancipatory, since they maintain the subordination of workers to employers and, as Lenin shows, create other forms of dependence and servility, in addition to opportunities for political corruption. From sleep cycles to dress codes, the capitalist enterprise constantly attempts to exert control over workers for the benefit of production, and labor laws come to codify this control, giving legitimacy and juridical backup to the arbitrary power of employers, who are quick to circumvent the law or bribe inspectors and judges to bypass regulations.

Lenin's sharp critique of the inherent limitations of laws that codify existing power relations seems to have been rethought after the revolutionary rupture of 1917 and the coming into power of the Bolsheviks. Oppressive labor laws endured, but the source of domination gravitated toward the state, which eventually became the main owner and manager of the productive forces. The power to discipline workers, now resting primarily in the prerogative of the courts to punish workers who break their contracts, was seen as necessary to achieve the goals of the revolutionary government. Lenin rethought the courts as "an instrument *for inculcating discipline*"[6] in the workers, a function that would reach its maximal expression under Stalinism, during which quitting a job without a proper, preapproved justification became a criminal offense.[7]

Even if in comparison to the legal domination of workers under the Tsarist regime and the Soviet Union between 1940 and 1956, workers in liberal capitalist democracies such as the United States seem freer, the conditions of an important section of the workforce, particularly within the emergent "gig economy," in which employers act as brokers between "independent contractors" and "services requesters," do not appear radically different from those Lenin observed at the end of the nineteenth century when labor relations were being legally codified. After analyzing Lenin's observations on the new labor laws in late—nineteenth-century Russia, the chapter addresses the relevance of his approach to the study of law by briefly engaging with labor practices prevalent in the "gig economy," exploring the consequences of the potential legalization of exceptions from current regulations. I argue that Lenin's materialist approach to law, which not only incorporates historical context and rich textual and prudential analyses, but also offers recommendations for adequate enforcement of pro-proletarian provisions, is especially important at a moment in which the structural scaffolding of liberal democracy is fracturing and new forms of domination are being invented and tried out in the marketplace, waiting to be validated or deterred by legality and the disciplinary power of the courts.

Legalizing Subordination: Law on Fines

There is much controversy within critical theory about the meaning of materialism and its centrality within the Marxist tradition.[8] I do not wish to intervene in this philosophical debate but rather to use materialism as a method to study legality, as a lens to analyze labor law and rights as framed in a specific conjuncture,[9] conditioned by existing power relations and their ideological justificatory structures. In his analysis of the law Lenin followed Marx's critical assessment of individual rights as providing only for partial liberty and obscuring relations of domination;[10] his approach to the legal system was also informed by his studies in law and his brief experience practicing it.[11] After he obtained his law degree in 1891 from the University of St. Petersburg, Lenin worked for one and a half years as an assistant defense lawyer in the Samara circuit on fourteen minor cases of property claims and petty thefts.[12] The only case he won was his personal legal battle against a steamship owner who had monopoly rights over the crossing of the Volga River, who had illegally seized Lenin when he attempted to get across by hiring a boatman. The merchant, despite his wealth and status, was convicted and sentenced to one year in prison.[13]

In 1893, Lenin moved to St. Petersburg where he also worked as an assistant lawyer; however, he spent most of his time writing and debating on revolutionary populism and Marxism, and lecturing in workers' circles from which he obtained data to support his ideas on the extent of capitalist development in Russia.[14] It was during that period that Lenin wrote his first material legal analysis of a law regulating the imposition of fines on workers—*Explanation of the Law on Fines Imposed on Factory Workers* (1895)—grounding his insights both on his study of Marxism and on the empirical knowledge of labor relations he obtained from interviewing workers. In this text, Lenin analyzes the legalization of fines in the aftermath of one of the largest worker unrests—a "terrific outbreak of some ten thousand workers"—that took place in 1885 in the Nikolskoye Mill, where workers went on strike to protest the reduction of wages and the imposition of arbitrary fines.[15] During the labor unrest, "the workers in their fury went so far as to start wrecking the factories and machinery, setting fire to goods and materials, and attacking managers and mill owners." The strike was powerful enough that the employers were forced to negotiate collectively with their employees, who presented management with "conditions drawn up by the workers themselves."[16] After brutal repression by the state, thirty-three workers were brought to trial. Their acquittal, after testimonies disclosed to the jurors "the abominable oppression to which the workers had been subjected,"[17] was seen as a legitimate "condemnation" not only of the owners of that particular mill, but "of the old factory system as a whole." The impression caused by this strike was so strong that other factory owners also agreed to concede demands to their workers to avoid strikes. As a result, the "government had to make concessions" and passed a law in 1886 regulating the imposition of fines on workers.[18]

After reminding workers that laws aimed at protecting them were not gifts from the government but the result of class struggle, which forced the government to cave to the workers' demands, Lenin tackles the problems of evasion of the law, its inadequate enforcement, and the false protection afforded by formal equal rights. More specifically, in his analysis of the law on fines, Lenin shows how the government effectively legalized subordination by enforcing the rights of employers instead of protecting workers from their power, and leaving loopholes everywhere for employers who were "anxious to violate the law" to exploit them.[19] The law, he explains, did not prohibit fines, but legalized them, setting three grounds for imposing fines on workers: defective work, absenteeism, and offenses against good order.[20] This not only did not limit much the arbitrary power of employers over workers but deepened it by giving it legal form.

Lenin argues that fines are an expression of a relation of subordination. While "compensation for damage is demanded of an equal" in court, fines are "imposed on a subordinate" without the need of damages, out of court.[21] Fines are levied to "establish discipline, i.e., to secure subordination of the workers to the employer" and are equivalent to the physical punishment landlords were able to impose on serfs decades prior.

> If anybody goes to work for an employer, it is clear that he loses his freedom; he must obey his employer, and the employer may punish him. The peasant serfs worked for landlords, and the landlords punished them. The workers work for capitalists, and the capitalists punish them. The only difference is that formerly it was a man's back that suffered, whereas now it is his purse.[22]

The subordinate position of the worker to the employer is clear when analyzing the grounds for imposing fines on workers. The law applies to workers with the same severity as to "soldiers in barracks, and not to free men," and its "attitude" toward them is the same as toward criminals.[23] When analyzing "absenteeism" as ground for imposing fines, Lenin specifies the valid reasons why a worker may be absent without penalty and argues they are the same rules governing nonappearance in court.

Everybody understands why the rules about appearance in court are so strict; it is because the prosecution of crime concerns the whole of society. The failure, however, of a worker to appear at his place of work does not concern the whole of society, but only a single employer.[24]

With this law the state granted employers the legal power to command the presence of workers in the factory with the same severity with which the state commands soldiers and criminals. Moreover, the law also states that "fines are imposed 'on the authority' of factory managements 'themselves,'"[25] which means that the grounds for applying fines are in themselves interpreted exclusively by employers. While the employer has the discretion to decide "whether the article is of good or bad quality" and apply a fine accordingly for "defective work,"[26] the imposition of fines for "offenses against good order" gave the employer vast control over workers' behavior, since whatever was stipulated in the factory rules—which were decided upon only by the employer—became the legitimate basis for imposing fines. Consequently, far from eliminating arbitrary punishment on workers, the law in fact legalized the employers' power over workers, "leav[ing] the worker unprotected, and giv[ing] the employer a loophole for oppressing him."[27]

And if this loophole were not enough for employers to have sufficient freedom to operate their business, the law also gives the state the prerogative to free any employer from subordination to the law if it is "really necessary," leaving the definition of what is necessary to the employer, and removing all oversight once this exemption has been granted.

> In one of his interpretations the minister states that he only frees such factory owners regarding whom the Factory Board "*is certain that the owner: of the establishment will not transgress the workers' interests.*" The factory owners and inspectors are such close boon companions that they take each other's word. Why burden the factory owner with regulations, when he "gives the assurance" that he will not transgress the workers' interests? Now, what if the worker should try to require of the minister or the inspector that he be released from the regulations, after "giving the assurance" that he will not transgress the factory owner's interests? Such a worker would very likely be considered insane.[28]

The "insanity" of demanding equal rights for workers and employers through the law is even clearer when it comes to the lack of means for workers to resist unlawful subordination and exploitation. The law did not include provisions for formal redress, so if a fine was wrongly imposed there was no mechanism for the worker to receive a reimbursement for lost wages. According to Lenin, this was not an oversight. When the law was "discussed in the Council of State, it was deliberately decided to be silent on this point" so as not to undermine the authority of managers.[29] Giving the express right to workers to challenge employers' rules and demand to be refunded for unfair fines—rather than leaving redress to the good will of inspectors and judges—would have given workers grounds for insubordination. Therefore, through the omission of enforcement provisions the law allowed for employer's authority to remain uncontested.

In the same way the law allowed the employer to legally oppress the worker through the imposition of fines, it also allowed employers to extract profit from this oppression by making it easy for them to *evade* the rule that prohibited fines from going into employers' coffers. While before 1886 the money collected through fines "went into the pockets of the factory owners,"[30] the new law stated that money was to go to a special fund for the use of the workers, who would need to "apply for grants to the employer, who makes them by permission of the inspector."[31] However, given insufficient enforcement, some employers kept pocketing the fines by recording them not as fines but as "money issued to the worker," while others failed to record fines for absenteeism and did not "credit the worker with all his days worked."[32] More creative employers evaded the law by refusing to use the word *fine* and "replacing it by other words" so to formally escape the reach of the law.[33] For instance, instead of charging the worker with a fine for defective work, which would go to the worker-controlled fund, the employer would pay the worker an arbitrary "lower rate" and pocket the difference. This adaptative "method" of avoiding specific terminology to evade the law became popular among employers and according to Lenin "was even improved on by a certain St. Petersburg factory owner of genius."[34]

The only way the workers could try to prevent such fraud was by leveling a claim to the labor inspector. However, since employers were not forced to keep a public record of fines, it was almost impossible for the workers to know if fraud was being committed.[35]

> The inspector himself admits his inability to discover fraud if the workers do not point it out. And the workers cannot do so if the factory owners are not obliged to put up notices about fines imposed.[36]

But even if there were evidence for fraud or a claim for wrongful imposition of fines, the right of workers to make appeals, Lenin argued, was merely formal, "a paper one." Workers can certainly lodge appeals to the inspector and the courts, but without the time, resources, and knowledge needed to follow up on appeals, they would probably not succeed. While the right to appeal was not negated in the law, the lack of rules establishing the ways workers could force employers to obey the law left them without tools to resist illegal oppression.

> First of all, [the worker] has no time to make the round of the inspectors and offices. He works and is fined for "absenteeism."
> He lacks the money to obtain a lawyer's services. He does not know the laws, and therefore cannot stand up for his rights.[37]

By not spelling out any mechanism for worker redress, the law leaves the workers at the mercy of the inspector or the judge, the fate of the case depending on the good faith of individuals who work for an oligarchic state that had been "evidently very slow in abandoning the old factory system"[38] in which the employer had the "right to uncontrolled (arbitrary) fining" of workers.[39]

Finally, even in the case where the law is respected and properly enforced, and employers effectively put the fines in a fund to be used "only for the needs of the workers themselves,"[40] the law is still pernicious because it creates new forms in which workers are subservient to their employer. By forcing the workers to apply for grants to be able to take advantage of the money from the fines fund, the employer imposes discipline, makes the workers compete for the funds, and in this way asserts a new type of domination.

> Instead of abolishing the workers' dependence on the employers in the matter of fines, we get a new dependence, which splits the workers and creates the servile and the go-getter types.[41]

If the law gives legal means to the employer to dominate and oppress the worker, either by imposing fines or making workers subservient to the employer through the grant application mechanism, what should the workers do to protect themselves? According to Lenin, the weavers from the Nikolskoye Mill advanced among their demands to have worker oversight, specifically to push back against arbitrary decisions on what is considered "defective work." In case of disagreement between worker and employer, there must be "witnesses from among the operatives working close at hand"[42] to make the final call on a defective product.

> This demand is quite a fair one, because there can be no other way of averting the employer's arbitrary conduct than to bring in witnesses when a dispute arises about quality, the witnesses without fail having to come from the workers' ranks: foremen or clerks would never dare to oppose the employer.[43]

Lenin takes this oversight function a step farther and argues that workers need to choose deputies not only to oversee the imposition of fines and make sure that the money goes to the fines fund and not to the employer's pocket, but also to "receive and check workers' applications for grants, and report to the workers about the state of the fines fund and its expenditure."[44] Evasion through loopholes and lack of proper enforcement can only be resisted if workers are able to choose deputies to oversee labor relations. And only by transferring the management of the fines fund to these deputies can the workers remain united "to uphold their rights, to combat oppression by the employers, and to win more decent earnings and shorter working hours."[45]

Legalizing Biopolitical Domination: Schedules and Overtime

Ten years after the *Law on Fines*, another massive workers' strike, this time in the cotton mills of St. Petersburg, resulted in another labor law, this time regulating working schedules. For the coronation of Tzar Nicolas II, textile mills closed down on May 16 and 17, 1896. Workers went on strike when their demands for holiday payment for those two days were denied. Shortly afterward, more than fifteen thousand workers in eighteen textile factories were on strike.[46] Following the experience of the Nikolskoye Mill workers, and aided by the League of Struggle for the Emancipation of the Working Class,[47] the workers presented to the government a set of demands that included not only paid holidays (as was customary) but also shortening daytime labor to eight hours and the prohibition of night work. Even after police "arrested masses of workers right and left and exiled them without trial,"[48] the government was ultimately forced to make concessions. Lenin writes:

The government realized that no amount of police persecution would break the determination of the working masses, once they had become conscious of their interests, had united for a struggle, and were led by the party of Social-Democrats, the champions of the workers' cause.[49]

While the workers had learned from the recent revolts that gains were possible despite state repression, the government understood that further concessions would only strengthen the labor movement. According to Lenin, the government "forbade the employers to yield, so as not to create a precedent for the workers," and announced a new factory law.[50] The content of the law did not take into account the workers' demands, but took the opportunity to further increase the legal subordination of workers. Instead of the eight-hour working day demanded by workers, which would have decreased maximum labor time for a majority of workers, the law "restricted" daytime working hours to eleven and one-half and nighttime shifts to ten hours, which effectively *increased* the legal time employers could demand their workers to stay on the job. I will focus here on Lenin's analysis of how the law negatively affected the work schedule and increased the degree of subordination of the working class to capital as a result of this legalization of labor relations. By analyzing the working conditions at the time the law was being discussed, Lenin showed that this law did not really improve the working conditions of the proletariat, but rather based its regulation in the *average degree of exploitation* already present in labor relations. For workers who were forced to be on the job for fourteen hours, the law formally reduced their shifts. However, the law simultaneously exposed the majority of workers to potential longer hours by explicitly allowing for it.

In addition, the state regulation of labor relations deepened the legal subordination of workers not only to their employers but also to the factory system as a whole. With the setting of daytime and nighttime shifts, the law structured the life of the worker to fit the demand of industrial production (something the workers would still endure under the Soviet state), even against biological and cultural sleep patterns.

> But the Russian law lays it down that the worker must adjust his whole life to the interests of capital; the worker must believe that day-time begins *without fail* after four in the morning, even if it may still be several hours before sunrise . . . and believe that the "day" has only just ended—for so the law decrees.[51]

The biopolitical nature of the law,[52] the juridical rationality aimed at managing human beings in the service of capital, determined directly by the mode of production, was not only designed to force workers to fit the continuous operation of the machines of industry, but also established different conceptions of time for the working class. The law redefined nighttime labor depending on the amount of work shifts required, which not only regimented the workers' life but also separated the working class from the oligarchy in terms of this new labor-based definition of "night."

> "Night" for the common people, who have to toil all their lives for others, and "night" for the fine folk, who live on the labor of others, are, according to the "law," two entirely different things.[53]

The subordination of workers to capital through the legal restructuring of their life cycle, and to their individual employers for almost all of their waking hours, was expanded even further by a clause allowing for the employer to force the laborer to work overtime by "special agreement" between employer and worker when "necessitated by the technical conditions of the industry."[54] By allowing the possibility of overtime in the labor contract, this clause not only did not restrict the practice of forcing workers to labor longer or risk being fired, but legalized it, extending the practice to all industries and deepening the subordination of the working class.

> The law has only *strengthened* the arbitrary powers of the employers by suggesting to them a *particularly reliable* way of oppressing the workers. . . . The government has therefore quite legally endowed the employers with arbitrary powers as regards overtime.[55]

According to Lenin, the argument the government used for "openly legaliz[ing] the complete subjection of the workers" by giving employers the loophole of "overtime" was that it would be "unfair to the worker" not to be able to choose to work more if she so desired it, and that "to deprive the worker of the right to work" more hours would be "difficult in practice."[56] The government legalized the use of arbitrary power by employers and framed it as enabling the freedom of workers, who now had the "right" to work any number of "extra" hours a day.[57] The same way as the law on fines enabled the employer to impose fines arbitrarily due to "defective work," or could force the worker to labor long hours or risk to be fined for "absenteeism," or exert total control over individual behavior in the factory to secure "good order," the overtime clause gave the right to employers to demand complete submission of the worker if it was necessary for industry, even if going against the natural human need to rest and sleep. Consequently, the formal restrictions on daytime and nighttime labor, which could potentially improve working conditions for those who were being forced to routinely labor for fourteen hours a day, were in practice eliminated if the contract contained a clause allowing for overtime, since then it was left to the employer to insist that overtime was "necessitated by the technical conditions of the industry."

Despite the vast arbitrary powers given to employers over workers, some workers would still be protected from overtime if able to prove that working longer hours were not really necessary in their trade. From a materialist perspective, Lenin showed that even when there was a case for appeal, the law was likely to be disregarded when it came to its enforcement in favor of workers, because the observance of laws is guaranteed by "supervision" over its compliance and "punishment" for its infringements—both of which were lacking in Russia.[58] Regarding state oversight over the observance of the law, Lenin noted that there were too few factory inspectors and that they were controlled by the oligarchic-enabling government that imposed the new factory law legalizing the employers' unrestricted right to their workers' time.

> The factory inspectors are completely under the jurisdiction of the Ministry of Finance, which turns them into servitors of the employers, compels them to report strikes and unrest to the police, to prosecute workers for leaving the factory even when the employer himself does not prosecute them; in a word, it turns them, in a manner of speaking, into police officials, into factory police.[59]

As agents of the oligarchic state, inspectors are not allies of the workers but rather part of the disciplinary, repressive force of the state, cooperating with employers to secure a stable and cheap workforce to keep the industries running at full speed. Even if the role of the inspectors were to assure the observance of the law, this does not mean that they would protect the workers, but rather that they would see that the law is enforced to assure that the industrializing project of the state was not undermined by labor unrest. The interests of the industrial class and the oligarchic state were brought together, which meant that the workers were left with "no legal means of exerting pressure on the government."[60] The workers lacked the resources to influence government, while their employers had "thousands of ways of exerting pressure on the government" through their organizations, personal connections, the press, and their capacity to bribe inspectors.[61] However, not all was lost for the workers on the legal front:

> The introduction of new factory regulations . . . will provide a splendid, convenient and *lawful* opportunity for the workers to present their *demands,* to uphold *their interpretation of the law,* to uphold the *old customs* when they are more advantageous to the worker . . . to press for more favorable terms when concluding *new agreements* on overtime, and to press for *higher pay.*[62]

The only way to effectively press for their demands legally, however, was for workers to join forces to "put up united resistance to the government and the employers," since "only by struggle will they be able to secure the actual enforcement of the law, and its enforcement in the interests of the workers."[63] Without the social power of organization to exert pressure on employers and the government, the law would remain unenforced, a "parchment barrier."[64] Lenin advises this time not only that workers elect their own deputies to oversee the observance of the law, but also to "convey the *general* decision of all the workers to the employer" as the only way to prevent further oppression.[65] Given that independent trade unions were prohibited at the moment of Lenin's writing,[66] it was clear to him that as long as workers "stand disfranchised in face of a police government," legal reforms cannot be effective; without the enforcement provided by the collective power of the working class, even a genuinely proletarian law would not be able to protect individual workers from the double oppression of capital and its police state.[67]

Labor Legislation as Legal Domination

In his analysis of the law on fines and work schedules, Lenin identified strategies and loopholes through which employers were able to exert domination over workers in an extralegal manner. In addition to the issues of employers evading the law, the law's silence on mechanisms and resources for workers' redress, and the lack of enforcement by the state to protect workers' rights, employers could use the law to exert uncontestable authority over their workforce. Even if the labor laws analyzed here seem draconian or far removed from both the Soviet and the liberal states, their structure as well as the loopholes and strategies that Lenin identified in them, have endured. In what follows I provide an analysis of penalties for "absenteeism" in the Soviet Labor Code and in a current labor contract in the Unites States' gig economy to show how this form of discipline and extraction of value is present regardless of who owns the means of production in society—even if the degree of domination differs greatly depending on the material conditions of workers and the level of decommodification of daily life.

The endurance of oppressive labor conditions well into the socialist era supports Evgeny Pashukanis's theory of law, which he developed after the Bolsheviks took control of the government. Pashukanis argues that material conditions are at the origin of the legal structure, and that the premises of law are always "rooted in the material relations of production."[68] Law—even law made by the Soviet government—is determined by relations of production and therefore cannot be truly proletarian. According to Pashukanis's commodity exchange theory of law, "the logic of juridical concepts corresponds to the logic of the social relations of a commodity producing society";[69] therefore, establishing a new legality would not be a proper tool for emancipatory structural change if relations of production and exploitation were to be kept intact.

In spite of his early insights into the exploitative nature of labor laws, once in power Lenin moved away from critique and adopted a modified view of labor law. New labor provisions establishing the eight-hour working day and other protections against exploitation were passed immediately following the October Revolution. However, in 1922 Lenin approved the new Labor Code, which, I argue, was based on the essentially capitalist idea of labor power as a resource for the production of commodities, and incorporated, alongside stronger labor protections, many of the existing provisions that Lenin had previously denounced as enabling exploitation. According to Burbank, Lenin's new approach to law was a response to the extreme pressure of simultaneously maintaining control of government against oligarchic and imperialist attacks, and avoiding a crisis of starvation and civil unrest.[70] Confronted with a complex reality of counterrevolution and crisis, Lenin chose a hierarchical and centralized mode of organization that relied on specialists, over horizontal management and workers' control over production. Under these historical conditions there emerged, as a result, a view of law in which courts had considerable power.[71] Labor discipline seemed an absolute necessity for the survival of the Bolsheviks' project, and therefore Lenin charged the courts to "mercilessly punish" anyone violating labor discipline.[72] Because the immediate goal of labor discipline was to raise production within an increasingly planned economy, judges were called to enforce severe measures on transgressors and only to mitigate punishment in cases of severe hardship to avoid hurting the "morale of the factory population."[73]

In what pertains to absenteeism, the new code did not contemplate pecuniary fines as under Tzarist law; however, it introduced other harsh punishments, which resulted in a similar kind of system of control over the worker and her labor. According to these new laws, management could dismiss a worker if she was absent without justifiable reason[74] for three consecutive days or for six days during a month.[75] Five years later (during Stalin's era), this provision was modified to allow management to fire workers who were absent for any three days in one month. In 1932, control over workers was further tightened, with only one absence per month constituting legitimate grounds for dismissal.[76] If dismissed, the worker could be immediately evicted from her housing when such was connected to her employment[77] (which was increasingly the case with the Soviet state as employer and provider of public housing) and deprived of ration coupons. Furthermore, with the establishment of a personal labor record in 1934, workers had to carry a "labor passport" in which managers needed to record penalties for absenteeism.[78]

The system of labor recruitment and retention was transformed into a system of labor conscription when Russia entered World War II.[79] During Hitler's invasion, high rates of production, especially in war industries, became existential, and therefore severe penalties were imposed to prevent labor turnover. In 1941 the new *Standard Rules of Internal Labor Organization* made absenteeism and tardiness punishable by law,[80] signaling to the merger of industrial production and the state, and the subordination of the worker to the producer-state and its juridical enforcers. While workers enjoyed strong labor protections and welfare benefits associated with a socialist state, their freedom of movement was effectively curtailed with the introduction of a system of registration and residence restrictions.[81] Quitting a job without prior authorization became an offense punishable by up to four months in prison for ordinary workers, and with up to eight years for workers in the defense industry.[82] By 1943, 7.6 million urban and rural residents had been drafted as labor conscripts. In addition, a system of Labor Reserve schools was implemented. In the course of the war, 2.5 million adolescents were compulsory trained for up to two years to become skilled laborers, and then given an obligatory placement for four years in government factories and mines.[83]

Regulations restricting labor mobility and punishing absenteeism were repealed in 1956, while the adolescent labor draft was finally abolished in 1959. A complete overhaul of the labor code came in 1971 with the *Principles of Labor Legislation*, which strengthened the rights of workers and expanded the role of trade unions in determining labor conditions.[84] As a result, in addition to protections against arbitrary transfers and dismissals, and the right to exit the labor contract with only two week's notice, workers were entitled to considerable benefits, such as paid sick leave, state-funded pensions, paid maternity leave, free childcare, free housing, a month-long vacation, and professional development.

Even if skipping work is not a criminal offense in any liberal democratic regime, this does not mean workers can meaningfully exercise the freedom to choose where to work and under which conditions, or that wages are sufficient to cover basic social needs. In countries such as the United States, employer-employee relations are a private matter of agreement between the parties, and are, therefore, not subject to review by federal or state enforcement agencies except for cases in which clauses are discriminatory or anti-union. Moreover, proper enforcement of antidiscrimination rules is mostly achieved after considerable pressure from labor has been exerted. Workers today sign all types of disciplinary clauses in contracts that are backed up by the threat of enforcement through the juridical state. For example, Uber, the platform-based taxi service established in 2009, which currently employs more than three million drivers around the world, has not only broken up local taxi service oligopolies by increasing competition, but also has allowed for "independent contractors" to work flexible schedules. However, this also means that these "contractors" are doing this work without labor protections.[85] Newer enterprises such as Handy, established in 2012 and currently employing around five thousand cleaners and housekeepers in Canada, the United States, and the United Kingdom, charge fees to its employees for defective work or lateness; its labor agreement also bars contractors from bargaining collectively and from engaging in class-action lawsuits. If the new legality surrounding the gig economy comes to legalize existing practices in the industry, establishing exceptions to labor protections, laws would allow for the legal entrenchment of precarity, enabling workers to become caught in a network of dependence in which the juridical power of the state is used to discipline labor.

Handy, a platform that hires people to do all kinds of manual labor for clients (from home cleaning to furniture assembly) is particularly oppressive to the workers. Aiming to connect "service professionals" with "service requesters," this broker platform for household chores appropriates about 20 percent of the average booking, a figure in line with what Uber, the main platform for taxi services today, typically takes for rides on its platform. In addition to this high "broker's fee," absenteeism—not showing up for the job—can cost workers fifty dollars under Handy's labor agreement,[86] the equivalent to more than three hours of work at a minimum-wage rate.[87] To repay the company, workers would need to labor three hours for free. If the worker needs to reschedule the service, fines are between ten and forty dollars. Also, workers who receive poor reviews from customers might earn less per hour and risk removal from the platform—as in prerevolutionary Russia workers would get fined, or paid less, for "defective work." According to Lenin, if the assessment of the quality of the work is only one-sided, fees for "defective work" become a tax on employees. If workers' pay is pegged to their rating, and their rating depends on the good will of customers, laborers are at the mercy of customers' reviews they cannot contest. Just like the need to apply for grants to inspectors and employers to use the workers' funds, in Lenin's analysis, establishes an attitude of subordination and flattery toward management among workers, the "reputation rating mechanism" in gig economy platforms such as Uber and Handy plays a similar role. It enshrines an attitude of subordination and flattery (for instance, creating the incentive to do extra work for free just to get a better rating). If wages are pegged to consumer ratings, this gives to consumers and, via their ratings, employers arbitrary power over service providers, which can then lead to exploitative extracontractual practices.

In today's liberal capitalist states, freedom of contract and the new gig economy allows employers to hire workers as "independent contractors" but to discipline them as "employees." Once they have signed the labor agreement, workers are subordinated to their employer, prohibited from providing services to clients outside of the broker's platform, without having any of the security associated with full-time employment. By allowing for freedom of contract and accepting this new type of labor relations as outside of current labor law protections, the liberal capitalist state has enabled the legal subordination of gig economy workers not only to their employers but also to the labor market system, in which precarity itself is a pervasive form of labor discipline. Even if freedom of contract has been paired with juridical procedures that give formal means for redress, individual litigation remains de facto inaccessible for the majority of workers. While in Soviet Russia the courts were effective enforcers of stringent labor protections as well as punishments to discipline workers, in today's free market economy workers are seemingly free to enter into almost any type of contract with little to no state oversight. Abusive labor relations are thus allowed to exist and proliferate until they are litigated in court in expensive and time-consuming processes dominated by lawyers specialized in using the law to minimize employers' liabilities. This weakened right to seek redress in court was further undermined beginning in the 1990s when employers begun to include in contracts mandatory arbitration clauses to resolve disputes—a procedure that yields lower win rates for employees when compared to litigation.[88] Consequently, even if workers are *formally* protected by the law against abuse coming from employers, achieving redress in cases of abuse is far from guaranteed, especially if workers have voluntary forfeited their right to sue their employer.

Labor laws not only offer weak protection for workers but also proceduralize forms of domination, effectively legalizing a relation of exploitation. Lenin's analysis of labor law allows us to better understand that legality and the courts are inadequate means for liberating workers from oppression because the rule of law tends to reproduce the relations that sustain our commodity-producing societies, which rely heavily on cheap labor. As I have shown in this chapter, Lenin's materialist approach to law makes evident the need to incorporate into legal studies not only the analysis of enforcement practices and the accessibility of judicial redress, but also the effects of law on the liberty of workers vis-à-vis the arbitrary power of employers, the tyranny of the market, and the repression of a complicit state unable to escape the implacable commands of economic growth.

Notes

1. See for example Jane Burbank, "Lenin and the Law in Revolutionary Russia," *Slavic Review* 54, no. 1 (Spring 1995): 23–44; Piers Beirne and Alan Hunt, "Law and the Constitution of Soviet Society: The Case of Comrade Lenin," in *Revolution in Law: Contributions to the Development of Soviet Legal Theory, 1917–1938*, ed. Piers Beirne (New York: M. E. Sharpe, 1990).

2. Burbank, "Lenin and the Law," 40.

3. For further reading on the materialist critique of law see Camila Vergara, *Systemic Corruption. Constitutional Ideas for an Anti-Oligarchic Republic* (Princeton: Princeton University Press 2020), ch. 3.

4. Lenin, "Explanation of the Law on Fines Imposed on Factory Workers," in *Collected Works*, vol. 2 (New York: Verso, 2018), 72.

5. Lenin, "Explanation of the Law on Fines," 53. This is the same argument James Madison used when arguing against adding a bill of rights into the Constitution of the United States. Legal protections are "parchment barriers," *Federalist 48*. In *The Federalist Papers*, ed. Clinton Rossiter (New York: Signet Classic, 2003), 305; Madison's *Letter to Jefferson Regarding the Proposed Bill of Rights* (October 17, 1788).

6. Lenin, "The Immediate Task of the Soviet Government," in *Collected Works*, vol. 27 (Moscow: Progress Publishers 1972), 235–77.

7. *Standard Rules of Internal Labor Organization*, 1941. A comprehensive analysis of Soviet labor law is beyond the scope of this chapter. For a fuller account of the contextual evolution of labor law and the complex coexistence of labor protections, social rights, and mandatory labor provisions in court cases see John N. Hazard, *Law and Social Change in the USSR* (Toronto: Carswell, 1953), ch. 7.

8. For an overview of this debate see Sebastiano Timpanaro, *On Materialism* (London: Verso, 1980). Timpanaro makes an important contribution to the conception of materialism by reincorporating biological and ecological conditions into the materialist analysis. I fundamentally disagree with his natural determinism.

9. I follow Louis Althusser's conception of the conjuncture as a historical singularity in which social power struggles are recognized, and the overdetermination of the contradictions of the system as well as the imprints this imbalance leaves behind on the structure are revealed. See Mikko Lahtinen, *Politics and Philosophy. Niccolò Machiavelli and Louis Althusser's Aleatory Materialism* (Chicago: Haymarket Books, 2011).

10. Karl Marx, *On the Jewish Question*. In *The Marx-Engels Reader* (New York: Norton, 1978), 33. For a discussion on relations of production as "effective power" and legal ownership see G. A. Cohen, *Karl Marx's Theory of History. A Defense* (Princeton: Princeton University Press, 2000), 63.

11. The influence his legal work had on Lenin's thinking remains largely unrecognized as researchers favor the sources that influenced his ideas on revolution. See for example Nikolaj Valentinov's account in *The Early Years of Lenin*, trans. R. H. W. Theen (Ann Arbor: University of Michigan Press, 1969). Neil Harding's otherwise excellent *Lenin's Political Thought* (Chicago: Haymarket Books, 1977) does not even mention his time as a prosecutor.

12. Conservative interpreters provide valuable facts about Lenin's early years that more favorable biographers tend to mostly neglect. For such an account see Victor Sebestyen, *Lenin: The Man, the Dictator, and the Master of Terror* (New York: Vintage Books, 2018), ch. 6.

13. Ibid.

14. Harding, *Lenin's Political Thought*, ch. 3; Paul Le Blanc, *Lenin and the Revolutionary Party* (Chicago: Haymarket Books, 1993), ch. 2.

15. Lenin, "Explanation of the Law on Fines," 36.

16. Ibid., 37.

17. Ibid., 38.

18. Ibid., 39. For labor laws in the 1880s and 1890s see Gaston V. Rimlinger, "Autocracy and the Factory Order in Early Russian Industrialization," *Journal of Economic History* 20 (1960): 67–92; Frederic C. Giffen, "The 'First Russian Labor Code': The Law of June 3, 1886," *Russian History* 2 (1975): 83–102. For labor relations see Robert R. Johnson, *Peasant and Proletarian: The Working Class of Moscow in the Late Nineteenth Century* (New Brunswick: Rutgers University Press, 1979); Rose L. Glickman, *Russian Factory Women: Workplace and Society, 1880–1914* (Berkeley: University of California Press, 1984).
19. Lenin, "Explanation of the Law on Fines," 71.
20. Ibid., 40.
21. Ibid., 33.
22. Ibid., 34.
23. Ibid., 43.
24. Ibid., 43.
25. Ibid., 50.
26. Ibid., 41.
27. Ibid.
28. Ibid., 68–69.
29. Ibid., 51–52.
30. Ibid., 55.
31. Ibid., 57.
32. Ibid., 60.
33. Ibid., 63.
34. Ibid.
35. Ibid., 61.
36. Ibid.
37. Ibid., 54.
38. Ibid., 67.
39. Ibid., 68.
40. Ibid., 55.
41. Ibid., 66.
42. Ibid., 41.
43. Ibid., 42.
44. Ibid., 66.
45. Ibid., 54–55.
46. *The Great Soviet Encyclopedia*, 3rd Ed. (New York: Macmillan, 1979).
47. Marxist group founded by Lenin in 1895 with the objective to distribute leaflets among workers and agitate against oppression.
48. Lenin, "New Factory Law," 271. For an analysis of labor violence see Daniel R. Brower, "Labor Violence in Russia in the Late Nineteenth Century," *Slavic Review* 41, no. 3 (Autumn 1982): 417–31.
49. Lenin, "New Factory Law," 271.
50. Ibid., 277.

51. Ibid., 279.

52. Lenin's insight on the biopolitical nature of law foreshadows Michel Foucault's conception of biopolitics as a rationality used to manage populations, in that it unveils the law as a technique that puts "life in order" by subjugating workers to economic processes. Foucault, *The Birth of Biopolitics: Lectures at the College De France, 1978–1979* (New York: Palgrave Macmillan, 2011), 138.

53. Lenin, "New Factory Law," 279.

54. Ibid., 282.

55. Ibid., 283.

56. Ibid., 284.

57. Ibid., 285. This "right to work" argument was used in England, developed from the freedom of contract theory, which was denounced as a form of domination by T. H. Green in 1881 in his "Lecture on Liberal Legislation and Freedom of Contract." Even if right-to-work laws in the United States are anti-union, their philosophical grounds are the same: freedom to contract without interference of regulations or unions.

58. Lenin, *New Factory Law*, 295.

59. Ibid., 296.

60. Ibid., 289.

61. Ibid., 288.

62. Ibid., 303.

63. Ibid., 289–90.

64. See the same realist critique of individual rights by James Madison, *Federalist 48*.

65. Lenin, *New Factory Law*, 291.

66. Labor organizing was prohibited until 1906. For Lenin on trade unionism see Thomas Hammond, *Lenin on Trade Unions and Revolution, 1893–1917* (New York: Columbia University Press, 1957). For an analysis of the role of trade unions in labor relations see Hazard, *Law and Social Change in the USSR*, 160–73.

67. Lenin, *New Factory Law*, 285.

68. Evgeny Pashukanis, *The General Theory of Law & Marxism* (London: Routledge 2017), 94.

69. Ibid., 96. For an extended analysis of Pashukanis see Michael Head, *Pashukanis: A Critical Reappraisal* (New York: Routledge, 2008).

70. Burbank, "Lenin and the Law," 40.

71. Ibid.

72. Lenin, "Immediate Tasks of Soviet Government," cited in Burbank, "Lenin and the Law," 40.

73. Hazard, *Law and Social Change in the USSR*, 179.

74. Death or severe sickness of parents, husband, wife, or children.

75. Vladimir Gsovski, *Elements of Soviet Labor Law: Penalties Facing Russian Workers on the Job*. In *Bulletin of the United States Bureau of Labor Statistics*, No. 1026 (1951).

76. In addition to dismissals due to absence, employers could fire workers arguing their lack of capacity to perform the job. Different from absenteeism, which could be objectively recorded in labor books, lack of capacity is more difficult to prove, therefore this type of dismissals was one of the most litigated. See Hazard, *Law and Social Change in the USSR,* 179.

77. Ibid.

78. Hazard, *Law and Social Change in the USSR,* 175.

79. For the sake of space, I have left out of my analysis the Gulag and only concentrated on the conditions of free labor. The use of convict labor in Russia might be compared to the massive use of convict labor in the United States after emancipation, using a loophole in the Thirteenth Amendment that allowed for "involuntary servitude" if convicted of a crime.

80. "[E]very violation of labor discipline shall entail either a disciplinary penalty or prosecution in court." Section 19. Cited in Vladimir Gsovski, "Elements of Soviet Labor Law."

81. For example, while urban dwellers needed a permit to reside in cities, peasants needed to register in their rural communes and needed authorization to leave the countryside. For a detailed analysis of labor regimes see Sheila Fitzpatrick, "War and Society in Soviet Context: Soviet Labor before, during, and after World War II," *International Labor and Working-Class History* 35 (Spring 1989): 37–52.

82. Penal consequences for labor insubordination were dropped in 1951.

83. Gsovski, "Elements of Soviet Labor Law," 11; Fitzpatrick, "War and Society in Soviet Context," 43.

84. Emily Clark Brown, "Fundamental Soviet Labor Legislation," *Industrial and Labor Relations Review* 26, no. 2 (Jan. 1973): 778–92.

85. C. Schwellnus et al. "Gig Economy Platforms: Boon or Bane?" *OECD Economics Department Working Papers,* No. 1550 (2019).

86. Handy Technologies, Inc. *Service Professional Agreement U.S.* https://www.handy.com/pro_terms.

87. New York's minimum wage is fifteen dollars per hour (2019).

88. According to the data provided by the American Arbitration Association, employee win rate is about 21 percent. See A. J. Colvin, "An Empirical Study of Employment Arbitration: Case Outcomes and Processes," *Journal of Empirical Legal Studies* 8 (2011): 1–23.

Bibliography

Beirne, Piers, and Alan Hunt. "Law and the Constitution of Soviet Society: The Case of Comrade Lenin" in *Revolution in Law: Contributions to the Development of Soviet Legal Theory, 1917–1938,* edited by Piers Beirne. New York: M. E. Sharpe, 1990.

Brower, Daniel R. "Labor Violence in Russia in the Late Nineteenth Century." *Slavic Review* 41, no. 3 (Autumn 1982): 417–31.

Brown, Emily Clark. "Fundamental Soviet Labor Legislation." *Industrial and Labor Relations Review* 26, no. 2 (January 1973): 778–92.

Burbank, Jane. "Lenin and the Law in Revolutionary Russia." *Slavic Review* 54, no. 1 (Spring 1995): 23–44.

Cohen, G. A. *Karl Marx's Theory of History. A Defense.* Princeton: Princeton University Press, 2000.

Colvin, A. J. "An Empirical Study of Employment Arbitration: Case Outcomes and Processes." *Journal of Empirical Legal Studies* 8 (2011): 1–23.

Fitzpatrick, Sheila. "War and Society in Soviet Context: Soviet Labor before, during, and after World War II." *International Labor and Working-Class History* 35 (Spring 1989): 37–52.

Foucault, Michel. *The Birth of Biopolitics: Lectures at the College De France, 1978–1979.* New York: Palgrave Macmillan, 2011.

Giffen, Frederic C. "The 'First Russian Labor Code': The Law of June 3, 1886." *Russian History* 2 (1975): 83–102.

Glickman, Rose L. *Russian Factory Women: Workplace and Society, 1880–1914.* Berkeley: University of California Press, 1984.

Green, T. H. "Lecture on Liberal Legislation and Freedom of Contract." In *Miscellaneous Works*, edited by R. L. Nettleship. Cambridge: Cambridge University Press, 2015.

Gsovski, Vladimir. *Elements of Soviet Labor Law: Penalties Facing Russian Workers on the Job.* In *Bulletin of the United States Bureau of Labor Statistics*, No. 1026 (1951).

Hammond, Thomas. *Lenin on Trade Unions and Revolution, 1893–1917.* New York: Columbia University Press, 1957.

Harding, Neil. *Lenin's Political Thought.* Chicago: Haymarket Books, 1977.

Hazard, John N. *Law and Social Change in the USSR.* Toronto: Carswell, 1953.

Head, Michael. *Pashukanis: A Critical Reappraisal.* New York: Routledge, 2008.

Johnson, Robert R. *Peasant and Proletarian: The Working Class of Moscow in the Late Nineteenth Century.* New Brunswick: Rutgers University Press, 1979.

Lahtinen, Mikko. *Politics and Philosophy. Niccolò Machiavelli and Louis Althusser's Aleatory Materialism.* Chicago: Haymarket Books, 2011.

Le Blanc, Paul. *Lenin and the Revolutionary Party.* Chicago: Haymarket Books, 1993.

Lenin, Vladimir. "Explanation of the Law on Fines Imposed on Factory Workers"; "The New Factory Law." In *Collected Works*, vol. 2. New York: Verso, 2018.

———. "The Immediate Task of the Soviet Government." In *Collected Works*, vol. 27. Moscow: Progress Publishers 1972.

Madison, James. "Federalist 48" In *The Federalist Papers*, edited by Clinton Rossiter. New York: Signet Classic, 2003.

———. *Letter to Jefferson Regarding the Proposed Bill of Rights* (October 17, 1788).

Marx, Karl. *On the Jewish Question*. In *The Marx-Engels Reader*. New York: Norton, 1978.
Pashukanis, Evgeny. *The General Theory of Law and Marxism*. London: Routledge 2017.
Rimlinger, Gaston V. "Autocracy and the Factory Order in Early Russian Industrialization." *Journal of Economic History* 20 (1960): 67–92.
Schwellnus, C. et al. "Gig Economy Platforms: Boon or Bane?" *OECD Economics Department Working Papers*, No. 1550 (2019).
Sebestyen, Victor. *Lenin: The Man, the Dictator, and the Master of Terror*. New York: Vintage Books, 2018.
The Great Soviet Encyclopedia, 3rd Edition. New York: Macmillan, 1979.
Timpanaro, Sebastiano. *On Materialism*. London: Verso, 1980.
Valentinov, Nikolaj. *The Early Years of Lenin*. Translated by R. H. W. Theen. Ann Arbor: University of Michigan Press, 1969.
Vergara, Camila. *Systemic Corruption. Constitutional Ideas for an Anti-Oligarchic Republic*, Princeton: Princeton University Press 2020.

Chapter 11

Facing the Test

The Leninist Party as Proctor

DEREK R. FORD

Introduction

At the First All-Russia Congress of Soviets of Workers' and Soldiers' Deputies in June 1917, Lenin makes a scandalous speech. He is responding to a claim made by Tsereteli, the Menshevik leader serving as the minister of posts and telegraphs in the Provisional Government. Tsereteli "said there was no political party in Russia expressing its readiness to assume full power. I reply: 'Yes, there is. No party can refuse this, and our Party certainly doesn't. It is ready to take over full power at any moment.'"[1] The crowd erupts in applause and laughter. "You can laugh as much as you please," Lenin retorts, but "no party can refuse this."[2] A few minutes later, when the chair announces Lenin's time is up, the crowd intervenes and forces the chair to allow him to finish. The speech is scandalous in part because the Bolsheviks are admittedly a minority in the Soviets at this time. Moreover, it marks pointedly the distinction between the Bolsheviks and the other two main "opposition" parties of what Lenin calls the "near-socialists," the Mensheviks and the Socialist-Revolutionaries (Narodniks): Lenin makes clear that any real communist party has to be organized around what Georg Lukács calls the *actuality of revolution*.[3]

That the revolution is actual does not mean it is guaranteed or inevitable; it is not an empirical claim but an organizing theory. Jodi Dean calls it "*anticipation,* the capacity of the future revolution to coordinate the actions that will bring it about."[4] As an organization of advanced elements of the proletariat and allied sections of other classes, the role of the Leninist Party is to provide leadership based on the actuality of the revolution. Leadership, however, is a vague term. It is more helpful to think of the Party as a kind of *teacher* who *teaches totally to the test: the test of revolution.* The Party, premised on the actuality of revolution, must always stand ready for the test of revolution.

That revolutions and social movements are educational is an implicit assumption of radical political theory. It is hard to find a revolutionary or even reformist text that does not make some mention of learning, teaching, studying, critical reflection, pedagogy, transformation, and so on. Yet rarely are these educational components explicated or interrogated closely, particularly at the general level of theory. What learning is and how it happens in such contexts is left unexamined. As such, the links between revolutionary and educational practice and theory remain implicit. This is not merely an interesting research gap; unexamined assumptions about teaching and learning can create practical problems for those who organize with the purpose of achieving social transformation. It is quite possible to sneak reactionary conceptions of teaching and learning into revolutionary struggles. It is also possible to eschew useful educational dynamics, such as the test, because of their contemporary association with reactionary educational systems and practices that increase inequality, alienate students, and facilitate the privatization of education.

In recent years, educational scholars and activists have been examining the varied educational processes and logics at work in reproducing or challenging capitalism, rather than merely attending to the *content* of education and politics.[5] In this chapter, I want to explore the relationship between testing and revolutionary struggle by working toward a Leninist theory of testing. I do this through an examination of Lenin's writings in the early months of the Russian Revolution with a focus on the operation of testing during protests. The Leninist Party, I argue, does not write the test, but *preps* for and *proctors* it. The Party knows that the test will come and organizes itself entirely around teaching to the upcoming test. Seen from this perspective, Lenin is therefore not a free agent, but a teacher confined to the changing and opaque determinations of the test. The test will determine every word and deed, every polemic, every slogan, every demonstration. Testing is both a means and an end. When protests reveal a weakness within the Party's internal organization, Lenin works to promptly identify and remedy the particular faults that prevented the Party from passing the test. Lenin, for example, viewed the turbulent days of April 1917 as a test that revealed weaknesses in the Party's organization. In response, he writes that the Party's internal "ties must be permanent, must be strengthened and tested every day and every hour."[6] The Party has to continually embrace the test.

Unlike the standardized testing regime that dominates so many educational systems, the content, form, and time of arrival of the revolutionary test is not known. Yet, the revolutionary teacher who teaches to that ultimate test is not stripped of agency or judgment. On the contrary: teaching to the revolutionary test requires that the teacher constantly anticipate potential content of the future test and try out, assess, and revise pedagogical strategies. In the field of education, one of the most important parts of test preparation is the pre-test. The revolutionary equivalent is the pro-test. As a pre-test of a sort, the protest allows the Party to test itself, the masses, its opponents, and to examine the political landscape of the moment. Where do the masses stand? How about the Party's organization, slogans, and pedagogy? How intense is the force of the state? What is the content of the test? To develop a Leninist theory of the test, I draw from Avital Ronell's writing on testing, which identifies a general *test drive* that, according to Ronell, both affirms and produces reality. Unlike in Ronell, for Lenin there is no testing for the sake of testing, however. Lenin's theory of the test, I argue, is a particular appropriation of the test drive, not a general but a *partisan drive*. To begin, we will briefly examine the history of the test and some contemporary debates about the use of testing in education, which can help us identify the ontology of testing and clear the way for a Leninist reconceptualization of the test.

Toward a Revolutionary Test Drive

Today, testing has a bad rap. Testing is associated almost exclusively with soul-crushing high-stakes standardized tests in schools, those forms of bubbles we fill in that abstract knowledge and subjectivity from the world, produce educational inequality, and facilitate the privatization of public education. In the United States, impressive grassroots movements have erupted against the test, the "opt-out" movement being the most significant. There are few progressives today who would defend testing as a form of assessment—let alone embrace it—and critical theorists within and around the field of education have on the whole rejected testing in favor of alternative assessments such as portfolio reviews. While the struggle against these tests in schools is surely important and progressive, we can't collapse one particular manifestation of testing together with the general educational logic of testing.

Ronell shows us that testing has an ontological status and force. What she terms the test drive is a "*nearly* unavoidable" condition of human being.[7] The test drive is "a kind of questioning, a structure of incessant research . . . [that] scans the walls of experience, measuring, probing, determining the 'what is' of the lived world."[8] As it scans the world, it both affirms and undermines what is. To test means to push, and sometimes when you push, you break. And when you break, you discover something else. This something else only holds until it, too, is tested. This is why testing is a *drive*—an evolving loop determining and challenging the contours of reality. At one point she puts it even more radically: "It is not clear even that something is known until there is a test for it."[9]

The test drive can be avoided or short-circuited. On the one hand, dogmatism tries to hold the test drive at bay with its own legitimating claims on truth. It is, in part, the modern era that gives birth to the impetus to test, to experiment. With the Reformation's challenge to the Church, authority began to need proof, had to submit itself to questioning. As the scientific pursuit overtook the church, it required that not just religious truth, but truth in general, must submit to the test. On the other hand, Ronell points out that the scientific regime itself tries to escape the test drive by fixing the rules of the test. The scientific test becomes a methodological and epistemological form of restraint. This is exemplified in Popper, who poses the test as "the answer to the answer" that "is never considered from the angle of a possible collapse."[10] What does it really mean to test? Are there different kinds of tests, and if so, do these produce different kinds of truths? If a hypothesis passes one kind of a test but fails another, what is its status?

While modernity entails liberating the truth (via the test) from the Church, it also encloses and fixes it within the scientific method. Science becomes the arbiter of truth, eclipsing philosophy. As science as such becomes an untestable maxim, Ronell argues, the test drive is taken over by the "normatively secured test," which "does not generate knowledge but confirms what already exists as 'knowable.'"[11] A key task for Ronell is thus to reassert the role of philosophical questioning, a practice that, building on Nietzsche, she argues shares an affinity with the test drive. "Rather than describing and merely computing," she writes, "the genuine philosopher tests the limits of intelligibility, making things happen with decisive positings that are by no means enslaved to what is."[12] Failure is the lifeblood of the philosopher, who risks everything—even themselves—in the process. There is literally nothing sacred here, no final ground that cannot be swept away or principles that cannot be broken. The test is aggressive, attacking "epistemological meaning with a kind of ontological fervor."[13] She wants to reclaim this fervor, use it to attack the juridico-scientific appropriation of the test drive. To do this, she points to the aporetic ethos of the test: "If the test really tested, then we would not need the test."[14]

How can we use Ronell's theory of the test drive to develop a Leninist concept of testing? Seen as drive, the test's impulse has no direction or content. We can view the Leninist test as a particular appropriation of the test drive, a *partisan* drive that both unleashes the impulse for change and gives it form or shape. While Lenin's teaching will be disciplined to the test, the test itself will be disciplined to the communist project. It is not that communism is a predetermined standard to be achieved. Instead, communism is the matrix—or, better, a rubric—for engaging and transforming reality. To make this clearer and more specific, let us turn to Lenin's writings during the early months of the 1917 Revolution as the Party faced several key pretests during which they tested their Party, the masses, and their enemies. Along the way, we can extract a Leninist appropriation of the test drive that can wrest the test away from its reactionary manifestations and inform Left organizing in the twenty-first century. For the prerevolutionary Party, the ultimate test is the revolution: Will we overthrow the bourgeoisie or not? Yet the revolutionary process as a movement of testing is not readily transparent. The Party has to deploy testing as a framework to assess its own capacities and strengths and to evaluate the character and relative power of the different social forces at play. The Party is thus both a proctor and a subject of testing. Conceptualizing the revolution as a test and the revolutionary process as a series of pre-tests enables the Party to build its internal organization, learn the shifting coordinates within which its operating, and intervene and push forward the revolution in response to these shifts. The concept of protest as a pre-test is especially useful today: it allows us to understand the role mass protests can play when they are disciplined to the test of the coming revolution.

Testing the April Theses

Lenin arrived in Petrograd on April 3, 1917, just weeks after the February Revolution overthrew the Tsar and his monarchy. What arose in its place was what Lenin—for a while—diagnosed as "dual power," a situation wherein power was shared between the Provisional Government and the Soviets of Workers' and Soldier's Deputies. This was a unique situation of interlaced power, in which the two independent forms of state existed together and, to varying degrees, depended on each other. The Provisional Government emerged out of the Duma (The House of Representatives) immediately after the February Revolution to organize a Constituent Assembly and govern in the interim. The *Soviets* (councils) were an organic form of sovereign and direct rule of the masses that first emerged in the 1905 revolution.

The day after Lenin's arrival, he was asked to report to a meeting of the Bolshevik delegates to the All-Russia Conference of Soviets of Workers' and Soldiers' Deputies. The meeting's chairman then asked Lenin to repeat the report to a meeting of Bolshevik and Menshevik delegates. This report contained a series of "personal theses" today known as the April Theses, which cover a range of topics: the communist position on the war, the stage of revolutionary Russia, the Party's immediate program, and the Socialist International, among others.[15] The Theses sparked controversy even within the Bolsheviks, and the Russian Social-Democratic Labor Party decided to host a public debate on them. Their controversial nature notwithstanding, as theses, they needed to be tested both in theory and practice, and over the course of the next four months some would stand and others would fall. The theses were an attempt to deduce the nature of the situation in Russia to provide a basis for communist tactics and strategies. It was Lenin's first attempt to ask and answer: What is the nature of the upcoming test? What questions will be on it? What are the standards? How do we prepare the Party, Soviets, and the broader masses for it? In this section, I isolate the first four theses, which speak most broadly to Lenin's test-driven revolutionary pedagogy.[16]

The first thesis concerns the war. The war is going to be part of the test. What is the nature of the war? What is the nature of annexations? How do we end the war? The war, Lenin says, is imperialist and predatory *because the capitalist class is waging it*. There can thus be no "concession to 'revolutionary defencism' "—an idea propagated by Menshevik Tsereteli and others that Russia must continue the war in order to defend the revolution—but that it must reject any annexations or territorial expansions. "Revolutionary defencism," Lenin argues, is nothing but an alliance with the bourgeoisie, a way to provide "socialist" support for an imperialist war. The Bolsheviks have to "*prove* that without overthrowing capital" the war will not end.[17] The second thesis confirms that Russia is in a transitional period between revolutionary stages. Tsarism has been overthrown and the bourgeoisie has been empowered. Now the bourgeoisie must be overthrown and the workers empowered. With the bourgeois-democratic revolution there is unprecedented freedom in Russia, which allows for the third thesis: a refusal to support the Provisional Government. All support, all power, must be to the Soviets. Yet, and this is the fourth thesis, the Bolsheviks are a minority in the Soviets. "As long as we are in the minority," Lenin says, "we carry on the work of criticizing and exposing errors and at the same time we preach the necessity of transferring the entire state power to the Soviets of Workers' Deputies, so that the people may overcome their mistakes by experience."[18]

With the situation of legal openness in which revolutionaries could openly organize and agitate, teaching to the test meant two things: patient explanation and experience of the moment's contradictions. Recognizing the lack of control they have over the situation and doubling down on the faith they have in the masses, Lenin again calls for power to the Soviets even though that, in essence, means power to the "near-socialists." The Mensheviks and Narodniks are positioned between the proletariat and bourgeoisie, and thus don't deserve the scorn the Bolshevik leader dishes out to the Provisional Government. As organs of power, Soviets are where the masses teach themselves how to govern. Through participating in the Soviets, the Bolsheviks' explanation and critique will give meaning, form, and direction to the experiences in the struggle in the months to come. This will prepare the masses for the test.

The first pre-test takes place just a few weeks later, and allows the Party to assess and evaluate their internal organization, their slogans, and their pedagogy. On April 18, the Provisional Government's foreign minister, Paul Milyukov, sends a note to Russia's allies reaffirming its commitment to fighting and winning World War I and reinforcing the annexations. On April 20, after the note leaks, the streets of Petrograd erupt for two days, during which the streets are packed with meetings, marches, and battling demonstrations. During the crisis, the masses instinctively gravitate away from the capitalists and toward the workers. Soldiers are the first in the streets. While the poorer sections of town and the suburbs fill with workers, reactionary elements that supported the Czar, led by military officers and The Black Hundreds, group in the rich areas. Street demonstrations erupt into violence and reports of shootings and deaths trickle in. As the crisis intensifies, the Soviets—under the leadership of the Mensheviks and Socialist-Revolutionaries—crack under the pressure and capitulate: they vote confidence in the government and ban street demonstrations for two days. Through reflections and debate in resolutions, newspaper articles, speeches, and a Party conference, Lenin and the Bolsheviks grade the pre-test and draw appropriate lessons. How did the Party, the Provisional Government, and the masses do on the pre-test?

The results showed first of all that the masses were opposed to the war, and that this was "strong enough to be a *decisive* factor, that caused the crisis."[19] The events also vindicated the Bolsheviks' distinction within the "defencist" camp between the masses and the leaders. The masses, Lenin concluded, do not understand the nature of the war, "that wars are waged by *governments*, that governments represent the interests of certain *classes*," and that the current war is a capitalist war.[20] The Provisional Government's April 18 note was a betrayal, they "were surprised, shocked, indignant. They *felt*—they did not understand it quite clearly, but they felt that they had been tricked."[21] Lenin inferred that the imperialists were well aware of the nature of the war while the "revolutionary defencist" leaders, by contrast, refused to admit its true nature, and so vacillated between the imperialists and the workers. The crisis confirmed the accuracy of the Bolsheviks' leader's thesis on both the war and the government's inability to end it at all—let alone without annexations.

There were also serious ways in which the Party failed the pre-test of the crisis. Party resolution on the morning of April 22 boldly states: "The organisation of our Party, the consolidation of the proletarian forces, clearly proved inadequate at the time of the crisis."[22] Even as their political opponents taunted them, the Bolsheviks embraced their failures. "We have no reason to fear the truth," Lenin wrote a few days later, "the crisis has revealed certain shortcomings in our organisation. We must set about to correct them!"[23] The primary error was a lack of centralization, which prevented an effective coordinated intervention. Because they weren't properly centralized, the Bolsheviks were not able to correctly ascertain the exact dimensions of worker support in different areas. The Central Committee "advanced the slogan for peaceful demonstrations," but the Petrograd Committee put forward a different slogan, "Down with the Provisional Government."[24] The second slogan was cancelled, but not before some workers got behind it. This showed a deficiency in intra-Party communication and unity. The Petrograd slogan was premature and made the Party vulnerable to accusations of adventurism and insurrectionism. There were also too many unknowns. Lenin said that the Party wanted "a peaceful reconnoitering of the enemy's forces; we did not want to give battle."[25] The goal of the protest was reconnaissance—to determine the size, strength, composition, and determination of the enemy. What forces are in the enemy camp in what numbers? How far will they go? The lack of coordination between various parts in the Party led to a failure that exposed the Party's vulnerability and taught the Party how to correct its errors.

The Party had to readjust. For instance, they needed to withdraw their slogan, "Turn the imperialist war into a civil war." The slogan was still correct in general and the retraction was only temporary, tactical. The only way out of the imperialist war was still through a revolutionary transfer of power from the bourgeoisie to the proletariat and its allies. However, the country was right now *in between* civil wars, and in fact the Provisional Government *needed* the Soviets and thus could not resort to violence against the workers. While the government could not repress the workers and soldiers, it could and wanted to repress the Bolsheviks, precisely because the Bolsheviks represented the revolutionary point of view. This was all the more reason for the temporary withdrawal of the slogan. "The government," Lenin said to the Congress, "would like to see us make the first imprudent move towards revolutionary action, as this would be to its advantage. It is exasperated because our Party has put forward the slogan of peaceful demonstrations."[26] Despite the fact that the Bolsheviks wanted a revolutionary struggle, they concluded that they should not be getting ahead of the objective conditions.

What about pedagogy? The Menshevik- and SR-guided Soviets capitulated, during the April protests, to the bourgeoisie. They corralled the workers, directing them out of the streets with the imperialists' promises that they would end the war. The pedagogical form of explanation, patience, and experience were once again affirmed by the Bolsheviks. The Party needed to engage in "peaceful, prolonged, and patient class propaganda."[27] Comrades needed to "explain more precisely, more clearly, more widely the proletariat's policy, *its* way of terminating the war."[28] The same went with dual power. The Soviets, Lenin claimed, *are* a real form of power, an embryonic socialist state. They "stand at the centre of the revolution," yet Lenin noted "that we have not sufficiently studied or understood them."[29] By this he meant that both the Bolsheviks and the broader struggle needed a better understanding of what the Soviets represent as a new kind of state, a workers' state along the lines of the Paris Commune. As if to provide an example of what it means to study the Soviets, Lenin offered the story of a coal miner who, speaking plainly, relayed how the miners took over the mine: "They seized the mine, and the important question to them was how to keep the cables intact so that production might not be interrupted. Then came the question of bread, which was scarce, and the miners also agreed on the method of obtaining it. Now that is a real programme of the revolution, not directed from books."[30] The "programme" came not from the enlightened Lenin but from the enlightened coal miner. The Party was a conduit through which the working class as a whole learned not only analysis but also about and through their own experience. "The Soviets must take power," and, "in this respect fear is the worst enemy."[31] It was not only the absence of a proper conception of imperialism and dual power, but also of the self-confidence of the masses. Or, it was the combination of these two aspects: without consciousness of class dynamics, the oppressed classes could not experience and flex their own power. The illusion that the imperialists could end the war was the illusion that the oppressed could not run their own affairs.

Finally, Lenin urged patience. "So far we are in the minority; the masses still do not believe us. We can wait."[32] There would be more pre-tests. Dual power, as a "state of unstable equilibrium," necessitated them.[33] Part of the revolutionary teacher's task is to affirm this again and again, to maintain momentum and keep pushing and preparing for the test. Others want to avoid or prevent the test, or keep the workers ill-prepared. There were three answers circulating after the April 20–21 crisis: (1) make no changes and give the government more time, (2) form a coalition government with representatives of the workers' parties, and (3) give all power to the Soviets. As it goes, answer 2 won, and the Mensheviks and Narodniks joined in a coalition government on May 6. This was another victory for the bourgeoisie, and another failed opportunity for the Soviets. What Lenin called the "near-socialists"—or what today we might call the left wing of imperialism—moved farther into the camp of the bourgeoisie.

The answer, of course, was wrong, and it was not long before it was exposed as such. Not even a month later, the government announced an upcoming offensive in the war. In response to a series of strikes, the Bolsheviks mobilized against the offensive and called for a peaceful demonstration on June 10. The night before, however, the First All-Russia Congress of Soviets headed them off by banning demonstrations for the next three days. The "near-socialists" said the Bolsheviks were planning a coup and that counterrevolutionaries were going to infiltrate the protests and cause violence. The Bolsheviks disciplined themselves to the Soviets and called off the demonstration. Comrades were understandably upset, but Lenin said that it was a strategically necessary retreat. The struggle was heightening and entering a new period. Tsereteli moved to ban the Bolsheviks from participating in the Congress. The war offensive was coupled with an offensive against the Bolsheviks. This was a vindication of the Bolsheviks' position, a testament that they really were the revolutionary opposition to imperialism. Lenin called for restraint and caution. As he suggested that the time for peaceful demonstrations had passed, he called for a change in agitation. The Mensheviks and Narodniks formed the ruling bloc and they had majority support. This means that *they were responsible* for the present situation, for the war offensive and the increasing economic disaster. They had shifted even further into the camp of the bourgeoisie.

Unable to contain the outrage at the offensive and the economic crisis, the Soviets called for a "general demonstration" of all parties for June 18, the day the war offensive was launched. This was another key pre-test for the Party, and one that the Party *administered*: A planned action with multiple parties would allow them to test their slogans on the masses, to see where they stood right then relative to other classes and parties. This time the Bolsheviks passed. Their standing increased. This pre-test showed they had a higher standing with the masses, and moreover, that the masses were *learning the content*. Although the action only lasted a few hours, the Party's slogans prevailed among the workers and soldiers.[34] Yet as a test of the struggle's state, it showed something new. It was the first protest that was forward-looking, "the first political demonstration of *action,* an explanation of how the various classes act . . . an explanation not given in a book or newspaper, but on the streets, not through leaders, but through the people."[35] Whereas previous actions emerged as reactions or reflections, this one was planned as a pre-test. The "near-socialists" had put their slogans up and failed.

The offensive went forward. While initially successful, it ended in absolute failure with around sixty thousand people dead within ten days. It sparked a new round of revolt with an insurrectionary character. Armed soldiers and workers took to the streets. They called on the Bolsheviks to take power. The Bolsheviks, after initially helping protest committees organize, quickly withdrew their support. The time was not right for insurrection. The protests were too concentrated in Petrograd and the Bolsheviks still did not have the majority of the Soviets. A severe reaction set in, as military forces loyal to the bourgeoisie repressed the protests and burned down the Bolsheviks' printing press and headquarters. Bolshevik leaders were accused of conspiracy. Some were successfully arrested while others were driven underground. The "near-socialists" were in complete support of the repression. The events signaled another major turning point: the coordinates of the revolutionary test had changed.

Reflecting on the three pre-tests, Lenin says each had unique features. While the first was spontaneous and chaotic, the second one was organized and orderly, and the third ushered in a counterrevolution. More important, however, were the continuities and what, taken together, they revealed. For one, each showed an increasing opposition to the Provisional Government and its inability to end the war and solve the economic crisis. For two, they were all demonstrations or protests. They were "something considerably more than a demonstration, but less than a revolution."[36] They were an eruption "of revolution and counterrevolution *together*, a sharp, sometimes almost sudden elimination of the middle elements."[37] The first four April theses no longer held. A military dictatorship now reigned as the counterrevolutionaries have consolidated power. The "near-socialists" have completely betrayed the revolution. No peaceful transfer of power was possible. The Soviets were with the counterrevolution. The Bolsheviks must prepare for violent insurrection, combining legal and illegal activity: "Let us muster our forces, reorganize them, and resolutely prepare for the armed uprising, *if* the course of the crisis permits it on a really mass, country-wide scale."[38] Propaganda must shift and intensify against the "near-socialists." The slogan, "All power to the Soviets" must be withdrawn. The era of the protest as a pre-test was over, was no longer an effective method of test preparation.

The Leninist Test

We witness the test drive each time the masses take to the streets to challenge and push at the boundaries of what is, every time political factions put forward their slogans and banners in a protest, and each time the Provisional Government takes another step toward war or against the Bolsheviks. At each juncture, the Bolsheviks utilized demonstrations or protests as pre-tests in which they tested their own slogans, internal organization, the composition and strength of their supporters and enemies, the different classes taking to the streets, and the coordinates in which the struggle was unfolding. That the Bolsheviks embraced the test drive means that they did not try to control it, but ride it, so to speak, and orient it into a revolutionary direction by assessing the states and trends of the objective and subjective forces. Only by submitting to the test drive did they have any chance of passing the ultimate revolutionary test.

As drive, the test drive has a permanent kind of consistency and is not the product of one particular mode of production, stage of social development, and so on. The political implication that follows is that the drive needs direction and organization. Any system can be tested in a variety of ways from any number of orientations. As pre-tests, protests do not presuppose any particular content. Thus, not only before but after the revolutionary event the Party has to continually reorient the test drive, directing it toward egalitarian ends. It has to become a permanent mechanism of the Party's outlook. It is not surprising, then, that in his political report to the Bolshevik Central Committee at the Eleventh Congress of the Russian Communist Party in 1922, we find Lenin framing the New Economic Policy also as a test, or a series of tests. Instituted one year prior, the NEP was a widely criticized retreat from socialism—one that instituted capitalist reforms to energize and expand productive capacities. Lenin frames the NEP *in the first instance* as a test: "First, the New Economic Policy is important for us primarily as a means of testing whether we are really establishing a link with the peasant economy."[39] Because the NEP allows for capitalist enterprises, the new state enterprises are put to the test as well. The NEP puts the entire revolution "to the test from the point of view of the entire economy."[40] The Party has launched a grand experiment and is relinquishing control of the test, which will ultimately be evaluated by an entire class (the peasants) and a rather abstract entity (the entire economy).

Just as in the heated moments in 1917, Lenin urged his comrades to *embrace the test*. "We need a real test," he said, "not the kind the Central Control Commission makes when it censures somebody . . . we want a real test from the viewpoint of the national economy."[41] It all came down to this test: "Either we pass this test in competition with private capital, or we fail completely."[42] Even once the working class and the Bolsheviks held state power, they still could not predict or control the outcome of this test. The Party must continue to test itself. Yet the Party was not only the proctor of testing, but the subject of it as well. After the revolutionary seizure of power, the Party continued to be tested by competing social forces and organizations. Immediately after October 1917, internal counterrevolutionary forces colluded with foreign imperialists who, through more than a dozen invasions, tried to overthrow Soviet power. At the same time, the Party had to completely reorganize society and the economy. It did not only look inward, however, but also began to help reconfigure the entire socialist movement. By passing the test of revolution, the Party verified and produced a new reality that came with new coordinates of testing. With state power, the Party's ability to test itself and others changed as well. They had to defend the results of the revolutionary test and continue to test themselves and the new order of things as they were subjected to the tests of rival forces and objective conditions.

The actuality of revolution is a framework for understanding the Party's role in building revolutionary momentum and organization. The Revolution is a test for which the Party—and their enemies—prepare. Yet the particular components of the test are impossible to tell in advance. The moment of insurrection cannot be determined in advance. Viewing the revolutionary process as a series of pre-tests helps the Party build itself and the movement. If the actuality of revolution is the test the organized Left is in fact preparing for, then everything leading up to it can be conceptualized as a pre-test. If we understand mass protests as pre-tests, we can more explicitly and precisely draw appropriate lessons about the Party, the relation of forces between competing leadership bodies, the consciousness and activity of the masses, and the overall objective conditions for the struggle. Where does mass consciousness stand? Who is in the streets, what banners are they following, and what slogans are they chanting? What forces and tactics are the state deploying? How did the movement's leadership respond? Were our tactics appropriate, were they too timid, or were they too radical? If a revolutionary crisis broke out right now, where would the various factions in society stand? Viewed through the test drive, each protest and action—whether organized by the Party or the spontaneous result of broader crises—can be placed in an overarching developmental sequence and can help us determine the evolution of that sequence. We can assess and evaluate the different factors at play, decipher the strengths and weaknesses of competing organizations and ideologies, and anticipate future developments. Protests and struggles are not isolated or singular events but rather part of an unfolding process of revolution.

Notes

1. V. I. Lenin, "First All-Russia Congress of Soviets of Workers' and Soldiers' Deputies," in *Lenin: Collected Works (Vol. 25)*, trans. and ed. S. Apresyan and J. Riordan, 15–24 (Moscow: Progress Publishers, 1980), 20.

2. Ibid.

3. Georg Lukács, *Lenin: A Study on the Unity of his Thought* (London: Verso, 2009), 26.

4. Jodi Dean, "The Actuality of Revolution," in *Storming the Gates: How the Russian Revolution Changed the World*, ed. J. Cutter (San Francisco: Liberation Media, 2017), 129.

5. See, for example, Tyson E. Lewis, *On Study: Giorgio Agamben and Educational Potentiality* (New York: Routledge, 2013); Derek R. Ford, *Communist Study: Education for the Commons* (Lanham, MD: Lexington Books, 2016); Fred Moten and Stefano Harney, *The Undercommons: Fugitive Planning and Black Study* (Los Angeles: Autonomedia, 2013); David I. Backer, *Elements of Discussion* (Charlotte: Information Age Publishing, 2015).

6. V. I. Lenin, "Foolish Gloating," in *Lenin: Collected Works (Vol. 24)*, trans. Bernard Isaacs (Moscow: Progress Publishers, 1980), 224.

7. Avital Ronell, *The Test Drive* (Chicago: University of Illinois Press, 2005), 5; emphasis added.

8. Ibid.

9. Ibid., 187.

10. Ibid., 41–42.

11. Ibid., 187.

12. Ibid., 137.

13. Ibid., 186.

14. Ibid., 224.

15. V. I. Lenin, "The Tasks of the Proletariat in the Present Revolution," in *Lenin: Collected Works (Vol. 24)*, trans. Bernard Isaacs (Moscow: Progress Publishers, 1980), 21.

16. Theses 5–9 address programmatic issues, while thesis 10 contains the same content as thesis 1 in a different context.

17. Ibid., 22; emphasis added.

18. Ibid., 23.

19. V. I. Lenin, "Lessons of the Crisis," in *Lenin: Collected Works (Vol. 24)*, trans. Bernard Isaacs (Moscow: Progress Publishers, 1980), 214.

20. V. I. Lenin, "Honest Defencism Reveals Itself," in ibid., 205.

21. Ibid.

22. V. I. Lenin, "Resolution of the Central Committee of the R.S.D.L.P. (Bolsheviks) Adopted in the Morning of April 22 (May 5), 1917," in ibid., 211.

23. V. I. Lenin, "Foolish Gloating," in ibid., 223.

24. "The Seventh (April) All-Russia Conference of the R.S.D.L.P.(B.)," in ibid., 244.

25. Ibid.

26. Ibid., 237.

27. Ibid., 236.

28. Lenin, "Lessons of the Crisis," 216.

29. Lenin, "The Seventh (April) All-Russia Conference of the R.S.D.L.P.(B.)," 241.

30. Ibid., 243.

31. Ibid.

32. Ibid., 232.

33. V. I. Lenin, "The 'Crisis of Power,'" in *Lenin: Collected Works (Vol. 24)*, trans. Bernard Isaacs (Moscow: Progress Publishers, 1980), 332.

34. V. I. Lenin, "The Eighteenth of June" in *Lenin: Collected Works (Vol. 25)*, trans. Stepan Apresyan and Jim Riordan (Moscow: Progress Publishers, 1980), 110.

35. Ibid., 111.

36. V. I. Lenin, "Three Crises" in ibid., 173.

37. Ibid.

38. V. I. Lenin, "The Political Situation" in ibid., 180.

39. V. I. Lenin, "Eleventh Congress of the R.C.P.(B.), in *Lenin: Collected Works (Vol. 33)*, trans. David Skvirsky and George Hanna (Moscow: Progress Publishers, 1980), 267.

40. Ibid., 272.

41. Ibid., 273.

42. Ibid., 277.

Bibliography

Backer, David I. *Elements of Discussion*. Charlotte: Information Age Publishing, 2015.

Dean, Jodi. "The Actuality of Revolution." In *Storming the Gates: How the Russian Revolution Changed the World*, edited by Jane Cutter, 129–40. San Francisco: Liberation Media, 2017.

Ford, Derek R. *Communist Study: Education for the Commons*. Lanham, MD: Lexington Books, 2016.

Lenin, V. I. "Eleventh Congress of the R.C.P.(B.)." In *Lenin: Collected Works (Vol. 33)*, translated by David Skvirsky and George Hanna, 259–329. Moscow: Progress Publishers, 1980.

———. "First All-Russia Congress of Soviets of Workers' and Soldiers' Deputies." In *Lenin: Collected Works (Vol. 25)*, translated and edited by Stepan Apresyan and Jim Riordan, 15–24. Moscow: Progress Publishers, 1980.

———. "Foolish Gloating." In *Lenin: Collected Works (Vol. 24)*, translated by B. Isaacs, 223–24. Moscow: Progress Publishers, 1980.

———. "Honest Defencism Reveals Itself." In *Lenin: Collected Works (Vol. 24)*, translated by Bernard Isaacs, 204–206. Moscow: Progress Publishers, 1980.

———. "Lessons of the Crisis." In *Lenin: Collected Works (Vol. 24)*, translated by Bernard Isaacs, 213–16. Moscow: Progress Publishers, 1980.

———. "Resolution of the Central Committee of the R.S.D.L.P. (Bolsheviks) Adopted in the Morning of April 22 (May 5), 1917." In *Lenin: Collected Works (Vol. 24)*, translated by Bernard Isaacs, 210–12. Moscow: Progress Publishers, 1980.

———. "The 'Crisis of Power.'" In *Lenin: Collected Works (Vol. 24)*, translated by Bernard Isaacs, 332–34. Moscow: Progress Publishers, 1980.

———. "The Eighteenth of June." In *Lenin: Collected Works (Vol. 25)*, translated by Stepan Apresyan and Jim Riordan, 110–12. Moscow: Progress Publishers, 1980.

———. "The Political Situation." In *Lenin: Collected Works (Vol. 25)*, translated by Stepan Apresyan and Jim Riordan, 178–80. Moscow: Progress Publishers, 1980.

———. "The Seventh (April) All-Russia Conference of the R.S.D.L.P.(B.)." In *Lenin: Collected Works (Vol. 24)*, translated by Bernard Isaacs, 225–73. Moscow: Progress Publishers, 1980.

———. "The Tasks of the Proletariat in the Present Revolution." In *Lenin: Collected Works (Vol. 24)*, translated by Bernard Isaacs, 19–26. Moscow: Progress Publishers, 1980.

———. "Three Crises." In *Lenin: Collected Works (Vol. 25)*, translated by Stepan Apresyan and Jim Riordan, 171–75. Moscow: Progress Publishers,

Lewis, Tyson E. *On Study: Giorgio Agamben and Educational Potentiality*. New York: Routledge, 2013.

Lukács, Georg. *Lenin: A Study on the Unity of his Thought*. London: Verso, 2009.

Moten, Fred, and Stefano Harney. *The Undercommons: Fugitive Planning and Black Study*. Los Angeles: Autonomedia, 2013.

Ronell, Avital. *The Test Drive*. Chicago: University of Illinois Press, 2005.

Chapter 12

The Production of "Leninism" and Its Political Journeys

ZHIVKA VALIAVICHARSKA

Introduction

Several generations of Western scholarship on the histories of radical and revolutionary thought have seen the legacies of Lenin and Stalin as historically and theoretically conjoined. Yet a quiet but profound instability defines their juncture, an instability that leaves a question mark after claims about their necessary relation or their predetermined historical linearity. This essay joins recent contributions in reopening and rethinking Lenin's revolutionary thought away from canonical and Western-centric readings. It joins a project of recovering Lenin's work from its canonical forms by studying the historical formation and political uses of those very forms. Treating the Lenin-Stalin juncture as an object of inquiry, as a historical and discursive figure with its own formation and with different political uses and "roles," opens a new set of questions: How was the theoretical and historical juncture between Lenin and Stalin discursively produced? What is the genealogy of this formation? Why did it turn out to be so tenacious, especially in some West European Marxist traditions? What kind of political work did it do and to what political ends? Twentieth-century and contemporary Western narratives of revolutionary political thought continue to retain assumptions about Lenin's political work and writings, locating in Lenin the split between a dogmatic

Soviet Marxism-Leninism and innovative West-European Marxisms. The latter, the argument goes, carried on Marx's project of social critique while the former degenerated into an unfortunate dogmatic distortion, a failure discarded along with the histories and social realities it forged. From the Frankfurt School and the Hungarian School, to Maurice Merleau-Ponty, to Ernesto Laclau and Chantal Mouffe's *Hegemony and Socialist Strategy*, Lenin's work has been consistently associated with the Party vanguard and its hierarchical relations between masses and leaders, and with an authoritarian, centralized, and oppressive state. In short, Marxism-Leninism in Western Marxist discourse came to signify a whole historical narrative, which was blamed for the unfortunate errors in political thinking for the failure of the socialist revolutions in the "East." Due to these conceptual errors, the project of socialism became unhinged from the project of democracy and took its unfortunate turn toward authoritarianism and terror. Even with Lenin's considerable impact on key political thinkers of the 1920s such as Georg Lukács and Antonio Gramsci, long considered among the "originators" and "pillars" of Western Marxism, and later, with Lenin's significant influence on figures such as Henri Lefebvre, Louis Althusser, and C. L. R. James, the disavowal of Lenin remains foundational to the broadly accepted divisions between the "good" Western Marxism and its bad, dogmatic, static, and historically catastrophic counterpart, Soviet Marxism.

This essay argues that "Leninism" is a discursive production, which began to take shape between 1924–1934 as part of the formation of the Stalinist canon of Marxism during the Stalinist period. Known as Marxism-Leninism, Stalinist philosophy reduced Lenin's thought to a system of stable ahistorical and general principles, obliterating much of its complexity, dynamism, and historical context. Contrary to the Western Marxists' idea that Soviet Marxism was static, however, in the socialist countries Marxism-Leninism began to lose its legitimacy in the late 1950s, giving way to an array of alternative and original interpretations of Marx, Engels, and Lenin in conversation within a diversity of philosophical traditions. In the early post-Stalinist period, "revisionist" scholars opposed to Stalinism in Eastern Europe and Soviet Russia republished the works of Marx, Engels, and Lenin, reopening them in multiple directions and liberating them from their canonical renditions. While in the former socialist contexts in Eastern Europe and the Soviet Union a humanist framework dominates these interpretations, they bear the mark of political experimentation and the unruly spirit of the era.

By contrast, in their critiques of Lenin (and of Soviet and East European Marxism), Western Marxist narratives overtly or tacitly continued to use the

"Stalinist" versions of Lenin's work. Regrettably, Soviet Marxism-Leninism has remained a stable referent even in the most careful studies, typically manifested in lumping together the philosophical legacies of Lenin and Stalin. This conflation, I argue, has played a key role in delegitimatizing the radical histories of the East, in their Western Eurocentric seizure and appropriation, and their subordination to revolutionary narratives produced in the West. Not altogether surprisingly, the dismissal of the socialist countries and their intellectual legacies among the Western Left has converged with Cold War and anticommunist political agendas.

Reopening the radical promises in Lenin's political works, this essay emphasizes the dynamism and instability of his thought, his concrete and situated analyses, and his deep commitments to principles of direct democracy, self-determination, and autonomous governance. It also highlights the value of Lenin's work for not only Eastern Marxists, but for anticolonial revolutionaries and writers during the anticolonial liberation struggles in the global South. By uncovering these submerged histories, the essay contributes to dismantling Western Eurocentric narratives of radical thought and decolonizing Lenin and the history of the socialist world.

Lenin in the Tumults of History

When reading Lenin, one needs to keep in mind that he does not offer a well-elaborated philosophical system. Anyone who would attempt to extract a coherent "Leninist" theory out of Lenin's work would have to confront a vast corpus of writings—forty-five volumes of essays, letters, telegrams, pamphlets, fragments, polemical addresses, and speeches written over the span of thirty-something years, virtually impossible for one scholar to grasp in its entirety.[1] These documents have also left a record of Lenin's political growth, of the internal shifts and turns in his political and theoretical commitments, at times subtle and at times quite abrupt. One would inevitably have to struggle with the immense tensions and contradictions even within some of his most systematic theoretical treatises and political analyses. Any attempt to extract an overarching system exposes itself to multiple contradictions to underscore the impossibility of constructing a "Lenin," a thinker, a line of thought, a corpus of systematic theoretical premises divorced from a situated historical understanding. Together with other letters and historical documents written in a dozen languages, Lenin's writings should be seen as a historical archive of a tumultuous stretch of time. As historian Lars T. Lih has put it in a detailed reconstruction of Lenin's *What Is to Be Done?*, "Lenin cannot be understood just by reading Lenin."[2] There is no such a thing as a "Lenin" autonomous from the shifts and tensions of a historical era marked by a dynamic unfolding of events constantly reconfiguring past history, political alliances, openings and possibilities, dead-ends, backlashes, and defeats. His interventions are intertwined with the fabric of a rapidly evolving maze of political positions, theoretical confrontations, and microevents.

This is not to say that it is impossible to trace the historical itinerary of Lenin's intellectual growth or political thinking, but to note that we should be cautious not to treat Lenin as a philosopher or a political theorist in the traditional sense. Althusser has pointed out philosophy's quite pronounced intolerance to Lenin.[3] He observed that Lenin has been "philosophically intolerable" to all who had philosophical encounters with him in one form or another, and this was the case precisely because Lenin would remain sarcastically indifferent to all philosophical objections. This aversion to Lenin is not surprising, considering that he offered "a different practice" of philosophy, one that threatens the status quo of current philosophical practice, marked by philosophy's refusal to recognize its own preconditions in the political. "Between Lenin and established philosophy there is a peculiarly intolerable connection: the connection in which the reigning philosophy is touched to the quick of what it represses: politics."[4]

Lenin's writings carry a sense of political mission, a calling; his pamphlets, letters, telegrams, and orders call into being, summon, and steer rather than describe and analyze historical events. His urgent and instructive voice throughout, as well as his relentless attacks on his theoretical opponents, shows a keen awareness that the revolution is a delicate, precarious project that lies in the ambiguous space between collective political forces and a terrain of historical openings. The imperative force of his voice permeated with anxiety and urgency throughout suggests that there is very little margin for "error." It conveys the pressing feeling that, as Lukács phrased it in a book published on the occasion of Lenin's death, a "chance" might be missed, a chance to seize on the unique possibility of driving history into a daring social vision.[5]

Back in 1924, Lukács called this kind of knowledge a revolutionary *Realpolitik*, the power of which carried "a world-historical responsibility."[6] It is the responsibility of having grasped a precarious possibility—to bring about, for the first time in the course of history, a better life and a present that belongs to the dispossessed and the oppressed. Lukács saw Lenin as a kind of expression of collective political agency that, by following the dialectical principle of realizing the struggle on a daily basis, in a number of concrete decisions within concrete historical situations, fully enacts Marx's philosophy of praxis—and by becoming its practitioner, abolishes its reified status. According to this conception, the analysis of the concrete historical situations is extremely important as it can guide one through the labyrinth of historical openings and mobilize the revolutionary potentials residing in the diversity of social forces. Lenin's work therefore conceived of the revolutionary project not as a historical inevitability but as a field of historical openings. The arrival of the new society could not be "promised," Lenin cautioned in his *State and Revolution*, and we have to always remember that it was not a historical necessity but required enormous collective political will and insight and strategy and militant struggle.[7]

"Leninism" in Western Marxism

Despite this rich and interesting archive, the intellectual histories of Marxist thought in the West have demonstrated a sustained aversion to Lenin for decades, refusing to recognize the complexity of his thought. They have continued to reproduce a simplistic, ahistorical account of his work, typically subsuming Lenin under a Stalinist frame of reference. Even with Lenin's considerable impact on key political thinkers of the 1920s such as Lukács or Gramsci, long considered among the "originators" and "pillars" of "Western" Marxism, and later, with Lenin's significant influence on Lefebvre, Althusser, C. L. R. James, and revolutionary writers in the formerly colonized countries such as Frantz Fanon and Amilcar Cabral, the disavowal of Lenin is foundational to the broadly accepted divisions between the "good" critical traditions of (Western) Marxist thought and its rigid and doctrinaire counterpart, Soviet Marxism.[8] This is in line with the broader dismissal of the intellectual traditions of the socialist world. Russian theorists and philosophers Maria Chehonadskih, Keti Chukhrov, and Alexei Penzin argue that in a Cold War context, "the philosophy of the USSR was mostly known only as an exotic object labelled as 'Eastern' or 'Soviet' Marxism. In the presupposed dichotomy, 'Western' Marxism was typically attributed an unconditional innovative value, whereas Soviet Marxism was seen under the vast umbrella of dogmatism or Stalinist Diamat."[9]

This tendency is perhaps most pronounced in the Western Marxist traditions influenced by the Frankfurt School and the Hungarian School. But it can also be seen in a range of thinkers who have engaged the history of Marxist thought in one way or another (from Merleau-Ponty to Laclau and Mouffe to Hardt and Negri). Hungarian School Marxists, trained and influenced by Lukács himself, have struggled with Lukács' own sympathies for Lenin and saw Lukács's embrace of Lenin as an unfortunate turn toward dogmatism and an endorsement of the authoritarian state. For some of them, the "Lenin" Lukács spoke about was "a virtual construction," an invention, mythology, or projection informed by a realization that all revolutionary potentials in Europe had been irretrievably lost.[10]

Similarly, members and followers of the Frankfurt School, in their effort to distance themselves from and articulate themselves against orthodox Marxism, have shared the rejection of Lenin's political work and writings—so much so that their legibility as a school of thought was premised on this shared rejection.[11] Herbert Marcuse, while a senior fellow at the Russian Institute at Columbia University in the early 1950s undertook a study of Soviet Marxism's philosophical foundations, and, partially refusing to accept the tacit premises of Cold War oppositions, attempted an "immanent critique" of Soviet Marxism. However, for him, too, "Leninism" was the fatal antiphilosophical turn: Lenin's work engendered the vanguardism of the Party, and pushed orthodox Marxism's economic determinism to an extreme by giving the economic domain a "primary" status and seeing it as objective reality, which in turn determined consciousness and knowledge. "A straight road seems to lead from Lenin's 'consciousness from without' and his notion of the centralized authoritarian party to Stalin's personal dictatorship," Marcuse said of Lenin's *What Is to Be Done?* It was "a road where 'scientific determinism' gives way . . . to decisions on the ground of shifting political and even personal objectives and interests."[12] In other words, Lenin opened the door to the formation of the authoritarian state and justified the arbitrary power of the authoritarian ruler.

Around the same time Merleau-Ponty published his *Adventures of the Dialectic* with a similar critique in mind. "He [Lenin] never asks himself by what miracle knowledge carries on a relationship with a suprahistorical object," Merleau-Ponty wrote of *Materialism and Empiriocriticism* while lamenting the loss of the dialectic, "a relationship which is itself removed from history. This new dogmatism puts the knowing subject outside the fabric of history and gives it access to absolute being, releases it from the duty of self-criticism, exempts Marxism from applying its own principles to itself, and settles dialectical thought, which by its own movement rejected it, in a massive positivity."[13] Lenin's legacy according to Merleau-Ponty committed the act of *destroying* radical philosophy—as opposed to realizing it—by relocating the dialectic to "the place where it is least capable of residing, namely, in the object, in being."[14] The effects of this move included "replacing total praxis by a technician-made action, replacing the proletariat by the professional revolutionary. It means concentrating the movement of history, as well as that of knowledge, in an apparatus."[15]

In the 1980s, Ernesto Laclau and Chantal Mouffe opened new and imaginative pathways for Marxism and the Left with their book *Hegemony and Socialist Strategy*. Yet, they also positioned Lenin within the lineage of orthodox Marxism from Plekhanov and Kautsky to Stalin. They found in Lenin the beginnings of the most problematic aspects of orthodox Marxism, which according to them predictably led to the authoritarian state. These were the primary and universal position of the working class in the revolutionary struggle, the shift toward party vanguardism, and the turn toward economic determinism in the two-dimensional, nondialectical relationship between base and superstructure.[16]

What unites these otherwise diverse traditions in Western Marxism is that they denounced the former socialist countries as the unfortunate failures of history that degenerated into authoritarian governments and totalitarian societies. They have become part of an unabashedly Western-centric narrative of revolutionary history and political thought, dismissing the radical, communal, and revolutionary histories of the East, their autonomous and community-based traditions of self-governance, and their historical and political connections to the anticolonial liberation movements in the global South. The irony is that they have lent themselves to Cold War political agendas, forming a sort of continuity with Western liberal and right-wing arguments about the socialist countries. Chehonadskih, Chukhrov, and Penzin call "the optics" of these arguments "colonial and exoticizing."[17] These optics have converged with colonial and orientalist phobias toward the East—a vast, vaguely defined region rendered as the seat of backward, dictatorial top-down governments with tyrannical rulers, and with unruly populations that need authoritarian regimes because they cannot govern themselves.[18]

The Formation of Leninism in the Marxist-Leninist Doctrine

The "Lenin" and "Leninism" known to these Western traditions is a product of the Stalinist doctrine of Marxism-Leninism. Stalin's pamphlets *Foundations of Leninism* and *Lenin and Leninism* (1924) are among the first systematic efforts to construct a coherent theory of "Leninism." This is the "Lenin" of the dictatorship of the proletariat, the Party vanguard, and the economic determinism of the "base-superstructure" model. Its formulations rested on several of Lenin's earlier writings such as *What Is to Be Done?* (1902), *One Step Forward, Two Steps Back* (1904), and *Materialism and Empiriocriticism* (1908), which were taken out of their historical context, their arguments simplified and generalized. The doctrine was fully elaborated in the *History of the Communist Party of the Soviet Union (Bolsheviks)*, known as the *Short Course*, what one might call the exemplary work in the Stalinist tradition.[19] The book, an ambitious project, came out in multiple editions between 1938 and 1956 and was reprinted more than three hundred times. It was also translated into sixty-seven languages and widely disseminated around the world. The *Short Course* provided a narrative of the history of the communist movement in Russia and also outlined the foundations and the general methodology for the natural sciences and the historical and social disciplines—Dialectical Materialism and Historical Materialism, known as Diamat and Istmat.

Diamat and Istmat became the main philosophical subfields that organized Stalinist epistemology. They rejected idealist philosophies of history and proposed a simplistic, dichotomist theory of "materialism." They constructed a dichotomy between the "base," or the economic and material organization of life, and the "superstructure," which included knowledge, consciousness, political institutions, culture, arts, and more. The latter was seen as derivative of and secondary to economic development and the "base."[20] Even though it called itself "dialectical," Stalinist philosophy thus affixed a two-dimensional, nondialectical relationship between "base" and "superstructure," where the "superstructure" was derived from the primary economic, material relations.[21]

Diamat instructed that all social processes were objectively knowable by means of scientific method, and thereby, in Stalin's words, "the history of society ceases to be an agglomeration of 'accidents'; [it] becomes a development of society according to regular laws, and the study of the history of society becomes a science." Hence, "the science of the history of society, despite all the complexity of the phenomena of social life, can become as precise a science as, let us say, biology, and capable of making use of the laws of development of society for practical purposes."[22] Similarly, Istmat put forward a philosophy of history by advancing a teleological understanding of history as a mechanistic progression of successive phases, where "the dying away of the old and the upgrowth of the new is a law of development."[23] Because it was scientifically knowable, historical progress could be studied by a science of social phenomena with the aid of a systematic methodology, which identified the "correct" vanguard historical elements, analyzed them, transformed them into instruments, and redeployed them back onto reality to accelerate the movement of history: "We must not base our orientation on the strata of society which are no longer developing, even though they at present constitute the predominant force, but on those strata which are developing and have a future before them, even though they at present do not constitute the predominant force."[24]

According to a projected historical teleology, historical contingencies became "deviations" and departures from the "correct" and "truthful" line of development. The undesired parts of the multiplicity of social forces were seen as contaminations and the spectrum of political forces was mapped onto an evolutionary plane of retrograde and vanguard forces, where all critique, alternative interpretation, and political multiplicity became a threat, an enemy, a deviation.[25]

The doctrine also took political agency away from the ordinary people. It was not the collective actions of the people, and certainly not collective struggle, that made change possible. Instead, Stalinist philosophy proffered a teleological understanding of history, which made the arrival of socialism inevitable. At the same time, it claimed that this arrival should be forced into existence—this is one of the many contradictions within the Stalinist philosophical system, a remnant of Marx's dialectical critique. The only active agent in history that remained was the Party, whose legitimacy was grounded in the inevitable arrival of communism and its access to the "correct" course of history. Perhaps the most defining feature of Stalinist theory, the "advanced detachment of the Party," was a "vanguardist" concept that imagined the "masses" as an unknowing subject that had to be "led" in the right direction.[26]

Marxism-Leninism also developed the concept of the "class enemy," which helped the Stalinist regime imagine itself as being in a perpetual state of war and constantly needing to reinvent the enemy. As Stalin himself unambiguously put it, the Party is not an "organization of order" but an "organization of war."[27] From the start, the Stalinist project then acquired enemies and a battlefield, and in fact, the entire social field becomes a war field. The class battle had a "forefront" and a "rear," "revolutionary positions" and "fortifications," and the Party, at the forefront of the class war, was an organization of vanguard order and military hierarchy.

It is important to recognize that the military language of the doctrine, particularly the language of "class war" and the "vanguard," was a result of a specific history rooted in the USSR's experience between the 1917 Revolution, the Civil War and the Allied Intervention, and World War II, which required massive reorganization of society according to the logic of war, militant battle, and defense. Daniel Egan (in this volume) shows that Lenin's use of the "vanguard" as a military metaphor, adopted by Stalin, was developed on the battlegrounds of World War I and the 1917 Revolution.[28] As Robert Tucker points out, Stalin himself developed an excessive affinity for military terminology in the context of the war communism of the Civil War. He consistently worked to generalize and extend the militant logics of war communism to the problems of social transformation in the context of early Soviet socialism.[29] The language of war, conquest, and expansion permeates his *Foundations of Leninism* to such a degree that one could read the booklet as a combat manual—a language that is certainly not unique in the history of revolutionary theory, especially during the period marked between the two world wars. For him, building communism was a revolutionary process "replete with civil wars and external conflicts, with persistent organizational work and economic construction, with advances and retreats, victories and defeats."[30]

While it produced a set of rigid formulations, the doctrine was far from coherent or stable. A clear contradiction structures the foundations of Diamat and Istmat: defining socialism both as a historical inevitability and a prescriptive call, they proclaimed its inevitable historical arrival and yet they insisted that it ought to be; they repeatedly announced that socialism had fully arrived in the present moment, while deferring it interminably into the future. And while insisting that the "ought" and the "is" have fully coincided, they retained the gap between the two wide open. This structural tension—between, on the one hand, asserting that socialism was already here and it was ours, and on the other, deferring it perpetually into the future—remained a defining structural tension in the intellectual production and material culture of Stalinist socialist discourse and socialist realism.

These inconsistent or dissonant moments attest to the fact that even in its most doctrinaire version, the epistemology of Stalinist Marxism was an evolving formation filled with tensions and contradictions, which David-Fox has called a "hybrid rather than a coherent, unified phenomenon."[31] During the Stalinist years, the philosophy underwent significant transformations, and even when its basic foundational principles remained unquestioned—because their status was unquestionable—those who adhered to its principles did not reproduce them blindly but tried, through their own understanding, to expand it in different directions and build upon its foundations, applying it to different spheres of knowledge. The ritualization of the doctrine in certain spheres of political and everyday life was inevitable, especially after it lost its legitimacy in the 1960s but nevertheless continued its life in coexistence and conflict with other philosophical ideas. And even then, as anthropologist Alexei Yurchak has demonstrated, these simplified ideologemes, seen as reiterative practices, produced unpredictable effects that subverted their official messages and acquired new meanings in everyday life.[32]

Western Critiques

What became obvious to scholars of Marx in the West was that the Marxist-Leninist doctrine had eliminated the dialectical foundations of Marx's philosophy of history, which grasped the manifest contradictions of social forces as the enabling conditions for historical change while relocating history's metabolic force in the practical activity of ordinary people. They were left over as remnants of an obliterated dialectical method. Henri Lefebvre, in his book *Dialectical Materialism*, thoroughly critiqued this move. This small and now marginalized study seems to be one of the earliest humanist critiques of the central currents in Stalinist thought and contains an astute diagnosis of Stalinism's reductionist rewritings of Marx. Lefebvre published parts of his critique as early as 1935, which put him in sharp conflict with the French Communist Party, which supported Stalinism. In the 1961 "Foreword" to the fifth edition of the booklet, twenty-five years after its first publication, he noted that we are just "beginning to see and know better what took place [under Stalinism]."[33] Marxism-Leninism's drive toward a positivist methodology, even if it called itself "dialectical," had developed tremendous hostility to the dialectic:

> [Stalinists] became more contemptuous than ever of Hegel and Hegelianism, they rejected Marx's early writings as being tainted with idealism and as having preceded the formulation of dialectical materialism, they drew a line between Marx and his predecessors and another one between the so-called philosophical and so-called scientific works in the Marxian corpus.[34]

Lefebvre saw that *Diamat* had declared a war on Hegel and the Hegelian aspects of Marx's thought, suppressing the continuities and tensions that define the relationship between Marx, Hegel, Feuerbach, and other young

Hegelians in Marx's early writings. Lefebvre devoted a significant number of years to restoring Hegel's influence in the French-speaking historiography of Marx, publishing the first French translation of Lenin's *Philosophical Notebooks* in 1938. At a time when "dogmatism is crumbling and dissolving," Lefebvre wrote, "the early writings of Marx have become of the first importance."[35]

The Hegelian influences in Marx's and Lenin's work had already begun to suffer considerable repression within the wider political context of the European Left from 1918 onward. Karl Korsch, a contemporary of Lenin and Lukács, signaled this tendency as a kind of "Hegel amnesia."[36] Georg Lukács's *History and Class Consciousness* and Karl Korsch's *Marxism and Philosophy*, which appeared independently but synchronically in 1923, sought to address this erasure and reinvent the dialectic in materialist terms.[37] Korsch speaks of the deeper prehistory of this tendency, showing that from the 1850s onward, Hegel almost disappeared from the philosophical debates in Germany. It was inconceivable for bourgeois philosophers of history, treating philosophy as a self-referential chain of ideas divorced from their social foundations, to imagine philosophy departing from the terrains of "purely" philosophical questions. They failed to notice that the Hegelian dialectic, rather than "decaying," formed a symbiosis with social practice while inaugurating forms of knowledge immediately concerned with social processes. As for the Marxists, Korsch argues, they got completely carried away in their attempts to supersede philosophy altogether, as was the case with the economic determinism and positivism of orthodox Marxism. What both philosophical trends missed was Marx and Engels's attempt to come up with "a theory of social development seen and comprehended as a living totality, or, more precisely . . . a theory of social revolution comprehended and practiced as a living totality."[38]

Lukács responded precisely to this general move away from Hegel in *History and Class Consciousness*. As a result of the rationalization of the labor process, the specialization and fragmentation of knowledge and production, and the commodification of needs, the bourgeois subjects had acquired a fragmented and reified knowledge of reality that they could not transcend. Plugged into an increasingly preexisting and self-sufficient rationalized production process, bourgeois subjects found themselves gradually deprived of all agency, becoming progressively more passive, their thought more contemplative. The proletarian class, on the contrary, was the only collective historical subject that embodied and could grasp the links between interrelated social phenomena at this particular historical juncture. Confronted with the "brute fact of the most elementary gratification of his needs," with their own exploitation and misery, the worker was able to "[perceive] the split of his being preserved in the brutal form of what is in its whole tendency a slavery without limit."[39] The irreducibly unique, accidental nature of life clashed with the rational, quantified, and systematized process of capitalist production in the experience of the worker; their labor was objectified and quantified in a regime of exchange value; the needs crucial for their survival were only met in the form of commodities. Hence, they embodied—in their physical, living being, in their material needs, and in the material liminality of their life constitution—the very historical contradictions that capitalism produced. This is how the proletarian class, according to Lukács, was able to grasp the material and sociohistorical preconditions for its own existence and gain self-knowledge as a collective subject, that is to say, become conscious as a "class."

The works of Lukács and Korsch stirred up controversy for the right reasons—namely, because they appeared as an unrelenting critique of proponents of reductive evolutionary materialism, who pressed for economic determinism as a way of eliminating all traces of Hegelian idealism. Korsch explicitly distanced himself from any association with Lenin at a time when a narrow version of Leninism was coalescing in Europe during the 1920s, as is evident in his reply to criticisms of *Marxism and Philosophy* in 1930, and in his critical review of Pannekoek's *Lenin as Philosopher*.[40] Lukács, by contrast, took a more difficult path—of recuperating the Lenin that had been lost in the doctrinization of Leninism. Almost immediately after publishing *History and Class Consciousness*, he began to move away from the "ethical idealism" and Party elitism he had endorsed in his loyalty to Hegel. He regretted that he had failed to account for "labor" and the praxis of social life and thus formulate a truly materialist notion of history. In the 1967 Preface to the long-awaited second edition of the book, he stressed the importance of labor in Marx's radical reformulation of the Hegelian dialectic. Seeing labor as the mediator between social activity and "nature" in its historically specific forms could help shed ontological conceptions of "nature" and deliver an effective critique of deterministic reductions of the economy seen as an objective process with internal laws. In a gesture that disowned his famous book almost in its entirety, Lukács declared: "This completely shattered the theoretical foundations of what had been the particular achievement of *History and Class Consciousness*."[41] "The book," he says, "became wholly alien to me just as my earlier writings had become by 1918–19. It suddenly became clear to me that if I wished to give body to these new theoretical insights I would have to start again from scratch."[42]

Yet it was as early as 1924, in Lukács's book on Lenin, that signs of a practical, materialist conception of the historical process appeared. Lukács undertook the study of Lenin without being aware of his *Philosophical Notebooks*—a voluminous record of Lenin's close study of Hegel's *Logic* in 1914–16—which were published in Russian only in 1929 and in German in 1931, nor, it seems, of *State and Revolution*.[43] "It is undoubtedly one of the great achievements of *History and Class Consciousness* to have reinstated the category of totality in the central position it had occupied throughout Marx's works and from which it had been ousted by the scientism of the social-democratic opportunists," Lukács reflected later. "I did not know at the time that Lenin was moving in a similar direction. . . . But whereas Lenin really brought about a renewal of the Marxian method, my efforts resulted in a—Hegelian—distortion, in which I put the totality in the center of the system, overriding the priority of economics."[44] He wrote, "All attempts to gain knowledge of socialism which do not follow this path of dialectical interaction with the day-to-day problems of the class struggle make a metaphysic of it, a utopia, something merely contemplative and non-practical." Instead, Lukács saw Lenin's life and work as embodying the "final elimination of all utopianism, the concrete fulfillment of the content of Marx's program: a theory become practical."[45]

Eastern Revisions and Anticolonial Visions

In the Soviet Union and the socialist countries in Eastern Europe, the collapse of the doctrine began in the mid-1950s, when a number of anti-Stalinist philosophers and social thinkers began reclaiming the works of Marx and Lenin back from their Stalinist renditions. New and expanded Soviet editions of the collected works of Marx-Engels and Lenin were prepared as previously unpublished works emerged. From the 1950s to the 1980s in the Soviet Union and other socialist countries, prominent scholars of Marx, still barely known to readers outside the former socialist world (some of them were Soviet scholars Nikolay Lapin, Georgii Bagaturia, Merab Mamardashvili, Evald Ilyenkov, Victor Vaziulin, among many others) revisited the context of the nineteenth and early twentieth century and reinterpreted the works of Marx, Engels, and Lenin in conversation with different philosophical traditions, including humanism, existentialism, and structuralism, and through questions of subjectivity.[46] Many of these scholars were involved in the collective labor of transcribing, translating, and republishing the entire corpus of Marx's and Lenin's writings. Marx's early works, which had been previously suppressed or marginalized by the doctrine (most importantly, the *Philosophical and Economic Manuscripts* of 1844), were published for the first time in their full versions. They shed new light on Marx's revolutionary thought, which helped the new generations to radically revise the canonical interpretations of both his earlier and later works. By studying closely the *1844 Manuscripts* and their historical context, post-Stalinists reconstructed the genealogy of materialist critique and the historical origins of its formation, bringing to light the conceptual and historical links between Hegelian dialectical thought and Marx's materialist method.[47]

In a similar way, post-Stalinist revisionists reclaimed Lenin from the Stalinist dogma and studied his work "holistically"—as a philosopher, political economist, sociologist, dialectician, and revolutionary. They underscored the dynamism of his thought while placing his writings in historical context.[48] The work of Bulgarian sociologist Petur-Emil Mitev reclaimed Lenin from the economic determinism of the Stalinist tradition and its evolutionary and monistic theories of history. For Mitev, Lenin was a thinker and organizer acutely aware of the dynamism of the historical process, the unpredictability of history, and the rift between theoretical formulas and political reality. According to him, Lenin's concept of history was a kind of "poliversity" with "a multiplicity of possibilities opened by the specific historical conditions." Lenin's lesson of truth, Mitev stated, was that "reality is much richer than any theoretical knowledge, and the emergence of every new political moment presents itself as a challenge to existing theory."[49]

Mitev also saw in Lenin a theorist of subjectivity. In *What Is to Be Done*, Lenin was the first person to introduce the "subjective" factor in the historical process from a revolutionary perspective and offer something close to a theory of hegemony. For Lenin, Mitev argued, consciousness and practice were always mediated through social forms such as political discourses and the specific shape of organized life. Political organization was nothing other than a mediated form of social consciousness, which was subject to its own dynamic.[50] Mitev's argument resonates with Perry Anderson's essay from the 1970s, which reminds readers that Gramsci borrowed the concept of "hegemony" from Lenin—Lenin had used it as early as 1901 to forge a collective "working-class" subject out of disparate and dynamic collective forces on the ground.[51]

Furthermore, Lenin's writings on imperialism and the national question became an important inspiration in the anticolonial national liberation movements in the Global South during the 1950s and 1960s. Lenin's texts *Imperialism, the Highest Stage of Capitalism* and *The Right of Nations to Self-Determination* circulated as pamphlets among anticolonial revolutionaries in Africa and the Caribbean. This is not surprising, considering the hegemonic role of the national idea in anticolonial revolutionary thought. Anticolonial intellectuals and revolutionaries Frantz Fanon, C. L. R. James, and Amilcar Cabral used Lenin to articulate intersections of racism, colonialism, capitalist accumulation, and class power. The humanist revolutionary C. L. R. James studied closely Lenin's writings on the national question from 1912–16 and also published a marvelous study of his *Philosophical Notebooks* from 1914.[52] Indebted to the humanist tendency that James belonged to, intellectual historian Kevin Anderson has studied the link between these texts. Anderson treats Lenin's encounter with Hegel as a watershed period in Lenin's political thought and argues that the *Notebooks* have left a record of Lenin's profound rethinking of his earlier understanding of dialectical materialism.[53] This deeper understanding, Anderson argues, helped Lenin develop his position on the new political subjectivities emerging with national self-determination movements.[54]

In Lenin's writings on the national question, the dynamic between "oppressor" and "subjugated" nations and ethnicities became a central problem for both anticapitalist revolution and anti-imperialist struggle. His *Right of Nations to Self-Determination* speaks of mobilizing the revolutionary potentials of national self-determination movements as they connected with peasant and working-class social unrest among ethnic and racial minorities in the Russian empire. Lenin recognized their rebellious anti-imperialist potentials in the peripheries of the empire—to him, they were articulated both against the extractivist and exploitative logic of Russian imperialism and against the ethnic and racial supremacy of Russian imperial nationalism. In them he saw a socially radical element and a major revolutionary subject without whom, in the conditions of world capitalism, a world socialist revolution was unthinkable.[55] Because of these decolonial elements, political philosopher Matthieu Renault reads Lenin as a decolonial thinker of his own time and in his own political context.[56] To Lenin, national liberation movements appeared as heterogeneous revolutionary formations that created their own temporalities and disrupted Eurocentric linearity and stagism. By recognizing and foregrounding these peripheral forces, Lenin "decentered the revolution."[57]

∼

Lenin's work should be seen as a dense bundle of collective history that continues to this day—because its archive has been collected, assembled, and published more than several times by dozens, if not hundreds, of people;

because it captures a vast range of collective political experiences of its times; because its meanings continue to shift in light of the political histories that succeed it; and because its echoes continue to rupture, disturb, and resonate in the present.[58] Excavating the erased, forgotten, neglected, or suppressed afterlives of this work and history contributes to a project of decolonizing socialist revolutionary thought and the histories of the socialist countries in the East. The genealogies traced in this essay have made visible some reified and ahistorical thought-forms that continue to overshadow Lenin's legacy in the West, which have participated in Eurocentric and orientalizing narratives of radical political history of the socialist countries. Recovering Lenin's dynamic and polemical history in Eastern Europe and the socialist world, its travels in the Global South, and its political value for the anticolonial liberation movements widens the horizons for decolonizing the historiographies of the radical political movements during the twentieth century.

Notes

1. I thank Robert Maclean for parts of this formulation, and to him and Alla Ivanchikova for the generative engagement and feedback.

2. Lars T. Lih, *Lenin Rediscovered: What Is to Be Done? in Context* (Chicago: Haymarket Books, 2008), 21. For discussion on Lih's intervention, see also "Symposium on Lars Lih's *Lenin Rediscovered*," special issue of *Historical Materialism* 18, no. 3 (2010).

3. Louis Althusser, "Lenin and Philosophy," in *Lenin and Philosophy and Other Essays* (New York: Monthly Review Press, 2001), 11–43.

4. Ibid., 18.

5. Georg Lukács, *Lenin: A Study of the Unity of His Thought* (Cambridge: MIT Press, 1971), 34.

6. Lukács, *History and Class Consciousness: Studies in Marxist Dialectics* (Cambridge: MIT Press, 1972), 34.

7. Lenin, "State and Revolution," *Collected Works*, vol. 25, 469.

8. For alternative readings of Lenin's political thought, see Kevin Anderson, *Lenin, Hegel, and Western Marxism: A Critical Study* (Urbana and Chicago: University of Illinois Press, 1995); "Lenin's Encounter with Hegel Eighty Years Later: A Critical Assessment," *Science and Society* 59, no. 3 (1995): 298–319. More recent contributions to recovering Lenin's political legacy and thought include Slavoj Zizek, ed., *Revolution at the Gates: A Selection of Writings from February to October 1917* (London and New York: Verso, 2002); Sebastian Budgen, Stathis Kouvelakis, and Slavoj Zizek, eds. *Lenin Reloaded: Towards a Politics of Truth* (Durham and London: Duke University Press, 2007).

9. Maria Chehonadskih, Keti Chukhrov, and Alexei Penzin, "Introduction: Antiquity and Modernity of Soviet Marxism," *Stasis* 5, no. 2 (2017): 4.

10. Arato and Breines, "The Lukács Debate," *The Young Lukács and the Origins of Western Marxism* (New York: Seabury Press, 1979), 195–96.

11. See, for example, Martin Jay's work on Western Marxism and dialectical totality, in *Dialectical Imagination* (Berkeley, Los Angeles, and London: University of California Press, 1996 [first published in 1973]), 173–93; *Marxism and Totality* (Berkeley and Los Angeles: University of California Press, 1984), 67 and 81–127.

12. Herbert Marcuse, *Soviet Marxism: A Critical Analysis* (New York: Columbia University Press, 1958), 145–46.

13. Maurice Merleau-Ponty, *Adventures of the Dialectic* (Evanston: Northwestern University Press, 1973), 60.

14. Ibid., 65.

15. Ibid.

16. Ernesto Laclau and Chantal Mouffe, *Hegemony and Socialist Strategy: Towards a Radical Democratic Politics* (London and New York: Verso, 1985), 19–20; 55–65; 58–59.

17. Chehonadskih, Chukhrov, and Penzin, "Introduction: Antiquity and Modernity of Soviet Marxism," 4.

18. See Natasa Kovacevic, "Anti-Communist Orientalism: Shifting Boundaries of Europe in Dissident Writing," in *Marx's Shadow: Power, Knowledge, and Intellectuals in Eastern Europe and Russia*, ed. Costica Bradatan and Serguei Oushakine. Lexington Books, 2010.

19. *History of the Communist Party of the Soviet Union (Bolsheviks): Short Course* (New York: International Publishers, 1939), 114. The chapter "Dialectical Materialism and Historical Materialism" is attributed to Stalin.

20. For some early studies of Stalinist thought seen as intellectual history, see Gustav Wetter, *Dialectical Materialism: A Historical and Systematic Survey of Philosophy in the Soviet Union* (New York and London: Frederick Praeger, 1958); David Joravsky, *Soviet Marxism and Natural Science: 1917–1932* (New York: Columbia University, 1961); and Robert Tucker's traditional biographical work with elements of intellectual history, *Stalin as Revolutionary, 1879–1929: A Study in History and Personality* (New York: Norton, 1973). For a recent return to the intellectual history of Marxism in pre- and postrevolutionary Russia and the Soviet Union, see Igal Halfin, *From Darkness to Light: Class, Consciousness, and Salvation in Revolutionary Russia* (Pittsburgh: University of Pittsburgh Press, 2000); on Stalinist political thought, Erik van Ree, *The Political Thought of Joseph Stalin: A Study in Twentieth-Century Revolutionary Patriotism* (London, Routledge, 2002); "Stalin as Writer and Thinker," *Kritika* 3, no. 4 (2002): 699–714. Michael David-Fox has raised anew the question of "ideology," giving a thorough account of the multiple and intersecting ways in which ideology has been conceptualized and deployed in understanding social

relations and cultural and political realities in Soviet and socialist history, especially during the Stalinist period. *Crossing Borders: Modernity, Ideology, and Culture in Russia and the Soviet Union* (Pittsburgh: University of Pittsburgh Press, 2015), 75–103.

21. Various "theories of reflection" emerged out of this framework—they established the theoretical foundations of Marxist-Leninist humanities and aesthetics and provided a lens for literature and the arts. One of the main authors of the "theory of reflection" was Stalinist philosopher Todor Pavlov, who used the pseudonym P. Dosev in his early writings. P. Dosev, *Teoriia otrazheniia: Ocherki po teorii poznaniia dialekticheskogo materializma* (Moscow: Gosudarstvenoe sots.-ekon. izdatel'stvo, 1936). First publication in Bulgarian is in 1945, Todor Pavlov, *Teoriia na otrazhenieto: Osnovni vuprosi na dialektichesko-materialisticheskata teoriia na poznanieto* (Sofia: Narizdat, 1945).

22. *Short Course*, 114.

23. Ibid., 110.

24. Ibid.

25. Ibid., 111.

26. See Daniel Egan, this volume, for a reconstruction of Lenin's dialectical use of the vanguard metaphor in contradistinction to the "vanguardist" elevation of Party over class.

27. Stalin, *Works*, vol. 6, 104.

28. Daniel Egan, "Saving the Vanguard: The Contemporary Relevance of Lenin's Military Metaphors" (current volume).

29. Robert Tucker, *Stalin as Revolutionary*, 400–402.

30. Stalin, *Works*, vol. 6, 115.

31. David-Fox, *Crossing Borders*, 42.

32. Alexei Yurchak, *Everything Was Forever until It Was No More: The Last Soviet Generation* (Princeton: Princeton University Press, 2006).

33. Henri Lefebvre, *Dialectical Materialism* (Minneapolis and London: University of Minnesota Press, 2009), 1.

34. Ibid., 2.

35. Ibid., 7.

36. Arato and Breines, "The Lukács Debate," 172.

37. For some informative although contested intellectual histories of Korsch, see Jay, "The Revolutionary Historicism of Karl Korsch," in *Marxism and Totality* (Berkeley and Los Angeles, 1984), 128–49; Douglas Kellner, *Karl Korsch: Revolutionary Theory* (Austin: University of Texas Press, 1977). Kevin Anderson has also addressed Korsch's political relationship to Lenin, which shifted considerably between his 1923 *Marxism and Philosophy* and his 1930 introduction to the new edition of the book. Anderson, *Lenin, Hegel, and Western Marxism*, 173–80.

38. Karl Korsch, *Marxism and Philosophy* (New York and London: Monthly Review Press, 1970), 57.

39. Georg Lukács, *History and Class Consciousness: Studies in Marxist Dialectics* (Cambridge, MIT Press, 1972), 166.
40. Korsch, *Marxism and Philosophy*, 98–145.
41. Lukács, *History and Class Consciousness*, xxxvi.
42. Ibid.
43. Anderson, *Hegel, Lenin, and Western Marxism*, 173–209.
44. Lukács, *History and Class Consciousness*, xx.
45. Ibid., 73.
46. For an informative discussion, see the conversation between Keti Chukhrov, Alexei Penzin, and Valery Podoroga on Soviet philosophy, "Marx against Marxism, Marxism against Marx," *Stasis* 5, no. 2 (2017): 266–88. See also "Antiquity and Modernity of Soviet Marxism," a thematic issue of the journal *Stasis* dedicated to Soviet Marxism, *Stasis* 5, no. 2 (2017). Also, Zhivka Valiavcharska, Chapter 1 of *Restless History: Political Imaginaries and Their Discontents in Post-Stalinist Bulgaria* (Montreal: McGill-Queen's University Press, 2021), 27–56.
47. On the humanist turn during the 1960s, see Zhivka Valiavicharska, "Herbert Marcuse, the Liberation of 'Man,' and Hegemonic Humanism," *Theory and Event* 20, no. 3 (2017): 804–27; and *Restless History: Political Imaginaries and their Discontents in Post-Stalinist Bulgaria*.
48. Mark Rozental, *Lenin kak filosof* (Moskva: Izdatel'stvo politicheskoi literatury, 1969); Teodor Oizerman, "V.I. Lenin i gegelevskaia kontseptsiia universal'nosti praktiki," *Voprosy Filosofii* 11 (1977): 76–87; Evald Ilyenkov *Leninist Dialectics and the Metaphysics of Positivism: Reflections on V.I. Lenin's book 'Materialism and Empirio-Criticism'* (London: New Park Publications, 1982).
49. Petur-Emil Mitev, *Ot sotsialniia problem kum svetogledni otkritiia* (Sofia: Nauka i izkustvo, 1984), 128.
50. Ibid., 120–28. On the social analysis and social critique in Lenin's work, Petur-Emil Mitev, "Sotsiologicheskiiat analiz v proizvedeniiata na Lenin," *Sotsiologicheski problemi*, no. 2 (1980): 3–14; B. I. Koval, "V. I. Lenin kato izsledovatel na sotsialnite strukturi i na tiakhnata rolia v politikata," *Sotsiologicheski problemi* 2 (1980): 15–30.
51. Perry Anderson, "The Antinomies of Antonio Gramsci," *New Left Review* 100 (Nov. 1976): 5–78. See also Alan Shandro's discussion of Lenin's thoughts on building proletarian hegemony. Alan Shandro, "Text and Context in the Argument of Lenin's *What Is to Be Done?*," *Historical Materialism* 18, no. 3 (2010): 84–89; "Lenin and Hegemony: The Soviets, the Working Class, and the Party in the Revolution of 1905," in *Lenin Reloaded*, ed. Budgen, Kouvelakis, and Zizek, 308–32.
52. C. L. R. James, *Notes on Dialectics: Hegel, Marx, Lenin* (London: Allison and Busby, 1980); Henri Lefebvre's introduction to his own translation of the *Notebooks* in French from 1938, in Lenine, *Cahiers sur la Dialectique de Hegel* (Paris: Éditions Gallimard, 1967), 7–135. For an extended discussion, see Kevin Anderson, "Lenin's Encounter with Hegel after Eighty Years," *Science & Society* 59, no. 3 (Fall 1995): 298–319.

53. Anderson, *Lenin, Hegel, and Western Marxism;* "Lenin's Encounter with Hegel after Eighty Years."

54. Ibid., 123–47.

55. On the significance of Lenin's positions on the national question to the decolonial project, see Pheng Cheah, *Spectral Nationality: Passages of Freedom from Kant to Postcolonial Literatures of Liberation* (New York: Columbia University Press, 2003), 208–32.

56. Matthieu Renault, "Revolution Decentered: Two Studies on Lenin," *Viewpoint Magazine,* February 2018; https://www.viewpointmag.com/2018/02/01/revolution-decentered-two-studies-lenin/.

57. Ibid.

58. I thank Robert Maclean and Alla Ivanchikova for inspiring this formulation.

Bibliography

"Antiquity and Modernity of Soviet Marxism," special issue of *Stasis* 5, no. 2 (2017).

Althusser, Louis. *Lenin and Philosophy and Other Essays.* New York: Monthly Review Press, 2001.

Anderson, Kevin. "Lenin's Encounter with Hegel Eighty Years Later: A Critical Assessment." *Science and Society* 59, no. 3 (1995): 298–319.

———. *Lenin, Hegel, and Western Marxism: A Critical Study.* Urbana and Chicago: University of Illinois Press, 1995

Anderson, Perry. "The Antinomies of Antonio Gramsci." *New Left Review* 100 (November 1976): 5–78.

Arato, Andrew, and Paul Breines. *The Young Lukács and the Origins of Western Marxism.* New York: Seabury Press, 1979.

Budgen, Sebastian, Stathis Kouvelakis, and Slavoj Zizek, eds. *Lenin Reloaded: Towards a Politics of Truth.* Durham and London: Duke University Press, 2007.

Cheah, Pheng. *Spectral Nationality: Passages of Freedom from Kant to Postcolonial Literatures of Liberation.* New York: Columbia University Press, 2003.

Chehonadskih, Maria, Keti Chukhrov, and Alexei Penzin, "Introduction: Antiquity and Modernity of Soviet Marxism." *Stasis* 5, no. 2 (2017).

Chukhrov, Keti, Alexei Penzin, and Valery Podoroga, "Marx against Marxism, Marxism against Marx." *Stasis* 5, no. 2 (2017), 266–88.

David-Fox, Michael. *Crossing Borders: Modernity, Ideology, and Culture in Russia and the Soviet Union.* Pittsburgh: University of Pittsburgh Press, 2015.

Dosev, P. *Teoriia otrazheniia: Ocherki po teorii poznaniia dialekticheskogo materializma* Moscow: Gosudarstvenoe sots.-ekon. izdatel'stvo, 1936.

Egan, Daniel. "Saving the Vanguard: The Contemporary Relevance of Lenin's Military Metaphors" (current volume).

Girginov, Girgin, and Kiril Vasilev, eds. *Lenin i niakoi problema na marksistkata filosofiia. Sbornik.* Sofia: Izdatelstvo na BKP, 1970.
Halfin, Igal. *From Darkness to Light: Class, Consciousness, and Salvation in Revolutionary Russia.* Pittsburgh: University of Pittsburgh Press, 2000.
History of the Communist Party of the Soviet Union (Bolsheviks): Short Course. New York: International Publishers, 1939.
Ilyenkov, Evald. *Leninist Dialectics and the Metaphysics of Positivism: Reflections on V. I. Lenin's book 'Materialism and Empirio-Criticism.'* London: New Park Publications, 1982.
James, C. L. R. *Notes on Dialectics: Hegel, Marx, Lenin.* London: Allison and Busby, 1980.
Jay, Martin. *Dialectical Imagination.* Berkeley, Los Angeles, and London: University of California Press, 1996.
———. *Marxism and Totality.* Berkeley and Los Angeles: University of California Press, 1984.
Joravsky, David. *Soviet Marxism and Natural Science: 1917–1932.* New York: Columbia University Press, 1961.
Kalaikov, Ivan, Svetoslav Slavkov, and Stoiko Popov, eds. *100 godini "Anti-Diuring i 70 godini "Materializum i empiriokrititsizum."* Sofia: BAN, 1981.
Kellner, Douglas. *Karl Korsch: Revolutionary Theory.* Austin: University of Texas Press, 1977.
Korsch, Karl. *Marxism and Philosophy.* New York and London: Monthly Review Press, 1970.
Koval, B. I. "Lenin kato izsledovatel na sotsialnite strukturi i tiakhnata rolia v politikata." *Sotsiologicheski prolblemi* 2 (1980): 15–30.
Kovacevic, Natasa. "Anti-Communist Orientalism: Shifting Boundaries of Europe in Dissident Writing." In *Marx's Shadow: Power, Knowledge, and Intellectuals in Eastern Europe and Russia,* edited by Costica Bradatan and Serguei Oushakine. Lexington Books, 2010.
Laclau, Ernesto, and Chantal Mouffe, *Hegemony and Socialist Strategy: Towards a Radical Democratic Politics.* London and New York: Verso, 1985.
Lefebvre, Henri. *Dialectical Materialism.* Minneapolis and London: University of Minnesota Press, 2009.
Lenin, Vladimir. *Collected Works,* vol. 25. Moscow: Progress Publishers, 1974.
Lih, Lars T. "Symposium on Lars Lih's *Lenin Rediscovered."* *Historical Materialism* 18, no. 3 (2010).
———. *Lenin Rediscovered: What Is to Be Done? in Context.* Chicago: Haymarket Books, 2008.
Lukács, Georg. *History and Class Consciousness: Studies in Marxist Dialectics.* Cambridge: MIT Press, 1972.
———. *Lenin: A Study of the Unity of His Thought.* Cambridge: MIT Press, 1971.

Marcuse, Herbert. *Soviet Marxism: A Critical Analysis*. New York: Columbia University Press, 1958.
Maydansky, Andrey. "The Ilyenkov Triangle: Marxism in Search of its Philosophical Roots." *Stasis* 5, no. 2 (2017): 136–63.
Merleau-Ponty, Maurice. *Adventures of the Dialectic*. Evanston: Northwestern University Press, 1973.
Mitev, Petur-Emil. "Sotsiologicheskiiat analiz v proizvedeniiata na Lenin." *Sotsiologicheski problemi* 2 (1980): 3–14.
———. *Ot sotsialniia problem kum svetogledni otkritiia* (Sofia: Nauka i izkustvo, 1984).
Oizerman, Teodor. "V.I. Lenin i gegelevskaia kontseptsiia universal'nosti praktiki," *Voprosy Filosofii* 11 (1977): 76–87.
Pavlov, Todor. *Teoriia na otrazhenieto: Osnovni vuprosi na dialektichesko-materialisticheskata teoriia na poznanieto*. Sofia: Narizdat, 1945.
Renault, Matthieu. "Revolution Decentered: Two Studies on Lenin." *Viewpoint Magazine*, February 2018; https://www.viewpointmag.com/2018/02/01/revolution-decentered-two-studies-lenin/.
Rozental, Mark. *Lenin kak filosof*. Moskva: Izdatel'stvo politicheskoi literatury, 1969.
Shandro, Alan. "Lenin and Hegemony: The Soviets, the Working Class, and the Party in the Revolution of 1905," in *Lenin Reloaded*, edited by Sebastian Budgen, Stathis Kouvelakis, and Slavoj Zizek, 308–32. Durham and London: Duke University Press, 2007.
———. "Text and Context in the Argument of Lenin's *What Is to Be Done?*" *Historical Materialism* 18, no. 3 (2010): 84–89
Stalin, J. V. *Works*, vol. 6. Moscow: Foreign Languages Publishing House, 1953.
Tucker, Robert. *Stalin as Revolutionary, 1879–1929: A Study in History and Personality*. New York: Norton, 1973.
Valiavcharska, Zhivka. *Restless History: Political Imaginaries and Their Discontents in Post-Stalinist Bulgaria*. Montreal: McGill-Queen's University Press, 2021.
———. "Herbert Marcuse, the Liberation of 'Man,' and Hegemonic Humanism." *Theory and Event* 20, no. 3 (2017): 804–27.
van Ree, Erik. "Stalin as Writer and Thinker," *Kritika* 3, no. 4 (2002): 699–714.
———. *The Political Thought of Joseph Stalin: A Study in Twentieth-Century Revolutionary Patriotism*. London, Routledge, 2002.
Wetter, Gustav. *Dialectical Materialism: A Historical and Systematic Survey of Philosophy in the Soviet Union*. New York and London: Frederick Praeger, 1958.
Yurchak, Alexei. *Everything Was Forever until It Was No More: The Last Soviet Generation*. Princeton: Princeton University Press, 2006.
Zizek, Slavoj, ed. *Revolution at the Gates: A Selection of Writings from February to October 1917*. London and New York: Verso, 2002.

Chapter 13

Looking for Lenin in Bishkek

TEXT AND PHOTOS:
JOHANN SALAZAR AND HJAL(MAR) JORGE
JOFFRE-EICHHORN

October 2019. Whenever we stopped a local on the streets of Bishkek, the capital of Kyrgyzstan (called Frunze during Soviet times), to ask where we could find Lenin, we were always directed to the big statue behind The State History Museum (Figure 13.1). This statue, which once occupied pride of place in the main square of Bishkek, formerly known as Lenin Square, Площадь Ленина (Figure 13.2), was moved to its current location in 2003—an astonishing twelve years after Kyrgyzstan's independence[1] in 1991. The square was since renamed after the Ala-Too Mountains that form the backdrop to the city, and a statue of Manas (Figure 13.3), the hero of the Kyrgyz national epic, was placed where Lenin once stood.[2] This is perhaps why it was the only statue of the great вождь, leader, of the Bolshevist Revolution that seemed to stand out in the consciousness of people. Even when pressed about it, no one seemed to know about the existence of any other statues or monuments, in a city that only twenty-five years prior was host to dozens of them. Could it be that Bishkek, like so many other places in the former Soviet Union (post-2014 Ukraine being the most recent), was de-Leninized, with no traces remaining? If that were true, this Lenin shouldn't be here either, and neither should there be bouquets of flowers at the feet of the ten meter high (33 feet), twenty ton trademark Vladimir guiding us with his noble, some will insist bloodstained, but undoubtedly tireless right hand into the glorious future his teacher Marx had proclaimed

Figure 13.1.

Figure 13.2.

Figure 13.3.

in the third volume of *Das Kapital*: the Kingdom of Freedom. Surely, we thought, if we looked closely enough, some other Lenins would be found in Bishkek, continuing their patient labor of "bring[ing] political knowledge to the workers," by "go[ing] among all classes of the population . . . in all directions."[3]

From a number of previous trips to Kyrgyzstan, we were conscious of the fact that the country is one of the few remaining places in the world where almost every town still hosts a monument to товарищ (comrade) Ulyanov. And so walking the streets "in all directions," of a city of juxtaposed modernities—Soviet, Western, Indigenous—we did eventually find more Lenins. It was on the very first day of our visit—aimed at documenting these Lenin monuments in Kyrgyzstan for a book project to mark the occasion of the old man's 150th birthday in 2020—and only by a stroke of luck that we spied, through the porthole-sized opening of a back gate of the bulky, socialist realism–style Sport Palace Kozhomkul (Figure 13.4) an uncharacteristically idle Lenin, no adoring masses in sight, standing two stories tall in the shade of a pine tree among abandoned furniture (Figure 13.5), long-expired building materials, and the empty chrysalis of what used to be a bus, possibly an old ЛАЗ (LAZ). And yet no one nearby seemed to know anything about him, where he'd come from or why he was there. Even the caretaker of the palace, who nearly locked us inside with the Lenin, couldn't shed any light on it. He did know, however, that it had been around for a few years now, with nobody ever coming to visit let alone rescue him from yet another enforced, this time round, symbolic exile (Siberia, Kraków, Munich, London, Geneva, Berne, Zurich, Finland, and now here. How many more?). After this we were convinced that there were more Lenins to be found in Bishkek, if only we knew where to look and in which direction to walk. This is a story about our quest to locate one such Lenin—one that we spotted in a faded photograph—because it provides a visual metaphor of the place of Lenin in Bishkek and possibly in the whole of the former Soviet republic of Kyrgyzstan.

If you look closely, Lenin still occupies a lot of space in the landscape of Bishkek—his name and likeness still visible, embedded in other

Figure 13.4.

Figure 13.5.

monuments (Figure 13.6), on buildings (Figures 13.7 and 13.8), in place names and in memorabilia of varying sizes in flea markets and thrift shops (Figures 13.9, 13.10, and 13.11). Yet, at the same time there seems to be something akin to a collective amnesia, or perhaps a generalized indifference, regarding the statues of Lenin among large parts of the general population. What explains it? After all, the superhuman figure of Lenin would not be unfamiliar to the people in Kyrgyzstan who experienced the Soviet Union firsthand, and who would thus be aware of what Lenin represented to its people and/or what he was claimed to represent by multiple Soviet leaders intending to further their own project in keeping the embattled USSR from losing the Cold War.[4]

Figure 13.6.

Figure 13.7.

Figure 13.8.

Figure 13.9.

Figure 13.10.

Figure 13.11.

While preparing for this project we knew that we wanted to shoot at least some of the pictures on consumer grade 35mm film using old Soviet cameras[5] because for many young photographers this equipment, which is still used today and sought after for its affordability and quality, accounts for their only contact, and a visceral one at that, with the communist project. And so we spent some time looking for old camera equipment in flea markets and antique shops. These antiques dealers have a unique position in that they transact in relationships that people cultivate with the past and are therefore forced to engage with it. This includes having to take a position on the ambivalent and contested history of the USSR in general and of Lenin in particular. When we asked the two proprietors of one such establishment, an elderly ethnic Russian couple who had been employees of the Soviet state, about how the new Kyrgyz Republic fared in comparison to the old Kyrgyz SSR, they put up a united democratic front by agreeing that things were better now, although one of them, Valentina, was clearly more enthusiastic than her husband, a respected archaeologist in Soviet times, whom she nudgingly encouraged to agree with her, "улыбáйся, Александр," "Smile, Alexander." Different views about the past glories of the USSR notwithstanding, the two of them invited us to return to the shop for further conversations. We dutifully obliged and were privileged to witness firsthand how the discussion of the Soviet experiment, and Lenin's role in it, certainly among those who actually lived through it, can still ignite great passions as well as heated and powerfully embodied disagreements. In short, there may be relative indifference among the people of Bishkek vis-à-vis the whereabouts of the physical remnants of Lenin in the city, but there was certainly no lack of interest in arguing over the legacy that seventh-plus years of state-sanctioned Leninism bequeathed to the inhabitants of contemporary Kyrgyzstan. In any case, thanks to such pleasurable discussions, we resumed our search with renewed vigor and it was in another antique shop, specializing in Soviet memorabilia (Figure 13.12), that we spotted an old photograph of a group of men standing in front of a statue of Lenin. The Lenin in the photo was barely visible and the clearest indication of it being Lenin was the plaque bearing his name (Figure 13.13).

When we got home that day we began searching online for where this statue might be today. We found one photo of a statue with a similarly styled platform with the chimney of a factory rising in the background. In a city whose skyline was generously dotted with chimneys, thanks to the World War II–era industrialization of Central Asia, we wondered if there might have been, and continue to be, many others like it. After some

Figure 13.12.

Figure 13.13.

searching we managed to find out that the photo was taken by someone on a walking tour, and after hours of digging online, we located and contacted the ever-industrious tour guide, a Kyrgyz woman named Rahat.[6] She was appreciative of Lenin for supporting the modernization of Central Asia and informed us that this particular Lenin was to be found near the outskirts of the capital, in the former communist cooperative neighborhood of Interhelpo, built by internationalist industrial workers and farmers from Czechoslovakia coming to the then-Kara-Kirghiz Autonomous Oblast in the 1920s. By 1935, the Interhelpo cooperative was involved in the production of bricks, textiles, leather goods, metalwork, woodwork, and furniture, and had built railroads, hospitals, schools, and even a few main government buildings. When we got there, courtesy of a middle-aged taxi driver, Nurkan (Figure 13.14), who told us that for him "Lenin is like God," a dramatic statement that further consolidated our growing understanding of the multiplicity of views that Bishkek residents hold about Ilyich, we were pleased to find the Lenin statue standing, unmoved, in the quiet compound of a football club, whose origins date back to the founding of the *zavod* (factory) just opposite the stadium (Figures 13.15, 13.16 and 13.17). Excited about our find and convinced that it was the Lenin in the photo we headed home.

It was only later when we compared it against the old photo that we realized that this was not in fact the same statue: the platform looked different

Figure 13.14.

Figure 13.15.

Figure 13.16.

Figure 13.17.

and the posture was not quite the same. Too bad, we thought, that would have made a great story. But perhaps this meant that there were still other Lenins lurking, hidden from perception if not from view; still there, part of the landscape. So we continued hunting for Lenin, taking inspiration in the idea that Lenin himself enjoyed hunting for heather cocks during his young days in Alakayevka.[7] Slowly and patiently we kept on the lookout. And sure enough, a few days later, accompanied by a Kyrgyz friend, Dastan, who categorically preferred Lev Tolstoy over Volodya Ulyanov, we located another Lenin at a decrepit yet still functioning USSR-built *sanatorium* (health spa), in a village just outside Bishkek. The statue was obscured by thick fog and surrounded by an army of decaying, shrivelling—white—roses (Figure 13.18). It was almost certainly the Lenin from the old photo. So that's why we couldn't find him in the city; he was here, not in exile but in retreat at a health spa in the Kyrgyz countryside—breathing fresh air, taking it easy, recovering from years of unceasing, selfless dedication to the proletarian revolution. And he was not alone. A few meters away stood a statue of his old, faithful comrade: the poet Mayakovsky. One can imagine the two strolling around, when nobody's looking, talking ever so leisurely, now in prose, now in verse. And it is Mayakovsky who supplies the words to conclude our quest:

Грудой дел,
суматохой явлений
день отошел,
постепенно стемнев.
Двое в комнате.
Я
и Ленин—
фотографией
на белой стене.

[Awhirl with events,
packed with jobs one too many,
the day slowly sinks
as the night shadows fall.
There are two in the room:
I
and Lenin—
a photograph
on the whiteness of wall.

Figure 13.18.

Notes

1. See Sally N. Cummings, "Leaving Lenin: Elites, Official Ideology and Monuments in the Kyrgyz Republic," *Nationalities Papers* 41, no. 4 (2013): 613. Cummings affirms that the case of Kyrgyzstan's independence and its aftermath is somewhat unusual in comparison to its neighbors: "Among Central Asian republics, its first president, Askar Akaev, a laser physicist from the Academy of Sciences, was the only one not to have been a former Communist Party boss. The republic's vibrant culture of contestation, vocal parliament and active civil society in the 1990s earned it the titles of 'island of democracy' and 'darling of the international donor community.' " See also Ahmed Rashid, *The Resurgence of Central Asia: Islam or Nationalism?* (New York: New York Review Books, 2017). In recent years, however, the country has been beset by ethnic strife, corruption scandals, attacks on sexual minorities, and an alleged presence of the Islamic State in the country.
2. Cummings, 613.
3. V. I. Lenin, *What Is To Be Done*, 1902, 48, https://www.marxists.org/archive/lenin/works/download/what-itd.pdf.
4. See Christopher Smart, "Gorbachev's Lenin: The Myth in Service to Perestroika," *Studies in Comparative Communism* XIII, no. 1 (1990): 5–22.
5. Most of the photos in this essay have been shot on 35mm film using Fed 5, a Zenit M3, and a Zorki 10.
6. Rahat runs Bishkek Walks, which conducts walking tours around Bishkek. Similar walks were previously organized by the School of Theory and Activism (STAB)—an artistic, research, and activist platform co-directed by queer communists Oksana Shatalova and Georgy Mamedov.
7. See Leon Trotzky, *Der Junge Lenin* (Wien: Verlag Fritz Molden, 1969), 166.

Bibliography

Cummings, Sally N. "Leaving Lenin: Elites, Official Ideology and Monuments in the Kyrgyz Republic." *Nationalities Papers* 41, no. 4 (2013): 606–21.
Lenin, V. I. *What Is to Be Done?* 1902. https://www.marxists.org/archive/lenin/works/download/what-itd.pdf.
Mayakovsky, Vladimir. "Conversation with Comrade Lenin," 1929. https://www.marxists.org/subject/art/literature/mayakovsky/1929/conversation-comrade-lenin.htm
Rashid, Ahmed. *The Resurgence of Central Asia: Islam or Nationalism?* New York: New York Review Books, 2017.
Smart, Christopher. "Gorbachev's Lenin: The Myth in Service to Perestroika," *Studies in Comparative Communism* XIII, no. 1 (1990): 5–22.
Trotzki, Leo. *Der Junge Lenin.* Wien: Verlag Fritz Molden, 1969.

About the Editors

Alla Ivanchikova is an associate professor of English and Comparative Literature at Hobart and William Smith Colleges in upstate New York. She is the author of *Imagining Afghanistan: Global Fiction and Film of the 9/11 Wars* (Purdue University Press, 2019). Her articles appeared in *Modern Fiction Studies*, *Textual Practice*, *Camera Obscura*, and *College Literature*, among many others. She is currently working on a new monograph, tentatively titled *Technoimmortality: An Unfinished Project*.

Robert R. Maclean is a historian, independent scholar, organizer, and bartender based in the Finger Lakes region of New York State. He wrote his PhD at the University of Michigan in the 2000s, and currently pursues an eclectic range of interests, including Black experimental aesthetics, especially music; world history in the era of imperialism; Marxist and Leninist critical theory and philosophy; and emergent late capitalist modes of sociality, namely, online gaming. This is his first publication.

Contributors

Charisse Burden-Stelly is an assistant professor and Mellon Faculty Fellow of Africana Studies and Political Science at Carleton College. She is a scholar of radical Black critical and political theory, political economy, and intellectual history. She is currently working on two book projects: *W.E.B. Du Bois: A Life in American History* (co-authored with Gerald Horne) and *Epistemologies of Blackness*, which explores the conjuncture of epistemology, institutionalization, anti-Marxism, and class politics in Black Studies at the dawn of the neoliberal turn. She has several book chapters and articles forthcoming, and her published work appears in journals including *Souls: A Critical Journal of Politics, Culture, and Society* and *The CLR James Journal*.

Jodi Dean is a political theorist and professor at Hobart and William Smith Colleges in Geneva, NY. She is the author and editor of numerous books, among them *The Communist Horizon; Crowds and Party; Comrade: An Essay on Political Belonging;* and *Organize, Fight, Win: Black Communist Women's Political Writing*—an edited collection (with Charisse Burden-Stelly) that focuses on radical Black women's writing and organizing in the first half of the twentieth century.

Daniel Egan is a professor of sociology at the University of Massachusetts Lowell. He is the author of *The Dialectic of Position and Manoeuvre: Understanding Gramsci's Military Metaphor* (Haymarket, 2017).

Zeyad el Nabolsy is a PhD student at the Africana Studies and Research Center at Cornell University where he is working on African Marxism. He has published on classical German philosophy: "Why Did Kant Conclude the *Critique of Pure Reason* with 'the History of Pure Reason'?" (*Kant Studies Online*); "Hegel and the Historiographic Consequences of Systematicity"

(*Hegel-Jahrbuch*); Marxist historiography of philosophy, "Aristotle on Natural Slavery: An Analysis Using the Marxist Concept of Ideology" (*Science & Society*); and philosophy of education, "Listening" (*Keywords in Radical Philosophy and Education*, ed. Derek Ford).

Derek R. Ford is an assistant professor of education studies at DePauw University. He has written four books, including *Politics and Pedagogy in the "Post-Truth" Era: Insurgent Philosophy and Praxis* (Bloomsbury, 2019) and *Communist study: Education for the Commons* (Lexington, 2016).

Alexandar Mihailovic is professor emeritus of Russian and Comparative Literature at Hofstra University, and is visiting professor of Slavic Studies at Brown University. He is the author of *Corporeal Words: Mikhail Bakhtin's Theology of Discourse*, the editor of the volume *Tchaikovsky and His Contemporaries*, and co-editor of *Navid Kermani*, a volume of articles about the contemporary Iranian-German essayist and novelist. His most recent book is *The Mitki and the Art of Postmodern Protest in Russia* (University of Wisconsin Press, 2018). He is currently working on a book about whiteness, gender, and nationalism in the American and Russian Far Right. Additionally, he writes reviews for the online journal *Kinokultura: New Russian Cinema*, and has published numerous articles on nineteenth- and twentieth-century Russian and Ukrainian literature, cultural relations during the Cold War, and LGBTQ identities in Putin's Russia.

David J. Ost is a professor of political science at Hobart and William Smith Colleges in Geneva, New York, and frequent visiting professor in Poland. He has written widely on East European politics and society, with a focus on political economy, democratization, capitalism, and labor. His books include *Solidarity and the Politics of Anti-Politics*, *Workers After Workers' States*, and *The Defeat of Solidarity*; and he is the editor of "Class After Communism," a special issue of *Eastern European Politics and Societies* (2015). His articles have appeared in numerous scholarly and popular publications, and he is on the editorial boards of several scholarly journals in the United States and Poland.

Christian Sorace is an assistant professor of political science at Colorado College. His research focuses on ideology, discourse, urbanization, and aesthetics. He is the author of *Shaken Authority: China's Communist Party and the 2008 Sichuan Earthquake* (Cornell University Press, 2017) and co-editor of *Afterlives of Chinese Communism: Political Concepts from Mao to Xi* (Verso Press and ANU Press, 2019).

Kai Heron is a lecturer in politics at Birkbeck College, University of London. His research interests include political theory, political economy, and political ecology. He is a post-doctoral research associate on the "Pathways to Public-Common Partnerships" project conducted for Commonwealth and Rosa-Luxemburg-Stiftung.

Hjalmar Jorge Joffre-Eichhorn is a German-Bolivian theatre maker and author. Since 2010, he has been feeling at ease in the post-Soviet space, particularly in Central Asia and Ukraine. After much ideological soul-searching, he now considers himself a decolonial communist. In 2020, together with Patrick Anderson and Johann Salazar, he published *Lenin150 (Samizdat)* (1st edition KickAss Books, 2nd edition Daraja Press).

Johann Salazar is an independent researcher and photographer with a background in sociology and anthropology.

Zhivka Valiavicharska is an associate professor of political and social theory at Pratt Institute, New York. She teaches and publishes in the fields of modern political and social theory, critical theory, gender and sexuality, postcolonial studies, and Russian and East European studies. She is the author of *Restless History: Political Imaginaries and Their Discontents in Post-Stalinist Bulgaria* (McGill-Queen's University Press, 2021).

Camila Vergara holds a PhD in political theory from Columbia University, specializing in legal and constitutional thought within the radical republican tradition. She is co-editor of the volume *Machiavelli on Liberty and Conflict* with David Johnston and Nadia Urbinati (University of Chicago Press, 2017) and the author of *Systemic Corruption: Constitutional Ideas for an Anti-Oligarchic Republic* (Princeton University Press, 2020).

Giovanni Zanotti is a post-doctoral fellow at the University of Brasilia. He graduated at the Scuola Normale Superiore of Pisa and received his PhD in Philosophy by the University of Pisa. He is the author of *Il problema filosofico in Wittgenstein. Dialettica nel positivismo* (ETS, 2020) and of articles and book chapters in Italian, English, Portuguese, and French. His research focuses on political philosophy, dialectic, critical theory, aesthetics, German and Brazilian contemporary thought, and psychoanalysis.

Index

Note: Page locators in *italic* refer to figures and page locators followed by "n" refer to endnotes.

"abject," 91
"abolition" of state, 238, *239*
absenteeism, 261, 273; fines for, 263, 264, 267; laws, 18; penalties for, 270, 271
Acton Institute, 76
actuality of revolution, 69–70, 281–82, 294
"administration of things," Engels's idea of, 39–40, 237
Adorno, Theodor W., 175, 190, 241, 244, 249, 252n26, 252–53n27
advanced guard. *See* vanguard
Adventures of the Dialectic (Merleau-Ponty), 304
affective politics, 115
affect theory, 115
African Americans, 14, 157, 159, 161, 162; nationality, 201n17; political repression of, 168; predicament of, 195; STJ and, 165
African Black Brotherhood, 179
African culture, 218
"African Roots of War, The" (Du Bois), 155
African socialism, 206, 207, 215; Babu and Nabudere's role to criticism of, 215–16; characterization of life in village communes, 216; construction of, 218–19; metaphysics of difference, 218; modern individual subject, emergence of, 216–17; neocolonial culture of, 217
African socialism, critique of, 16
African Socialism or Socialist Africa? (Babu), 212
Africa World Review, 206
Afro-Pessimism, 199n4
Ahmed, Sara, 104, 115
Akaev, Askar, 337n1
Ali, Tariq, 7
All African Peoples Conference, 163
Allakhazam, 104
Allende, Salvador, 186
Allen, James S., 164
Allied Intervention, 308
All-Russia Congress of Soviets of Workers' and Soldiers' Deputies, 281, 290
alternative right, 11
Althusser, Louis, 80, 119, 253n29, 275n9, 300, 302, 303
alt-Right movement, 103; appropriation of leftist activist paradigms, 103;

alt-Right movement *(continued)*
  disgust with pluralism, 118–19;
  engagement with Leninism, 104;
  self-contradicting character of state
  of, 112
American conservatism, problem of, 111
American Greatest Generation, 201n14
American Renaissance, 103
American Right, 28, 29
Americans for Tax Reform, 109
Amin, Idi, 207
Anderson, Benedict, 183
Anderson, Brian C., 2–3
Anderson, Kevin, 314
Anderson, Perry, 313
anti-anarchist polemic, 238
anti-Blackness. *See* anti-Black racism
anti-Black racism, 179, 180, 196, 199n4
anticapitalism: pedagogies of, 9;
  romantic, 6, 11, 78, 79; sentimental, 11, 78, 86
anticipation, 10, 69, 70, 115, 282
anticommunism, 166, 179
Anti-Dühring: Herr Eugen Dühring's Revolution in Science (Engels), 113, 236–37
anti-imperialism, 13, 17, 21, 201n13
anti-opportunist polemic, 238
"anti-politics" of populist Right, 119
antiracism, 13, 33
antiradicalism, 180
anti-statism, 12, 71
Appasionata (Beethoven), 83
April Theses, 6, 286; Bolsheviks's
  position on war, 290–91; communist
  position on war, 286, 288;
  military dictatorship, 292; Party's
  "programme," 290; pre-test, 287–88, 290, 291; protest, 288–89; Soviets'
  call for general demonstration, 291; stage of revolutionary Russia, 286–87. *See also* testing, Leninist theory of
April Theses, The (Lenin), 79
Autobiography (Davis), 175
Avrich, Paul, 109

Babu, Abdul Rahman Mohamed, 16, 206; adopting Lenin's theory of imperialism, 208–10, 212; *African Socialism or Socialist Africa?*, 212; arguments about social formations in Africa, 219; assessment of Tanzanian "African socialism," 207; capitalism, views on, 214, 216; characterization of nationalism in colonies and neocolonies, 213; criticism of African socialism, efforts to, 215–15; cultural *vs.* political Pan-Africanism, views on, 213–14; in formulation of Marxist-Leninist critique, 207; neocolonial culture, views on, 217; revolutionary Marxism of, 206; socialism in Marxist theoretical framework, views on, 216
"backwardness," 190–91, 202–3n23
Badger, Honey, 122n43
Badiou, Alain, 2, 6–7, 17, 42, 70–71
Bagaturia, Georgii, 312
Bagehot, Walter, 116
Bakhchiev, Bakyt, 20
"balance of power," concept of, 245
Bannon, Steve, 6, 11, 12, 28, 102, 103, 114, 122n43; admiration for Trump's thuggish demeanor, 118; affinities with Althusser, 119; argument for postcolonial nationalism, 112; characterization of relations with Trump, 117; conflation of state capitalism, 110–11; conversation with Radosh, 105–7; engagement with Leninism, 104, 105; idealistic understanding

of grass-roots spirituality, 110; and Marxism-Leninism, 102, 111; positive assessments of Leninism, 108; preoccupations and essential beliefs, 107–8; quasi-Jacobinism, 105; self-declared Leninism, 108–9; style of contestation, 118–19; sympathy for aspects of socialism, 111; taking conservative biographical accounts of Lenin, 116; on unhappy "affect aliens," 104

Basel Manifesto (1912), 155

"base-superstructure" model, 306

Bass, Charlotta, 165

Bebel, August, 113

Berardi, Franco Bifo, 3

Berlant, Lauren, 115, 119–20

Bernstein, Eduard, 254n39

Biehl, João, 89

Biennio Rosso of 1919–1920 in Italy, 30

biopolitical domination, legalization of: biopolitical nature of law, 267; factory inspectors as agents of oligarchic state, 268–69; law redefined nighttime labor, 267; legalizing use of arbitrary power, 267, 268; need of workers union, 269; overtime clause, 267–68; state regulation of labor relations, 266; worker's demands for working schedules, 265–66. *See also* subordination, legalization of

biopolitics: of capitalism, 84; Foucault's conception of, 277n52

Bishkek (Kyrgyzstan), 20, 323, 326, 327

Bishkek Walks, 337n6

Black Americans. *See* African Americans

Black Belt thesis, 14, 177, 195; African Black Brotherhood of, 179; Haywood's role in formulation of, 196–98; impact in U.S. imperialism, 198; nationality policy, 196. *See also* Black Leninist struggle for liberation

Black Book of the American Left, The (Horowitz), 105

Black Hundreds, 287

Black Leninism, 6, 13–14, 176–77, 180; for Black liberation, 16; epoch of, 15; faith in international working class, 182; Hall's question of, 186, 188; Haywood's role in, 180–81; history of, 194; implications of, 189; legacy of, 187; materialist analysis of blackness, 186–87; neoliberalism and, 186; as Pan-African concept, 183; prospects for renewal of, 198; Robinson's interpretation of nationality, 181–82; Rodney's role in, 184, 185–86; struggles against national oppression, 184–85; struggles against racism, 180–81; working definition of, 183–84

Black Leninists: formation in United States, 190; internationalism, 187; opinion about racism, 198

Black Leninist struggle for liberation: aiming destruction of white supremacy, 179; Angela Davis, contribution of, 175–76; Du Bois, contribution of, 176, 177–78; James, contribution of, 176; objectification of Black personhood, 178–79; Rodney, contribution of, 177; Wells-Barnet, contribution of, 176

Black liberation, 196; centrality of struggle, 176; internationalism of, 181; Leninism and, 169–70; through social revolution, 184; struggles for, 13, 176; time and place in, 186–88; from U.S. empire, 194

Black Lives Matter movement, 7
Black Marxism (Robinson), 14, 201n11
Black Nationalism, 181
Black National Liberation, 201n12; African Black Brotherhood of, 179
Black Panther Party, 65, 176, 184, 185, 190, 202n22; community political education projects, 191; Jackson's role in, 192–93; political education programs, 190
Black radical tradition, 14, 152–53, 181–82
Black Reconstruction (Du Bois), 177, 200n10
Black self-determination, 189, 190, 196
Blinded by the Right: The Conscience of an Ex-Conservative (Brock), 108
Blood in My Eye (Jackson), 192
Bolsheviks, 3, 37, 41, 136, 281, 290; controversy over April Theses, 286; embracing test drive, 292; fact of revolution for, 70; historical materialism of, 69–70; Kaczyński's admiration of, 29; preparation for violent insurrection, 292; status in Russia, 287; victory of, 33, 34, 259
"bolshevization" of communist parties by Communist International, 139
Bonior, David, 108
bourgeois(ie), 184, 127, 128, 287; duality of, 239–40; forces, 200n7; ideology, 127, 132–33; law, 17, 18; nationalism, 183, 213
bourgeois-democratic revolution, 130–31, 287; transition to socialist revolution, 131–32
bourgeois state, 238, 240, 246, 248; "abolition" of, 238, *239;* "withers away," 236
Bozell III, L. Brent, 110
Breda, Stefano, 243, 246, 252n26

Breitbart, Andrew, 118, 122n43
Brest-Litovsk Treaty, 63, 136
Brink, The documentary (Klayman), 107
Brock, David, 108
Browder, Earl, 168
Buckley Jr., William F., 110
Budgen, Sebastian, 6
Bukharin, Nikolai, 136
Burbank, Jane, 257, 270
Burden-Stelly, Charisse, 14, 15
Burke, Edmund, 102
Burnham, James, 102
Burroughs, William S., 108

Cabral, Amilcar, 184–85, 303, 314
Caceres, Berta, 59
Capital (Marx), 80, 127–28, 210, 241, 242, 253n27
Capital (Piketty), 7
capital, 242, 245; accumulation, 134; knowledge of, 245; Postone's emphasis on, 253n28; subordination of workers to, 266, 267
capitalism, 11, 84, 127; contemporary, 62; crony, 109, 111; definition of, 242; dialectical ambivalence about, 93; enlightened, 112; excesses of (*See* capitalist excess); globalization and, 84–85; integral features of, 177; introduction in Russia, 190–91; kernel of objectivity in, 244; Lenin's idea of economic proportion, 86–87; metastatic global, 111; monopoly, 161–62; need of instability in, 87–88; overproduction issue in, 87; positive and negative valences, 84; postindustrial, 91; revolutionary potential of, 83; rise of, 83, 86; Robinson's views on, 152; state-sponsored, 109; viewing as utopian perspective, 85. *See also* racial capitalism

Index

capitalist: class, 58; compulsion, 85; domination, 243; ideology, 86–87; overpopulation. *See* capitalist excess

capitalist excess, 87–88, 89; capitalist accumulation and, 90, 91; and Green New Deal, 92; industrial reserve army and, 90, 91; and surplus populations, 89–90; thoughts of Lenin and Sismondi about, 89, 90–91

Castro, Fidel, 10

centralization: of labor, 128; principle of, 34–35

Césaire, Aimé, 201n13

Chambers, Whittaker, 102

Characterisation of Economic Romanticism, A (Sismondi and Our Native Sismondists) (Lenin), 82

chauvinism, 183; failure of U.S. Left to overcome, 191; racial, 190; struggle against, 165–67; white, 198–99

Chehonadskih, Maria, 20, 303, 305

Che-Lumumba Club, 176

Chiesa, Lorenzo, 80, 250n5, 250n9

Chretien, Todd, 254n39

Chukhrov, Keti, 20, 303, 305

Civilian Conservation Corp, 92

class antagonism, 238

"class enemy" concept, 307

Clausewitz, Carl von, 128–29

climate change, 60, 65, 66, 92

Clinton, Hillary, 106, 118

Cohn-Bendit, Daniel, 32

Cohn-Bendit, Gabriel, 32

collectivism, 47, 68

colonialism, 33, 111, 151, 153, 156, 163, 177, 184, 185, 212

Comintern. *See* Communist International (Comintern)

commodified labor, 83

commodity production, 88

communism, 32, 81, 83–84, 86, 89, 113; Black, 13, 15, 177, 187; relationship with anticolonialism, 17; support of U.S. millennials for, 77; war, 35, 43, 136

Communist Horizon, The (Dean), 10, 63

Communist International (Comintern), 139, 140

Communist Manifesto, The, 84, 128

Communist Party, 18, 133; Lenin's theory of, 19; power of, 36; Russian, 139, 293; serving as educational institution, 18; USA, 35

Communist Party of the United States of America (CPUSA), 176, 197, 199n1

competition, mechanism of, 243–44

complex networks in technology, 61–62

Comrade (Dean), 10, 63

Conference of Independent African States, 163

Conquest, Robert, 116

conservative epistemology, 116

conservative interpreters, 275n12

conservative reactionaries, 102

Constituent Assembly, 33, 36, 283

constitutionalism, 247, 254n39

constitutional reform, 247

contemporary capitalism, 62

contemporary imperialism, 61

Cooper, Esther V., 152

Corbyn, Jeremy, 7, 65

coronavirus pandemic. *See* COVID-19 pandemic

Coulter, Anne, 105

countercultural affect, 12

coup d'état, 3

COVID-19 pandemic, 8; failures of United States in handling, 55–57; Leninist's view on handling, 57–58

CPUSA. *See* Communist Party of the United States of America (CPUSA)
crony capitalism, 109, 111
Crowds and Party (Dean), 45, 63
culture, idea of, 242
"cumbersome" exegesis of Lenin's text, 80
Cummings, Sally N., 337n1

Das Kapital (Marx), 325
Dastan (Kyrgyz friend), 335
David-Fox, Michael, 308
Davies, Carole Boyce, 13
Davis, Angela, 13, 175–76, 190, 194; access to Marxism, 189; about Lenin's *State and Revolution*, 190
Davis, Horace B., 212
Davis, Mike, 175, 176, 189
Dean, Jodi, 7, 8, 10, 45, 282; account of Michels's remarks, 46; addressing problems with contemporary Left, 46; Climate Leninism, about usefulness of, 58–59; denunciation of liberal democracy, 46; about dramatic instability of temporal reference in U. S., 68; *Imperialism*, about value of Lenin's, 61–62; inconsistency of Leninist revival, 48; Krupskaya and Kollontai, about thoughts of, 65–68; organizing working class, about importance of, 71–72; pandemic/crisis, about Leninist views on handling, 55–58; about party dictatorship, 45–46; proletarian democracy, about building, 70–71; recommending Lenin's texts for young comrades, 72–73; return to Lenin, opinion about cautions against, 59–61; about "revolutionary temporality," 69–70; right-wing Leninism, opinion about, 72; solidarity in U.S., about need for, 64–65; about things to follow current leftists about Leninism, 62–63; views on left realism, 45
defective work, 261, 265; fees to employees for, 272; fines for, 262, 263, 267, 273
Deleuze, Gilles, 9
democratic centralism, 73; guiding principle of, 35; Lenin's concept of, 144n35; national self-determination for, 162–63
democratic despotism, 156
democratic socialism, 48, 76, 77, 79
Democratic Socialists of America (DSA), 7
Demon Revoliutsii television miniseries (Khotinenko), 106
Derrida, Jacques, 86
determinism, 241, 245–46, 248, 304, 305, 306, 310
Development of Capitalism in Russia, The (Lenin), 6, 83
deviationism, 160, 168
Devil's Bargain: Steve Bannon, Donald Trump, and the Storming of the Presidency (Green), 102
"dialectical ambivalence" about capitalism, 93
Dialectical Materialism. *See* Diamat
Dialectical Materialism (Lefebvre), 309
Diamat, 116, 306–7, 308, 309
"dictatorship of the proletariat." *See* proletarian democracy
Dilemmas of Lenin, The (Ali), 7
Dilthey, Wilhelm, 242
discontinuity: fundamental relation of, 246; Lenin's insistence on, 240; need for, 248
Discourse on Colonialism (Césaire), 201n13
divorce, right of, 195–96

"doctrinaire positivism" of Leninism, 107
dogmatism, 284, 303, 310
domination, capitalist, 243
domination, objectively mediated, 243
domination of really objectified relations, 243
Dosev, P. *See* Pavlov, Todor
DSA. *See* Democratic Socialists of America (DSA)
D'Souza, Dinesh, 103
duality of bourgeois and proletarian state, 239–40
dual power, 286, 290
Du Bois, W. E. B., 155, 169, 176–78, 187, 201n11; analysis of roots of imperialism, 157; analysis of World War I, 155–56
Duck Dynasty (television series), 105
Duma (The House of Representatives), 286
Dupuy, Jean-Pierre, 69

Economic Content of Narodism and the Criticism of It in Mr. Struve's Book, The (Lenin), 215
economic romanticism, 88, 93
economic sentimentalism, 83, 85
economic structure, 176, 212, 216, 253n28
Edelman, Lee, 115
Egan, Daniel, 8, 12, 308
el Nabolsy, Zeyad, 9, 15–16
emancipatory egalitarian political change, 58
"End of History, The" article (by Fukuyama), 58
Engels, Frederick, 67, 75, 80, 83, 104, 192, 236–37, 312; and *The Communist Manifesto*, 84, 128; understanding of capitalism, 127; views about bourgeoisie and proletariat, 127–28; views about military metaphors, 128
"epiphenomenon," 253n27
Eurocentrism, 15; response to charge of, 205–6, 219–20
excesses of capitalism. *See* capitalist excess
exclusionary nationalism, 28
Explanation of the Law on Fines Imposed on Factory Workers (Lenin), 258, 260, 265. *See also* subordination, legalization of

Fanon, Frantz, 151, 187, 192, 303, 314
February Revolution, 12, 285, 286
federalism, 57, 162
federation, 158, 162, 163, 170
Feuerbach, Ludwig, 309
"fictionalization of politics," 119
fines, laws on: absenteeism, fines for, 261, 263, 264, 267, 270, 271; defective work, fines/penalties for, 261–63, 265, 267, 273; imposed 'on authority' of factory managements, 262; offenses against good order, fines for, 261, 262, 267–68
Fire and Fury: Inside the Trump White House (Wolff), 106
Floyd, George, 65
Ford, Derek R., 18, 19
Ford, James, 14, 163; arguments about Black self-determination, 163–65
Foucault, Michel, 9, 277n52
Foundations of Leninism (Stalin), 305, 308
Fraser, Nancy, 154
freedom of contract, 272, 273–74; theory, 277n57
French Communist Party, 309
Freudian repression of social objectivity, 244

Friedman, Milton, 76, 90
Frunze. *See* Bishkek, Kyrgyzstan
Fukuyama, Francis, 58

Gagarin, Yuri, 62
Garvey, Marcus, 196
Geist (Hegel), 253n28
General Confederation of Labor, 32
German Ideology, The (Marx), 82
Getachew, Adom, 154, 163
Ghodsee, Kristen R., 62
gig economy, 259, 270. *See also* independent contractors, workers as
"glass of water" theory of sex, 67
globalization, 84–85, 178
Global South, 62, 208, 219–20; anticolonial national liberation movements in, 313–14; recovering Lenin's dynamic and polemical history in, 315
Gohmert, Louie, 105, 106
Gomez, Michael, 201n17
Gorbachev, Mikhail, 51n39
Gottfried, Paul, 11, 101, 102, 103
gradualism, 240, 254n40
Gramsci, Antonio, 29, 32, 128, 186, 199n4, 300, 303, 313
Greene, Graham, 111
Green, Joshua, 102
Green New Deal, 76, 79, 82, 92–93
Green, T. H., 277n57
Guattari, Félix, 9
Gulag, 46, 47, 278n79

Habermas, J., 60, 244
Haitian Revolution, 200n10
Hall, Stuart, 186
Harcourt, William, 75–76
Hardt, Michael, 7, 17
Hassan, Salah M., 205
Haywood, Harry, 14, 159, 196, 201n15, 202n22, 203n29; arguments about Negro question, 159–61; and Black Belt thesis, 196–98; struggle against racial capitalism, 180–81
Hegel, Georg Wilhelm Friedrich, 80, 250n8, 309
Hegelian "point of view of whole," 247
Hegelian aspects of Marx's thought, 309–10
Hegelian idealism, 311
hegemony, 191, 254n36, 313; socialist ideological, 33
Hegemony and Socialist Strategy (Laclau and Mouffe), 64, 300, 305
Heller, Nathan, 19
Hell, Julie, 114, 117
Heron, Kai, 8, 10–11, 59
Historical Materialism. *See* Istmat
History and Class Consciousness (Lukács), 242, 310, 311, 312
History of the Communist Party of the Soviet Union (Bolsheviks) (Stalin), 306
Hobsbawm, Eric, 31
Hobson, J. A., 183
Hook, Sydney, 102
horizontalism, 45
Horne, Gerald, 153
Horowitz, David, 103, 105
household labor, 73
Huiswoud, Otto, 160
humanity, 89, 178, 180, 194, 215

iconoclasm, 2, 3, 20
Ilyenkov, Evald, 312
imperial expropriation, 154
imperialism, 61–62, 158, 193–94, 313; contemporary, 61; countering in Russia, 191; industrial, 159; and Tradition of Radical Blackness, 155–57. *See also* Lenin's theory of imperialism

Imperialism: The Highest Stage of Capitalism (Lenin), 61, 73, 85, 111, 162, 210, 313
independent contractors, workers as, 272, 273. *See also* gig economy
individualism: American, 64, 65; of capitalist, 64
Intelligencer magazine, 76, 77
Interhelpo cooperative, 333
internal counterrevolutionary forces, 293
internationalist/internationalism, 61, 196, 201n12; of Black liberation struggle, 181; character, 183; critique of racial capitalism, 157; "forgotten" problematic of, 178; industrial workers, 333; Marx's conceptions of, 164; pluralistic, 112; proletarian, 183, 189
International Socialist Congress, 167
intra-European ethnonationalism, 152
Istmat, 306–7, 308
Ivanchikova, Alla, 315n1

Jackson, Esther V. Cooper, 166
Jackson, George, 191–93, 194
Jacobin magazine, 77
James, C. L. R., 152, 176, 200n10, 201n11, 203n29, 300, 303, 314
James C. Scott, 88
Jameson, Fredric, 60, 93
Jappe, Anselm, 91–92
jingoism, 183
Johnson, Boris, 11, 102
Johnson, Ron, 105
Jomini, Antoine Henri, 128–29
Jones, Claudia, 13, 14, 152, 167, 169, 202n22; arguments about self-determination and deviationism, 168–69; defending self-determination in Black Belt, 169; thesis of "super-exploitation" of Black women, 184

Journal of African Marxists, The, 206
Journal of the Left Arts, The (LEF), 80
Jowitt, Ken, 3
Judt, Tony, 107
July Days, 136

Kaczyński, Jarosław, 28–29
Kautsky, Karl, 107, 117, 118, 160, 208, 254n39, 305
Kelley, Robin D. G., 152
Kennedy, Ted, 118
Kerensky, Alexander, 117
Keynesianism, 76, 247, 254n39
Khotinenko, Vladimir, 106
Kingdom of Freedom, 325
Klayman, Alison, 107, 112
Koch, Charles, 28
Koffler, Keith, 109
Kollontai, Alexander, 65, 66, 67
Korsch, Karl, 310
Koteska, Jasna, 3
Krausz, Tamás, 40; pointing Lenin's inconsistency, 41–42; views on Lenin's concern of democracy, 40–41
Kristol, Irving, 103
Kristol, William, 111
Kronstadt rebellion, 33, 39, 109
Krupskaya, Nadezhda, 65, 66, 67, 73
Kuomintang (Chinese political party), 30
Kurz, Robert, 91–92
Kyrgyzstan, 20–21, 331

labor: conscription system, 271; discipline, 270–71; law(s), 59, 258, 269, 274; recruitment and retention system, 271; regulations analysis, 258; superexploitation, 154
labor legislation, 269–74; enforcement of antidiscrimination rules, 272; freedom of contract, 272, 273–74; labor conscription system, 271;

labor legislation *(continued)*
  Labor Reserve schools system, 271;
  as legal domination of employers,
  269–70; new labor provisions,
  270–71; Pashukanis's theory of law,
  270; *Principles of Labor Legislation*,
  272
labor relations, legal codification of,
  258–59
Labor Reserve schools system, 271
Lacan, Jacques, 84
Laclau, Ernesto, 64, 300, 305
Lapin, Nikolay, 312
Latin Tridentine Mass, 107
law(s): labor, 258, 269, 274; law
  redefined nighttime labor, 267;
  Lenin's biopolitical nature of,
  277n52; liberal rule of, 257;
  Pashukanis's theory of, 270;
  regulating imposition of fines
  on workers, 261. *See also* fines;
  materialist approach of Lenin to law
League of Struggle for Emancipation
  of the Working Class, 265
Lefebvre, Henri, 300, 303, 309
Leftist abandonment of Leninism, 9,
  29, 144n35; activities of Western
  communist parties, changes in, 32;
  conflicts over democracy, 33–34;
  failure of seizing state power, 30–31;
  lack of centralization, 34–35;
  Leftist turn to Gramscian policy,
  32–33; New Left, emergence of, 32;
  nonrevolutionary mindset of Leninist
  parties, 31–32; transitional demands,
  31
Leftist re-embracement to Leninism,
  42; inconsistencies of Leninist
  revival, 48; Jodi Dean, 45–47, 48;
  Slavoj Žižek, 42–44, 46, 48
"*Leftwing Communism: An Infantile
  Disorder*" (Lenin), 73, 192

legality: concept of, 242; structural,
  242, 243
legal subordination of workers, 266,
  267
Lenin 2017 (Žižek), 2, 7
"Lenin and East African Marxism"
  (Nabolsy), 15–16
Lenin and Leninism (Stalin), 305
Lenin and the End of Politics (Polan),
  39
Lenin as Philosopher (Pannekoek), 311
Lenin in Zürich (Solzhenitsyn), 106,
  115–16
Leninism, 9, 14, 102, 125, 183,
  202n22, 300; antidemocratic nature
  of, 35; Bannon's views about, 104;
  and Black liberation, 169–70; in
  colonized world, 9; doctrinaire
  positivism of, 107; eradication
  of, 3; historical conflicts of,
  301–2; influence on anticolonial
  revolutionaries, 191; Left arguments
  against, 144n35; left-wing critics
  of, 46; Lukács views on, 302–3; in
  Marxist-Leninist doctrine, 305–9;
  philosophical intolerance of Lenin,
  302; for radical Black thinkers, 155;
  sine qua non of, 202n22; Tugal's
  support of, 29; Western critiques
  of, 309–12; in Western Marxism,
  303–5. *See also* Marxist/Marxism
"Leninist extinction" essay (by Jowitt), 3
Leninist party, 63, 282–83, 285
Leninist thinking, 60–61
Lenin Museum in Gorki complex, 4;
  living room of Lenin in, 4, *5;* statue
  of Lenin in, 4. *See also* statues/
  sculptures of Lenin in Bishkek
*Lenin Rediscovered: What Is to Be Done?
  in Context* (Lih), 73, 202n22
*Lenin Reloaded: Toward a Politics of
  Truth*, 6

"Lenin's Cabinet in the Kremlin," removal of, 3
Lenin's legacy in West, 315
Lenin Square, 323, *324*
"Lenin's shame" phrase by Koteska, 3
Lenin's theory of imperialism, 207; African Marxists adoption and implementation of, 208–11, 212; features of, 211–12; historical significance for East African Marxism, 208. *See also* imperialism
Leonard, Elmore, 106
"*Letters from Afar*" (Lenin), 73
"*Letter to a Comrade on Our Organizational Tasks, A*" (Lenin), 12, 73
Levitz, Eric, 76
Lewin, Moshe, 51n39
liberal democracy: capitalist democracy, 43; Dean's denunciation of, 46; legacy, 43; structural scaffolding of, 259
liberal rule of law, 257
libertarian socialism, 109
libidinal economy, 176, 199n4
Lih, Lars T., 63, 73, 81, 202n22, 301–2
Li, Tania Murray, 89
"live and let live" libertarian variant, 88
localism, 57, 58
Logic (Hegel), 312
Losurdo, Domenico, 180, 201n14
Löwy, Michael, 81
Lukacs, Georg, 20, 36, 38, 69, 242, 253n27, 254n35, 281, 300, 302, 303, 304, 310
Luporini, Cesare, 244
Luxemburg, Rosa, 34, 212

MacLean, Nancy, 28
Maclean, Robert R., 14, 315n1

"Make way for Winged Eros: A Letter to Working Class Youth" (Kollontai), 67
Mamardashvili, Merab, 312
Manas, statue of, 323, *325*
Mao Zedong, 192
Marcuse, Herbert, 176, 190, 304
Marcus Garvey Pan-African Institute, 207
Martinsville Seven, 166
Marxism and Philosophy (Korsch), 310, 311
Marxism and the National Question (Stalin), 214
Marxism-Leninism, 21, 102, 103, 177, 300; African Marxists contribution to, 206–7; developing "class enemy" concept, 307; dichotomy of form and content of, 103; discursive production of, 19; drive toward positivist methodology, 309; Eurocentric claim of, 215; justification of Pan-Africanism from, 212–14; response to charge of Eurocentrism leveled at, 205–6, 219–20; Stalinist doctrine of, 305–6; twentieth-century intellectuals engagement with, 14; views of el Nabolsy, 16; in Western Marxist discourse, 300
Marxist-Leninist doctrine, 186; anticolonial national liberation movements, 313–14; "class enemy" concept, 307; Diamat and Istmat, 306–7, 308; formation of Leninism in, 305–6; historical contingencies of, 307; military language of, 307–8; revisions in Eastern Europe, 312–13; ritualization of, 309
Marxist/Marxism, 60, 84, 200n7; African socialism, *vs.*, 16; Fanon's analysis of, 151; as foreign

Marxist/Marxism *(continued)*
ideological import into Africa, 207;
Left, 180; legacy, 103–4; Lenin's
conception of, 184; Robinson's views
on, 14, 153; traditional, 253n28
Marx, Karl, 13, 75, 80, 83, 104, 152,
200n10, 250n8, 309, 312, 323;
analysis of Paris Commune, 239;
and *The Communist Manifesto*, 84,
128; conceptions of internationalism
and socialism, 164; critique of
political economy, 244; critique
of "utopian socialists," 244;
statement on political power,
36–37; understanding of capitalism,
127; views about bourgeoisie and
proletariat, 127–28; views about
military metaphors, 128
Massive Multiplayer Online Games
(MMORGs), 104
materialism, 259–60; of Bolshevik
women, 66; dialectical, 116;
dichotomist theory of, 306;
historical, 69, 185, 220, 244
Materialism and Empiriocriticism
(Lenin), 304, 306
materialist analysis, 192–93
materialist approach of Lenin to law,
257–58; biopolitical domination,
legalization of, 265–69; on inherent
limitations of laws, 259; on legal
codification of labor relations,
258–59; subordination, legalization
of, 259–65. *See also* law
material manifestation of real global
struggle, 192
material power of revolutionary theory,
191
Mayakovsky, Vladimir, 335; poem of,
336
Mbembe, Achille, 89
McGee, Willie, 166

mechanicism, objection of, 240
Mensheviks, 34, 61, 281, 287; forming
ruling bloc, 291; joined in coalition
government, 290; leadership of, 287
Merleau-Ponty, Maurice, 300, 304
Mészáros, István, 36, 41, 47; pointing
Lukács's defense of dictatorship,
38; question of organizing political
power, 36–37; concerning state
socialist economies, 38–39; views
on Lenin's proletarian state power,
37–38
Michels, Robert, 46
Miéville, China, 7, 27
Mihailovic, Alexandar, 8, 11, 12, 17
military metaphors, 12, 126–28, 183,
308
military vanguard, 125, 126, 128–30,
133, 134, 137, 141, 317n26
"millennials," 66
Milyukov, Paul, 287
misogyny, 66–67
Mitev, Petur-Emil, 313
MMORGs. *See* Massive Multiplayer
Online Games (MMORGs)
modern individual subject, 216–17
Modzelewski, Karol, 39
monopolization, 158
monopoly capitalism, 161–62
Moore, Harriet, 166
Moore, Harry, 166
Moscow Regional Bureau, 63
Mouffe, Chantal, 64, 300, 305
Müller, Jan-Werner, 119
Mussolini, Benito, 32

Nabudere, Dani Wadada, 16,
206–7; adopting Lenin's theory of
imperialism, 208–11; capitalism,
views on, 216; East African societies,
views on, 219; efforts to criticism
of African socialism, 215–16; in

formulation of Marxist-Leninist critique, 207; neocolonial culture, views on, 217; *Political Economy of Imperialism, The*, 210; on recognition of right to national self-determination, 213; role in founding UNLF, 207; socialism in Marxist theoretical framework, views on, 216

Narodism, 215–16

Narodniki/Narodniks, 78, 81, 85, 287; forming ruling bloc, 291; joined in coalition government, 290; Lenin's critique of, 207, 215–16; as "utopians" by Lenin, 81–82

national independence, 160, 185

nationalism: Black, 181; bourgeois, 183, 213; characterization of nationalism, 213; exclusionary, 28; for Leninists, 183; postcolonial nationalism, 112; Stalin's definition of, 214; struggle against, 165–67. *See also* internationalist/internationalism

National Liberation Front, 192

national oppression, 161; Black peoples' predicament as, 182–83; English, 184; liberation from, 193–94

national question, 14, 16, 152, 196, 213; Lenin's writings on, 313, 314; Negro question as, 159, 168

National Review, 2, 76, 102, 106, 110, 117

national self-determination, 6, 162, 183, 213, 314

national socialism, 44, 72

near-socialists, 281, 287, 290, 291, 292

necessity, concept of, 242

necropolitics, 89

Negro in a Soviet America, The (Ford and Allen), 164

Negro liberation movement, 160

Negro People and the Communists, The (Wilkerson), 161

Negro question: Communist position on, 168; Haywood's arguments about, 159–61; as national question, 159, 168

neocolonial(ism), 212; absorption of capital risk, 154–55; culture, 217

Neo-Colonialism: The Highest Stage of Imperialism (Nkrumah), 162

neoliberalism, 64, 186

neo-statism, 17

neostatist Left position, 235, 236

Neue Marx-Lektüre. *See* New Marx Reading

New Economic Policy (NEP), 34, 136, 293

New Factory Law, The (Lenin), 258. *See also* subordination, legalization of

New Left, emergence of, 32. *See also* Left (left-wing)

New Left Review, 36

New Marx Reading, 236, 241, 252n26

Newsweek Magazine, 76

New Yorker, 19

New York Times, 7

Nicolas II, Tzar, 265

Nietzsche, Friedrich, 80, 122n43, 284

Nikolskoye Mill strike issue, 260–61, 264

Nkrumah, Kwame, 14, 152, 162–63, 169

nomenklatura, 8

non-Eurocentric Lenin, need of, 21

Norquist, Grover, 108, 109

North, David, 42

Nurkan (taxi driver), 333, *333*

Nyerere, Julius K., 206, 207, 215, 216

Obama, Barack, 106

objective feasibility of redistributive policies, 244

Objectivism, 109
objectivity: form of, 242; transcendence of, 244. *See also* social objectivity/objectivities
"object's preponderance" concept, 253n27
"Obsolete Communism: The Left-Wing Alternative" (Cohn-Bendit brothers), 32
Occupy movement, 7, 65, 68, 87
"October! To Commemorate the Future" (Hardt), 7
October (Miéville), 7, 27
October Revolution, 1, 9, 20, 27, 125, 133–36, 180, 191, 239, 257, 270, 285, 323; 2017 centennial of, 7, 27; developmental benefits of, 30
Offe, Claus, 47
offenses against good order, 261; fines for, 262, 267–68
Old Gods, New Enigmas: Marx's Lost Theory (Davis), 175
Olgin, Moishe, 117
One Step Forward, Two Steps Back (Lenin), 306
opportunism, 80, 160, 168
oppressed Black working class, 178
"opt-out" movement in United States, 283
organization, 71–72
Organization of African Unity, 163
orthodox Marxism, 305, 310
Ost, David J., 8–9, 10, 70, 71
O'Toole, Fintan, 102
overproduction, 87

Palmer Raids, 30
Pan-Africanism, 207; cultural *vs.* political, 213–14; formulation, 16; from Marxist-Leninist standpoint, 212–14
Paris Commune, 38, 70, 104, 239, 289

partisan drive, 283, 285
party bureaucracy, 45
party dictatorship, 45–46
Party for Socialism and Liberation (PSL), 7
Parvus, Aleksandr, 106, 116, 117
Pashukanis, Evgeny, 270
Passos, Dos, 106
patriotism, enlightened, 112
Pavlovsky, Gleb, 3
Pavlov, Todor, 317n21
pedagogy, 282, 287, 289
Penzin, Alexei, 20, 303, 305
perfectibility of human nature, 249
petty bourgeoisie, 217; intellectuals, 209
Phaedrus (Plato), 112
philistinism, 117
Philosophical and Economic Manuscripts (Marx), 313
Philosophical Notebooks (Lenin), 310, 312, 314
Piketty, Thomas, 7
"Pink Tide" wave in Latin America, 27
PiS. *See* Poland's Law and Justice Party (PiS)
Platten, Fritz, 116
Plekhanov, Georgi, 107, 117, 305
plutocratic state, 43
Polan, A. J., 39–40
Poland, double-face of PiS government in, 44–45
Poland's Law and Justice Party (PiS), 28–29, 44
Polish United Workers Party, 39
political culture, ephemerality of, 120
political economy, Marx's critique of, 244
Political Economy of Imperialism, The (Nabudere), 210
poliversity, 313
Pollock, Friedrich, 254n32
Popper, Karl, 284

populist Right, 29, 66
Portuguese colonialism, 184
postcolonial nationalism, 112
postindustrial capitalism, 91
Postone, Moishe, 252n24, 253n28
postrevolutionary democracy, Lenin's theorization about, 37
postrevolutionary repression, Lukács's defense of, 38
poststructuralist affirmation of difference, 244
Poulantzas, Nicos, 48
"power relations" concept. *See* "balance of power," concept of
Pravda, 161
pre-test, 283, 285, 287, 290, 291
Principles of Labor Legislation (Commons), 272
"prison-house of nations." *See* Late imperial Russia
productive consumption, need of, 87
productive forces, 218, 242, 247; of labour, 84; unfettering of, 254n41
professional revolutionaries, 134
"projected time" by Dupuy, 69
Proletarian Revolution and the Renegade Kautsky, The (Lenin), 42, 73, 155, 160
proletarian state, 238, 240, 246, 248, 251n18; duality of, 239–40; Lenin's theory of, 39; withering away of, 238, *239*
proletariat/proletarian, 127, 128; class, 310; creating possibility for abolition of national oppression, 208; democracy, 28, 32, 37, 42, 70–71, 184, 202n22, 238; dictatorship, 113; ideological vanguard of, 132–33; internationalism, 183; law, 18, 258; revolution(ary), 73, 132, 163–64; as vanguard fighter, 130–31; vanguard of dictatorship of, 133–34

protest, concept of, 283, 285, 288–89
Proud Boys, 66
Provisional Government, 286–88
PSL. *See* Party for Socialism and Liberation (PSL)
psychological wage, 177
public exploitation, 258
putative universals, 194, 195

QAnon, 66

Rabinowitch, Alexander, 34
Radical Blackness, tradition of, 14, 15, 151–52; anticapitalists in, 155; Black radical tradition *vs.*, 152–53; imperialism and, 155–57; racial capitalism and, 153–55
racial capitalism, 14, 153, 199n4, 201n11; dependent extraction, 154; imperial expropriation, 154; labor superexploitation, 154; neocolonial absorption of capital risk, 154–55; theory of, 161; white supremacist accumulation, 154
racial/racism, 177; chauvinism, 190; discrimination, 196; hierarchy, 153–54; racialization, 153; subjection, 151
radical philosophy, act of destroying, 304–5
radical Right, 30
Radosh, Ronald, 11, 105–7, 108, 111
Rahat (photographer), 333, 337n6
Rand, Ayn, 105, 109–10
Razem (political party in Poland), 44
re-embracement of Leftist to Leninism, 42; inconsistencies of Leninist revival, 48; Jodi Dean, 45–47, 48; Slavoj Žižek, 42–44, 46, 48. *See also* abandonment of Leninism by Leftist, reasons for

Reactionary Mind, The: Conservatism from Edmund Burke to Donald Trump (Robin), 102
Realpolitik, 302
Rebirth of History, The (Badiou), 2, 6–7
Reconstructing Lenin (Krausz), 40
Red Army of Soviet Union, 31, 136
"rediscovery of imperialism" by Western Left, 210
"Red Summer" (1919), 180
Rees-Mogg, Jacob, 12, 102
reform, concept of, 240
reification, Lukács's "idealistic" emphasis on, 253n27
Reminiscences of Lenin (Krupskaya), 73
Renault, Matthieu, 314
"reputation rating mechanism" in gig economy platforms, 273
Review of African Political Economy, 206
revisionism, 80, 160, 177, 197, 200n7
revisionist, 200n7
revolution(ary), 19, 21, 238, *239*, 254n40, 302; actuality of, 281–82, 294; bourgeois-democratic, 130–31; concept of, 246, 248; conceptualization as test in, 285; defencism, 286; political, 77; proletarian, 73, 132; proletariat, 163–64; reading Lenin's text as revolutionary practice, 79–83; self-governance issues, 71; self-organization of subordinate classes, 142; socialist, 131–32; state, 4, 6; strategy of revolutionary defeatism, 183; temporality of Lenin, 69–70. *See also* testing, Leninist theory of
revolutionary theory: actuality of, 197; material power of, 191; relevance to predicament of America's oppressed masses, 192; revival of, 195; universality of, 191, 193

"Revolution or Ruin" (Heron), 59
Right (right-wing), 8, 11, 30, 32, 33; American, 28, 29; capitalism and, 76; ideologues of, 17; international, 11; Leninist/Leninism, 6, 8, 11, 29, 43, 72; neofascist political, 28; populist, 29, 66, 119; radical, 28, 30; taking ideas from Left, 72; in United States, 44
Right of Nations to Self-Determination (Lenin), 313, 314
"right to work" argument, 267, 277n57
Robertson, Phil, 105, 106
Robeson, Eslanda, 167, 169
Robeson, Paul, 202n22
Robin, Corey, 102, 105, 111
Robinson, Cedric, 14, 152, 201n11; excavation of Black radicalism, 182; interpretation of nationality, 181–82
Rodney, Walter, 153, 177, 184, 185
romantic anticapitalism, 6, 11, 78; Lenin's critique of, 78–79; romantic impulses and restraints, 92–93
romantic anticapitalist position, 8
romanticism, 93; economic, 88, 93; Hegel's critique of, 226n82
Ronell, Avital, 283, 284
Rothbard, Murray, 28, 29
RSDLP, 136–37
Russia(n): capitalism, 131; late imperial, 190, 203n29; Lenin's critique of Narodniks in, 207, 215–16
Russian Social-Democratic Labor Party, 286

sachlich vermittelte Herrschaft. *See* domination, objectively mediated
Sanders, Bernie, 7, 65, 66, 76; as alternative for Trump, 44; claim of democratic socialism, 77; and Green

New Deal, 76, 79, 82, 92–93; social welfare proposals of, 85; thought about anticapitalism, 76–77; U.S. presidential election campaigns of, 10–11; views on capitalism, 82–83
Sankara, Thomas, 184
Sante, Luc, 107–8
Saur (April) Revolution (1978), 9
Sayre, Robert, 81
Scalia, Antonin, 102
Scheidemann, Phillip, 107
School of Theory and Activism (STAB), 337n6
scientific determinism, 304
"Scottsboro boys," 197, 203n31
"Scramble for Africa" (1881–1914), 208, 212
Sebestyen, Victor, 112
secession, 158, 163
Second Congress, 139
"second nature," concept of, 253n27
Second Reconstruction, 176, 179
self-determination, 14, 152, 158, 160, 163, 169; conceptual apparatus of, 157; right of, 195–96; right to, 212, 213
sentimental anticapitalism, 11, 78, 86
sentimentalism, economic, 85
Service, Robert, 118
"seudo-leftists," 42
Sexton, Jared, 199n4
Shaw, Tamsin, 122n43
Short Course, 306
Simpsons, The 1998 episode, 2
Sismondi, Jean Charles-Leonard Simonde de, 78, 82, 87; Lenin's criticisms of, 83, 87, 89, 92; political-economic explanation of surplus populations, 89–90; romantic anticapitalist disposition in, 82; sentimental impulse of, 87; thoughts about capitalist excess, 89

Smadiyarov, Sydyk, 20
Social Contract (Rousseau), 112
Social Democrats, 132, 137
Socialist Revolution and the Right to Self-Determination, The (Lenin), 151; about democratic rights for Black people in, 161–62; Leninism and Black liberation movement, 169–70; Lenin's position on federation in, 162–63; about necessity of struggle against chauvinism and nationalism, 165–67; about recognition of right to self-determination of nations, 167–69; about rights to self-determination and secession in, 163–65; about self-determination and political secession, 158–61; theses, 157–58. *See also* Tradition of Radical Blackness
Socialist-Revolutionaries, leadership of, 287
socialist/socialism, 75, 127, 200n7, 200n8, 308; democratic, 48, 76, 77, 79; ideological "hegemony," 33; libertarian, 109; in Marxist theoretical framework, 216–17; organizations, 7; politics in UK and U.S., 65; popularity in United States, 77; project of, 300; revolution, 131–32; support for imperialist war, 286. *See also* Marxist/Marxism
socialization of production, 248
"social justice"–oriented "radical liberal" formation, 182
social movements, 282
social objectivity/objectivities, 236, 241, 249, 252–53n27; Adorno's concept of, 242; "balance of power" concept in, 245; definition of, 241–42; determinism *vs.* voluntarism, 245–46; Freudian repression of, 244;

social objectivity/objectivities *(continued)* kernel of objectivity in capitalism, 244; mechanism of competition, 243–44; objectively mediated domination, 243; possibilities vs. impossibilities, 245; revolutionary break of barrier by, *249;* structural legality, 242, 243; suppression of, 248; systemic nature of, 246–47; theory of, 242, *243*, 245, 253n28; transcendence of objectivity, 244. See also "withering away of state"

social power struggles, 275n9

society, concept of, 241

Sohn-Rethel, Alfred, 252n27

Sojourners for Truth and Justice (STJ), 14, 165; and anticommunism, 166–67; against chauvinism and nationalism, 165–66; political strategy to Black Cold War liberals, 167; task of "educate the masses," 167

Solzhenitsyn, Aleksandr, 106, 115–16

Sontag, Susan, 107

Sorace, Christian, 8, 10–11

Soviet Labor Code, penalties for "absenteeism" in, 270

Soviets of Workers' and Soldier's Deputies, 286

Spencer, Richard, 103, 117

Sport Palace Kozhomkul, 326, *326*

Srnicek, Nick, 7

STAB. *See* School of Theory and Activism (STAB)

Stalinist philosophy, 300, 306, 307

"Stalinist" versions of Lenin's work, 301

Stalin, Joseph, 63, 305, 308; definition of nationalism, 214; liquidation of withering-away thesis, 251n15

Standard Rules of Internal Labor Organization, 271

State and Revolution (Lenin), 6, 73, 79, 102, 105, 107, 117, 251n12, 303, 312; affinities between Lenin's characterization of equality in, 119; audience response, 112–13, 115, 118; conceptualization of withering away, 17–18; depicting danger to revolution, 81; discussions of withering away of state in, 110, 113–15; duplication of concept of state, 238; imaginary postrevolutionary outcome, 47; instructions to read Marx, 80; Lenin's style of argumentation in, 112–13; Lenin's theory of proletarian state in, 39; Lenin's use of soviets as form of social self-management in, 133; materialist idea of state, 193; postrevolutionary polity of equality in, 37; rejection of parliamentary democracy, 33; Service's views on, 118; theoretical contribution of, 236; theoretical foundation of, 238; ultra-democratic, 36

State and Revolution. The Marxist Theory of the State, and the Tasks of the Proletariat in the Revolution. See *State and Revolution* (Lenin)

state, concept of, 235–36; consequences for, 246; duplication of, 238; as economic class domination, 237; elements of, 237; "two states" concept, 238–41

State History Museum, The, 323, *324*

state-sponsored capitalism, 109

state, transformation of, 240; problem of, 247; suppression of social objectivity defining, 248

statism, 35

statues/sculptures of Lenin in Bishkek, 326, *327*, 333, *334–35*, *336*; in antique/thrift shops, 327, *330*, 331,

332; in buildings, 327, *328, 329;* in memorabilia/monuments, 325, 327, *328, 329,* 331, *332*
Steinmetz, George, 114, 117
STJ. *See* Sojourners for Truth and Justice (STJ)
structural analogy, 252n27
structural causality, 253n29
structural legality, 242, 243
structured organizational thinking of Lenin, 60–61
'structure of feeling', 199n4
structure/superstructure causal determination, 242, *243*
subordination, legalization of, 259; absenteeism, fines for, 261, 263, 264, 267, 270, 271; defective work, fines/penalties for, 261–63, 265, 267, 273; fines imposed 'on authority' of factory managements, 262; "insanity" of demanding equal rights, 262–63; Nikolskoye Mill strike issue causes, 260–61; offenses against good order, fines for, 261, 262, 267–68; ways to control fraud imposition of fines, 263–64. *See also* biopolitical domination, legalization of
substitutionism, danger of, 45
"Sunbelt," 195
superexploitation, 15, 156, 160; Black oppression as, 14, 17, 161; of Black peoples, 13, 182, 184; labor, 153, 154, 170
"superstructural" forms, 252n27
surplus populations, 89–90
Swedberg, Richard, 81
syncretic national consciousness, 201–2n17
Syriza (political party in Greece), 43, 48

tail-ism, 137

Táíwò, Olúfémi, 218
Talbot, Margot, 102
Taraki, Nur Muhammad, 9
Tenth Party Congress, 34
Tereshkova, Valentina, 62, 331
test drive, 283; aporetic ethos of test, 285; Bolsheviks embracing, 292; Leninist appropriation of, 285; Ronell's theory of, 283–85
testing, Leninist theory of, 282–83, 292; actuality of revolution, 294; NEP, 293; using partisan drive, 285; support and rejection of, 283–84. *See also* April Theses
Theory of the Subject (Badiou), 70
Thottbot, 105
Time Machine, The (Wells), 5
Tolstoy, Lev, 335
Torchbearer, The documentary (Bannon), 106
Tory anarchists/anarchism, 12, 102, 116
Toward a Strategy for Libertarian Social Change (Rothbard), 28
"traditional two-facedness," 166–67
triple oppression, 184
Tronti, Mario, 245
Trotskyism, 103
Trotsky, Leon, 41, 50n38, 103
Trump, Donald, 29, 48, 56, 66, 103, 105
Tsarism, 287
Tsereteli, Irakli, 281, 286, 290
Tucker, Robert, 308
Tugal, Cihan, 29
"two states" concept of Lenin, 238–41, 247–48
Tynanov, Yuri, 80

Uber (ride sharing service), 18, 273
Uganda National Liberation Front (UNLF), 207

Ujamaa ("familyhood"), 16, 215
Ulyanov, Volodya, 335
unhappy "affect aliens," 104
United States (US): "antirevisionist" communist organizations, 200n7; Black Leninist formation in, 190; Black radicalism in, 182; imperialism in, 62; individualisms in, 64; "opt-out" movement in, 283; plutocratic right-wing in, 44; popularity of socialism in, 77; racist ideologies and policies in, 160; realization of socialism in, 165; response to Bolshevik Revolution, 179; socialist politics in, 65
universality of (white, European) theory, 195
UNLF. *See* Uganda National Liberation Front (UNLF)
unrealized universality of revolutionary theory, 193–94
U.S. Civil War, 159, 200n10
utopia(n), 43, 75, 88, 248, 249, 312; right-wing criticism as withering away, 235; socialists, 244; vision of balance and harmony, 87
utopianism, objection of, 240, 248
"utopian socialists," Marx's critique of, 244

Valiavicharska, Zhivka, 19–20
Vandervelde, Emile, 107
vanguard, 12–13, 125, 126, 128–30, 133, 134, 137, 141, 191, 307–8; dialectical analysis of class-party relationship, 134, 137–38; of dictatorship of proletariat, 133–34; in discussion of soviets, 133; functions for, 129, 134–35, 140–41; ideological vanguard of proletariat, 132–33; lagging behind main force, 136–37; Lenin's use of, 130; military, 12, 125–26, 128–30, 133, 134, 137, 141–42, 183, 317n26, 308; organization, 139; party as, 183; proletariat-as-vanguard, 130–32; risks associated with, 135–36
vanguardism, 125, 138–39, 142, 144n32
Vardon, Philippe, 28
Vaziulin, Victor, 312
Velvet Revolutions (1989), 9
Vergara, Camila, 18
virtual construction, 304
voluntarism, 245–46

War and Revolution (Losurdo), 201n14
Wark, McKenzie, 61
Warren, Elizabeth, 76
Washington Post, 77
"We Charge Genocide" campaign, 176
Weekly Standard, 106
Wells-Barnet, Ida B., 176
Wells, H. G., 5
Western European Social Democrats, 59
Western Marxism, 19, 303; currents of, 239, 241, 254n41; Leninism in, 303–5; "originators" and "pillars" of, 300, 303
What Is to Be Done? (Lenin), 71, 79, 81, 302, 304, 306, 313; Lenin's mention about class consciousness in, 133; "vanguardist" model in, 138–39
white chauvinism, 198–99
white-dominated class-first social democratic electoralism, 182
white Left, 189
white racism, 190
white supremacist accumulation, 154
Why Women Had Better Sex Under Socialism (Ghodsee), 62
Wilderson III, Frank, 199n4

Wilkerson, Doxey, 14, 161–62
Williams, Alex, 7
winged Eros, 67–68
Wingless Eros, 67
Winter Palace in Russia, 1, 2
withering away thesis, 39, 110, 113–15, 235, 237–38, *239*, 248, 251n12; bourgeois state, 236, 238, 246; consequences for theory of state, 246; criticism from Right and Left, 235; Lenin's conceptualization of, 17–18; need for discontinuity, 248; objections raised against, 240–41; proletarian state, 238, 246; Stalin's liquidation of, 251n15. *See also* social objectivity/objectivities
Wodak, Ruth, 119
Wolff, Michael, 106
workers' state, 60, 184, 192, 236, 257, 289
working class, 37, 41, 65, 290; Black, 178, 182; class-conscious vanguard of, 133–34; conceptions of time for, 267; defeat of, 64; degree of subordination of, 266; importance of organizing, 71–72; imposing socialist ideology onto, 133; merging of democratic activities with other classes, 131; multinational, 178, 195, 199; primary and universal position of, 305; Russian, 131; spontaneous activity of, 132; white, 12, 104, 156, 164
World and Africa, The (Du Bois), 177
World War I: analysis of Du Bois and Lenin, 155–56; democracy in context of, 162; ending Russia's participation in, 136; Russia's involvement in, 106
World War II: anti-imperial formation during and after, 201n13; democracy in context of, 162; ending in favor of Left, 31
Wowhead, 104
Wright, Erik Olin, 47–48, 85
Wright, Richard, 201n11

Yeltsin, Boris, 3
Yurchak, Alexei, 309

Zanotti, Giovanni, 17–18
Zanzibar Revolution, 206
Zetkin, Clara, 72
Žižek, Slavoj, 2–3, 42, 6, 7, 56, 79; inconsistency of Leninist revival, 48; opinion about resurrection of Lenin, 43–44; views on Lenin's democratic thought, 42–43
"Zombie Lenin" essay (by Brian C. Anderson), 2–3